Telling the EU's Story by Others

Telling the EU's Story by Others

The Jean Monnet Programme and European Union Public Diplomacy

Yifan Yang

LEXINGTON BOOKS
Lanham • Boulder • New York • London

Published by Lexington Books
An imprint of The Rowman & Littlefield Publishing Group, Inc.
4501 Forbes Boulevard, Suite 200, Lanham, Maryland 20706
www.rowman.com

6 Tinworth Street, London SE11 5AL, United Kingdom

British Library Cataloguing in Publication Information Available

Library of Congress Cataloging-in-Publication Data Available

ISBN 978-1-4985-9341-0 (cloth)
ISBN 978-1-4985-9342-7 (electronic)

Contents

Acknowledgments

This book has been developed based on my PhD thesis defended at King's College London in 2016. I would like to express my deepest appreciation to my supervisor, Dr. Ramon Pacheco Pardo, whose guidance, support, and encouragement have been invaluable in developing the research and finishing my thesis. I would also like to thank the member of my thesis defense committee, Professor Alister Miskimmon and Dr. Paul Irwin Crookes, whose comments on a previous version help me improve the quality of my thesis and subsequently this book.

Special thanks go to all my interviewees in China and Belgium for kindly agreeing to be interviewed for this research and their insightful opinions during the conversation and constructive comments on my research. I would like to acknowledge my appreciation to professors and students at Renmin University of China, Fudan University, and Sichuan University. Without their help, this book would never be possible.

My biggest debt of gratitude goes to my parents and my younger sister, for their love and understanding. As teachers at a primary school, my parents always influence my sister and me by their words and deeds, which encourage us to obtain our doctoral degrees and start our own academic careers.

Furthermore, I want to thank one anonymous reviewer for his/her critical comments on a previous version of the manuscript. I am also grateful to Mr. Joseph Parry and Ms. Bryndee Ryan, my editors at the Lexington Books, for their help and patience in turning the thesis into a book.

Chapter One

Introduction

1.1 PUBLIC DIPLOMACY IN
EU-CHINA STRATEGIC PARTNERSHIP

Public diplomacy is crucial for all actors in world politics; the European Union (EU) is no exception. Arguably, the practice of public diplomacy extends back as far as the First World War, with some scholars believing that the wartime "propaganda" constituted an earlier form of it since they share a similar root in influencing foreign public opinion through external communication.[1] Meanwhile, the innovation in international broadcasting based on shortwave radio introduced between the two world wars accelerated the speed of transnational information transmission.[2] Since then, public diplomacy, carrying "information" and "ideas" towards foreign publics has been very widely employed, whether it is implemented under the name of "propaganda," "psychological warfare," or "strategic communication," even though distinctions do exist among these terms.

Nowadays, even a cursory observation of professional periodicals and monographs can tell us that public diplomacy research gives priority to the study of historical experience, with a particular focus on US-USSR relations during the Cold War, the contemporary practice of the US following the September 11 attack, and the ongoing China's "Charm Offensive." The great powers need public diplomacy to create a favourable international climate for the implementation of their policies.[3] For medium and small nations, public diplomacy is an effective means for them to increase their visibility on the world stage and fulfill their national interests.[4] In addition, both inter-governmental and non-governmental organizations are all leveraging public diplomacy instruments to attract attention and win public support for the issues that concern them. Even terrorist groups use public diplomacy through social

1

media to recruit new members and broadcast their doctrines.[5] Conversely, the EU—despite being an unprecedented entity in international affairs—has not received similar attention from both academic and political circles.

The term "public diplomacy" was first coined by Edmund A. Gullion, the former Dean of the Fletcher School of Law and Diplomacy at Tufts University in 1965, when the Edward R. Murrow Centre of Public Diplomacy was established at the Fletcher School. The Centre emphasized the importance of the influence of public attitudes on the formation and implementation of foreign policy.[6] Henceforward, scholarly attempt in defining the concept of public diplomacy has never stopped. The concept of public diplomacy has been updated due to the role of government,[7, 8] its impact on soft power,[9, 10, 11, 12, 13, 14] its interaction with international relations,[15, 16] as well as its interaction with the Internet in a social media era.[17]

As a supranational organization, the EU needs public diplomacy. Internally, nation states' public diplomacy is merely aimed foreign publics, but the EU is responsible for promoting the formation and development of European identity through communicating directly with European citizens. Externally, the EU's role at world level depends on international activities, and their impact or, more specifically, "what the EU does" and "what foreign publics see." In this sense, the EU requires public diplomacy in order to communicate itself to world audiences, while studying the EU's practice could also enrich the content of public diplomacy research, considering its unique features as an international player, any discussion of public diplomacy which does not look at the EU simply will not suffice.

To be more specific, the role of the EU in the world is based on its own internal capability and external influence beyond its border.[18] The creation of the European Economic Community, and subsequently, the EU, was aimed at securing economic prosperity and long-lasting peace among European countries.[19] Meanwhile, thanks to its process of enlargement, the EU (currently consisting of 28 member states) has the autonomy to transfer certain competences from member states, as well as the relevant resources, such as the EU's own revenue, with which to operate collectively in international arena.

With regard to the EU's influence in East Asia, both its Asia strategy and its China policy include improving the perception of the EU, which is expressed in terms of strengthening mutual awareness between the EU and Asia,[20] and improving the EU's image in China.[21] Both these aspects demand public diplomacy. According to Pacheco Pardo, China perceives the EU differently from the way in which the latter self identifies.[22] Meanwhile, due to China's increasing global impact and overlapping interests between the EU and China on global and regional issues, mutual understanding between the two has become increasing necessary.[23] Furthermore, the EU is not perceived as having an active role in East Asia affairs. Using public diplomacy as a channel of introducing the EU to a Chinese audience is a means whereby the EU can increase its impact on China and even East Asia as a whole.

As research results showed, the motivations behind EU public diplomacy are quite complicated. It has been argued that EU public diplomacy aims to improve external perceptions of the EU;[24, 25] and the EU as a normative power and model in regional integration also helps to improve the common good of the whole world in global governance.[26] Besides, EU public diplomacy has two dimensions since it needs to address both domestic and international audiences.[27, 28] Also, there is a debate about whether EU public diplomacy needs a single voice or a single message,[29] albeit it seems that a single voice in public diplomacy does not apply to the EU since it is not a nation state.[30] Nevertheless, the EU is currently experiencing a serious decline in influence, evident in "the failure of the Copenhagen Climate Conference, the Greek and Eurozone financial crisis, and the marginalisation because of the US on developing agreements with other emerging powers on the international scene,"[31] let alone the UK EU membership referendum and its unexpected outcomes.[32] The US National Intelligence Council has gone even so far as to predict that by 2050, Europe will be "a hobbled giant distracted by internal bickering and competing national agenda and less able to translate its economic clout into global influence."[33] Furthermore, the growing Euro-scepticism inside and outside the EU cannot be dismissed.[34] Hence, public diplomacy, including information transmission, international public opinion research, and analysis activities, as well as cultural and educational exchange, are vital for the EU to exert its influence on world politics. All these reasons make EU public diplomacy a tough job.

These problems attributable to internal capacity building and institutional design need solutions based on further policy adjustment and institutional change, while those related to how the EU is viewed by the rest of the world can only be solved through a change in these perceptions. Given that both "what the EU does" and "what foreign publics see" help to mold the external image of the EU, the capacity of the public diplomacy to deal with "ideas" and "information" may provide a possible solution. No wonder Margot Wallström, former vice president of the European Commission, even argues that "we Europeans believe that public diplomacy plays a special role in the external relations of the EU."[35]

When it comes to EU-China relations, public diplomacy has been gradually playing a significant role. Europe as a geographical concept had a historical link with ancient China, but the EU, which was originally established in the 1950s, had no diplomatic relations with China for over two decades because of the Cold War and the ideological differences between the East and the

West. Following US President Richard Nixon's visit and the recognition of China by the United Nations in 1972, EU-China relations were officially established in May 1975,[36, 37] and the opening of the Delegation of the European Commission to Beijing occurred on 4th October 1988, which was followed by a general trend of steady development since then. Albeit EU-China relations encountered some difficulties in the immediate aftermath of the Tiananmen events in June 1989, they resumed in 1992 as both sides were keen to re-establish bilateral relations.[38] In other words, albeit the punitive measures that had been taken the member states of the EU either collectively or bilaterally in the weak of Tiananmen Square issues had soon been resolved, due to that both sides had strong wishes to restore bilateral relations for economic and diplomatic purposes. After that, thanks to the reform and opening-up policy, China's economic growth has astonished the world.[39] It is now an important economic power that cannot be overlooked. Besides, as an economic giant, China plays an increasingly important role in regional and global issues, all of which make cooperation with China necessary.

To enhance bilateral relationship, in 1995, the European Commission launched a Communication titled *A long-term policy for EU-China relations*, the first of its kind.[40] In the Communication, the Commission declaimed that "Europe's relations with China are bound to be a cornerstone in Europe's external relations, both with Asia and globally," and the Europe "needs an action-oriented, not a merely declaratory policy, to strengthen that relationship."[41] Besides indicating the European interests at stake in the bilateral relationship including shared global and regional security interests, shared interests on other global issues, global economic stability, and competitiveness, the EU, more importantly, also emphasized mutual understanding between Europeans and Chinese and raised the EU profile in China.[42] The intensification of EU-China relations was further updated to a comprehensive partnership in the Commission's Communication released in 1998, which stressed five key suggestions for EU policy towards China: "engaging China further, through an upgraded political dialogue, in the international community; supporting China's transition to an open society based upon the rule of law and the respect for human rights; integrating China further in the world economy by bringing it more fully into the world trading system and by supporting the process of economic and social reform underway in the country; making Europe's funding go further; and raising the EU's profile in China."[43] Despite the development of bilateral relations, the Commission's 2001 communication recognized that "China is not always an easy partner for the EU . . . and EU concerns over key issues such as human rights affect and strain relations at times,"[44] which, according to Michalski and Pan, reflected a downbeat forecast for bilateral relations.[45]

However, two years later, another policy paper had been released by the Commission, with a title of *A maturing partnership—shared interests and challenges in EU-China relations*, which updated the previous two papers regarding EU-China relations launched in 1998 and 2001 respectively. In this updated version, the EU effectively presented China as a "strategic partner," with calls for the upgrading of relations across a very wide spectrum of issues and problems.[46] Besides, it called for "new efforts to raise EU visibility in China" with a few targeted messages.[47] Following China's entry to the World Trade Organisation (WTO) in late 2001, a deepening EU-China relations and economic interdependence also caused competition in a globalized world. Thus, the 2006 Communication stands as the most recent comprehensive statement of the framework for EU-China relations, calling for an increase in responsibilities on both sides, along with a re-emphasis on "a strategic partnership." In the latest communication, the EU emphasized bilateral co-operation at different levels ranging from global to regional to bilateral, and expanding people-to-people links has been particularly mentioned to underpin bilateral relations.[48] By reviewing all these five Commission Communications, raising the EU's visibility in China consistently located in the EU's interests, though the specific rhetoric had been developed along the time.

From the Chinese side, the first ever EU "White Paper," with a title of *China's EU Policy Paper* had been released in 2003. In this paper, China indicated that "there is no fundamental conflict of interest between China and the EU and neither side poses a threat to the other," but "given their differences in historical background, cultural heritage, political system, and economic development level," both consensus and disagreements over some issues including human rights co-exist.[49] Following this policy paper, two more policy paper on the EU had been launched in 2014 and 2018 respectively, but the statement on their differences over such issues as human rights because of distinctions in history, cultural tradition, political system and stage of economic development had been retained, accompanied by some new issues in economic and trade field.[50] In short, these three policy papers affirmed a "strategic partnership" between the EU and China, echoing the EU's statement on bilateral relations.

After proclaiming a "strategic partnership" by both sides, official definition of the term "strategic partnership" has also attracted scholarly attention. It has been seen four process of conceptualization and operationalization of the term "strategic partnership": what has been shaping the foreign policy outlook of the each actor in this relationship; the conceptualization of the strategic partnership, on top of the shaping of the actor that is being analyzed; mutual expectations of the strategic partners involving in the partnership in the consideration; and the issues that need to be dealt together in the strategic partnership.[51]

From the EU side, the *2003 European Security Strategy* indicated the necessity of working with partners as saying that "there are few if any problem we [the EU] can deal with on our own. The threats described above are common threats, shared with all our closet partners" and "these relationships are an important asset to build on. In particular we should look to develop strategic partnerships, with Japan, China, Canada and India as well as with those who share our goals and values, and are prepared to act in their support."[52] Javier Solana, former EU Higher Representative for the Common Foreign and Security Policy (CFSP) listed two reasons: "First, the issues which we discuss together and on which we push action forward are global strategic issues," ranging from the proliferation of weapons of mass destruction and international terrorism; and second, because China and the EU are "partners with significant global strengths, capabilities and responsibilities."[53] Even so, the term "strategic partnership" is ill-defined in the EU's discourse. In practice, it can either mean boosting a foreign country's diplomatic status, organizing summits and extra minister-level and expert-level meeting or mean an alternative to fully-fledged EU membership, which makes an EU diplomat say that "it's like love—no one can define it. You only know what it is when you experience it."[54]

From the Chinese side, Wen Jiabao, former Premier of the State Council delivered a speech at the China-EU Investment and Trade Forum in Brussels in May 6, 2004. He indicated that:

> By "comprehensive," it means that the cooperation should be all-dimensional, wide-ranging and multi-layered. It covers economic, scientific, technological, political and cultural fields, contains both bilateral and multilateral levels, and is conducted by both governments and non-governmental groups. By "strategic," it means that the cooperation should be long-term and stable, bearing on the larger picture of China-EU relations. It transcends the differences in ideology and social system and is not subjected to the impacts of individual events that occur from time to time. By "partnership," it means that the cooperation should be equal-footed, mutually beneficial and win-win. The two sides should base themselves on mutual respect and mutual trust, endeavour to expand converging interests and seek common ground on the major issues while shelving differences on the minor ones.[55]

Albeit so, it has been argued that EU-China relationship has not been either "comprehensive" or "strategic." By claiming that it is not "comprehensive," Holslag thinks that both sides fail to identify a common ground in terms of interests and concerns, and joint priorities continue to be concentrated in the business sector.[56] Moreover, the problems revolving around internal institutional competition, external shifts in the global balance of power and preferences and pressure on the EU's capacity to assert its normative distinctiveness faced by the EU put restraints on its pursuit of "strategic partnerships" in general and its partnership with China in particular, so the EU-China "strategic partnership" is at best a partial rather than a comprehensive one.[57] When saying that it is not "strategic," first of all, their different understandings of political values and ideology have limited and will continue to limit the scope and depth of bilateral cooperation; second, both the EU and China are either unable or unwilling to contribute much to the main security interests and concerns of the other, in that they have pursued different strategies in response to some of the most pressing security problems; third, the EU and China do not share a common vision for the composition and management of the current international order.[58]

Moreover, it seems that the development of bilateral cooperation has encountered a bottleneck in recent years. The EU has now become China's largest trading partner and China is the second largest trading partner of the EU,[59] only after the US, but the EU is increasingly concerned about a widening trade deficit which accumulated to over 130 billion euros in 2017. At the same time, China is getting more and more impatient in terms of the EU's refusal to grand it market economy status (MES).[60] Besides, the 2006 Communication proposed the negotiations for a new Partnership and Cooperation Agreement to update the 1985 Trade and Cooperation Agreement, with its specific focus on trade and investment issues.[61] However, the negotiations advanced slowly because of some different concerns from both the EU and China. Although both the European and Chinese leaders frequently speak of a strategic partnership between Brussels and Beijing, there is a big gap between rhetoric and reality in bilateral relationship.[62]

Albeit the differences over values and ideology constitute a serious obstacle to the realization of a genuine strategic partnership, some scholars still believe that the growing interdependence between the EU and China and the multidimensional nature of the relationship in the economic, political, and social areas will overshadow these differences, considering that both sides highly value their relationship.[63, 64] To be more specific, as the two most unlikely powers in the world, the EU and China differ in a number of their key preferences for a desirable world order, including their nature (post-sovereign Union versus sovereign state), internal systems (post-industrialised democracies versus developmental party-state), and international cooperation (alliance versus partnership).[65] However, their mutually approaching tendencies in global governance are narrowing differences between the EU and China, leading to a much better concerted relationship on wide-ranging bilateral and multilateral issues. Thus, the EU and China have expanded exchange and cooperation continuously through political, economic, and cultural approaches and various channels have become a close and inseparable bond between two sides, which, in the long run, will help them deal with complex bilateral and global issues.

For the EU, enhancing its role as a global actor necessitates increasing its influence in East Asia and the world. To be more specific, the EU has crucial interests in East Asia, not only in trade, finance, and energy but also in politics, human rights, and security.[66] However, the EU has not been viewed as an active player in East Asian affairs.[67] The perceptions in China of the EU—a new, unique, and post-modern entity and a model of economic prosperity, regional cooperation and integration—as a central pole in a desired multi-polar world, have given way to a more critical view of the EU due to its incoherence in foreign policies, its perceived decline in centrality in world politics and its economic troubles.[68] Therefore, raising the EU's visibility locates centrally in its Asian and China policies,[69, 70, 71] and cooperating with China and projecting a favorable image to the Chinese public is crucial.

It is no doubt that Europe is not in the center of East Asia's security interests based on academic research.[72] Both the EU and China (more broadly East Asia) have to pay more attention to the constraints on bilateral relationship which is inherent in the nature of the EU as an institution and in the nature of the newly rising regionalism in East Asia. If they failed to do so, bilateral relationship between the EU and China would remain as the lofty level of "common" or "shared" interests in political and academic discussions, which are potentially infinite.[73] Therefore, public diplomacy has a significant role to play in enhancing the comprehensive strategic partnership between the EU and China, since it will help eliminate the prejudice over each other's culture, history, and political system and increase mutual understanding based on the growing knowledge and frequent communication and exchange, which will be of the most important policy implications for the EU to deal with its relations with East Asia in general and China in particular. Among all these public diplomacy programs, the Jean Monnet Programme deserves more scholarly attention.

1.2 THE CASE OF THE JEAN MONNET PROGRAMME

The research uses the implementation of the Jean Monnet Programme as EU public diplomacy to look at whether and how EU public diplomacy can exert influence on foreign students' knowledge and perceptions of the EU. In so doing, the practice of the Jean Monnet Programme in China will be employed as a case for empirical study. As the Jean Monnet Programme puts the promotion of "European integration and EU studies" as one of its priorities, this program, as one of EU public diplomacy programs, aims to tell the story of European integration from political, economic, social, and cultural aspects, which will eventually benefit the general aim of the EU as a global actor in world politics.[74]

What is the rationale or this? Although the Jean Monnet Programme is not, strictly speaking, a public diplomacy program implemented by the public diplomacy section in the European External Action Service (EEAS) established by the Treaty of Lisbon, it does maintain the function of public diplomacy in practice.[75,76] The Jean Monnet Programme is named after Jean Monnet (1888–1979), one of the founding fathers of the EU,[77] and Jean Monnet played a fundamental role in the initial stage of post-Second World War European integration. Because of being involved in France's economic plan after 1945, Jean Monnet began to believe that economic development and prosperity can best be achieved at a continental rather than a national level.[78] According to Cini and Perez-Solorzano Borragán, Jean Monnet's concept of supranationality was the driving force for the Schuman Plan which led to the establishment of the European Coal and Steel Company (ECSC) (which became the European Economic Community (EEC) and then the EU), and Monnet became the first head of the ECSC's High Authority.[79]

By conducting interviews in Brussels and referring to official archives released by the EU, a brief history of the Jean Monnet Programme has been presented. As Renato Girelli, program manager of the Jean Monnet Programme in the Directorate General for Education and Culture (DG EAC), has said, those pioneers who founded this program retired several years ago and are no longer able to recount the specific details, but nevertheless some anecdotes remain of the early stages.[80] Girelli and his colleagues conducted some interviews with EU staff members who had worked on the Jean Monnet Programme from the very beginning.

> People who designed the Jean Monnet activities (later the Jean Monnet Action and then the Jean Monnet Programme) 25 years ago and eventually put them into action, knew each other very well. Suddenly they realised that the European project should not only be linked to policy but also reach the citizens. Eventually, they figured out that education was the only way to inform the citizens about what they (the EU officials) were doing.[81]

Although directly approaching the original designers of this program is problematic due to the time and budget constraints, the booklet entitled *Thinking about Europe: Jean Monnet support to European studies* which was edited by Renato Girelli and his colleagues in 2014 by interviewing these pioneers can be used to show the development of the Jean Monnet Programme.

According to Jean Monnet, the development of European integration required the universities of the original six member states to work cooperatively to solve the problems faced by the newly built institutions.[82] Meanwhile, Jean

Monnet also believed that economic integration was only one aspect of the European integration project and the integration process was a concern of everyone in society. Since the EU was a project of future generations, students would have to be engaged more than anyone else. Against this backdrop, Jacques-René Rabier, one of Jean Monnet's close asides, signed a contract with a professor from *Sciences Po* in Pairs for his research about the origins of the Schuman Plan which was published in the *French Journal of Political Science*.[83] Since then, Rabier's work has been expanded to academia.

The independence of the Jean Monnet Programme, even long before it was named after Jean Monnet, was addressed by Luciano Di Fonzo, who worked as a project manager of the Jean Monnet Programme from 1994 to 2013. Di Fonzo stated that:

> Of course, the academic programmes including the Jean Monnet Programme communicate the message of the EU and reach the people in and outside the EU. However, it is not the propaganda of the EU but possesses its independence and freedom. The Jean Monnet Programme conveys the EU's messages to the outside world and plays an important role in EU public diplomacy, but its operation independent from political circles ensures the European studies in academia.[84]

However, at that time, the idea of bringing the EU to its citizens was mainly attributed to a group of leaders. In fact, it was the goal Monnet set that led the information service to engage the people and foster a European consciousness, which ultimately aimed to gain the support of public opinion for European integration and secure its future development.[85] Again, as Renato Girelli emphasized, the early creation of European studies and eventually the innovation of the Jean Monnet Programme aimed to bring the European project to Europeans.[86] In general, the information policy at the supranational level towards member states and third parties was multi-layered: explaining the structure, institutions, and aims of European Community, presenting the process of decision-making in the EU and establishing a permanent dialogue with the public to make the European Communities and their institutions known and thus requiring reputation and mobilizing support for European integration in general and the EU in particular.[87]

At the very earliest stage of European integration, high level officials in the European Commission believed that the role of universities in European information action could be divided into two branches: the first was to be the training ground for the rising generation of European leaders; the second was to produce knowledge and information about European integration in order to increase public acceptance of the European project because of the legitimacy and reputation of universities in knowledge production.[88] Even so, the early endeavors of promoting academic research and study on European integration were random and fragmented. After all, considering that the EEC was a giant project on the way to full European integration, the cooperation between the academic world and the institutions of the EEC and later the EU had been a long process.

Renato Girelli, who interviewed some of the pioneers of the Jean Monnet Programme and edited a booklet about its 25-year history, said that:

> At the very beginning, the idea of creating this programme [which was not named as the Jean Monnet Programme at its preliminary stage of still being a draft] was to bring the idea of the European project to citizens through academic channels.[89]

The Jean Monnet Action received a very positive response from the academic world. After the first call for projects was made in 1990, 1354 proposals were received by DG Information, Communication, Culture, Audiovisual (DG X) for Chairs, Modules, and research grants, and 220 of these were launched in 1990. A year before the first call, the European University Council was founded for leading and administering the Jean Monnet Action according to the suggestions of Jacqueline Lastenouse and Emile Noël. Noël himself became the first president of the European University Council. Besides the unexpected response from the universities, the financial support from the community increased during the three years of its first trial. Finally, the budget from the first year was extended annually with extra funds from the European Parliament.[90]

From 1990 to 1998, the Jean Monnet Action developed rapidly. According to a survey conducted in 1999, around 500 professors received support from the Jean Monnet Action and produced at least 1400 seminars, which eventually covered around 251,000 students based on the data of 1998.[91] Moreover, during this period, over 1,200 PhD theses were written under the supervision of the Jean Monnet professors.[92]

In 2006, the Education and Culture Executive Agency (EACEA) within the DG EAC was created and took over the day-to-day management of the Jean Monnet Activities, and the Lifelong Learning Programme was adopted in the same year. One year later, the Jean Monnet Action became the Jean Monnet Programme with the same status as the Erasmus and Leonardo da Vinci programs, and they all formed part of the Lifelong Learning Programme.[93] However, under the single umbrella of the Lifelong Learning Programme, the Jean Monnet Programme is the only one that can reach beyond the borders of the EU and covers scholars and students directly and indirectly across the world.

After 2014, the Jean Monnet Programme has been integrated into a new programme, "Erasmus Plus," and its objective has been moved slightly from supporting European integration studies to EU studies, while its specific aims include innovation (studying the EU from a new angle and methodologies); cross-fertilization (boosting the knowledge of the EU); and knowledge dissemination. Meanwhile, the predicted direct and indirect beneficiaries of this program extend to students, policy-makers, professionals, civil society, and the general public at large rather than the narrow group of research institutions and academics.[94] Also, the Jean Monnet Chair "Ad Personam" as one of the actions of the Jean Monnet Programme is no longer in existence. Vito Borrelli, Head of the Jean Monnet and the China Desk in DG EAC, explained that,

> According to the previous regulation, professors who held a Jean Monnet Chair position once were not allowed to apply for the funding from the Action of Jean Monnet Chair again. Thus, we created the Jean Monnet Chair "Ad Personam" for professors who had many achievements in European integration studies and were in need of further support for their research. However, the Erasmus Plus Jean Monnet Programme has changed the regulation in order to allow former Jean Monnet Chair holders to apply for the Jean Monnet Chair again, so the Action of Jean Monnet Chair "Ad Personam" is not a need anymore.[95]

With regard to the sponsored research topics that have changed from European integration studies to EU studies, Borrelli said that,

> There is a debate about the content of European integration studies and EU studies before officially making changes to objectives of the Jean Monnet Programme. It seems that European Integration studies focus on political and economic aspects of European integration while EU studies also stress other aspects of low politics such as culture and identity.[96]

Besides, Girelli added that,

> "EU studies" is a much broader concept than European integration studies. Usually, European integration studies place emphasis on EU member states and its candidate states and tries to understand the process and results of integration. However, after five times enlargement, the border of the EU had been largely extended, Thus, EU studies, which includes the relations between the EU and non-EU member states, is more suitable to be one of the objectives of the Erasmus Plus Jean Monnet Programme.[97]

These new changes give rise to new objectives: research innovation, boosting the knowledge of the EU and information dissemination. From the perspective of supporting academic research and study, there is little difference, since studying the European project has always been its main aim.

The EU centers, which are launched by the Service of Foreign Policy Instruments (FPI) in the European Commission, serve as EU public diplomacy under the policy of cooperating with industrialized countries.[98] In other words, the EU centers are the only action labelled as public diplomacy by EU officials despite other EU programs also having the function of public diplomacy in communicating the EU to a world audience. However, this program would have been slightly changed in the following years because of the success of the Jean Monnet Programme.[99]

> Although the EU's educational programmes are coordinated by the DG EAC, other DGs in the European Commission also implement different educational programmes with their own budget. On the one hand, they have their own budget plan; on the other hand, they also want to increase their own competence.[100]

However, the EU Centres have the same objectives of supporting European studies around the world as the Jean Monnet Programme which has gained recognition due to its successful implementation.

> We [the Jean Monnet Sector in DG EAC] have already negotiated with the Service of Foreign Policy Instrument about transferring the administration of the EU Centres from the FPI to the Jean Monnet Programme. Therefore, these EU Centres of Excellence in the industrialised countries and areas will gradually become the Jean Monnet Centre of Excellence in the following years.[101]

Nevertheless, the Jean Monnet Programme has harvested more than expected. In fact, after being moved to the DG EAC, the role of the Jean Monnet Programme as a political instrument increased.[102] Calligaro considers that support of European studies beyond the limits of the Union is a form of public diplomacy.[103] At the 2009 conference celebrating the 20th anniversary of the Jean Monnet Action, José Manuel Barroso, the President of European Commission, emphasised the diplomatic dimension of the Jean Monnet Action and its role in creating an international network of European ambassadors for the EU,[104] which is agreed by some scholars who believe that, in the knowledge era, the EU is prepared to lead the world through building world-class foundations and links in education and training on a global scale thanks to such programs as the Jean Monnet Programme and the Erasmus Mundus Programme with academic credentials and global vision.[105]

Therefore, as an educational program under the management of EACEA within the DG EAC of the European Commission, the activities of the Jean Monnet Programme have always been aimed at supporting academic study and research on European integration and the EU as a whole through selecting the teaching positions and modules in universities around the world and establishing the Jean Monnet Centres of Excellence. However, the objective of the Jean Monnet Programme at the current stage of European integration, according to José María Beneyto, Jean Monnet Chair and Director of Jean

Monnet Centre of Excellence, is to bring the Union closer to its citizens and to reinforce the role and presence of Europe in the world.[106]

As the EU's diplomatic service, the EEAS has indicated that EU public diplomacy aims to cooperate with industrialised countries and areas (Australia, Canada, United States of America, Russia, New Zealand, Singapore, Japan, South Korea, Taiwan, Hong Kong, and Macau) through the establishment of EU centers in these countries and areas. Although the program of establishing EU centers around the world is implemented by the FPI in the European Commission,[107] China and other developing countries are not on the list. According to an official working in a unit in of the EEAS which is in charge of its relationship with China, the EU's public diplomacy practice indicated in the official statement on its website of the EEAS did not include China or other emerging economies simply because of budgetary concerns and a new public diplomacy program specifically toward China would be implemented soon.[108] In other words, besides EU Centres Programme, EU public diplomacy towards developing countries has been implemented through other channels including international educational cooperation programs.

Therefore, although the Jean Monnet Programme is not directly designed or implemented by the divisions of foreign affairs within the framework of public diplomacy at the EU level, it does have the function of public diplomacy and plays a role in EU public diplomacy practice. Thus, studying the implementation of the Jean Monnet Programme in China can reveal how well the Jean Monnet Programme works in that country and whether it offers lessons for EU public diplomacy in the future.

In terms of the content, three key activities took place over the period 2007–2013 when the Jean Monnet Programme was a sub program of the Lifelong Learning Programme of the European Commission: The Jean Monnet Action; Support for Specific Institutions Dealing with Issues Relating to European Integration; European Associations Active at the European Level in the Field of European Integration and Education and Training. The Jean Monnet Action, including the creation of Jean Monnet Chairs, Centres of Excellence, Modules, Information and Research Activities as well as Support for Academic Associations for Professors and Researchers in Researching European Integration, was originally launched in 1989 within the EU and extended to countries outside the EU in 2001 with the purpose of stimulating teaching, research, and reflection on European integration in higher education institutions across the world.[109] In 2014, the Jean Monnet Programme had been incorporated into the new programme of "Erasmus Plus" or "Erasmus for All." Under this new program, its objective has been moved from "supporting European integration studies" to "EU studies," which seems that this program becomes more inclusive, albeit it still gives particular emphasis on the European integration process.[110]

According to the official data of the European Commission, at the time of writing, the Jean Monnet Action helped establish 165 Jean Monnet Centres of Excellence, 879 Jean Monnet Chairs and 2,139 Jean Monnet Modules between 1990 and 2011.[111] As for the mainland China, it has three Jean Monnet Centres, two Jean Monnet Chairs "Ad Personam," fifteen Jean Monnet Chairs and eleven Jean Monnet Modules and several other activities.[112] China is one of the first few non-EU member states being covered by the Jean Monnet Programme, so looking at its practice in China will help us understand whether (and/or how) the teaching and research activities sponsored by the EU in non-EU countries affects perceptions of the EU among future generations.

In the Jean Monnet Programme, the scholars and experts who obtain financial support from this program serve as intermediaries of EU public diplomacy in their countries. They have multiple functions in their home countries: they are professors who deliver knowledge about the EU to young students; they work as commentators in mass media who analyze the various issues related to the EU and set the agenda and framework for public discussion; they serve as a bridge which connects the EU with outside countries and provide intellectual support for European integration. Also, some PhD students supervised by the Jean Monnet professors go on to teach EU-related courses after graduation. The program has also started training teachers from primary and junior schools in Western China in order to deliver knowledge about the EU to teenagers. In other words, the intermediaries of EU public diplomacy in China can, in turn, become trainers training more scholars and researchers to teach and do research on the EU.

This program was established to bring the "European project" to its citizens due to the endeavor of some pioneering EU leaders in late 1980s and had been officially promoted to non-EU member states including China in 2001, which promoted educational export and educational exchange since then. Furthermore, this program has been under-research, despite calls for research on how identity creation and ideology transfer are at work in the context of EU studies centers and the Jean Monnet Chairs.[113] More importantly, this program had been deployed in Poland and Hungary in 1993 and the Czech Republic in 1997 before these countries became EU member states,[114] but China is qualitatively different from EU member states and candidate countries where the Jean Monnet Programme has been implemented for over 25 years. The Chinese context characterized by Chinese history, cultural, economic development model, and political ideologies, provides a new arena within which the Jean Monnet Programme has been exercised.

Hence, evaluating EU public diplomacy by analyzing the implementation of the Jean Monnet Programme in China will be useful because of its comparatively long time span, the continuously adjusted program design and the particularity of the Chinese context. Moreover, cultural background is a vital factor in the localization of educational programs.[115] As traditional Chinese culture still has a great influence in East Asian nations, researching the Jean Monnet Programme in China can be helpful for understanding its effect in an East Asian context. The EU's global governance ambitions cannot be fulfilled without cooperating with China, but a clash of cultural identities may hinder cooperation.[116] Information-based educational programs may offer a way out of this dilemma.

China is an Asian country which is different from its European counterparts in terms of its cultural background and development path, so the effect of the Jean Monnet Programme will partially reveal some features of transcultural communication. As a regional and even global superpower, China's economic and military development largely determines the role of China in East Asia; hence the EU's influence in East Asia will depend on its cooperation with China and other East Asian countries. Therefore, the Chinese view of the EU and the EU's attempt to improve this view through the use of soft power via the Jean Monnet Programme is important. Therefore, even though studying the Jean Monnet Programme cannot give a big picture of EU public diplomacy, it does analyze the achievements of the program in the Chinese context and cast light on the design and implementation of EU public diplomacy for the future.

Besides, studying the Jean Monnet Programme in China will have to consider the national political context. On the one hand, citizenship education in China that aims to sustain the leadership and legitimacy of the Chinese Communist Party does not accept the universality of norms or values,[117] but these so called Western values that have been banned directly or indirectly in Chinese official and academic discourse overlap with the norms promoted by the EU. In this sense, whether and how the EU norms can be disseminated in Chinese universities need to be addressed. On the other hand, the EU's knowledge dissemination and EU norm diffusion are different concepts/processes, so the relationship between them helps understand how EU norms as a part of the knowledge of the EU can be disseminated in China. These two aspects will be elaborated in empirical chapters later.

Again, the EU as a unique international actor on the world stage has its special features of implementing public diplomacy, making its practice different from public diplomacy practice of nation states in the world. However, EU public diplomacy deserves more analysis than it already gained in academia. In this sense, this research, by studying the implementation of the Jean Monnet Programme in China as a case, will add new theoretical and empirical knowledge to public diplomacy literature. On the one hand, in the fieldwork for data collection, the author interviewed participants covered by the program and EU officials who were or have been working on it, which is the most important contribution of this research. On the other hand, this research also studies the Chinese context for the implementation of the Jean Monnet Programme given that China is qualitatively different from EU member states where this program has been implementing for over 25 years, and China has different understanding of EU norms in its political discourse. Against this background, whether/how the knowledge of the EU including descriptive knowledge and normative knowledge has been disseminated in China will shed light on the research on the particularity of the Chinese context.

There is no doubt that EU public diplomacy, through promoting European study and research at the level of higher education, will help increase the EU's presence and visibility and enable it to play a greater role on the world stage. The study of the Jean Monnet Programme in China, and whether and how the EU's public diplomacy works, can be explained and better understood with the empirical data. Moreover, this research will also contribute to the scholarly understanding of EU public diplomacy and its practice in the context of China that has not been given enough attention in the golden age of public diplomacy research.

As aforementioned, this book takes the implementation of the Jean Monnet Programme in China as a case for the study of EU public diplomacy, including how EU public diplomacy has been carried out through this program and why this program works (or why it does not work). At the time of writing, it incorporates several Jean Monnet Chairs and Modules in the universities and three Jean Monnet Centres of Excellence locating at Renmin University of China in Beijing, Fudan University in Shanghai, and Sichuan University in Chengdu, Sichuan. Hence, the research will focus on these three universities. Interviews were conducted in China over a period of seven months including the first round interview (December 2013–February 2014) which aims to find out the descriptive knowledge dissemination of the Jean Monnet Programme and second round interview (March–April 2016) to address the concern that whether the normative knowledge of the EU has been hindered by the Chinese governmental regulations due to the conceptual differences between the EU and China. Furthermore, in order to obtain first-hand information from EU officials responsible for this program, a two-week interview (February 2015) was conducted in Brussels, Belgium.

To be more specific, the Chinese professors who had received funding from this program were interviewed so as to obtain their views of the program and its impact on the Chinese students' perceptions. The Jean Monnet Centres of Excellence in China has opened compulsory and elective courses at the undergraduate level and has also trained masters and PhD students since this program was established, and information and knowledge about the EU have also been transmitted to the Chinese students through the Jean Monnet Modules. The aim of interviewing undergraduate and postgraduate students is to find out the effect of the relevant modules on the students. The influence of the Jean Monnet Professors on PhD students can be figured out by interview PhD students who pursued their degrees in the Jean Monnet Centres of Excellence at these three universities.

In this sense, objectives determine measures of success, or more specifically, "when you set out to measure the effectiveness of an activity, what you measure should reflect the purpose of that activity."[118] The study will use the objectives of EU public diplomacy as general criteria along with the objectives of the Jean Monnet Programme as specific criteria in order to discover whether the program works in China, and these objectives will be correlated and reflected in the interview questions. Moreover, the general criteria of public diplomacy will be discussed in the conceptualization process of public diplomacy, so the specific criteria will be elaborated here. As indicated before, the Jean Monnet Programme under the "Erasmus Plus" will aim to promote "EU studies" through knowledge dissemination, knowledge innovation, and cross-fertilization of knowledge regarding the EU, so two aspects consist of descriptive knowledge and normative knowledge of the EU knowledge will be mentioned through the interview process.

In philosophical studies, the division between descriptive and normative sciences had been used as one of the commonest devices in classification over one century ago, as that the former referred to physics or "what is" and the latter emphasized ethics or "what ought to be."[119] Put differently, descriptive knowledge indicates "what it is" by stating the facts or functions while normative knowledge is not to state any kind of fact but to express an emotion, exhort, command, a wish, prescribe, etc.[120]

Admittedly, descriptive knowledge and normative knowledge has been fused to some extent.[121] Chinese philosophy also identifies knowledge as either descriptive knowledge referring things outside one's mind or normative knowledge entailing the cultivation of one's intentions and the ratification of mind, but a kind of synthesis between descriptive and normative knowledge always exists because knowledge things descriptively can bear upon one's action by making correct judgment possible.[122] On the one hand, a pure statement of EU norms can be descriptive knowledge; on the other hand, a statement of cognition of EU norms is naturally loaded with values since "normative way" is viewed as a "good thing" that are evaluative than factual,[123] which has been enhanced due to different understandings of norms between the EU and China.

Even so, China's response to liberal values which overlap with EU norms is not counter-ideology but counter-norm.[124] China rejects the universal values not by challenging liberalism in the sense as communism did in the Cold War. Rather, China accepts that norms based on liberalism are a part of the pluralist international order but rejects the promotion of universal values with a counter-norm of international diversity.[125] In other words, China emphasizes the appropriateness of liberal values in the Western context constructed by its culture and history and stresses the particularity of the Chinese context characterised by Chinese culture and history. Thus, the EU's normative knowledge dissemination is different from norm diffusion of the EU, which will be fully elaborated in the empirical chapter.

However, distinguishing descriptive knowledge from normative knowledge of the EU is not meaningless albeit it is a tough job. As EU public diplomacy stresses both "what the EU is" and "what the EU stands for," the classroom teaching and learning of the EU will cover descriptive knowledge of the EU including the history and current status as well as normative knowledge of the EU consisting of EU founding norms that guide the EU's internal and external behaviors and are promoted by the EU in its relations with a third party. Given that the EU and China have different understandings of EU norms and the Chinese government does issue regulations on the dissemination of EU norms (also known as "Western values") in higher education institutions, studying the EU's descriptive and normative knowledge dissemination in the Chinese classroom separately will help understand the particularity of knowledge dissemination and the implementation of the Jean Monnet Programme in the Chinese context, which will be discussed with empirical data later.

Therefore, the reminder of this book consists of seven chapters. By reviewing the scholarly debates on public diplomacy and EU public diplomacy practice, it conceptualizes public diplomacy and its relations to soft power, which also offers the general criteria of evaluating public diplomacy programs in chapter 2. The third chapter will look at the role of public diplomacy in the EU's external relations, giving a big picture of EU public diplomacy. Combining with evaluation criteria of the public diplomacy program in general and the Jean Monnet Programme in particular, the fourth one examines the status of the Jean Monnet Programme and its contributions to EU public diplomacy and soft power before moving to look at the implementation of the Jean Monnet Programme in China in chapter 5. On top of this analysis, chapters 6 and 7 will discuss the descriptive and normative knowledge dissemination of the EU through the Jean Monnet Programme with empirical data from the fieldwork, which will be followed by a conclusion regarding the practical implications of the Jean Monnet Programme.

NOTES

1. Mull, C. and Wallin, M. (2013), "Propaganda: A Tool of Strategic Influence," *Fact Sheet of American Security Project*, available at: http://www.scribd.com/doc/165110783/FACT-SHEET-Propaganda-A-Tool-of-Strategic-Influence, [accessed Nov. 4, 2014]: 2.

2. Headrick, D. R. (1994), "Shortwave Radio and Its Impact on International Telecommunication between the Wars," *History and Technology: An International Journal*, 11(1): 26.

3. Burman, A. (2007), *The State of the American Empire: How the USA Shapes the World*, Oxon and New York, Earthscan: 102.

4. Bátora, J. (2005), *Public Diplomacy in Small and Medium-Sized States: Norway and Canada*, Discussion papers in diplomacy, Netherland Institute of International Relations, "Clingendael": 21.

5. McPhail, T. L. (2010), *Global Communication: Theories, Stakeholders and Trends*, West Sussex: Wiley-Blackwell: 95.

6. Edward Murrow Centre, (1965), *What is Public Diplomacy?* Available at: http://fletcher.tufts.edu/Murrow/Diplomacy, [accessed Oct. 10, 2013].

7. Tuch, H. (1990), *Communicating with the World: US Public Diplomacy Overseas*, New York: St. Martin's Press: 2.

8. Malone, G. (1985), "Managing Public Diplomacy," *The Washington Quarterly*, 8(3): 199.

9. Nye, J. (1990), "Soft Power," *Foreign Policy*, No. 80: 168.

10. Nye, J. (2004), *Soft Power: The Means to Success in World Politics*, New York: Public Affairs: 5.

11. Nye, J. (2010), *The Future of Power*, New York: Public Affairs: 100.

12. Melissen, (2005): *Wielding Soft Power: The New Public Diplomacy*, Netherland Institute of International Relations, "Clingendael": 1.

13. Jia, Q. (2010), *Continuity and Change: China's Attitude toward Hard Power and Soft Power*, Brookings East Asia Comment, No. 44.

14. Lynch, D. (2005), *Communicating Europe to the World: What Public Diplomacy for the EU?* EPC Working Paper, No. 21: 14.

15. Yun, S. H. (2006), "Toward Public Relations Theory-Based Study of Public Diplomacy: Testing the Applicability of the Excellent Study," *Journal of Public Relations Research*, 18(4): 307.

16. Fitzpatrick, K. R. (2007), "Advancing the New Public Diplomacy: A Public Relations Perspective," *The Hague Journal of Diplomacy*, 2(3): 210.

17. Melissen, J. (2005), "The New Public Diplomacy: Between Theory and Practice," in Melissen, J. (ed.), *The New Public Diplomacy: Soft Power in International Relations*, New York: Palgrave Macmillan: 12.

18. Bretherton, C. and Vogler, J. (2005), *The European Union as a Global Actor*, London and New York: Routledge: 2.

19. Toje, A., (2010), *The European Union as a Small Power*, London: Palgrave Macmillan: 1.

20. Europa.eu, (2014), *Enhancing the Asian Strategy*, available at: http://europa. eu/legislation_summaries/external_relations/relations_with_third_countries/asia/ r14202_en.htm, [accessed Nov. 3, 2014].

21. Delegation of the EU to China, (2015), *The European Union and China: A Maturing Partnership*, available at: http://eeas.europa.eu/delegations/china/eu_china/ political_relations/index_en.htm, [accessed Mar. 31, 2015].

22. Pacheco Pardo, R, (2009), "The Political Weakness of the EU in East Asia: A Constructivist Approach," *Asia Europe Journal*, 7(2): 273.

23. European Commission, (1995), *A Long Term Policy for China-Europe Relations, Communication of the Commission*, COM (1995) 279/final, available at: http:// eeas.europa.eu/china/docs/com95_279_en.pdf, [accessed Mar. 23, 2015]: 4.

24. Fioramonti, L. and Lucarelli, S, (2010), "Self-representations and External Perceptions—Can the EU Bridge the Gap?" In Lucarelli, S. and Fioramonti, L. (eds.), *External Perceptions of the European Union as a Global Actor*, Hoboken: Taylor and Francis: 224.

25. De Gouveia, P. F. and Plumridge, H. (2005), *European Infopolitik: Developing EU Public Diplomacy Strategy*, London: Foreign Policy Center, available at: fpc.org. uk/fsblob/657.pdf. [Accessed Dec. 12, 2012]: 3.

26. La Porte, T. (2011), *The Power of the European Union in Global Governance: A Proposal for a New Public Diplomacy*, Los Angeles: Figueroa Press: 16.

27. Michalski, A. (2005), "The EU as a Soft Power: The Force of Persuasion," in Melissen, J. (ed.), *The New Public Diplomacy: Soft Power in International Relations*, New York: Palgrave Macmillan: 125.

28. Duke, S. (2013), *The European External Action Service and Public Diplomacy*, Discussion Papers in Diplomacy, No. 127, Netherlands Institute of International Relations, "Clingendael": 3.

29. Vončina, T. (2011), "Speaking with One Voice: Statement and Declarations as an Instrument of the EU's Common Foreign and Security Policy," *European Foreign Affairs Review*, 16(2): 169.

30. Rasmussen, S. B. (2010), "The Messages and Practices of the European Union's Public Diplomacy," *The Hague Journal of Diplomacy*, 5(3): 269.

31. La Porte, T. (2011), *The Power of the European Union in Global Governance: A Proposal for a New Public Diplomacy*, Los Angeles: Figueroa Press: 7.

32. Pisani-Ferry, J., Röttgen, N., Sapir, A., Tucker, P. and Wolff, G.B. (2016), *Europe after Brexit: A Proposal for a Continental Partnership*. Available at: https:// ces.fas.harvard.edu/uploads/files/Reports-Articles/Europe-after-Brexit.pdf, [accessed July 11, 2018]: 1.

33. United States National Intelligence Council, (2008), *Global Trend 2025: A Transformed World*, available at: http://fas.org/irp/nic/2025.pdf, [accessed April 18, 2015]: 32.

34. Lucarelli, S. and Fioramonti, L. (2010), "The EU in the Eyes of the Others— Why Bother?" In Lucarelli, S. and Fioramonti, L. (eds.), *External Perceptions of the European Union as a Global Actor*, Hoboken: Taylor and Francis: 1.

35. Wallström, M. (2008), *Public Diplomacy and its Role in the EU's External Relations*, Mortara Center for International Studies, Georgetown University, available

at: http://europa.eu/rapid/press-release_SPEECH-08-494_en.pdf, [accessed April 3, 2015]: 2.

36. Snyder, F. (2009), *The European Union and China, 1949–2008: Basic Documents and Commentary*, Oxford and Portland: Hart Publishing: 7.

37. EEAS, (2015), *EU-China 2020 Strategic Agenda for Cooperation*, available at: http://www.eeas.europa.eu/china/docs/20131123_agenda_2020__en.pdf, [accessed Mar. 29, 2015].

38. Song, X. (2012), "Challenges and Opportunities in EU-China Relations," in Vogt, R. (ed.), *Europe and China: Strategic Partners or Rivals?* Hong Kong: Hong Kong University Press: 19–20.

39. Deng, K. G. (2010), "Globalisation, China's Recent Miracle Growth and Its Limits," in Deng, K. G. (ed.), *Globalization—Today, Tomorrow*, Available at: http://www.intechopen.com/books/globalization--today--tomorrow/globalisation-china-s-recent-miracle-growth-and-its-limits-, [accessed Aug. 6, 2014]: 140.

40. European Commission (1995), *A Long-Term Policy for EU–China Relations*, COM (1995) 279 final.

41. Ibid, 1995: 3.

42. Ibid, 1995: 5.

43. European Commission (1998), *Building a Comprehensive Partnership with China*, COM (1998) 181 final: 4.

44. European Commission (2001), *EU Strategy towards China: Implementation of the 1998 Communication and Future Steps for a More Effective EU Policy*, COM (2001) 265 final: 7.

45. Michalski, A. and Pan, Z. (2017), *Unlikely Partners? China, The European Union and the Forging of a Strategic Partnership*, Singapore: Palgrave Macmillan: 47.

46. Smith, M. (2016), "EU Diplomacy and the EU-China Strategic Relationship: Framing, Negotiation and Management," *Cambridge Review of International Affairs*, 29(1): 82.

47. European Commission (2003), *A Maturing Partnership—Shared Interests and Challenges in EU-China Relations*, COM (2003) 533 final: 4.

48. European Commission (2006), *EU-China: Closer Partners, Growing Responsibilities*, COM (2006) 631 final: 9.

49. Ministry of Foreign Affairs of P. R. China. (2003), *China's Policy Paper on EU*, available at: www.chinamission.be/eng/zywj/zywd/t1227623.htm, [accessed March 6, 2019].

50. Ministry of Foreign Affairs of P. R. China. (2014), *China's Policy Paper on the EU: Deepen the China-EU Comprehensive Strategic Partnership for Mutual Benefits and Win-Win Cooperation*, available at: http://www.chinamission.be/eng/zywj/zywd/t1143406.htm, [accessed March 6, 2019]. Ministry of Foreign Affairs of P. R. China. (2018), *China's Policy Paper on the European Union*, available at: http://www.chinamission.be/eng/zywj/zywd/t1623330.htm, [accessed March 6, 2019].

51. Stumbaum, M. U. and Xiong, W. (2012), "Conceptual Differences of Strategic Partnership in EU-China Relations," in Pan, Z. (ed.), *Conceptual Gaps in China-EU Relations: Global Governance, Human Rights and Strategic Partnership*, Basingstoke: Palgrave Macmillan: 157.

52. European Union. (2003), *European Security Strategic—A Secure Europe in a Better World*, available at: https://europa.eu/globalstrategy/en/european-security -strategy-secure-europe-better-world, [accessed March 10, 2019].

53. Solana, J. (2005), *Speech by Javier Solana, EU Higher Representative for the Common Foreign and Security Policy: Driving forwards the China-EU strategic partnership*, Sept. 6, available at: http://www.omct.org/files/2005/09/3088/omct _euro_week_newsletter_30_05.pdf. [accessed March 6, 2019].

54. Rettman, A. (2010), "Ashton Designates Six New 'Strategic Partners,'" *EU Observer*, available at: https://euobserver.com/institutional/30828, [accessed March 10, 2019].

55. Wen, J. (2004), *Vigorously Promoting Comprehensive Strategic Partnership between China and the European Union*, at the China-EU Investment and Trade Forum in Brussels, May 6, available at: https://www.fmprc.gov.cn/ce/cebe/eng/zt/ Topics/t101949.htm, [accessed March 6, 2019].

56. Holslag, J. (2011), "The Elusive Axis: Assessing the EU-China Strategic Partnership," *JCMS: Journal of Common Market Studies*, 49(2): 293.

57. Smith, M. and Xie, H. (2010), "The European Union and China: The Logics of 'Strategic Partnership,'" *Journal of Contemporary European Research*, 6(4): 434; 445.

58. Maher, R. (2016), "The Elusive EU-China Strategic Partnership," *International Affairs*, 92(4): 959–976.

59. Griese, O. (2006), "EU-China Relations—An Assessment by the Communications of the European Union," *Asia Europe Journal*, 4(4): 546.

60. Men, J. (2012), "The EU and China: Mismatched Partners?" *Journal of Contemporary China*, 21(74): 335.

61. European Commission (2006), *Commission Working Document, Accompanying COM(2006) 631 Final: Closer Partners, Growing Responsibilities, A Policy Paper on EU-China Trade and Investment: Competition and Partnership*, COM (2006) 632 final: 14.

62. Men, J. (2012), "The EU and China: Mismatched partners?" *Journal of Contemporary China*, 21(74): 335.

63. Taneja, P. (2010), "China-Europe Relations: The Limits of Strategic Partnerships," *International Politics*, 47(3/4): 372; 385.

64. Zhou, H. (2017), "An Overview of the China-EU Strategic Partnership (2003–2013)," in Zhou, H. (ed.), *China-EU Relations: Reassessing the China-EU Comprehensive Strategic Partnership*, Singapore: Springer: 13.

65. Chen, Z. (2016), "China, the European Union and the Fragile World Order," *JCMS: Journal of Common Market Studies*, 54(4): 782–784.

66. Reiterer, M. (2012), *2012: The EU in Asia Year—Facts and Figures Concerning the EU's Engagement in the Asia Pacific*, available at: http://eeas.europa.eu/del egations/australia/documents/press_corner/20121025_eu-in-asia-facts-and-figures. pdf, [accessed 09-09-2014]: 2.

67. Pacheco Pardo, R, (2009), "The Political Weakness of the EU in East Asia: A Constructivist Approach," *Asia Europe Journal*, 7(2): 273.

68. Stumbaum, M. U. (2012), How *Does Asia View the EU? Security in an Interpolar World*. NFG Working Paper, Series, No. 01, March 2012, NFG Research Group "Asian Perceptions of the EU," Free University of Berlin: 12–13.

69. Reiterer, M. (2012), *2012: The EU in Asia Year—Facts and Figures Concerning the EU's Engagement in the Asia Pacific*, available at: http://eeas.europa.eu/del egations/australia/documents/press_corner/20121025_eu-in-asia-facts-and-figures. pdf, [accessed 09-09-2014]: 3.

70. Delegation of the EU to China, (2015), *The European Union and China: A Maturing Partnership*, available at: http://eeas.europa.eu/delegations/china/eu_china/ political_relations/index_en.htm, [accessed Mar. 31, 2015].

71. China.com, (2012), *the Wisdom of Public Diplomacy: The Dialogue Among Chinese, American and European Scholars*, available at: http://www.china.com.cn/ international/txt/2012-09/11/content_26492930.htm, [accessed Sept. 3, 2013].

72. Von Hofmann, N. (2007), "How do Asians Evaluate Europe's Strategic Involvement in East Asia," *Asia Europe Journal*, 5(2): 192.

73. Robles, A. C. Jr. (2003), "The ASEAN Regional Forum and the European Union as a security system and a security actor," *Dialogue and Cooperation*, Singapore: Friedrich-Ebert Stiftung Singapore: 30.

74. Cross, Mai'a K. D. (2013), "Conceptualising European Public Diplomacy," in Mai'a K. Davis Cross & Jan Melissen (eds.), *European Public Diplomacy: Soft Power at Work*, Hampshire: Palgrave Macmillan: 1.

75. Quintin, O. (2009), *20 Years of Support for European Integration Studies*, Jean Monnet Conference (Closing Session), http://ec.europa.eu/education/jean-monnet/ doc1567_en.htm, [accessed 10-02-2013]: 332.

76. Calligaro, O. (2013), *Negotiating Europe: EU Promotion of Europeanness since the 1950s*, New York: Palgrave Macmillan: 38.

77. Fransen, F. J. (2001), *The Supranational Politics of Jean Monnet: Ideas and Origins of the European Community*, Westport CT: Greenwood Press: 1.

78. Urwin, D. W. (2009), "The European Community: From 1945 to 1985," in Cini M. and Borragán N., (eds.), *European Union Politics (3rd edition)*, New York: Oxford University Press: 20.

79. Cini, M. and Borragán, N., (eds.), (2009), *European Union Politics (3rd edition)*, New York: Oxford University: 446.

80. Interview with Renato Girelli in Brussels, Feb. 6, 2015.

81. Ibid.

82. Maresceau, M. (2011), "Tracing the History of the Jean Monnet Programme," in in European Union, (ed.), *20 Years of Support for European Integration Studies*, Luxembourg: Publications Office of the European Union: 275.

83. European Union (2014b), *Thinking about Europe: Jean Monnet Support to European Studies*, Luxembourg: Publications Office of the European Union: 11.

84. Interview with Luciano Di Fonzo in Brussels, Feb. 17, 2014.

85. Calligaro, O. (2013), *Negotiating Europe: EU Promotion of Europeanness since the 1950s*, New York: Palgrave Macmillan: 20.

86. Interview with Renato Girelli in Brussels, Feb. 6, 2014.

87. Reinfeldt, A. (2014), "Communicating European Integration: Information vs. Integration," *Journal of Contemporary European Research*, 10(1): 48–49.

88. Calligaro, O. (2013), *Negotiating Europe: EU Promotion of Europeanness since the 1950s*, New York: Palgrave Macmillan: 21.

89. Interview with Renato Girelli in Brussels, Feb. 6, 2015.

90. European Union (2014), *Thinking about Europe: Jean Monnet Support to European Studies*, Luxembourg: Publications Office of the European Union: 21; 25.

91. ECOTEC Research and Consulting (1999), *External Evaluation Report of the Jean Monnet Action*, available at: http://ec.europa.eu/dgs/education_culture/evalreports/education/1999/jeanmonnet/JMintrep_fr.pdf, [accessed Oct. 20, 2014]: 22; 30.

92. Reinfeldt, A. (2014), "Communicating European Integration: Information vs. Integration," *Journal of Contemporary European Research*, 10(1): 35.

93. European Union (2014), *Thinking about Europe: Jean Monnet Support to European Studies*, Luxembourg: Publications Office of the European Union: 39.

94. EACEA, (2014), *Erasmus Plus: Actions,* available at: http://eacea.ec.europa.eu/erasmus-plus/actions_en#, [accessed Sept. 17, 2014].

95. Interview with Vito Borrelli in Brussels, Feb. 6, 2015.

96. Ibid.

97. Interview with Renato Girelli in Brussels, Feb. 6, 2015.

98. EU Centres-EEAS, (2014), available at: http://www.eeas.europa.eu/eu-centres/index_en.htm, [accessed Mar. 21, 2014].

99. Interviews with Vito Borrelli and Girelli Renato in Brussels, Feb. 6, 2015.

100. Ibid.

101. Ibid.

102. European Union (2014), *Thinking about Europe: Jean Monnet Support to European Studies*, Luxembourg: Publications Office of the European Union: 40.

103. Calligaro, O. (2013), *Negotiating Europe: EU Promotion of Europeanness since the 1950s*, New York: Palgrave Macmillan: 38.

104. Barroso, J. M. (2011), "Europe at the Crossroads—What I Think," in European Union, (ed.), *20 Years of Support for European Integration Studies*, Luxembourg: Publications Office of the European Union: 6–13.

105. Figel, J. (2011), "Critical Reflection and Reliable Information: The Jean Monnet Community and the Future Course of the European Union," in European Union, (ed.), *20 Years of Support for European Integration Studies*, Luxembourg: Publications Office of the European Union: 15.

106. Beneyto, J. M. (2011), "The Future of the Jean Monnet Programme and of European Integration Studies," in European Union, (ed.), *20 Years of Support for European Integration Studies*, Luxembourg: Publications Office of the European Union: 322.

107. EEAS, (2014), *Organisation Charts*, available at: http://eeas.europa.eu/background/docs/organisation_en.pdf, [accessed Mar. 12, 2015]; EEAS, (2014), website of EU delegations, available at: http://www.eeas.europa.eu/delegations/index_en.htm, [accessed Mar. 24, 2014]; general introduction of the EU delegations, available at: http://www.eeas.europa.eu/delegations/index_en.htm, [accessed Mar. 24, 2014]; Foreign Policy of cooperating with industrialised countries, available at: http://www.eeas.europa.eu/ici/publicdiplomacy/index_en.htm, [accessed Mar. 21, 2014].

108. Conversation with an EU official during a roundtable discussion affiliated to Europe China Research and Advice Network (ECRAN) annual conference on 17–19 June, 2014 in Brussels, Belgium. Interview in Brussels, Belgium, Feb. 5, 2015.

109. EACEA, (2014), *Information about the Jean Monnet Programme from 2007–2013*, available at: http://eacea.ec.europa.eu/llp/jean_monnet/jean_monnet_en.php, [accessed Sept. 29, 2014].

110. EACEA, (2014), *Erasmus Plus: Actions,* available at: http://eacea.ec.europa.eu/erasmus-plus/actions_en#, [accessed Sept. 17, 2014].

111. EACEA, (2014), *Information about the Jean Monnet Programme from 2007-2013*, available at: http://eacea.ec.europa.eu/llp/jean_monnet/jean_monnet_en.php, [accessed Sept. 29, 2014].

112. Interview with Vito Borrelli in Brussels, Belgium, Feb. 6, 2015; EACEA, 2014e.

113. Wiessala, G. (2013), "Social-Cultural and Educational Cooperation between the EU and Asia," in Christiansen, T. Kirchner, E. and Murray, P. B. (eds.), *The Palgrave Handbook of EU-Asia Relations*, Hampshire: Palgrave Macmillan: 213.

114. European Union (2014), *Thinking about Europe: Jean Monnet Support to European Studies*, Luxembourg: Publications Office of the European Union: 24.

115. Cheng, Y. C. (2001), *Paradigm Shift in Higher Education: Globalization, Localization, and Individualization*, presented at the conference of Innovation in African Higher Education, Ford Foundation, Nairobi, Kenya, Oct. 1st to 3rd: 10.

116. Wang, Y. (2012), "China and the EU in Global Governance: Seeking Harmony in Identities," in Wouters, J. de Wilder, T. and Defraigne P. (eds.), *China, the European Union and Global Governance*, Cheltenham: Edward Elgar: 54–59.

117. Law, W. (2013), "Globalization, National Identity, and Citizenship Education: China's Search for Modernization and a Modern Chinese Citizenry," *Frontiers of Education in China*, 8(4): 617.

118. Wilding, C. M. (2007), *Measuring the Effectiveness of Public Diplomacy: the UK Approach*, available at: http://www.global.asc.upenn.edu/fileLibrary/PDFs/wilding.pdf, [accessed April 3, 2015]: 1.

119. Sabin, G. H. (1912), "Descriptive and Normative Sciences," *The Philosophical Review*, 21(4): 433–450.

120. Emmons, D. C. (1972), "Normative Knowledge," *The Journal of Value Inquiry*, 6(4): 294.

121. Dibble, V. K. and Pekowsky, B. (1973), "What Is and What Ought to Be: A Comparison of Certain Characteristics of the Ideological and Legal Styles of Thoughts," *American Journal of Sociology*, 79(3): 547.

122. Cheng, C. (1991), *New Dimensions of Confucian and Neo-Confucian Philosophy*, NY: Albany: State University of New York Press: 269.

123. Pace, M. (2007), "The Construction of EU Normative Power," *Journal of Common Market Studies*, 45(5): 1043.

124. Dams, T. and Van Der Putten, F. P. (2015), *China and Liberal Values in International Relations, Clingendael Report*, Netherlands Institute of International Relations "Clingendael": 5.

125. Ibid: 17.

Chapter Two

Conceptualizing Public Diplomacy and Soft Power

2.1 THE CONCEPTUAL EVOLVEMENT OF PUBLIC DIPLOMACY

The EU needs public diplomacy to improve external perceptions and anchor its role on the world stage, so what public diplomacy is? Despite its long history in practice, and its earliest definition coined by Edmund A. Gullion in 1965, public diplomacy is still not a universally accepted term. On the one hand, the concept of public diplomacy has been constantly updated attributable to technology innovation and the structural changes of international politics. On the other hand, public diplomacy is under-theorized and under-criticized, albeit it matters for each international actor on the world stage based on historical experience. Therefore, the world is ready for public diplomacy, but public diplomacy might or might not be ready for the world.[1]

Defining "public diplomacy" is not an easy task due to its varied political and national characteristics. Based on his diplomatic practice, Edmund A. Gullion, a former Director of the United States Information Agency (USIA) and former Dean of Fletcher School in Tufts University, emphasized the influence of public attitudes on the formation and implementation of foreign policies. According to his understanding, evaluating the reporting of foreign affairs and their impact on policy, promoting cross-cultural communications, cultivation of international public opinion, the interaction between domestic non-governmental organizations and their counterparts abroad, and the communication between diplomats and foreign reporters are all included in the practice of public diplomacy. Gullion also stressed that "central to public diplomacy is the transnational flow of information and ideas."[2]

Admittedly, Gullion's definition was a watershed in the theory of public diplomacy. However, scholars and experts doing research on public diplo-

macy have never stopped adjusting this term to the new conditions of international politics and the requirements of foreign policies. Moreover, a multi-
and inter-disciplinary approach study conducted by scholars from a variety of
subjects also contribute to the conceptualization of public diplomacy.

Communication studies is the most important area for the conceptualization of public diplomacy since such key concepts as public opinion and news
management have been introduced to public diplomacy research, so it is easy
to understand that a large part of public diplomacy theory consists of the
application of the "5W" communication model, which was first coined by
Harold Lasswell in 1948 and further elaborated in his monograph published
in 1971 to explain government-initiated cross-border and global communication.[3, 4] The "5W" communication model includes "who," "says what," "in
which channel," "to whom," and "with what effect," so more and more scholars try to define public diplomacy by incorporating one or more elements in
the communication process.

According to Malone, public diplomacy is "direct communication with
foreign peoples, with the aims of affecting their thinking and, ultimately, that
of their government."[5] Malone also describes the objectives of public diplomacy as "promoting national interests abroad and achieving mutual understanding."[6] Based on Malone's definition, the effect of public diplomacy has
two stages: the first is to influence foreign publics and win their "hearts and
minds"; the second is to change the attitudes of foreign governments through
domestic pressure from their own informed citizens. However, his definition
does not indicate who would be the communicator in this process.

Tuch defines public diplomacy as "a government's process of communicating with foreign publics in an attempt to bring about understanding for its
nation's ideas and ideals, its institutions and culture, as well as its national
goals and current policies,"[7] but this definition describes public diplomacy
as a one-way transmission of information and confines the main actor of
public diplomacy to the government, which, because of the utilization and
prevalence of the Internet and the rise of civil society around the world, has
been largely revised by public diplomacy researchers in modern times. In the
twenty-first century, the target groups of public diplomacy are not passive
foreign publics or overseas countries. On the contrary, individuals and communities are active "participants" and potential collaborators with whom to
cooperate and co-create.[8]

Scholars of public relations studies also continue to explore the features in
common between public relations and public diplomacy. In 1992, Signitzer
and Coombs tried to understand public diplomacy from the perspective of
public relations, and they cited Delaney's definition of public diplomacy
as the "way in which both government and private individuals and groups

influence directly or indirectly those public attitudes and opinions that bear directly on anther government's foreign policy decisions."[9] According to them, implementers of public diplomacy include both private actors and governments, and the relationship building between a nation-state and its foreign publics is what brings public diplomacy and public relations together.[10] They were the first researchers to discuss the role of private actors and the effect of relationship building in public diplomacy, which will be further discussed from a transdisciplinary perspective—public relations studies.

With the coming of information age, researchers are now re-thinking the term "public diplomacy" and suggesting that its original definition is no longer applicable to the new functions of public diplomacy in the new era. Consequently, public diplomacy has been replaced by the term "new public diplomacy." Rhiannon Vickers was one of the first to identify the differences between the new definition of public diplomacy and its original version. She considers that developments in public diplomacy practice have created new and different recipients and actors, and she believes that the new public diplomacy can be characterized as the "blurring of traditional distinctions between international and domestic information activities, between public and traditional diplomacy, and between cultural diplomacy, marketing and news management."[11] However, the word "blurring" is still confusing because it does not accurately explain the distinctions between traditional public diplomacy and its new incarnation.

Against this backdrop, Jan Melissen concludes that there are three features of new public diplomacy: the enlarged groups of public diplomacy participants—sovereign state, large and small non-state actors, supranational and subnational players; changed targets—influencing foreign publics instead of domestic citizens, which differentiates it from public affairs or open diplomacy where diplomats interact with publics at home; altered information flow—from one-way information transmission to two-way information flow with the advancement and prevalence of social media.[12] Melissen's analysis systematically illustrates the new factors of public diplomacy, and to some extent, explains the necessity of using the term "new public diplomacy."

Gilboa offers an even more comprehensive approach to the concept of public diplomacy including the utilization of soft power, the participation of states and non-state actors, the function of mass media, two-way communication, the effect of public opinion, public relations, nation branding and cyber public diplomacy, regarding both short- and long- term issues.[13] As Gregory persuasively argues, public diplomacy "has come to mean an instrument used by states, associations of states, and some sub-states and non-state actors to understand culture, attitudes and behaviours; to build and manage relationships; and to influence thoughts and mobilize actors to advance their interest and values."[14]

Furthermore, some scholars try to understand public diplomacy in the field of nation branding—another interdisciplinary perspective of marketing theory. As Wang argues, a crucial element of nation branding is communicating a country's policies and culture to an international audience, and public diplomacy has been one of the primary tools for addressing such issues.[15] Ham indicates that the key element in both nation branding and public diplomacy is building personal and institutional relationships and dialogue with foreign publics.[16] Fan also says that beyond marketing, nation branding can play a potentially important role in cross-cultural communication, which is something that public diplomacy also emphasizes.[17]

Other scholars try to understand public diplomacy through distinguishing effective public diplomacy from ineffective public diplomacy. Nicholas Cull gives seven lessons of successful public diplomacy: listening as a start; public diplomacy should be reflected in policy; public diplomacy is not for domestic consumptions; effective public diplomacy needs credibility; credibility depends on intermediaries; public diplomacy is more than image projection; and last but not least, public diplomacy is everyone's business.[18] On top of this, Margot Wallström, first vice president of the European Commission, adds three more: public diplomacy should give as much attention to outside the capital as within it; public diplomacy should reflect not only what we do or want to do, but also what we are and what we stand for; public diplomacy should respect gender equality.[19] Their recommendations have no apparent direct connection with the conceptualization of public diplomacy, but they do offer some clues about what effective public diplomacy is and how to make it work. This helps us understand and define public diplomacy.

Among these different definitions, several parts of these issues related to public diplomacy concepts may have well been developed; others will be exploited below by discussing interdisciplinary contributions to public diplomacy.

2.1.1 Interdisciplinary Contributions to Public Diplomacy Research

Communication studies and public relations research have been leveraged to understand the deployment and operation of public diplomacy, while international relations scholars are using their respective theories to explain the effect of these transnational communication behaviors and cross-border public opinion campaigns in international politics. In its discussion of the concept of public diplomacy, this research will mainly focus on the contributions from the interdisciplinary studies of communication, public relations, and international relations. In sum, this chapter will establish a theoretical basis for further discussion about EU public diplomacy and the Jean Monnet Programme.

2.1.1.1 The Contributions of Communication Studies

The contribution from communication studies, which acts as a crucial precondition for public diplomacy, consists of four main elements: two-step flow of communication, international public opinion, mass media research, and the advancement of information and communication technologies. Even though public diplomacy is a branch of foreign policy and diplomacy study, the transnational flow of information and intercultural communication are what make its practice possible and operable. In other words, transnational information and the flow of ideas is a central aspect of public diplomacy practice,[20] albeit public diplomacy goes further than transnational information transmission.

Drawing on the different understandings of public diplomacy mentioned above, public diplomacy is a communication process, irrespective of specific channels, tools, and aims, although the audience is located within a different cultural context. Meanwhile, on top of the discussion above, public diplomacy stresses the role of messages in influencing foreign publics, which seems that public diplomacy is a direct information communication process from the communicator to the recipients with the messages. Following this logic, strategic narratives, representational force, and sociological construction closely relating to information-oriented public diplomacy are put forward as factors in strengthening the effect of messages.

Nevertheless, a good message does not necessarily lead to an expected effect. The message of the EU, whether it is reflected in information activities or carried by educational and cultural programs, aims to reach its foreign publics through a communication process. From the perspective of communication effect research, the effectiveness of public diplomacy is also affected by the credibility of information sources.[21] Thus, for the communicators who cannot reach their audiences directly, the credibility of messenger has a determining effect because the wrong messenger will ruin the meanings that the message carries, no matter how good the message is.[22] Put differently, public diplomacy does not always seek its mass audience directly, so we must consider the two-step flow model in the transnational communication context.

Since the EU is viewed as a model of regional integration and endeavors to promote EU norms, its message is loud and clear. Thus, this research concerns the question of how to ensure that the EU's message is communicated to its end recipients by an appropriate messenger. However, public diplomacy goes further than transnational information transmission. According to Lynch, public diplomacy consists of information, research and analysis, and cultural and educational activities, which are further explained by Cull as listening advocacy, cultural and educational diplomacy, and international new broadcasting. Information activities mainly emphasize short-term impact, while both cultural and educational programs carry the potential for long-term influence and relationship building. In this sense, the indirect communication process in public diplomacy also merits analysis, which can be understood from another interdisciplinary perspective—communication studies.

The two-step flow of communication, first formulated in 1944, implies that ideas often flow from radio and print to opinion leaders, and from these to less-active sections of the population,[23] emphasizing the effect of interpersonal communication as a channel of communication. In this process, opinion leaders are not only information providers but also information seekers.[24] Accordingly, it is opinion leaders who have the most influence on the media audience rather than the mass media.[25] More importantly, further research has proven that opinion leaders and the people they influence are very much alike, and typically belong to the same primary groups.[26] Although the two-step flow model is based on the study of interpersonal communication occurring within one country, its application to public diplomacy—a transnational communication practice—can offer different insights into the practice of public diplomacy.

Since public diplomacy is a form of cross-border communication, finding an appropriate messenger (i.e., an opinion leader influential with the target groups) can solve three problems. First, public diplomacy requires credibility, but official information channels always lack credibility.[27] Therefore, a credible intermediary who can speak on behalf of the implementers of public diplomacy will be helpful in sharing the total burden shouldered by the implementers and increasing the effect of public diplomacy.[28] Second, public diplomacy is a form of transnational and sometimes even transcultural communication, which means that its message not only needs to reach the target audience but it also needs to make sense to them. Messengers in similar cultures or the same countries as the audience can explain the message to them while speaking for the implementer of public diplomacy. Third, high visibility does not necessarily lead to a favorable image.[29] A messenger communicating the information on behalf of the implementer can help lower the visibility of the implementer behind the public diplomacy message. This chapter will not address this point further, but Manheim's findings remain persuasive.

It is worth noting that scholarly discussion has already begun to apply the two-step flow model to public diplomacy. The relationship between social media users and their followers in information sharing is comparable to that of opinion leaders and the people influenced in this model, which explains why social media—with its characteristics of interpersonal communication—is utilized to conduct public diplomacy in target countries.[30] Based on the two-step flow model, experienced public diplomacy officers know fully well that a credible human factor is important in effective communication, i.e., a message transmitted by the mass media is far more credible but would have a greater impact if it was relayed to audiences by key opinion leaders.[31] British public diplomacy also puts emphasis on elites, who then mediate and multiply the message in order to reach the wider masses, which is in line with the two-step flow.[32] Indeed, applying the two-step flow model to public diplomacy not only solves the credibility problems but also addresses certain ethical concerns.[33] These studies point out the similarity between the two-step flow model and public diplomacy as a cross-border communication process, and the necessity of looking for a credible message, yet they do not concentrate on it as an independent phenomenon of public diplomacy practice.

While researching EU public diplomacy practices, Rasmussen suggests that supporting civil society activities in target countries can help the EU deliver its message through civil society actors, because of the credibility of the latter; this is called "public diplomacy by proxy."[34] However, Winston Churchill, former Prime Minister of the UK, was already embracing public diplomacy by proxy when seeking aid from the US during the Second World War, in that, according to Churchill, it was helpful to use America's own voices—particularly those of journalists and reporters with good reputation—to convince the US public that it was in the best interests of the US to aid Britain.[35] Both these cases locate the proxies for public diplomacy inside the target countries.

The intermediary for public diplomacy can also be outside the target countries. Through studying the competition for diplomatic recognition between the People's Republic of China (P.R. China) and Taiwan in Central America, Alexander noticed that certain poor countries switched their diplomatic relations from Taiwan to Beijing, because of the promise of huge investments. This made other poor Central American republics diplomatically salivate, after witnessing the special treatment offered by Beijing, and many followed suit in establishing diplomatic relations with P.R. China.[36] Thus, public diplomacy by intermediary can also be understood as the performance of public diplomacy within one nation state, with the intention of creating favorable opinion among the public and elites of another nation state.[37] This research uses "intermediary" rather than "proxy" to manifest the independence of academics and academic activities sponsored by the academic programs of the EU. However, "proxy" may still be used due to the quotation of academic publications.

In the cases above, it is clear that there are two different kinds of intermediaries in public diplomacy. In the former case, civil society actors originating from the target countries can serve as internal intermediaries for EU public diplomacy, which highlights the influence of civil society actors within their home countries. In the latter case, the intermediaries for China's public diplomacy towards the other Central American countries is a nation state acting as external intermediaries, paying attention to the attractiveness of successful models. Yet, in a way, talking about public diplomacy by intermediaries, from its very outset, involves looking for solutions to the credibility problems. In other words, effective public diplomacy requires credibility, yet the most credible voice is not always one's own.[38]

In this way, public diplomacy by intermediary, as a phenomenon in practice, involves the indirect engagement with foreign publics through employing messengers—either inside or outside the target countries—on behalf of the implementers, so as to enhance the credibility of the message and improve the effect of public diplomacy. Under these circumstances, public diplomacy can be broken down into two steps: the message first travels from the original implementer of public diplomacy to the intermediary (messenger), and then it travels from the intermediary to its end recipient (foreign publics).

Public diplomacy is also driven by international public opinion and is based on the complex relationship between the government, mass media, and perceptions of foreign publics. Many effective studies of the interaction between public diplomacy practice and these three variables have been carried out. Tomoko Akami thinks that the change in the means of wartime propaganda in that time can be attributed to the increasing importance of international public opinion and its impact.[39] According to the author, as mass political participation increases, the idea of "international public opinion" becomes a crucial element in international relations, forcing nations to adjust their approaches to external propaganda, and this explains the origins of what is now called public diplomacy.[40]

Goldsmith and Horiuchi analyze US high-level visits to foreign countries and the relationship between the leader and foreign public opinion as a type of public diplomacy.[41] The result reveals the interaction between government leaders and foreign perceptions of US global leadership: the increasing credibility of US leaders in foreign countries can improve foreign perceptions of the US and its influence on international affairs and vice versa.[42] In fact, "credibility" is at the root of positive foreign public opinion and one of the most important attributes of successful public diplomacy, no matter who takes charge of public diplomacy practice or what kind of public diplomacy is deployed.

The interaction between the mass media and international public opinion has also been discussed by experts. The term agenda-setting theory was first put forward by McCombs and Shaw in 1972, who indicated that, to a certain extent, newsroom and press workers do not only present a given story, but they also decide how much significance to attach to it through their selection of what news to cover.[43] Agenda-setting theory explains the possible relationship between the mass media and public opinion and is used more for domestic political phenomena, but public diplomacy is "winning hearts and minds" of foreign publics.

A new phenomenon in public diplomacy is the advancement of communication technologies and their unanticipated influence.[44, 45, 46] Before the worldwide utilization of the internet, any improvement in communication technologies merely accelerated the pace of information transmission, but the role of the recipient remained unchanged. The availability of the internet and the prevalence of personal computers and then mobile phones, by lowering the cost of collecting and publishing information, totally changed this situation and brought public diplomacy into a new era. The new technologies affect not only the amount of information that is accessible, but they have also altered the relationship between communicator and receiver, which in turn affects the new model of public diplomacy.

As Seo Hyunjin has mentioned, the internet is the "prime mover" of the change in diplomacy. For non-state actors in public diplomacy practice, the development of information technology provides them with an opportunity to access and exert a positive influence on their foreign counterparts.[47] That means that the changes in the communication context of international politics make foreign policy and political operations more visible and accessible to more non-state actors and even ordinary people.[48] In this sense, communication technology improvement is basic and is the most crucial factor for what has been called "new public diplomacy."

2.1.1.2 *The Contributions of Public Relations Research*

The worldwide popularity of public diplomacy has been attributed to the advancement of communication technologies and the involvement of non-state actors, which shifts the model of information dissemination from monologue/one-way information flow to dialogue/two-way information exchange. Therefore, long-term relationship building rather than short-term influence becomes the main purpose of communicating with foreign publics in public diplomacy practice. Accordingly, the similarities between public relations theory and public diplomacy practice have impelled researchers to transfer ideas from one area to another so as to further the conceptualization of public diplomacy.

As far back as the early 1990s, Signitzer and Coombs argued that the similarity of objectives and utilization of the same tools have given rise to the conceptual convergence of the two, and public relations theories can now be applied to public diplomacy.[49] In their study, public diplomacy consists of political information and cultural communication, and the latter is made up of two sub-fields—cultural diplomacy and cultural relations. The authors argue that foreign ministries and embassies are responsible for communicating political information to foreign publics, and the function of cultural communication is theoretically consistent with the deployment of public relations. In order to prove this theoretical linkage, a comparison is made between Peisert's four models of cultural communication (one-way transmission of one's own culture abroad, self-portrayal, information, exchange, and cooperation) and Grunig and Hunt's four models of public relations (press agentry/publicity, public information, two-way asymmetric, and two-way symmetric).[50]

Signitzer and Coombs argue that two of the four models of public relations fit best with cultural diplomacy. Press agentry/publicity is comparable to one-way transmission of one's culture abroad in that it is all one-way and reflects an unbalanced relationship.[51] Public information is identical to self-portrayal because both are one-way information with little persuasion. The other two models of public relations fit best with cultural relations. Two-way "asymmetric" is similar to "information" because both acceptance and sympathy are their goals. Two-way symmetric is consistent with exchange and cooperation because they are based on dialogue and balanced effects. This argument resonates with some experts in public relations studies who believe that in many ways public diplomacy is a form of international public relations.[52]

Because these four models overlap in certain respects, the original four models of public relations, which were articulated by Grunig and Hunt in 1984, were reconstructed into four dimensions as a framework for public relations practice by Grunig in 1997. These new four dimensions of public relations are: direction, purpose, channel, and ethics. "Direction" means one-way information transmission and two-way information exchange in public relations; "purpose" includes symmetry and asymmetry: the former is the mutual effect of communication on both sides and the latter is one-sided; the "channel" refers to interpersonal and mediated communication; and the "ethical" dimension is the degree to which public relations behavior is ethical.[53]

Seong-Hun Yun operationalizes the four-dimensional framework of public relations into a six-factor measurement model (two-way, symmetrical, asymmetrical, ethical, interpersonal, and mediated communication) to test the applicability of public relations theories to the study of public diplomacy through empirical research.[54] The six-factor measurement model is then used to examine how well the model fits the public diplomacy behavior by embassies in Washington D.C., and the author concludes that "public relations frameworks are transferable to conceptualising and measuring public diplomacy behaviors."[55] Although the empirical research is only limited to one capital city of the US, it is useful for the empirical study of utilization of public relations theories in the field of public diplomacy.

In addition to examining the conceptual convergence of these two spheres in empirical research, image management and relationship building and management are the two means for delineating the similarities between public relations and public diplomacy. International image, which comprises cognitions and beliefs regarding the target nation's motives, leadership, and primary characteristics, can be used to justify a nation's desires, reaction, or treatment towards another nation. A positive international image in target nations can win overseas support for their foreign policy and international behaviors from these nations, create more opportunities for them to participate in the international system, and better protect their own national interests.[56]

Hence, image management becomes a consideration for public diplomacy. Noting that the function of public relations can be used to improve the international image of a nation through increasing the positive visibility of that country in target nations through the activities of public relations firms and associated communication processes, these two fields are closely linked within the framework of "image management." Manheim also places "image management" at the top level of strategic public diplomacy, and distinguishes strategic public diplomacy from propaganda with case studies, since strategic public diplomacy focuses on two-way communicative approaches and image management with professional advice from consulting firms instead of political advertising, which is the favored method of propaganda.[57]

Therefore, strategic communication is another term easily confused with public diplomacy. Based on a new agenda or certain messages proactively set by government, strategic communication aims to reinforce the core message and influence perception,[58] which is usually carried out by employing professional public relations firms.[59] Nevertheless, strategic communication fuses "pushing" and "delivering" because the government and their representatives, usually overseas PR firms, seems in a higher position than target audience, while public diplomacy concentrates on "dialogue" and "collaboration" instead of "monologue" of the governments.[60] Hence, public diplomacy emphasizes on interactive communication and pays attention to feedback from audience. However, during the implementation process of public diplomacy, strategic communication has never been ruled out.

A number of scholars have also researched public diplomacy from a relational perspective in public relations through challenging "image building" in public diplomacy. As Wang observes, public diplomacy is not just about projecting a favorable international image to foreign publics, but rather achieving a mutual understanding between nations and publics and building relationships.[61] Kathy R. Fitzpatrick argues that "the application of relational concepts and principles to public diplomacy demonstrates the potential for public relations' perspective to contribute to our understanding of the purpose of public diplomacy and how public diplomacy works (or should work)."[62] In this sense, public diplomacy provides a special perspective for understanding its long-term effects, which also explains the reason why some scholars emphasize relationship building in public diplomacy research.

2.1.1.3 The Contributions of International Relations Theories

Three mainstream theories of international relations include realism, liberalism and constructivism. However, when discussing contemporary international relations theories, researchers actually refer to neo-realism, neo-liberalism and constructivism. Among them, neo-realism concerns national security by the means of military power and liberal institutionalism cares about peace built on international laws and international institutions,[63] while constructivism as a new approach to understand international relations argues that identity is social constructed.[64] All these three theories offer some insights into the conceptualization of public diplomacy.

From the standpoint of realism, public diplomacy is a tool for sovereign states to pursue power and security. Based on the theory of realism, sovereign states as the key actors on the world stage have the capacity of controlling the objectives, contents, and approaches of public diplomacy, so realists aim to gain advantages in competition by employing public diplomacy approaches in order to communicate values, break trust, or create chaos.[65] In this sense, one-way information dissemination is a focus of public diplomacy for realists.

Albeit realism prioritized military power, it does not deny the importance of invisible power. With the deepening of globalization, information power/force becomes an integral part of the comprehensive power of a sovereign state, so realists emphasize the control on information storage and flow because they see information power as an extension of power.[66] Even for John Mearsheimer as one famous scholar of Offensive Realism, he believed that the US should adopt a "hearts and minds" strategy that concentrates on reducing Islamic hostility toward it instead of pursuing an empire with sword to defeat the terrorists.[67] Therefore, realism also contains some basic philosophy: propaganda or "psychological warfare" is the key activities of public diplomacy and national interests are the starting point and destination of public diplomacy.[68] However, realists overstress public diplomacy as a supplementary way of political competition instead of amending power politics according to the development of information society, which will not recover the essence of public diplomacy in a contemporary world.

Neo-liberalism, also known as liberal institutionalism, stresses complex interdependence to analyze the development of world politics after the 1970s. According to Robert O. Keohane and Joseph S. Nye, complex interdependence refers to a situation among a number of countries in which multiple channels of contact connect societies; there is no hierarchy of issues; and military force is not used by governments towards one another.[69] Therefore, the states as one type of international actors do not monopolize these contacts. Rather, a great number of non-state actors including international organizations, non-governmental organizations, and even multilateral corporations are participating in and exerting influence on international relations. Accordingly, no strict boundaries between high politics and low politics, and economic and cultural approaches that exceed military power become the means of dealing with international issues.[70]

One of the prominent contributions of liberal institutionalism to public diplomacy research is the inclusion of non-governmental organizations (NGOs) from two aspects: one is that the participation of NGOs in public diplomacy helps to project a favorable image of the state of origin of a particular NGO, since a state's recognition of NGOs in domestic and international politics is a part of its soft power resource. The other is that NGOs can play as a bridge between the public diplomacy implementer and its target in the form of financial, media, legal, or technical support.[71] From the perspective of liberal institutionalists, the actors of public diplomacy have been diversified, and public diplomacy can have a big role to play in negotiation and cooperation with the societal support.

For constructivists, culture, norms, identity, ideas, and the mutual understandings that accompany each of these currencies are the main factors in influencing state interactions and performances.[72] Public diplomacy can be viewed as a political instrument used by states, associations of states, and non-state actors to understand cultural, attitudes, and behaviors in order to influence opinions and actions to advance their interests and values.[73] In this sense, employing constructivism to understand public diplomacy reflects a continuous feedback loop between national identity construction and external image cultivation.[74]

Constructivism gives its attention to non-material factors including national identity, so public diplomacy aims to the formation of mutual understanding and recognition based on ideals, ideas, and culture beyond direct power and policy interaction among nations.[75] However, as argued by Gilboa, advocates of constructivism have ignored relevant communication theory, while communication experts have ignored constructivism. Thus, social construction of reality helps to bridge the different mechanisms of public diplomacy.[76] Accordingly, the EU's norm diffusion in its relations with the third parties reflects the EU's objectives of influencing its partners' internal understanding and norms and promoting the socialization of these norms in its partners.

When talking about international relations theories, "soft power" cannot be skipped. Soft power as an academic term or concept has been widely accepted in academic circles as a means of associating public diplomacy deployed by a single international actor with its global effect. Nye defined the term "soft power" in 1990 and re-explained and updated its content from time to time. Soft power is always used as a conceptual tool of international relations for analyzing public diplomacy, which is even considered as the most important contribution of liberal institutionalists by some scholars because of Joseph Nye as the father of soft power. However, soft power does not necessarily oppose realism or constructivism, since soft power which consists of culture, ideas, and identity emphasised by constructivism can also have hard impact of realism as analyzed above.

Moreover, soft power resources do not automatically translate into soft power, so public diplomacy is an effect way of wielding soft power resources. As Nye and Melissen have advised, public diplomacy means yielding soft power.[77, 78] According to the existing research on theoretical basis of public diplomacy, it is easy to conclude that soft power has not lost its explanatory force. Moreover, soft power has been widely used by public diplomacy researchers from different disciplines including communication studies, public relations as well as international relations, so the concept of soft power will be discussed by explaining why and how it links to the analysis of the EU's public diplomacy in details later.

Public diplomacy is neither a simple reflection of realism nor a combination of liberalism and constructivism. As a matter of fact, public diplomacy as a new diplomatic concept and approach meets the requirements of globalization, absorbing and merging together the ideas and propositions of different international relations theories and reflecting the convergence of theories.

2.1.1.4 *The Contributions of Nation Branding in Marketing Studies*

While nation branding has gradually gained popularity in recent years, discussion of the complex relationship between nation branding and public diplomacy is also attracting more attention.[79, 80] The Association for Place Branding and Public Diplomacy was established, and the *Journal of Place Branding* was also renamed the *Journal of Place Branding and Public Diplomacy* to explore the nature, purposes, and benefits of both areas. The discussion, however, has not yet reached clear conclusion among researchers from different academic areas. On the one hand, both public diplomacy and nation branding are still in the process of perfection, meaning that these two terms cannot have a clearly defined concept that can be used for comparison. Both academic fields draw upon the theories of other research areas, such as communication study, public relations, and even international relations, to further their development, which causes them to overlap in certain aspects (such as theoretical foundation and objectives). On the other hand, the two fields are utterly different because nation branding is mainly driven by marketing theory and public diplomacy is linked closely to international relations.

The concept of the "nation brand" originates from the discipline of marketing. A brand, according to the classic definition by the American Marketing Association, is a name, term, sign, symbol, or design, or a combination of these which aims to identify the goods or services of one seller or a group of sellers and to differentiate them from those of competitors.[81] It also can be described as being a customer's idea about a product, and the "brand state" implies what people around the world think and feel about a specific country.[82] In the book *Nation Brand*, Dinnie defines it as a "unique, multi-dimensional blend of elements that provide the nation culturally grounded differentiation and relevance for all of its target audience."[83]

Simon Anholt, an independent policy advisor, developed a Nation Brand Index to evaluate the comprehensive perception of a country by foreign publics across six dimensions of national assets: exports, governance, culture and heritage, people, tourism, investment, and immigration.[84] The concepts "nation-brand" and "nation-branding" have to be distinguished in order to avoid confusion. Nation brand is the image of your country that exists with or without any conscious endeavor in nation branding, and nation branding is the effort to improve the nation brand. From this standpoint, nation branding is selling a country as a product to the outside world, which is distinct from public diplomacy that is concerned with the understanding of a particular country.

Nevertheless, as mentioned earlier, nation branding is still in the process of being conceptualized through learning from other mature disciplines, which is the same as the current situation of public diplomacy. These two fields, therefore, overlap in certain aspects. Szondi analyzes and classifies the literature about nation branding and public diplomacy, and presents five relationships between the two, namely: distinct spheres; public diplomacy as a part of nation branding; nation branding as a part of public diplomacy; distinct but with overlapping concepts; and they are the same concepts.[85] Within the five relationships, the idea of nation branding and public diplomacy as being distinct spheres will not be discussed because this situation only existed when nation branding was in its nascent form in the 1990s. Also, the author quotes Donnie's discussion to prove that nation branding and public diplomacy are identical, which is unreasonable because Donnie thinks that some terms like "competitive identity," "public diplomacy," and "reputation management," which are the specific activities of nation branding practice, may supplant "nation branding" in the future, and no one actually regards these two terms as identical.

Theoretically, some nation branding professionals believe that public diplomacy is part of nation branding. The growing need for nations to brand themselves comes from deepened globalization, geopolitical rivalries and economic competition, and the nation branding comprises public diplomacy, tourism, exports, and direct foreign investment.[86] As argued by Jian Wang, a crucial element of nation branding is communicating a country's polices and culture to an international audience, and public diplomacy has been one of the primary tools for addressing such issues.[87] In practice, nation branding can be successfully used as a tool of public diplomacy. Apple Computer Inc. and its high-tech electronic products, Microsoft and fast food chains like KFC and McDonald's have become symbols of America; as have Samsung in South Korea and Toshiba and Canon in Japan. All these brand products are closely linked to their countries and serve as instruments of public diplomacy. Furthermore, many researchers point out that they are overlapping. Ham indicates that the key elements including building personal and institutional relationships and dialogue with foreign publics are the same in both nation branding and public diplomacy.[88] Fan also says that beyond marketing, nation branding can play a potentially important role in cross-cultural communication that is also emphasized by public diplomacy.[89]

Even though some experts have attempted to clarify these two terms, they are still confusing. Nation branding is an imperfect term to start with, because the activities associated with nation branding surpass the traditional view of branding as merely marketing of products.[90] On top of that, the advocates of nation branding keep trying to perfect the term, and some of them have even changed their original ideas about nation branding, redefining it with new content,[91] which complicates the relationship between nation branding and public diplomacy. No wonder Dinnie predicts that nation branding may be replaced by another more specific term. Be that as it may, currently nation branding and public diplomacy have some obvious conceptual similarities and differences.[92] Both nation branding and public diplomacy make use of image and relationship management and extensive use of mass media for success, but public diplomacy serves the strategy of general diplomacy for one country; in contrast, nation branding aims to increase sales, no matter what products are on a nation's shelves. As Fitzpatrick observes, "although the two disciplines share some common views regarding the importance of a nation's global reputation to its ability to advance national interest, fundamental differences in worldviews and functions preclude the adoption of nation branding as a viable strategic approach to public diplomacy."[93]

As we can tell, the definition of public diplomacy is so broad that it can include elements inimical to its ethics and subversive of its purpose and promise. According to Copeland, what differentiates public diplomacy from marketing, branding, or information warfare are the elements of dialogue, two-way information flows, and meaningful exchange, with feedback of the results of the dialogue operating in both directions, resulting in changes in the policy choices and behaviors of international actors at each end of the conversation.[94] In fact, while talking about public diplomacy in the EU's external relations, some diplomats insist that "this [public diplomacy] is not an exercise in "national branding"; it is not "propaganda," because we know that does not work."[95] Therefore, "nation brand" or "nation branding" will not be used herein to formulate the concept of public diplomacy or analyze the public diplomacy practice of the EU.

Based on the interdisciplinary approaches to the conceptualisation of public diplomacy, producing a definition seems to be one of the hardest tasks for most researchers in this field, but it is not impossible. Interdisciplinary studies on public diplomacy offer us a chance to define this term according to a specific situation in that the role of public diplomacy can be fully realized in practice and each country which leverages public diplomacy to achieve its own national interests emphasises different aspects of public diplomacy. Meanwhile, interdisciplinary studies also encourage us to define public diplomacy by distinguishing it from what it is not. For instance, public diplomacy is not "nation brand." In other words, cross-disciplinary study is definitely beneficial for enriching public diplomacy theory and promoting public diplomacy practice, albeit it may increase its difficulty. Nevertheless, besides reviewing the interdisciplinary approaches to public diplomacy research, it is also important to distinguish public diplomacy from concepts that might be confused with it before offering a final definition of public diplomacy. This will be done in the following section.

2.1.2 Three Related Concepts

The development of public diplomacy and its conceptualization are also closely related to the ever-changing field of international relations and the theoretical development and practical application of communication. Therefore, before defining public diplomacy for the purposes of this research, it is also necessary to distinguish public diplomacy from other related concepts. Based on existing scholarly research and academic publications, propaganda, media diplomacy, and cultural diplomacy are three terms which need to be discussed.

Among the three terms, propaganda and public diplomacy have the same root if we oversimplify both of them as a communication process, while media diplomacy and public diplomacy overlap in certain aspects yet are completely different in others. Cultural diplomacy is usually viewed as being public diplomacy through cultural means. In other words, these three terms do bear a close relationship to public diplomacy.

2.1.2.1 *Propaganda and Public Diplomacy*

Propaganda and public diplomacy have similar roots in that they influence foreign publics and win support from the outside world. That is why many researchers and students still view propaganda and public diplomacy as two different names for the same phenomenon: public diplomacy is a new bottle filled with the old wine of propaganda.[96]

At the theoretical level, if propaganda is defined in a broad sense, it is hard to distinguish it from public diplomacy. For instance, Jowett and O'Donnell state that "propaganda is a form of communication that attempts to achieve a response that furthers the desired intent of the propagandist. Public opinion and behavioural change can be affected by propaganda."[97] According to David Welch, propaganda is "the deliberate attempt to influence the opinion of an audience through the transmission of ideas and values for the specific purpose, consciously designed to serve the interest of the propagandists and their political masters, either directly or indirectly."[98] Both of these definitions of propaganda seen from the angle of information transmission are easily confused with public diplomacy. Actually, the term "propaganda" is widely used in the official discourse of some countries and also by some scholars as a substitute for communication,[99] given that propaganda can be understood as a neutral word associated with such benign activities as information transmission and the general shaping of ideology.[100]

Propaganda was historically used in wartime, particularly during World Wars I and II and the Cold War, and its potential was fully exploited by all the parties involved. After War World I, in 1927, Harold D. Lasswell, a famous American political scientist and one of the four founders of Communication, published his PhD thesis entitled *Propaganda Techniques in World Wars*, one of the first books to research the utilization of propaganda in wartime. In his book, propaganda, which is used to reveal the effect of mass communication through symbols, is a neutral word. But the term "propaganda" can be dated back to the first half of the seventeenth century when the Roman Catholic Church tried to re-establish its authority in the northern countries of Europe through the dissemination of religious doctrine. More recently, "propaganda" has become a pejorative term with the meaning of manipulating information and public opinion. In addition, Goebbels, the head of the Ministry of Popular Enlightenment and Propaganda in Hitler's first government, further sullied the image of "propaganda" in the Western world because of his propaganda activities during World War II.[101] Because of this negative historical burden, public diplomacy has to be differentiated from propaganda due to the negative connotations of the latter in the Western world.

Propaganda is thus distinct from public diplomacy according to popular understanding and historical significance. Negative memories of Nazi propaganda in World War II and Communist propaganda in the Cold War have reinforced the pejorative meaning of propaganda in the popular understanding. Because of the use of one-sided news or even falsified information and the repetition of political slogans in propaganda, it is also viewed as psychological warfare. In other words, propaganda makes use of lies. In propaganda, the communicator and the recipient of information have unequal status, and foreign publics are manipulated and deceived by inadequate or misleading information. In this sense, propaganda equals to "lies" and "brainwashing" in modern discourse.[102] In contrast, credibility, transparency, and informed publics are the basic requirements for the success of public diplomacy.

To sum up, the practice of propaganda practice in history has provided theoretical implications and successful experience for the emergence and development of public diplomacy. In some countries the original institutions responsible for propaganda in wartime are still employed in public diplomacy today. However, due to historical reasons, contemporary public diplomacy researchers insist that public diplomacy has to be separated from propaganda in order to avoid the possible failure of public diplomacy endeavors because of historical baggage.[103, 104, 105]

2.1.2.2 *Media Diplomacy and Public Diplomacy*

As previously mentioned, the conceptualization process of public diplomacy benefits from communication study and mass media research, and it also focuses on the relationship between mass media, governments, and public opinion. In this sense, public diplomacy has a complicated relationship with the mass media. Therefore, the term "media diplomacy" also has a complicated relation with public diplomacy.

The term "media diplomacy" is used to describe the interaction between foreign policy makers, the mass media and publics, but as such it has lost much of its analytical power. On the one hand, media diplomacy is equated with open diplomacy in that the mass media provides an effective channel for ordinary people to get to know and participate in foreign policy making processes, and it moves traditional diplomacy from secretive to open diplomacy. On the other hand, media diplomacy is also viewed as a component of public diplomacy in which state and non-state actors used the mass media to disseminate information and change perceptions about their own countries in a foreign state. In a pioneering study, Yoel Cohen argues that "media diplomacy includes all those aspects of public diplomacy where the media are involved as well as others not associated with public diplomacy, including the sending of signals of government through the media, and the use of the media as a source of information."[106] In his opinion, media diplomacy and public diplomacy overlap in certain aspects, such as using media as a channel for transmitting information, changing attitudes, and winning support from a foreign country, but molding opinion at home and disclosing sensitive diplomatic information through mass media for domestic public support and diplomatic advantage belong to the scope of media diplomacy or open diplomacy rather than that of public diplomacy.

Cohen's definition can be criticized for its ambiguity. For example, Rawnsley distinguished public diplomacy from media diplomacy by audience: in the former, he advised, policy makers use the media to address foreign publics, while in the latter they address government officials.[107] But in practice, the mass media is also used as a way of molding domestic public opinion, so this distinction is not persuasive. Besides, as Eytan Gilboa argues, Cohen's definition "is somewhat confusing because it means that media diplomacy is part of public diplomacy and can also reflect a separate and independent phenomenon."[108] Gilboa attempts to address the differences between media diplomacy and public diplomacy in five dimensions: context, time frame, goals, methods, and medium. He believes that public diplomacy is effective in ideological confrontation with long-term effect, but media diplomacy is used in negotiations with short-term impact; promoting a favorable image is the general goal of public diplomacy, but media diplomacy is useful for specific goals, particularly for conflict resolution; public diplomacy emphasizes multiple channels but media diplomacy only uses mass media.[109] These distinctions might have made sense several years ago, but now, considering the active role of mass media in public diplomacy practice, both conflict resolution and the short-term impact are addressed by public diplomacy in its practice. Hence, Gilboa's effort to distinguish these relevant concepts does not work in the present understanding of public diplomacy.

Attempts are being made to differentiate public diplomacy from media diplomacy, but in practice public diplomacy and media diplomacy have complex linkages and overlap in various aspects which are difficult to separate clearly. Mass media, as the main channel of information transmission, affects the design and execution of public diplomacy activities in many ways. Therefore, Cohen's analysis of the relationship between public and media diplomacy is still comparatively appropriate. That is, if mass media is used for certain diplomatic purposes in explaining one country's policy to foreign publics and influencing foreign perceptions about itself, then media diplomacy belongs to public diplomacy. If mass media is the medium for interaction between diplomats and domestic citizens, then media diplomacy is independent from public diplomacy. Specifically for the EU, public diplomacy includes both internal and external levels, but this research is concerned only with its external public diplomacy to China. Therefore, media diplomacy or international news broadcasting will be replaced by information activities in general.

2.1.2.3 Cultural Diplomacy and Public Diplomacy

Compared with media diplomacy, cultural diplomacy has a much clearer relation to public diplomacy, but it also has a much vaguer definition. In current studies most researchers and experts believe that cultural diplomacy is an integral part of public diplomacy. Some researchers view cultural diplomacy as an independent diplomatic form in certain countries due to its specific activities, for instance British cultural diplomacy designed and executed by the British Council is always discussed in academic papers as an independent diplomatic field, but for most researchers cultural diplomacy is identified as an effective approach in the "big family" of public diplomacy.[110]

Because cultural diplomacy is discussed under the overarching umbrella of public diplomacy, little work has been done to define its connotations. Schneider published a paper entitled Cultural Diplomacy in 2006 with the subtitle, "Hard to define, but you'd know it if you saw it," reflecting the difficulty of defining cultural diplomacy.[111] Cummings has produced the most frequently cited definition of cultural diplomacy. According to him, cultural diplomacy is the use of creative expression and exchanges of ideas, information, and people to increase mutual understanding.[112]

According to Banks, careful management of the approaches of culture and cultural expression are central aspects of cultural diplomacy, as they bring cultural workers from different societies together.[113] Cultural diplomacy recognizes the ability of these workers to affect the hearts and minds of their respective societies in a concrete and dramatic way, thereby affecting the direction of political, economic, and social interactions between countries. However, cultural diplomacy practice does not view cultural workers as being the only actors in this type of diplomacy.

Experts from Demos, a think tank based in the UK, describe the way cultural diplomacy operates. As they put it, "culture is both the means by which we come to understand others and an aspect of life with innate worth that we enjoy and seek out." Proceeding on the basis of this definition, cultural diplomacy includes activities such as cultural exchange and cultural contact in order to enhance cultural understanding among nations. More specifically, promoting cultural exchange provides an opportunity for different countries and their citizens to understand fundamental aspects of humanity that they share with others, making culture a critical means of negotiation and mediation. It also provides a more informal platform, based on cultural contact, where all parties can build relationships in situations where political connections are in difficulties.[114]

However, such efforts at defining cultural diplomacy do not clearly separate it from public diplomacy when they are compared with the concepts of public diplomacy that were reviewed earlier in this book. As Mark indicates, cultural diplomacy is "the deployment of a state's culture in support of its foreign policy goals or diplomacy." Although it is usually viewed as a diplomatic practice of single governments (nation states), cultural diplomacy can also be used by supranational organizations such as the EU.[115] By emphasising the role of culture in general diplomacy and realizing the policy goals of a country, Mark argues that cultural diplomacy is neither a synonym for public diplomacy, nor for international cultural relations, nor is the practice simply another form of propaganda.[116]

Cultural diplomacy had its heyday in the Cold War in US public diplomacy to the USSR. During the Cold War, the US government promoted its cultural works to the Soviet Union through cultural exchange programs, and some American scholars even believe that cultural diplomacy precipitated the collapse of Communism.[117] But can the effect of cultural diplomacy in practice be different from that of public diplomacy? Schneider thinks that public diplomacy does not benefit from relationship building in a crisis as compared with cultural diplomacy, since their experience of public diplomacy may even further alienate foreign publics.[118] But this empirical analysis misunderstands the relationship between cultural diplomacy and other components of public diplomacy. To be more specific, other components of public diplomacy, except cultural diplomacy, may not be effective in solving a crisis between nations, but it does not mean that public diplomacy is not effective because it never excludes culture as a factor in achieving its goals.

Both Mark and Cull view cultural diplomacy as being just one of the main public diplomacy instruments.[119, 120] Therefore, from both a theoretical and a practical aspect it is unnecessary to isolate cultural diplomacy from public diplomacy, but the role of cultural diplomacy needs to be discussed separately from other components of public diplomacy such as international broadcasting, international public relations, etc. In brief, cultural diplomacy makes use of culture as a tool of public diplomacy. In this book, the term cultural exchange will be used in order to avoid confusion, while cultural diplomacy may also appear in quotations.

To summarize, because of the wide range of approaches employed, public diplomacy has unavoidably been connected and even confused with other similar concepts. Although the discussion partially distinguished public diplomacy from the three terms mentioned above, this research might still contradict the understandings and explanations of other experts.

2.1.3 Concept of Public Diplomacy and Its Approaches

According to the above analysis, communication study and public relations can be used to define public diplomacy and explain how it operates. The concept of nation branding will not be considered in this conceptualization because of its different basis, which rules out any association with public diplomacy. Moreover, the study of public relations is a branch of communications in practice, meaning that public diplomacy, is entirely a communication process. To be more specific,

1. Public diplomacy is a cross-border communication process organized and carried out by different actors (states, IGOs and INGOs, terrorist groups, and even influential individuals) who participate in international relations;
2. Public diplomacy is carried out through various direct or indirect channels such as international broadcasting, cultural and educational exchange, tourism, international public relations, etc.
3. Public diplomacy aims to influence foreign publics and thus change the public opinion of target country/countries, improve the soft power of one country and public opinion environment and enhance mutual understanding and relationship building;
4. Public diplomacy serves the interests of its organizer, or sometimes the interests of all the participants in the process and may bring about a "win-win" situation.

Based on this definition, three aspects need to be stressed.

First, direct engagement of foreign publics by the implementers of public diplomacy programs fits precisely within the traditional definition of public diplomacy, but "public diplomacy through intermediary" is a special form of public diplomacy practice. In fact, making full use of an "intermediary" in target countries can solve the credibility problem that sometimes arises from direct communication. In this book, foreign professors sponsored by the Jean Monnet Programme act as the intermediaries of EU public diplomacy and increase the credibility of the message transmitted by this program, which will be more fully discussed in the empirical findings from the interviews.

Second, the above definition of public diplomacy fits the Commission's understanding of public diplomacy as provided in a booklet on the occasion of the EU's fiftieth anniversary celebration:

> Public diplomacy deals with the influence of public attitudes. It seeks to promote EU interests by understanding, informing, and influencing. It means clearly explaining the EU's goals, policies, and activities and fostering understanding of these goals through dialogue with individual citizens, groups, institutions, and the media. [121]

Third, EU public diplomacy is not only organized and executed by EU institutions. Within the EU different levels, including at member-state level, EU citizen level and grassroots organizations level all have their own public diplomacy targeting each other or even countries outside the EU. However, in this research, we are mainly concerned with public diplomacy at the EU level in order to understand the effect of public diplomacy on the EU's image projection and global influence. Thus, the EU organizes and carries out its public diplomacy through the Jean Monnet Programme so as to increase the understanding of Chinese people about the EU and finally enhance the influence of the EU in East Asia and the wider world.

With regard to the approaches of public diplomacy, although communication study and public relations can explain how public diplomacy is executed, the specific process of public diplomacy is more complicated. In designing and carrying out public diplomacy, different approaches are used in different situations.

Cull lists five core approaches to public diplomacy including listening, advocacy, cultural diplomacy, exchange diplomacy, and international news broadcasting.[122] These have been widely accepted and used in academic work. Among them: 1) listening is the process of collecting and collating information and data about foreign publics and their opinions and understanding, and managing the international opinion environment, which establishes the basis for foreign policy decision-making; Cull emphasises "listening" more than once in his different publications that understanding foreign public opinion is a starting point for effective public diplomacy. 2) advocacy, focusing on short-term influence, means an actor's attempt to influence and manage the foreign opinion environment by carrying out various international communication activities to promote ideas, a specific policy, or the actor's interests in the minds of foreign publics; 3) cultural diplomacy emphasizes the importance of cultural transmission and cultural exchange on the improvement of the international opinion environment. 4) Exchange diplomacy, including cultural diplomacy, gives more attention to two-way communication. One-way information transmission is helpful for explaining problems and reducing suspicion, but two-way communication benefits understanding and the building of mutual trust. 5) For Cull, international news broadcasting consists of the changes of international communication brought about by communication technology, and overlaps with other public diplomacy approaches in his classification.

At the same time, Gilboa classifies public diplomacy approaches according to the timeline of their effect.[123] For instance, advocacy, international broadcasting, and cyber public diplomacy aim for an immediate effect; international public relations, corporate diplomacy, and diaspora public diplomacy will produce an intermediate influence; and a long-term effect comes about through cultural diplomacy, exchange, and even branding. These two classifications mainly emphasize the extrinsic form of public diplomacy but neglect its intrinsic essence, which, to a certain extent, causes the different approaches or actions to overlap in some respects. As we can see, listening is the first step in Cull's classification, and cyber public diplomacy can be merely the application of international broadcasting or cultural diplomacy.

In addition to these definitions, Han classifies public diplomacy into two categories: information programs and educational and cultural programs.[124] Information programs are conducted through the mass media and publications in order to improve the understanding of current policies; educational and cultural programs are conducted through the exchange of students, experts and other visitors, research, and overseas language education to promote the understanding of culture, society, history, and institutions. According to his classification, public diplomacy can be analyzed via these two main activities without considering the timeliness of different approaches.

The EU's Jean Monnet Programme, based on academic research and educational exchange in higher education, mainly concentrates on long-term effectiveness. Therefore, in order to fully understand the essence of the public diplomacy approaches, this research will divide it into three parts: international public opinion analysis, information activities, and cultural and educational exchange.

1). International public opinion analysis. According to the definition of public diplomacy offered by other scholars and experts, as well as the discussion above, public diplomacy, aiming to influence international opinion about its organizer, is based on research and analysis of foreign perception. In other words, the first and most important step of public diplomacy is to conduct public opinion analysis. More specifically, the organizer of public diplomacy will do an accurate and general survey of the target country or countries before deploying a public diplomacy strategy. "Listening" in Cull's classification has the same meaning as public opinion analysis.

The vague definition of public diplomacy causes governments to believe that all programs that target foreign publics which list foreign public objectives as their goals can be viewed as public diplomacy programs without any detailed discourse analysis. This compels governments to design exchange and mobility programs based on a belief that public diplomacy alone can influence foreign perceptions and behaviors.[125] The truth is that, without carefully analyzing the specific situation of target countries and target groups, those programs may not work effectively or even not work at all.

2). Information activities. Information is the most crucial element for successfully realizing the objectives of public diplomacy. In the process of information communication, daily news dissemination and management, and the strategic communication of messages and images are all included. Methods such as international broadcasting, international public relations, cyber public diplomacy, and so forth are used. Usually, information activities refer to both passive reactions to the wrong message about the communicator as well as proactive information communication for explaining and understanding. Public diplomacy aims to build long-term relationships and project a favorable image, but the communicator is also concerned with correcting the wrong message from authoritative sources since negative messages do considerable damage to the national image and can ruin all past endeavors in seconds.

3). Cultural and educational exchange. Mark states that "cultural diplomacy is now considered to be both conceptually and practically a subset of public diplomacy, which can be defined as a government's communication with foreign audiences in order to positively influence them, some elements of public diplomacy such as reactive media briefings sit outside cultural diplomacy's rubric."[126] Therefore, from both a theoretical and a practical aspect it is unnecessary to isolate cultural diplomacy from public diplomacy. In this research, the term cultural exchange will be used in order to avoid confusion, while cultural diplomacy may also appear in quotations.

Cultural and educational exchange activities also include information dissemination and reception, but in contrast to information activities which mainly have a short-term effect, cultural and educational exchange may produce a long-term influence. Cultural and educational engagement aims at building a relationship between two societies which have different languages, cultural, political, and economic backgrounds with the purpose of achieving greater familiarity, more favorable views and better mutual understanding.

Considering that foreign public opinion analysis is a prerequisite for designing and implementing public diplomacy programs, public diplomacy actions which are easily observable are the activities of broadcasting (information activities) and bringing people into direct contact and facilitating dialogue (exchange programs, or to be more specific, cultural and educational programs). The latter two activities are important instruments of public diplomacy and are more easily identified.

Generally speaking, the information activities of public diplomacy are carried out by means of communication technologies and governments, as the originators of the information have the capacity to decide what is to be communicated or what the foreign publics may hear. While modern communication technologies make two-way communication possible, governments are still in a dominant position because they can monopolize the sources of news and also serve as the only official spokespersons for specific information and messages. The feedback of the recipients might be heard by the communicator, but it is hard to evaluate how this will affect future policy making. In this sense, the relationship between communicators and audiences in information activities through the mass media would seem to be asymmetric. On the other hand, cultural and educational programs which facilitate dialogue and personal contact can be viewed as symmetric since the participants of both sides are equal.[127] The respective advantages of asymmetric and symmetric public diplomacy activities as reflected in the Jean Monnet Programme will be discussed in chapter 4 and in the case study of this program in China in chapters 5–7.

As will be discussed in this book, EU public diplomacy to China via the Jean Monnet Programme has already incorporated all three approaches. Reviewing the existing literature has provided us with five general criteria for assessing EU public diplomacy practice: 1) listening is a start; 2) credibility is a basic requirement; 3) public diplomacy has to go local; 4) public diplomacy aims to influence external perceptions; 5) public diplomacy must be connected with policy. In chapter 4, the first four criteria of public diplomacy will be applied to the Jean Monnet Programme so that we can use the concepts and theoretical base of public diplomacy to analyze specific EU public diplomacy practices. In chapters 6-7, these rules, in concert with the specific objectives of the Jean Monnet Programme will be discussed further after analyzing the data from the fieldwork in order to make definite connections between the case study and the overall argument.

2.2 THE EVOLUTION OF SOFT POWER

Since "soft power" is the most frequently cited term in public diplomacy research and is also the theoretical term that will be used to analyse EU public diplomacy, this section will focus on the conceptual evolution of soft power.

Soft power, coined by Joseph Nye in 1990, was used to explain the power relations and respond to the discussion about the decline of America's role in the world after the Cold War. According to Nye, since traditional military power was costly and less fungible, along with increasing competition from the rise of non-state actors in world politics and the influence of economic power, technologies, transnational boundary communication, and even ecological security, the US leadership faced a number of challenges.[128] The changing nature of global power relations suggested a second and more attractive means of exerting power which Nye called "co-optive or soft power." In his view, co-optive power is the ability of a country to structure a situation so that other countries define their interests or develop their preference in ways consistent with its own, which mainly come from cultural and ideological attraction as well as the rules and institutions of international regimes.[129]

More than a decade later, Nye updated his definition of soft power to that of "rests on the ability to shape the preferences of others.[130] This soft power—

getting others to want the outcomes that you want—co-opts people rather than coerces them." He also described the three main sources of a country's soft power: culture, political values, and foreign policy. Soft power behaviors include agenda-setting, attraction, and persuasion[131] and soft power resources are used to set the agenda, persuade, and produce attraction.[132] The academic discussion about soft power has never stopped at the theoretical and practical levels. In fact, besides talking about the resources and instruments of soft power, questions about real influence (how to translate soft power resources into real influence) and how to exert the real influence of soft power have gradually emerged within the scholarly discussion. In this regard, soft power has been discussed from two approaches: how to wield soft power and how it influences the target country. From the angle of how to use soft power, or more specifically, use attraction in pursuit of its national interests, "strategic narratives" have been stressed.[133]

A narrative is a story, and strategic narratives of the EU should be stories all the Europeans can understand and identify within their own lives.[134] As argued by Freedman, an effective narrative works not only because it is appealing to the values, interests, and prejudices had by the recipients but also because it is still convincing to the public even if later information and events tell a different story.[135] Therefore, soft power resources may be attractive because they fit within a pre-existing or developing personal narrative.[136] More importantly, actors in international relations are given meaning to themselves and others by narrative—meaning through narrative can be tied to issues associated with identity in international relations.[137] Thus, utilizing narrative strategically needs to consider both the reception of interpretation of narratives and their formation and projection because "it is here that meaning is made and any attractiveness, engagement and scope for persuasion are located and experienced."[138]

Strategic narrative is soft power in the twenty-first century.[139] In a long term, strategic narrative, by shaping the interests and identity of others and their understanding of how world politics works and where it is heading, will get others both at home and abroad to buy in your strategic narrative,[140] which is exactly the same definition of soft power given by Nye. Some scholars argue that soft power can come from the ability to create consensus and shared meaning by using strategic narratives that shape the way human beings understand the world around them,[141] which is the same as Nye's statement that politics "may ultimately be about whose story wins" in the information era.[142] Furthermore, strategic narrative addresses the role of influence in international relations giving scholars insight into what underlies soft or normative power.[143] In light of the rules universally accepted by most international actors, it is hard to legitimize actions or behaviors that conflict with the rules. In other words, having the ability to create and promote rules can be converted to soft power. Admittedly, creating international rules will not be an easy job, but it does have a long-lasting effect.[144] In short, the strategic narratives methodology explains when and where these norms are in effect.[145]

The ever-changing conceptualization of soft power means that it has been widely used in explaining the global strategy of different countries since each can add a new dimension according to their own requirements. Nevertheless, the wide utilization of soft power in explaining each country's global strategy enriches the content of soft power while also increasing the complexity of understanding and defining it theoretically. According to some scholars, this means that soft power has become a catch-all term that has lost its explanatory power.[146] In this sense, soft power faces two challenges: one is whether it can work independently, which mainly focuses on its interaction with hard power; the other is whether soft power can be explained according to different national characteristics, which gives attention to the applicability of soft power to other countries beyond America.

The debate and criticism around the ambiguity of soft power as an academic term and the blurred border between soft and hard power has never ceased. Noya indicates that "soft power is not a type of power at all," in that any resource, including military power, can be soft when it is perceived as legitimate for a soft purpose like humanitarian aid.[147] To be more specific, for states with great military and economic power, soft power largely depends on hard power rather than being an independent power that can exert worldwide influence. The soft power resources, like culture, history, political value, and foreign policy (in specific contexts) may be attractive in some countries but may provoke other societies with very different cultural backgrounds. According to Noya, the role soft power plays in contemporary international relations largely depends on the increasing influence of public opinion in a global context along with increasing democratization, the prevalence of education as well as information and communication technologies, but the problems associated with the concept of soft power may decrease and even end the explanatory power of soft power.[148] Wielding soft power may possibly lead to accusations of "artistic hegemony" and "cultural imperialism." In other words, soft power does not necessarily increase the world's love for America, but on the contrary, it is still power and it can still make enemies.[149]

Nevertheless, there is no denying that these critics have forced Nye and other experts to revise the original concept and develop another term, that of "smart power." This implies that it is impossible to understand soft power without paying attention to its interaction with hard power.[150] Actually, the term "smart power" can be attributable to both Suzanne Nossel and Joseph Nye in that Nossel used "smart power" in her article entitled *Smart Power:*

Reclaiming Liberal Internationalism[151] while Nye argues that he coined this term in 2003 to counter the misperception that soft power alone can produce effective foreign policy.[152] Nye defines smart power as the capability of combining hard and soft power effectively and points out that military power can sometimes play a crucial role in the generation of soft power.[153] According to him, public diplomacy is an indispensable tool in the apparatus of smart power, and smart public diplomacy requires an understanding of the role of credibility, self-criticism, and civil society in the generation of soft power.

In this regard, Nye still emphasizes the relationship between soft power and public diplomacy but within the framework of smart power which is achieved by artfully combining soft and hard power through institutional re-arrangement rather than through simple conceptual integration. As Wilson III argues, soft power and public diplomacy often suffer from political naivety and institutional weakness, because institutions of soft power are often much smaller, receive less funding, and have limited influence compared with their hard power counterparts, but smart power based on long-term structural adjustment of governmental institutions is more strategic and intelligent.[154] Even so, the definition of smart power is still unclear, and the distinction between hard power and soft power in constructing the content of smart power has not yet been explained.

Since the concept of smart power is still vague and mainly understood in political discourse, it will not be employed to understand public diplomacy in this research. Rather, soft power will be used to illustrate the practice and influence of public diplomacy, though some academic concerns regarding soft power still need to be addressed. Gilboa states that "any analysis of soft or smart power is quickly evoking public diplomacy, but the conceptual and operational relationship between the two has not yet been sufficiently clari-fied."[155] On the contrary, some academic researchers deny power-based pub-lic diplomacy completely. Differing from traditional public diplomacy, new public diplomacy emphasizes mutual understanding and long-term relation-ship building; the protection of national interests and "win-win" outcomes are its ideal aims. However, power-based public diplomacy seems to help a coun-try acquire or retain power in a power-based international system, which is quite different from public diplomacy's fundamental purpose of establishing and maintaining mutually beneficial relations with strategic foreign publics that can affect the national interest.[156]

In terms of the applicability of soft power to different countries, Nye's con-clusion about the sources of soft power from American practice and national attributes of other countries have raised questions about whether the concept of soft power can be used widely. Nye's sources of soft power in one country include its culture, political values, and foreign policies, but they have different meanings in different countries.

More specifically, the concept of soft power has been developed along different trajectories based on the resources possessed by different international actors, which is exactly what happens in the EU and China (who are also involved in the Jean Monnet Programme and studied in this research).[157] China, as an emerging country, attracts world attention because of its soft power strategy. According to China's explanation of its own soft power, culture, especially traditional Chinese culture including Chinese characters, classical literature rather than contemporary or popular culture are the main sources of soft power in official statements,[158] and this is different from Nye's understanding. Although Nye viewed Europe as America's closest soft power competitor, since Europe has considerable soft power resources, describing the EU as a soft power—not in the sense that Nye intended—also shows that soft power changes shape from one global actor to another.[159]

To a large extent, Nye's definition of soft power which bears the footprint of American practice has worldwide influence, in both political and academic circles, but the concept of soft power has developed along different trajectories in China and the EU, each consistent with intrinsic economic, cultural, and political conditions.[160] In the case of China, Ding explains that "China has a different set of concerns and must tap different sources of soft power" due to the fact that it is a developing country and was a relatively marginalized actor on the world stage in the first few years after the Cold War.[161] Thus, China's soft power must be explained and re-conceptualized in the Chinese context rather than according to Nye's term. The EU's attractiveness is easily linked to its member states, so defining the EU's soft power requires integrating the activities of the EU, its notion of European history, culture, and lifestyles, as well as the deep-seated values of European societies. Obviously, the EU's practice has enlarged Nye's definition of soft power,[162] which means Ding's explanation about the situation of China's soft power seems also applicable to the EU's soft power research, given that the situation of the EU as a supranational organization which is distinct from the US.

In sum, even though soft power receives both emphasis and criticism during the process of conceptualization as well as its influence on public diplomacy research, Nye's definition of soft power as "the ability to affect others through the co-optive means of framing the agenda, persuading, and eliciting positive attraction in order to obtain preferred outcomes"[163] still makes sense albeit it also needs to cooperate with hard power in the global strategy of any one country. It has to be admitted that soft power is still the most frequently cited term for understanding the informational, cultural, and educational activities of different international actors, and this is also the case with the EU.

As previously mentioned, Michalski emphasizes that the EU is a soft power and that EU public diplomacy integrates EU values, norms, and principles into its policy, instrumentalized through its information and communication strategy in order to achieve its force of persuasion.[164] Chan also realizes that "soft power is not a magic wand but a sensible way to achieve part of the EU's global ambition,"[165] and the exercise of soft power depends on the capability of the EU to obtain public approval. Rasmussen believes that EU public diplomacy is an effective way for the EU to wield its soft power.[166] Therefore, soft power as a theoretical term will also be used in this research, although how to apply the theory of soft power to EU public diplomacy requires further discussion and analysis according to the specific situation of the EU and its public diplomacy practice.

2.3 THE RELATIONSHIP BETWEEN
PUBLIC DIPLOMACY AND SOFT POWER

In the previous two parts, the concepts of public diplomacy and soft power were reviewed. Since soft power as the theoretical framework, in concert with the application of the public diplomacy concept to EU public diplomacy practice, will be used to structure the process of analysis, we will proceed to a discussion of the relationship between public diplomacy and soft power.

As the "father" of the concept of soft power, Nye has continued to explain and revise his understanding about the interaction between soft power and public diplomacy. In his monograph entitled *Soft Power: The Means to Success in World Politics*, he mentions that soft power resources are slower and more diffuse because many of them are outside the government's control and work indirectly by shaping the environment for policy implementation, and therefore it is not easy to wield soft power resources.[167] A discussion about their interaction then appeared in a paper entitled *public diplomacy and soft power* published four years later. Although a large part of this article derived from his book of 2004, Nye adds "smart power" which is the artful combination of soft and hard power to rebut criticism of the exaggerated influence of soft power. Nye emphasizes that smart public diplomacy calls for a reconsideration of credibility, self-criticism, and civil society in the generation of soft power, but smart public diplomacy is still closely related to the utilization of soft rather than hard power.[168] In this sense, soft power is still a proper theory for explaining the function of public diplomacy in Nye's discourse.

"Wielding soft power" and "wielding soft-power resources" have been used interchangeably in his book of 2004 while the phrase "wielding soft power" has also been used by Melissen.[169] This can be understood as using public diplomacy as a way of making a country's soft power resources work, a process of converting soft power resources into real soft influence by public diplomacy, or as Nye said, to "create soft power through the instrument of public diplomacy."[170] Public diplomacy is not a subcategory of soft power but is rather the practical means to a strategic pursuit of soft power and as such is integral to the policy of each international actor.[171]

In fact, Melissen further explains that public diplomacy as an instrument of soft power has been recognized in practice long before the current debate on public diplomacy since, in his opinion, the propaganda competition—even if viewed equally as public diplomacy—was used by the US, Soviet Union and Europe's three major powers with huge investment in winning hearts and minds in the Cold War.[172] The relationship between soft power and public diplomacy has a long history from the perspective of diplomatic practice, but the term of soft power imbues public diplomacy with new meanings. According to Golan, the soft power approach causes public diplomacy research and practice to move from a global persuasion model to a government-to-citizen engagement model.[173] It is easy to tell from the terms he uses that the former refers to propaganda while the latter emphasizes equal dialogue and cooperation, such as in educational and cultural exchanges along with language training and development programs, something that is echoed by Hayden in his book about soft power and public diplomacy. For Hayden, soft power is a new term used to describe a phenomenon that has been in existence for a long time, but soft power and public diplomacy represent the inevitable convergence of transnational communication with the imperatives of international politics.[174] In other words, soft power endows public diplomacy with a theoretical basis.

Nevertheless, associating public diplomacy with soft power can confuse public diplomacy with propaganda in that exerting "power over" an audience might overlap with the definition of propaganda. Five different aspects lend meaning to power or soft power in concert with public diplomacy. These include maintaining consistency in message and action; the actions depend on the domestic constituency; exerting power using information activities while engaging a foreign audience needs exchange programs; the power relationship is rooted in networks with the participation of international actors as well as the prevalence of technologies; identifying who is important and what is successful in public diplomacy.[175] Reconsidering these five aspects can avert the mistake of focusing solely on the masculine sense of power and extend its connotation of the relationship between soft power and public diplomacy to empowerment, which seems more meaningful for understanding educational and cultural programs in public diplomacy.

Also, the relationship between soft power and public diplomacy has been touted by the proponents of hard power since the latter is viewed as an effective user of soft power.[176] However, advocating the marriage of smart power and public diplomacy does not come from conceptual changes alone but responds to the urgent need for national security. Nye defines smart power as the artful combination and strategic use of soft and hard power but he does not really illustrate the internal linkage between smart power and public diplomacy.[177] From the viewpoint of smart power, understanding the connection between smart power and public diplomacy cannot be isolated from the link to hard power. Therefore, one direction of soft power within the aegis of smart power focuses on the soft use of public diplomacy towards populations when traditional forms of combat are being carried out while the other direction of soft power within the framework of smart power emphasizes the function of public diplomacy without referring to war.[178] In the former situation public diplomacy is used to gain respect and support from hostile populations while it aims to better communicate and effectively engage with locals in the latter one. With the purpose of discussing the relationship between smart power and public diplomacy, Wilson tries to connect hard power (an integral part of smart power) with public diplomacy by raising the discussion of the utilization of public diplomacy in wartime, but this does not make the relations much clearer since, irrespective of appealing to war or living in peace, public diplomacy has always been discussed on the basis of soft power, and the only difference is in decreasing the hostility of the target country in wartime or increasing the favorable image in peacetime.

However, smart power is far from being clear and operational enough to resolve the weakness of ideas about soft power. On the contrary, because of the increasing popularity of smart power in political and ideological debate among scholars, politicians, and diplomats, smart power has been loaded with different and sometimes even misleading meanings.[179] In practice, solving the problems of how to make soft power have an impact on overall policy and how to make hard power more effective, require institutional change and more coordination among different governmental departments. Smart power is not easy to achieve given its complexity.[180]

As an academic term, soft power may not be the most clearly defined and tidy concept, but it does provide a form of non-material influence for analysis that can be distinguished from material ones. In other words, the most important meaning of soft power is that it is clearly sufficient to offer something other than military and economic force in world politics.[181] In the information era where ideas and minds do matter, soft power as an analytical concept and theoretical basis can be widely used to explain public diplomacy as well as other forms of communication that link to behaviors of international players in formulating a positive image. The frequent use of soft power to explain public diplomacy practice makes some scholars equate it with public diplomacy,[182] which is obviously, not the case. In fact, soft power and public diplomacy are not the same things in academic discussion or international practice. Other instruments other than public diplomacy can be used to increase soft power, but public diplomacy, without any doubt, is an active effort to cultivate soft power for nation states.[183]

Therefore, in comparison with the concept of smart power which is more frequently used by politicians and diplomats and is not appropriate for the discussion in this research, soft power is still one of the most useful concepts to explain the public diplomacy practice of different international actors on the world stage. From the explanation above, using soft power to understand public diplomacy can be examined from two perspectives: the first is to use public diplomacy as an instrument for transferring the soft power resources of an international actor, and the second one is to convert soft power to external influence through public diplomacy.

The discussion about the relationship between soft power and public diplomacy in general discourse helps us understand the role of public diplomacy in wielding EU soft power and producing actual external influence. However, EU public diplomacy has also to be put in the context of the understanding of soft power on the part of the EU itself. The perceived achievement of regional integration through peaceful approaches based on the cultural diversity of the formation of European identity as well as its founding norms constitute the core content of the EU's soft power. Thus, EU public diplomacy also takes responsibility for telling the story of European integration as well as promoting EU norms,[184] which exactly manifest Nye's understanding of soft power—creating consensus and shaping the preference of other.[185] Thus, EU public diplomacy, first and foremost, needs to project an image of the EU a global actor by telling the history and achievement of European integration;[186] while at the meantime, EU public diplomacy has the ambition of shaping the preferences of other by exporting its norms through public diplomacy and other means.[187]

The most significant aspect of EU soft power is the EU as a model of regional integration, and projecting the EU as a model of regional integration is also what EU public diplomacy does. Besides, the importance of norms, as the foundation of European integration, cannot be disregarded when considering soft power in the context of the EU. On the basis of this, the EU's policy—or its public diplomacy—is to communicate the EU as a normative power. As mentioned in the previous section, a compelling narrative used to describe the history of a country or the specifics of policy can be power resources and the process of communicating narratives is one way through which power resources can be understood to work more broadly.[188] In terms of EU norms, the discussion of the uniqueness of the EU in world politic has a long history. Besides creating a new political system, namely a subsystem of international relations,[189] the identity of the EU, from being regarded as a civilian power to being re-defined as a normative power (which will be elaborated later), reflects a better understanding of the role of the EU at the world stage. There is no denying normative power Europe, as a widely accepted term, has been used to provide theoretical framework for and will continue to provide insights into scholarly research related to the EU. Thus, as a normative power, the EU possesses two aspects of normative power: being normative (shaping the conceptions of "normal") and acting in a normative way (behaving in an ethically good manner).[190]

EU public diplomacy and norm diffusion correlate in the EU's educational programs. the Consolidated Version of the Treaty on European Union indicates that "the Union is founded on the values of respect for human dignity, freedom, democracy, equality, the rule of law and respect for human rights" (Article 2) and the Union "seeks to advance its principles in the wider world" (Article 21). However, norm diffusion is a more complicated process than knowledge dissemination, which may confuse some readers if they have not paid enough attention to the differences between these two concepts. Norm diffusion is a process that norms travel across physical and psychological borders, and it is the same situation as knowledge dissemination. Yet, the effect of knowledge dissemination is based on two types of studies: knowledge related studies and socially related studies. The former one includes curriculum, assessment, and cognitive purpose while the latter one consists of group characteristics of teachers, types of teaching methods, and student learning requirements.[191]

Norm diffusion is a concept or a process. Diffusion mechanisms are summarized as contagion and transference[192] and further generalized as coercion, competition, social learning, and emulation.[193] In fact, both classifications almost overlap, in that Manners defines norm diffusion from the angle of the EU's intentionality (transference) or non-intentionality (contagion)[194] while Gilardi conceptualizes it from the standpoints of promoter (coercion), receiver (competition and learning) and the appropriateness of the norm itself (emulation).[195] Moreover, transnational norm diffusion, which not only crosses the physical borders between nations but also penetrates the boundary existing psychologically, is more complicated in empirical study for two reasons: the first is that cross-cultural traveling of norms may imply a new understanding in the context of recipients;[196] and the second is that the recipients of norms are not only passive receivers but also proactive agents: who could influence the content and outcome of the socialization process.[197] Given that several domestic factors, such as the economic development of the recipients, their institutional structures, their views about norms, and their capacity of localizing these norms, all have impact,[198] any study of the success or failure of norm diffusion should look beyond the promoter and modalities of diffusion. Rather, domestic factors will explain adaptation or rejection of norm diffusion in developing countries.[199]

In this sense, the EU's normative knowledge dissemination and EU norm diffusion are different processes, but normative knowledge dissemination serves as the preliminary condition for EU norm diffusion. On the one hand, the EU norms have gone through the teaching process in concert with the specific events, making these intangible EU norms which had been learnt as "Western values" in general from other courses more concrete in the context of the EU and EU-China relations.[200] Although it cannot directly exert an impact on Chinese politics and society, an informed intellectual community in the long run may exert their influence on policy process of different fields since these students are studying at well-known Chinese universities and would stand a good chance of being future policy makers. On the other hand, EU-China cooperation establishes on a series of practical programs besides the Jean Monnet Programme,[201] and for these projects aiming to promote EU norms in China, a cultivated society favorable towards the EU and EU norms will be a preliminary condition for the EU's norm diffusion.

Therefore, on the one hand, teaching the EU to college students of the third parties cannot avoid mentioning EU norms. On the other hand, albeit norm diffusion is a long process beyond classroom teaching, EU norm or the normative knowledge of the EU that have been lectured in the classroom will serve a good start for the EU's norm diffusion in China and even the world outside of EU territory. The purpose of establishing the Jean Monnet Programme is supporting the research and teaching of European integration and EU studies, which helps communicate the image of the EU as a model of regional integration and a "force of good." Again, projecting a favorable image on the world stage is also regarded as a long-term objective of an international actor, which is related to the concept of soft power and requires the utilization of strategic narratives. Thus, public diplomacy falls into this category.[202]

During this process, public diplomacy, which is a means of producing real external influence, informs the target audience with an understanding and acceptance of who you are and what you are doing now through information activities—the informational procedure for promoting EU norms;[203] and influencing the target groups by educational and cultural activities over the long-term—transference procedure for promoting EU norms.[204] In fact, in the former, the power dimension of soft power is still obvious because "exerting power" through one-way information diffusion and transmission manifests the role of the executor of public diplomacy and has the capacity of dominating this information transmission process although the role of the one-way information flow which is gradually interrupted by a two-way information exchange due to the innovation and prevalence of new information and communication technologies. The executor, the EU in this case, can still have advantages in the communication process towards foreign publics because of the resources it has. In the latter, educational and cultural activities in public diplomacy can be viewed as engagement with the target group and empowerment endeavors by the executor.

This chapter took a close look at the multi-disciplinary contributions to and conceptual development of public diplomacy and the evolution of soft power before moving on to discuss the relationship between the two. The definition of public diplomacy and its relation to soft power as presented in this chapter have not only provided a conceptual basis for the arguments and discussions in the research but have also established a framework within which the whole book may be structured.

Furthermore, looking at public diplomacy through the lens of soft power is a process of using public diplomacy to convert soft power resources to soft power, then to real external influence. In practice, the activities of public diplomacy can be viewed as a story-telling process of letting others know the history, development, and standpoints of the EU. Before moving on to the discussion of the Jean Monnet Programme of the EU, the next chapter will look at the role EU public diplomacy plays in its external relations as well as its practice before and after the Treaty of Lisbon. In comparison with EU public diplomacy practice beyond the Jean Monnet Programme, it is much easier for us to understand why the Jean Monnet Programme works effectively in the pool of EU public diplomacy practice.

NOTES

1. Copeland, D. (2011), "The Seven Paradoxes of Public Diplomacy," in Fisher, A. and Lucas, S. (eds.), *Trials of Engagement: The Future of US Public Diplomacy*, Leiden: Martinus Nijhoff Publishers: 183.

2. Edward Murrow Center, (1965), *What Is Public Diplomacy?* http://fletcher. tufts.edu/Murrow/Diplomacy, [accessed Oct. 10, 2013].

3. Lasswell, H. (1948), "The Structure and Function of Communication in Society," in Bryson, L. (ed.), *The Communication of Ideas*, New York: Harper & Bros: 37.

4. Lasswell, H. (1971), *Propaganda Technique in World War, the New Edition*, MA: MIT Press.

5. Malone, G. (1985), "Managing Public Diplomacy," *The Washington Quarterly*, 8(3): 199.

6. Ibid.

7. Tuch, H. (1990), *Communicating with the World, U.S. Public Diplomacy Overseas*, New York, St. Martin's press: 3.

8. Fisher, A. and Lucas, S. (2011), "Introduction," Fisher, A. and Lucas, S. (eds.), *Trials of Engagement: The Future of US Public Diplomacy*, Leiden: Martinus Nijhoff Publishers: 1.

9. Signitzer, B. H. and Coombs, T. (1992), "Public Relations and Public Diplomacy: Conceptual Convergences," *Public Relations Review*, 18(2): 138.

10. Ibid: 143.

11. Vickers, R. (2004), "The New Public Diplomacy: Britain and Canada Compared," *The British Journal of Politics and International Relations*, 6(2): 182.

12. Melissen, J. (2005), "The New Public Diplomacy: Between Theory and Practice," in Melissen, J. (ed.), *The New Public Diplomacy: Soft Power in International Relations*, New York: Palgrave Macmillan: 12.

13. Gilboa, E. (2008), "Searching for a Theory of Public Diplomacy," *Annals of the American Academy of Political and Social Science*, 616(1): 74.

14. Gregory, B. (2011), "American Public Diplomacy: Enduring Characteristics, Elusive Transformation," *The Hague Journal of Diplomacy*, 6(3–4): 353.

15. Wang, J. (2005), "Localizing Public Diplomacy: The Role of Sub-national Actors in Nation Branding," *Place Branding*, 2(1): 32.

16. Ham, P. V. (2008), "Place Branding: The State of the Art," *Annals of the American Academy of Political and Social Science*, 616(1): 135.

17. Fan, Y. (2006), "Branding the Nation: What is being branded?" *Journal of Vocation Marketing*, 12(1): 12.

18. Cull, N. J. (2010), "Public Diplomacy: Seven Lessons for its Future from its Past," *Place Branding and Public Diplomacy*, Vol.6: 11.

19. Wallström, M. (2008), *Public Diplomacy and its Role in the EU's External Relations*, Mortara Center for International Studies, Georgetown University, available at: http://europa.eu/rapid/press-release_SPEECH-08-494_en.pdf, [accessed April 3, 2015]: 3–4.

20. Edward Murrow Center, (1965), *What Is Public Diplomacy?* http://fletcher.tufts.edu/Murrow/Diplomacy, [accessed Oct. 10, 2013].

21. Hovland, C. and Weiss, W. (1951), "The Influence of Source Credibility on Communication Effectiveness," *Public Opinion Quarterly*, 15(4): 635–650.

22. Council on Foreign Relations, (2001), *Improving the U.S. Public Diplomacy Campaign in the War against Terrorism*, Task Force Report No. 38.

23. Lazarsfeld, P. F., Berelson, B. and Gaudet, H. (1948), *The People's Choice*, New York: Columbia University Press 151.

24. Nisbet, E. C. (2005), "The Engagement Model of Opinion Leadership: Testing validity within a European Context," *International Public Opinion Research*, 18(1) 3–30.

25. Yepsen, E. A. (2012), *Practicing Successful Twitter Public Diplomacy: A Model and Case Study of U.S. Efforts in Venezuela*, CPD Perspectives on Public Diplomacy, University of Southern California, 3.

26. Katz, E. (1957), "The Two-Step Flow of Communication: An Up-To-Date Report on a Hypothesis," *Public Opinion Quarterly*, 21(1): 61–78.

27. Jungermann, H., Pfister, H. R., and Fischer, K. (1996), "Credibility, Information Preference, and Information Interests," *Risk Analysis*, 16(2): 251–261.

28. Council on Foreign Relations, (2001), *Improving the U.S. Public Diplomacy Campaign in the War against Terrorism*, Task Force Report No. 38.

29. Manheim, J. B. (1994), *Strategic Public Diplomacy and American Foreign Policy: The Evolution of Influence*, New York: Oxford University Press: 126–147.

30. Yepsen, E. A. (2012), *Practicing Successful Twitter Public Diplomacy: A Model and Case Study of U.S. Efforts in Venezuela*, CPD Perspectives on Public Diplomacy, University of Southern California: 24.

31. Rugh, W. A. (2014), *Front Line Public Diplomacy: How US Embassies Communicate with Foreign Publics*, Hampshire and New York: Palgrave Macmillan: 73.

32. Pamment, J. (2012), *New Public Diplomacy in the 21st Century: A Comparative Study of Policy and Practice*, New York and Abingdon: Routledge: 75.

33. Sevin, E. (2011), "Thinking About Place Branding: Ethics of Concept," *Place Branding and Public Diplomacy*, Vol.7: 155–164.

34. Rasmussen, S. B. (2010), "The Messages and Practices of the European Union's Public Diplomacy," *The Hague Journal of Diplomacy*, 5(3): 263–287.

35. Seib, P. (2012), *Real-time Diplomacy: Politics and Power in the Social Media Era*, New York: Palgrave Macmillan: 116.

36. Alexander, C. (2011), *China, Costa Rica, and the Race for U.N. Security General*, Centre on Public Diplomacy, University of South California, available at: http://uscpublicdiplomacy.org/blog/china_costa_rica_and_the_race_for_un_secretary_general, [accessed June 5, 2014].

37. Alexander, C. (2011), "Public Diplomacy and the Diplomatic Truce: Taiwan and the People's Republic of China in EI Salvador," *Place Branding and Public Diplomacy*, 7(4): 271–288.

38. Cull, N. J. (2010), "Public Diplomacy: Seven Lessons for its Future from its Past," *Place Branding and Public Diplomacy*, Vol. 6: 11–17.

39. Akami, T. (2008), "The Emergence of International Public Opinion and the Origins of Public Diplomacy in Japan in the Inter-War Period," *The Hague Journal of Diplomacy*, No. 3: 99–128.

40. Ibid: 128.

41. Goldsmith, B., and Horiuchi, Y. (2009), "Spinning the Globe? U.S. Public Diplomacy and Foreign Public Opinion," *The Journal of Politics*, 71(3): 863–875.

42. Ibid: 873.

43. McCombs, M. and Shaw, D. L. (1972), "The Agenda-Setting Function of Mass Media," *The Public Opinion Quarterly*, 36(2): 176.

44. Melissen, J. (2005), "The New Public Diplomacy: Between Theory and Practice," in Melissen, J. (ed.), *The New Public Diplomacy: Soft Power in International Relations*, New York: Palgrave Macmillan: 13.

45. Van Ham, P. (2005), "Power, Public Diplomacy, and the Pax Americana," in Melissen (ed.), *The New Public Diplomacy: Soft Power in International Relations*, New York: Palgrave Macmillan: 57.

46. Pamment, J. (2012), *New Public Diplomacy in the 21st Century: A Comparative Study of Policy and Practice*, New York and Abingdon: Routledge: 7–8.

47. Seo, Hyunjin, (2009), *How the Internet Changes Public Diplomacy: A Case Study of Online Community Run by U.S. Embassy in South Korean*, Conference paper, International Communication Association: 3.

48. Brown, R. (2004), "Information Technology and the Transformation of Diplomacy," *Knowledge, Technology & Policy*, 18(2): 17.

49. Signitzer, B. H. and Coombs, T. (1992), "Public Relations and Public Diplomacy: Conceptual Convergences," *Public Relations Review*, 18(2): 137–147.

50. Peisert, H. (1978). *Die auswärtige Kulturpolitik der Bundesrepublik Deutschland. Sozialwissenschaftliche Analysen und Planungsmodelle*. Stuttgart: Klett-Cotta.

51. Signitzer, B. H. and Coombs, T. (1992), "Public Relations and Public Diplomacy: Conceptual Convergences," *Public Relations Review*, 18(2): 141.

52. Wang, J. and Chang, TK. (2004), "Strategic Public Diplomacy and Local Press: How a High-Profile 'Head-of-State' Visit was Covered in America's Heartland," *Public Relations Review*, 30(1): 11–24.

53. Grunig J. E. (1997), "A Situational Theory of Publics: Conceptual History, Recent Challenges, and New Research," In Moss, D., Macmanus, T. and Vercic, D. (eds.), *Public Relations Research: An International Perspective*, London: International Thomson Business: 3–38.

54. Yun, S. H. (2006), "Toward Public Relations Theory-Based Study of Public Diplomacy: Testing the Applicability of the Excellent Study," *Journal of Public Relations Research*, 18:(4): 293.

55. Ibid: 307.

56. Alexander M. G. Levin, S. and Henry, P. J. (2005), "Image Theory, Social Identity, and Social Dominance: Structural Characteristics and Individual Motives Underlying International Image," *Political Psychology*, 26(1): 42.

57. Manheim, J. B. (1994), *Strategic Public Diplomacy and American Foreign Policy: The Evolution of Influence*, New York: Oxford University Press: 39.

58. Leonard, M., Stead, C. and Smewing, C. (2002), *Public Diplomacy*, London: Foreign Policy Centre: 11.

59. Manheim, J. B. (1994), *Strategic Public Diplomacy and American Foreign Policy: The Evolution of Influence*, New York: Oxford University Press: 14.

60. Cowan, G. and Arsenault, A. (2008), "Moving from Monologue to Dialogue to Collaboration: The Three Layers of Public Diplomacy," *Annals of the American Academy of Political and Social Science*, 616(1): 10.

61. Wang, J. (2006), "Managing National Reputation and International Relations in the Global Era: Public Diplomacy Revisited," *Public Relations Review*, 32(2): 92.

62. Fitzpatrick K. R. (2007), "Advancing the New Public Diplomacy: A Public Relations Perspective," *The Hague Journal of Diplomacy*, 2(3): 210.

63. Jackson, R. and Sørensen, G. (2016), *Introduction to International Relations: Theories and Approaches (6th edition)*, Oxford: Oxford University Press: 6–7.

64. Wendt, A. (1992), "Anarchy Is What States Make of It: The Social Construction of Power Politics," *International Organisations*, 46(2): 404.

65. Zhang, Q. (2012), "Jiangou Zhuyi Shijiaoxia Gonggong Waijiao De Xingainian (The New Concept of Public Diplomacy from the Perspective of Constructivism)," *Journal of University of International Relations*, No. 1: 29.

66. Han, F. (2011), *Gonggong Waijiao Gailun* (*Introduction to Public Diplomacy*), Beijing: Peking University Press: 20.

67. Mearsheimer, J. (2002), "Hearts and Minds," *The National Interest*, No. 69: 15.

68. Han, F. (2011), *Gonggong Waijiao Gailun* (*Introduction to Public Diplomacy*), Beijing: Peking University Press: 20.

69. Keohane, Robert, O. and Nye, J. (1987), "Review: Power and Interdependence Revisited," *International Organisations*, 41(4): 727.

70. Keohane, Robert, O. and Nye, J. (2011), *Power and Interdependence, 4th edition*, New York: Longman: 115.

71. Broś, N. (2017), "Public Diplomacy and Cooperation with Non-governmental Organisations in the Liberal Perspective of International Relations," *Journal of Education, Culture and Society,* No.1: 17.

72. Hopf, T. (1998), "The Promise of Constructivism in International Relations Theory," *International Security*, 23(1): 173.

73. Gregory, B. (2008), "Public Diplomacy: Sunrise of an Academic Field," *The Annals of the American Academy of Political and Social Science*, 616(1): 276.

74. Cross, Mai'a K. D. (2013), "Conceptualising European Public Diplomacy," in Mai'a K. Davis Cross & Jan Melissen (eds.), *European Public Diplomacy: Soft Power at Work*, Hampshire: Palgrave Macmillan: 6.

75. Zhang, Q. (2012), "Jiangou Zhuyi Shijiaoxia Gonggong Waijiao De Xingainian (The New Concept of Public Diplomacy from the Perspective of Constructivism)," *Journal of University of International Relations*), No. 1: 30.

76. Gilboa, E. (2008), "Searching for a Theory of Public Diplomacy," *Annals of the American Academy of Political and Social Science*, 616(1): 68.

77. Nye, J. (2004), *Soft Power: The Means to Success in World Politics*, New York: Public Affairs: 8.

78. Melissen, J. (2005b), *Wielding Soft Power: The New Public Diplomacy*, Netherlands Institute of International Relations, "Clingendael": 3.

79. Simonin, B. L. (2008), "Nation Branding and Public Diplomacy: Challenges and Opportunities," *World Affairs*, 32(3): 19.

80. Szondi, G. (2008), *Public Diplomacy and Nation Branding: Conceptual Similarity and Difference*, Netherlands Institute of International Relations, "Clingendael."

81. Fan, Y. (2010), "Branding the Nation: Towards A Better Understanding," *Place Branding and Public Diplomacy*, Vol.6: 5.

82. Ham, P. V. (2001), "The Rise of the Brand State: The Postmodern Politics of Image and Reputation," *Foreign Affairs*, 80(5): 2.

83. Dinnie, K. (2008), *Nation Branding: Concepts, Issues, Practice*, Oxford: Butterworth-Heinemann: 15.

84. Anholt, S. (2006), "Public Diplomacy and Place Branding: Where's the Link?" *Place Branding*, Vol. 2: 217.

85. Szondi, G. (2008), *Public Diplomacy and Nation Branding: Conceptual Similarity and Difference*, Netherlands Institute of International Relations, "Clingendael":14.

86. Simonin, B. L. (2008), "Nation Branding and Public Diplomacy: Challenges and Opportunities," *World Affairs*, 32(3): 22.

87. Wang, J. (2006), "Localizing Public Diplomacy: The Role of Sub-national Actors in Nation Branding," *Place Branding*, 2(1): 32.

88. Ham, P. V. (2008), "Place Branding: The State of the Art," *Annals of the American Academy of Political and Social Science*, 616(1): 135.

89. Fan, Y. (2006), "Branding the Nation: What is Being Branded?" *Journal of Vocation Marketing*, 12(1): 12.

90. Dinnie, K. (2008), *Nation Branding: Concepts, Issues, Practice*, Oxford: Butterworth-Heinemann: 15.

91. Anholt, S. (2006), "Public Diplomacy and Place Branding: Where's the link?" *Place Branding*, Vol. 2: 271.

92. Dinnie, K. (2008), *Nation Branding: Concepts, Issues, Practice*, Oxford: Butterworth-Heinemann: 251.

93. Fitzpatrick, K. R. (2010), *The Future of U.S. Public Diplomacy: An Uncertain Fate*, Leiden: Koninklijke Brill NV: 131.

94. Copeland, D. (2011), "The Seven Paradoxes of Public Diplomacy," in Fisher, A. and Lucas, S. (eds.), *Trials of Engagement: The Future of US Public Diplomacy*, Leiden: Martinus Nijhoff Publishers:185.

95. Wallström, M. (2008), *Public Diplomacy and its Role in the EU's External Relations*, Mortara Center for International Studies, Georgetown University, available at: http://europa.eu/rapid/press-release_SPEECH-08-494_en.pdf, [accessed April 3, 2015]: 2.

96. Melissen, J. (2005), "The New Public Diplomacy: Between Theory and Practice," in Melissen, J. (ed.), *The New Public Diplomacy: Soft Power in International Relations*, New York: Palgrave Macmillan: 3.

97. Jowett, G. S. and O'Donnell, V. J. (2011), *Propaganda and Persuasion, (fifth edition)*, CA: Sage Publication: 1.

98. Welch, D. (1999), "Power of Persuasion," *History Today*, 49(8): 26.

99. Azpíroz, M. L. (2015), *Soft Power and Public Diplomacy: The Case of the European Union in Brazil*, CPD perspectives on public diplomacy, Centre on Public Diplomacy, University of Southern California: 6.

100. Wang, Y. (2008), "Public Diplomacy and the Rise of Chinese Soft Power," *The Annals of the American Academy of Political and Social Science*, Vol. 616: 259.

101. Cull, N. J., D. Culbert, and D. Welch. (2003). *Propaganda and Mass Persuasion: A Historical Encyclopaedia, 1500 to the Present*. Santa Barbara, CA: ABC-CLIO: 39.

102. Welch, D. (1999), "Power of Persuasion," *History Today*, 49(8): 24.

103. Xing, G. (2009), "'Peaceful Rise': China's Public Diplomacy and International Image Cultivation," in Guo, S. and Hua, S. (eds.), *New Dimensions of Chinese Foreign Policy*, Lanham and Plymouth: Lexington Books: 141.

104. Snyder, J. T. (2013), *The United States and the Challenge of Public Diplomacy*, New York: Palgrave Macmillan: xx.

105. Cull, N. J. (2013), "Roof for a House Divided: How U.S. Propaganda Evolved into Public Diplomacy," in Auerbach, J. and Casteronovo, R. (eds.), *The Handbook of Propaganda Studies*, New York: Oxford University Press: 143.

106. Cohen, Y. (1986). *Media Diplomacy: The Foreign Office in the Mass Communications Age*, London: Frank Cass: 7.

107. Rawnsley, G. (1995), "Media Diplomacy: Monitored Broadcasting and Foreign Policy," *Discussion Papers in Diplomacy*. Leicester, UK: Centre for the Study of Diplomacy, University of Leicester.

108. Gilboa, E. (1998), "Media Diplomacy: Conceptual Divergence and Applications," *The International Journal of Press/Politics*, 3(3): 57.

109. Ibid: 62.

110. Zhong, X. and He, J. (2010), "Yingguo: Cong Wenhua Waijiao Dao Gonggong Waijiao De Yanjin (The UK: An Evolution from Cultural Diplomacy to Public Diplomacy)," Guoji Xinwenjie (*Chinse Journal of Journalism & Communication*), No. 7: 19.

111. Schneider, C. P. (2006), "Cultural Diplomacy: Hard to Define, but You'd Know It if You Saw It," *The Brown Journal of World Affairs*, 13(1): 191.

112. Cummings, Milton C. (2003), Cultural Diplomacy and the United States Government: A Survey, Washington, DC: Center for Arts and Culture, cited from Center for Arts and Culture, 2004, Cultural Diplomacy: Recommendations and Research, Washington. DC.

113. Banks, D. (2011), "The Questions of Cultural Diplomacy," *Theatre Topics*, 21(2): 111.

114. Bound, K. Briggs, R. Holden, J. and Jones, S. (2007), *Cultural Diplomacy*, London: Demos, available at: http://www.demos.co.uk/files/Cultural%20 diplomacy%20-%20web.pdf, [accessed Nov. 11, 2013]: 12.

115. Mark, S. L. (2010), "Rethinking Cultural Diplomacy: The Cultural Diplomacy of New Zealand, the Canadian Federation and Quebec," *Political Science*, 61(1): 62.

116. Ibid: 65.

117. Schneider C. P. (2005), "Culture Communicates: US Diplomacy That Works," In Melissen Jan, (ed.), *The New Public Diplomacy: Soft Power in International Relations*, New York: Palgrave Macmillan: 154.

118. Schneider, C. P. (2006), "Cultural Diplomacy: Hard to Define, but You'd Know It if You Saw It," *The Brown Journal of World Affairs*, 13(1): 192.

119. Mark, S. L. (2010), "Rethinking Cultural Diplomacy: The Cultural Diplomacy of New Zealand, the Canadian Federation and Quebec," *Political Science*, 61(1): 65–66.

120. Cull, N. J. (2008), "Public Diplomacy: Taxonomies and Histories," *Annals of the American Academy of Political and Social Science*, 616(1): 31.

121. European Commission, (2007), *A Glance at EU Public Diplomacy at Work*, http://europa.eu/50/around_world/images/2007_50th_anniv_broch_en.pdf, [accessed April 2, 2015]: 13.

122. Cull, N. J. (2008), "Public Diplomacy: Taxonomies and Histories," *Annals of the American Academy of Political and Social Science*, 616(1): 31.

123. Gilboa, E. (2008), "Searching for a Theory of Public Diplomacy," *Annals of the American Academy of Political and Social Science*, 616(1): 72.

124. Han, Z. (2011), "China's Public Diplomacy in a New Era," in Zhu, Z. (ed.), *The People's Republic of China Today: Internal and External Challenges*, Singapore: World Scientific Publishing: 293.

125. Wilson, I. (2010), *Are International Exchange and Mobility Programmes Effective Tools of Symmetric Public Diplomacy?* Aberystwyth University, available at: http://cadair.aber.ac.uk/dspace/handle/2160/7177, [accessed Sept. 18, 2014]: 9.

126. Mark, S. L. (2010), "Rethinking Cultural Diplomacy: The Cultural Diplomacy of New Zealand, the Canadian Federation and Quebec," *Political Science*, 61(1): 65–66.

127. Wilson, I. (2010), *Are International Exchange and Mobility Programmes Effective Tools of Symmetric Public Diplomacy?* Aberystwyth University, available at: http://cadair.aber.ac.uk/dspace/handle/2160/7177, [accessed Sept. 18, 2014]: 10–14

128. Nye, J. (1990), "Soft Power," *Foreign Policy*, No. 80:153–165

129. Ibid: 168.

130. Nye, J. (2004), *Soft Power: The Means to Success in World Politics*, New York: Public Affairs: 5.

131. Nye, J. (2011), *Why Europe is and Will Remain, Powerful? Utopian.org*. available at: http://www.the-utopian.org/post/2424081389/why-europe-is-and-will-remain-powerful, [accessed May 11, 2015]: 90.

132. Nye, J. (2004), *Soft Power: The Means to Success in World Politics*, New York: Public Affairs: 6.

133. Roselle, L., Miskimmon A., O'Loughlin, B. (2014), "Strategic Narrative: A New Means to Understand Soft Power," *Media, War & Conflict*, 7(1): 72.

134. Porter, W. and Mykleby, M. (2011), *A National Strategic Narrative*, Woodrow Wilson Centre, available at: https://www.wilsoncenter.org/sites/default/files/A%20National%20Strategic%20Narrative.pdf, [accessed April 19, 2016]: 4.

135. Freedman, L. (2006), "Networks, Culture and Narratives," *The Adelphi Papers*, 45(379): 23.

136. Roselle, L., Miskimmon A., O'Loughlin, B. (2014), "Strategic Narrative: A New Means to Understand Soft Power," *Media, War & Conflict*, 7(1): 74.

137. Miskimmon, A., O'Loughlin, B. and Roselle, L. (2013), *Strategic Narratives: Communication Power and the New World Order*, New York and London: Routledge: 30.

138. Skuse, A., Gillespie, M., and Power, G. (eds.), (2011), *Drama for Development: Cultural Translation and Social Change*, New Delhi: Sage India.

139. Roselle, L., Miskimmon A., O'Loughlin, B. (2014), "Strategic Narrative: A New Means to Understand Soft Power," *Media, War & Conflict*, 7(1): 7.

140. Miskimmon, A., O'Loughlin, B. and Roselle, L. (2013), *Strategic Narratives: Communication Power and the New World Order*, New York and London: Routledge.

141. Roselle, L., Miskimmon A., O'Loughlin, B. (2014), "Strategic Narrative: A New Means to Understand Soft Power," *Media, War & Conflict*, 7(1): 72&74.

142. Arquila, J. and Ronfeldt, D. (1999), *The Emergence of Noopolitik: Toward an American Information Strategy*, Santa Monica, CA: Rand: 62.

143. Miskimmon, A., O'Loughlin, B. and Roselle, L. (2012), *Forging the World: Strategic Narratives and International Relations*, Working Paper, Centre for European Politics/ New Political Communication Unit, available at: http://newpolcom. rhul.ac.uk/storage/Forging%20the%20World%20Working%20Paper%202012.pdf, [accessed Nov. 22, 2015]: 180.

144. Roselle, L., Miskimmon A., O'Loughlin, B. (2014), "Strategic Narrative: A New Means to Understand Soft Power," *Media, War & Conflict*, 7(1): 72.

145. Miskimmon, A., O'Loughlin, B. and Roselle, L. (2012), *Forging the World: Strategic Narratives and International Relations*, Working Paper, Centre for European Politics/ New Political Communication Unit, available at: http://newpolcom. rhul.ac.uk/storage/Forging%20the%20World%20Working%20Paper%202012.pdf, [accessed Nov. 22, 2015]: 5–6.

146. Roselle, L., Miskimmon A., O'Loughlin, B. (2014), "Strategic Narrative: A New Means to Understand Soft Power," *Media, War & Conflict*, 7(1): 70.

147. Noya, J. (2005), "The Symbolic Power of Nations," *Place Branding*, 2(1): 16.

148. Ibid.

149. Joffe, J. (2006), "The Peril of Soft Power," *The New York Times*, http://www. nytimes.com/2006/05/14/magazine/14wwln_lede.html?_r=1&pagewanted=print&oref=slogin, [accessed Dec. 10, 2013].

150. Roselle, L., Miskimmon A., O'Loughlin, B. (2014), "Strategic Narrative: A New Means to Understand Soft Power," *Media, War & Conflict*, 7(1): 71.

151. Nossel, S. (2004), "Smart Power: Reclaiming Liberal Internationalism," *Foreign Affairs*, 81(2): 131.

152. Nye, J. (2009), "Get Smart: Combining Hard and Soft Power," *Foreign Affairs*, July/August Issue, available at: http://www.foreignaffairs.com/articles/65163/joseph-s-nye-jr/get-smart?page=1, [accessed Aug. 18, 2014].

153. Nye, J. (2008), "Public Diplomacy and Soft Power," *Annals of the American Academy of Political and Social Science*, 616(1): 106–107.

154. Wilson III, E. (2008), "Hard Power, Soft Power, Smart Power," *Annals of the American Academy of Political and Social Science*, 616(1): 110.

155. Gilboa, E. (2008), "Searching for a Theory of Public Diplomacy," *Annals of the American Academy of Political and Social Science*, 616(1): 56–75.

156. Fitzpatrick, K. R. (2010), *The Future of U.S. Public Diplomacy: An Uncertain Fate*, Leiden: Koninklijke Brill NV.

157. Michalski, A. (2012), "China and the EU: Conceptual Gaps in Soft Power," in Pan, Z. (ed.), *Conceptual Gaps in China-EU Relations*, Hampshire and New York: Palgrave Macmillan: 66.

158. Gill, B. & Huang, Y. (2006), "Source and Limits of Chinese Soft Power," *Survival: Global Politics and Strategy*, 48(2): 17–19.

159. Smith, K. E. (2014), "Is the European Union's Soft Power in Decline?" *Current History*, March: 104–105.

160. Michalski, A. (2012), "China and the EU: Conceptual Gaps in Soft Power," in Pan, Z. (ed.), *Conceptual Gaps in China-EU Relations*, Hampshire and New York: Palgrave Macmillan: 66.

161. Ding, S. (2010), "Analysing Rising Power from the Perspective of Soft Power: A New Look at China's Rise to the Status Quo Power," *Journal of Contemporary China*, 19(64): 265.

162. Michalski, A. (2012), "China and the EU: Conceptual Gaps in Soft Power," in Pan, Z. (ed.), *Conceptual Gaps in China-EU Relations*, Hampshire and New York: Palgrave Macmillan: 68–69.

163. Nye, J. (2010), *The Future of Power*, New York: Public Affairs: 21.

164. Michalski, A. (2005), "The EU as a Soft Power: The Force of Persuasion," in Melissen, J. (ed.), *The New Public Diplomacy: Soft Power in International Relations*, New York: Palgrave Macmillan: 124–146.

165. Chan, K. (2010), "The Image, Visibility and the Prospects of Soft Power of the EU in Asia: The Case of China," *Asia Europe Journal*, 8(2): 144.

166. Rasmussen, S. B. (2010), "The Messages and Practices of the European Union's Public Diplomacy," *The Hague Journal of Diplomacy*, 5(3): 285.

167. Nye, J. (2004), *Soft Power: The Means to Success in World Politics*, New York: Public Affairs: 99–100.

168. Nye, J. (2008), "Public Diplomacy and Soft Power," *Annals of the American Academy of Political and Social Science*, 616(1): 108.

169. Melissen, J. (2005), *Wielding Soft Power: The New Public Diplomacy*, Netherlands Institute of International Relations, "Clingendael": 1.

170. Nye, J. (2010), *The Future of Power*, New York: Public Affairs: 100.

171. Michalski, A. (2012), "China and the EU: Conceptual Gaps in Soft Power," in Pan, Z. (ed.), *Conceptual Gaps in China-EU Relations*, Hampshire and New York: Palgrave Macmillan: 71–72.

172. Melissen, J. (2005), *Wielding Soft Power: The New Public Diplomacy*, Netherlands Institute of International Relations, "Clingendael": 3.

173. Golan, G. J. (2013), "An Integration Approach to Public Diplomacy," *American Behavioural Scientist*, 57(9): 1251.

174. Hayden, C. (2011), *The Rhetoric of Soft Power: Public Diplomacy in Global Context*, Plymouth: Lexington Books: 16.

175. Fisher, A. (2011), "Looking at the Man in the Mirror: Understanding of Power and Influence in Public Diplomacy," *in Fisher, A. and Lucas, S. (eds.), Trials of Engagement: The Future of US Public Diplomacy*, Leiden: Martinus Nijhoff Publishers: 273.

176. Wilson III, E. (2008), "Hard Power, Soft Power, Smart Power," *Annals of the American Academy of Political and Social Science*, 616(1): 120.

177. Nye, J. (2008), "Public Diplomacy and Soft Power," *Annals of the American Academy of Political and Social Science*, 616(1): 94.

178. Wilson III, E. (2008), "Hard Power, Soft Power, Smart Power," *Annals of the American Academy of Political and Social Science*, 616(1): 121.

179. Gilboa, E. (2008), "Searching for a Theory of Public Diplomacy," *Annals of the American Academy of Political and Social Science*, 616(1): 62.

180. Wilson III, E. (2008), "Hard Power, Soft Power, Smart Power," *Annals of the American Academy of Political and Social Science*, 616(1): 122.

181. Hayden, C. (2011), *The Rhetoric of Soft Power: Public Diplomacy in Global Context*, Plymouth: Lexington Books: 278.

182. Gilboa, E. (2008), "Searching for a Theory of Public Diplomacy," *Annals of the American Academy of Political and Social Science*, 616(1): 56.

183. Hayden, C. (2011), *The Rhetoric of Soft Power: Public Diplomacy in Global Context*, Plymouth: Lexington Books: 287

184. Manners, I. and Whitman, R. (2013), "Normative Power and Future of EU Public Diplomacy," in Mai'a K. Davis Cross & Melissen, J. (eds.), *European Public Diplomacy: Soft Power at Work*, Hampshire: Palgrave Macmillan: 189.

185. Nye, J. (2004), *Soft Power: The Means to Success in World Politics*, New York: Public Affairs: 5.

186. DG Research and Innovation, (2014), *A Global Actor in Search of A Strategy: European Union Foreign Policy between Multilateralism and Bilateralism*, available at: https://ec.europa.eu/research/social-sciences/pdf/policy_reviews/kina26572enc. pdf, [accessed April 19, 2016]: 44.

187. Krebs, R. R. and Jackson, P. T. (2007), "Twisting Tongues and Twisting Arms: The Power of Political Rhetoric," *European Journal of International Relations*, 13(1): 39.

188. Roselle, L., Miskimmon A., O'Loughlin, B. (2014), "Strategic Narrative: A New Means to Understand Soft Power," *Media, War & Conflict*, 7(1): 74.

189. Hill, C. and Smith, M. (2011), "International Relations and the European Union: Themes and Issues," in Hill, C. and Smith, M. (eds.), *International Relations and European Union (2nd edition)*, the New York: Oxford University Press: 8–9.

190. Whitman, R. G. (2011), "Norms, Power and Europe: A New Agenda for Study of the EU and International Relations," in Whitman, R. G. (ed.), *Normative Power Europe: Empirical and Theoretical Perspectives*, Basingstoke: Palgrave Macmillan: 6.

191. Neumann, R., Parry, S. and Becher, T. (2002), "Teaching and Learning in their Disciplinary Contexts: A Conceptual Analysis," *Studies in Higher Education*, 27(4): 405.

192. Manners, I. (2002), "Normative Power Europe: A Contradiction in Terms?" *Journal of Common Market Studies*, 40(2): 244–245.

193. Gilardi, F. (2012), "Transnational Diffusion: Norms, Ideas, and Polices," in Carlsnaes, W. Risse, T. and Simmons, B. (eds.), *Handbook of International Relations, 2nd edition*, Thousand Oaks: Sage Publication: 461.

194. Manners, I. (2002), "Normative Power Europe: A Contradiction in Terms?" *Journal of Common Market Studies*, 40(2): 244–245.

195. Gilardi, F. (2012), "Transnational Diffusion: Norms, Ideas, and Polices," in Carlsnaes, W. Risse, T. and Simmons, B. (eds.), *Handbook of International Relations, 2nd edition*, Thousand Oaks: Sage Publication: 461.

196. Zwingel, S. (2012), "How do Norms Travel? Theorising International Women's Rights in Transnational Perspective," *International Studies Quarterly*, 56(1): 124.

197. Pu, X. (2012), "Socialisation as a Two-way Process: Emerging Powers and the Diffusion of International Norms," *The Chinese Journal of International Politics*, 5(4): 347.

198. Gillespie, J. (2012), "Developing a Theoretical Framework for Evaluating Rule of Law Promotion in Developing Countries," in Zurn, M., Nollkaemper, A. and Peerenboom, R. (eds.), *Rule of Law Dynamics: In an Era of International and Transitional Governance*, New York: Cambridge University Press: 237–48.

199. Ibid: 233.

200. Interview in Beijing, Mar. 15, 2016.

201. Delegation of the EU to China, (2015), The European Union and China: A Maturing Partnership, available at: http://eeas.europa.eu/delegations/china/eu_china/political_relations/index_en.htm, [accessed March 31, 2015]

202. Miskimmon, A., O'Loughlin, B. and Roselle, L. (2013), *Strategic Narratives: Communication Power and the New World Order*, New York and London: Routledge: 9.

203. Manners, I. and Whitman, R. (2013), "Normative Power and Future of EU Public Diplomacy," in Mai'a K. Davis Cross & Melissen, J. (eds.), *European Public Diplomacy: Soft Power at Work*, Hampshire: Palgrave Macmillan: 190.

204. Ibid: 191.

Chapter Three

The Development of EU Public Diplomacy

Before proceeding to look at the case of the Jean Monnet Programme and its implementation in China, the role of public diplomacy in the EU's external relations needs to be addressed. First, public diplomacy aims to improve the foreign public opinion environment for the EU's foreign policy, by influencing foreign perceptions with information and narratives, which means that public diplomacy has to be considered in the EU's external relations as a whole. Second, the institutional changes that followed the entry into force of the Treaty of Lisbon provide a new administrative structure for EU public diplomacy, and identifying these new changes will help us understand the changes in EU public diplomacy in general and what role the Jean Monnet Programme can play in particular. Third, since the Jean Monnet Programme is one of the EU public diplomacy programs, looking at other public diplomacy practices of the EU will be useful in order to understand the special features of the Jean Monnet Programme within EU public diplomacy.

3.1 THE ACTORNESS OF THE EU IN PUBLIC DIPLOMACY

With the participation of non-state actors (international organizations, subnational organizations and even non-governmental organizations) in public diplomacy and the prevalence of Internet-based communication technologies, public diplomacy can be further defined as an instruments used by different actors on the world stage. Put differently, this concept is summarized based on the analysis above, not only providing a basis to understand the actorness of the EU in public diplomacy practice since it relates to the first research question, but also helping structure the criteria of evaluating the Jean Monnet Programme in chapter 4 and analyze the effect of this program in chapters

6–7 which relates to the second and third research questions. In order to grasp the essence of this concept, some details need to be considered. However, what role is public diplomacy playing in the EU's foreign policy?

In terms of EU external relations, the first question to be answered is what the EU is on the world stage. Secondly, what does the EU do in international relations? Generally speaking, the EU is a global actor, described as "Sui generis,"[1] an "unprecedented experience,"[2] an "ongoing project,"[3] and a "dynamic entity."[4] The terms including "Sui generis" and "unprecedented" illustrate its different attributes in comparison with other international actors, while "ongoing" and "dynamic" indicate the current stage of the EU. Such descriptions provide the basis for us to explore the importance and indispensability of researching EU public diplomacy, and also help explain the problems in EU foreign policy as well as public diplomacy practice in general.

Based on the Schuman Plan, six countries including Germany, France, Italy, Belgium, the Netherlands, and Luxembourg established the ECSC in 1951, which started the process of European integration. Since then, European integration has undergone primarily regional economic integration, gradually involving the political and foreign policy dimension in this process.[5]

Christopher Hill and Michael Smith present three perspectives of the EU: (1) The EU as a subsystem of international relations, meaning that it has to deal with internal "foreign" relations among member states as well as generate collective action directed at external actors. (2) The EU is a part of the wider process of international relations, indicating that it has its own mechanisms related to law, institutions, and politics to address the international problems of conflict and political economy. (3) The EU is a major power impacting upon contemporary international relations.[6]

According to their analysis, the notion of the EU as a power is based on other actors and the international setting. Smith discusses this in another paper in which he identifies the EU as one of the world's most accomplished interactors which has the capacity depended on its relational resources to shape it international environment and has already made considerable impact in its collective international activities.[7] With regard to the EU's impact, its actual performance is related to the resources deployed, stated strategy and the level of collective action, as well as the perceptions of the EU by the recipient of its actions.[8] Instead of putting a priority on the EU's impact and its role in international relations at an abstract level, Jan Orbie and other scholars concern the empirical aspects of the EU's external action and analyze the varied roles of the EU in different areas of external actions by means of assessing what the EU actually does based on the linkage between means and ends.[9]

After more than sixty years of development and five times enlargement, the need to speak and act more coherently has been continuously stressed and an EU identity is gradually being formed through interaction among member states and their citizens. No matter how the EU is perceived by the outside world, its resources and, to a greater or lesser degree, its impact on world politics makes it a global power. Along with these achievements, the image of the EU in the world, which is summarized as a civilian power because of its peaceful approaches to unsolved problems, and as a normative power due to its endeavors in promoting norms and as an ethical power in protecting the rights of individuals, makes it unique.[10] Since this research focuses on external activities towards a third country by studying EU public diplomacy in China, it places emphasis on the analytical level of the interactions. Hence, the EU is an international actor.

Different from the nation states in world politics, the EU has its own particular characteristics: (1) As a normative power, the EU tries to promote its traditions such as human rights protection, the rule of law, and democracy.[11, 12] (2) As a model of regional integration, the EU experience sheds lights on attempts at political cooperation in East Asia and other areas.[13] (3) as an activist of relevant policy making and a leader in global governance, the EU tries to exert influence on environmental governance and climate change.[14] In short, the EU has its own specific features, foreign policies, and instruments corresponding to its own ideas about what it is and what it stands for.

After the initial endeavor at European Political Cooperation (EPC) in 1970s, the Treaty of Maastricht came into force in 1993. With the creation of the European Union and its CFSP which became the second pillar, the EU came up with three pillars: European Community, the European Atomic Energy Community, and the ECSC, as well as police and judicial cooperation.[15] The CFSP was explicitly viewed by the EU member states and academic experts as the site of the EU's foreign policy. Even so, the CFSP was still faced with the problems of a lack of common actors and common instruments as did the EPC which were the two major problems that the Amsterdam Treaty tried to tackle in 1997.[16] Since the Amsterdam Treaty came into force with its main change being the creation of Secretary General/High Representative (SG/HR) for the CFSP, the CFSP was finally supported by a permanent actor and eventually had a "face."[17] In the year of 2010, the Treaty of Lisbon and its creation of the High Representative/Vice President (HR/VP) and EEAS once again made changes to the EU's institutional design regarding foreign policy decision-making and implementation, and it exerted influence on the making and deployment of the EU's foreign policy.

However, the international status of the EU as a global actor with relational resources and its contribution to regional integration and prosperity as well as global governance has been doubted and challenged by other world powers. Even though the EU tries to present a united face to the world and act coherently in terms of external relations through the CFSP, European Security, and Defence Policy (ESDP), as well as the creation of the EEAS and HR/VP, the EU's global influence as a whole has been restricted by its institutional design and conflicting interests among member states. Andrew Moravcsik believes that its internal bickering and different national agenda may be a hindrance to the EU to translate its giant economic clout into global influence.[18] Although Moravcsik believes that "the EU today is still more effective at projecting civilian power than any other state or non-state actors,"[19] these negative impressions of the EU draw the attention of EU leaders and its member states.

The key point is what the EU actually does with the purpose of safeguarding the EU's prestige in the world. In this sense, its internal achievements through negotiation and exchange, as well as its external impact through the making and implementation of the EU's foreign policy, are determining factors. However, promoting the EU's global influence depends on the impact of the EU's external actions based on foreign policy and its image as perceived by both an internal and external audience, implying that the EU is supposed to make people in the world know what it does and moreover, support its foreign policy instead of just focusing on the making and implementing of foreign policy. The second task of letting the world know about the EU belongs to public diplomacy. Put more specifically, since ideas matter in international relations, public diplomacy has the potential to provide and create an enabling environment for foreign policy implementation and needs to be considered during the policy process.[20]

In terms of the implementation of foreign policy, varieties of instruments are employed. Jose Calvet de Magalhaes, a retired ambassador from Portugal, classifies the instruments of foreign policy into two components: violent and peaceful. Evidently, deterrence, threat, economic war, military pressure, and war are violent instruments. Meanwhile, he divides the peaceful instruments into plurilateral and unilateral contacts. Plurilateral contacts and negotiation include: 1) direct negotiation; 2) Diplomacy; 3) Mediation. And unilateral contacts include: 1) propaganda; 2) Espionage, or intelligence; 3) Economic intervention; 4) Political intervention.[21] Due to the fact that his book was published before the end of the Cold War, he used "propaganda" in his classification, but it was given exactly the same meaning as public diplomacy.

With regard to the EU, it has to deal with different relations with different actors and areas in the world in order to fulfil its own interests. As we can tell from the official releases of the EEAS, the EU's foreign policies include Common Foreign & Security Policy, Development and Cooperation, European Neighbourhood, Global Challenges, Non-proliferation and Disarmament, Crisis Response, Human Rights Promotion, Cooperation with Industrialised Countries, and so on, each of these policies has its own objectives and targets.[22] Among them, public diplomacy is deemed to be a tool of the EU's foreign policy of Cooperation with Industrialised Countries.

According to the official statement, the main objectives of the public diplomacy unit of the FPI in the European Commission are to enhance the visibility of the EU as a whole, promote a better understanding of the EU's actions and positions, and exert a positive influence on how the EU is perceived in partner countries.[23] From this statement, we can see the objectives of the EU's foreign policy through public diplomacy, but we cannot tell how public diplomacy is deployed and carried out. Actually, in the EU's practice, industrialized partner countries are not the only targets and the EEAS is also not the only executor of EU's public diplomacy.[24] Accordingly, the official statements clarify the official guidance on the EU's public diplomacy, but its practice is varied and impressive.

If EU public diplomacy has been implemented by both the EEAS and other institutions or actors at the EU level, then talking about public diplomacy in cooperation with industrialized countries is obviously not sufficient for an understanding of the importance of public diplomacy in EU external relations. In fact, the EU's external activities including enlargement, trade, development and humanitarian aid, and culture and educational programs can have the function of increasing the EU's attraction and promoting favorable attitudes towards the EU whether these programs are deployed as public diplomacy activities by the EEAS or not. In this sense, EU public diplomacy can extend to various areas. However, this research is only concerned with actions that are closely related to public diplomacy, as discussed previously, including international public opinion analysis, information dissemination, as well as cultural and educational programs. As some scholars have argued, the EEAS and other relevant institutional transformations bring new opportunities, and the most distinctive contribution of the Treaty of Lisbon to EU public diplomacy is, to a certain degree, integrating the public diplomacy resources of the European Parliament, European Commission, and Commission's delegations.[25] That means, if we study EU public diplomacy today and try to figure out the new progress, it is necessary to review these new changes after the Treaty of Lisbon.

3.2 THE DEVELOPMENT OF EU
PUBLIC DIPLOMACY POST-LISBON

As indicated by scholarly research, EU public diplomacy before Lisbon was highly fragmented.[26, 27] First, while the EU's endeavors in promoting its norms and its external activities including trade, enlargement, and aid were programs of or had the function of public diplomacy, the term "public diplomacy" was rarely used in official statements or public speeches.[28] As a result of this avoidance of the term, "information activities" became the preferred official term because EU officials believed that public diplomacy might be misunderstood by the mass media as propaganda. This rendered EU public diplomacy passive and reactive since it merely emphasized information dissemination without giving attention to international public opinion analysis and long-term relationship building accompanied by proactive actions.[29] Second, the role of the European Commission Delegations in third countries was not fulfilled. Third, the "pillarisation" of the EU into different policy areas which included the foreign and security policy meant that EU public diplomacy was conducted by various actors, but with a coordinating body.

Put differently, EU public diplomacy before Lisbon was mainly information-oriented and was implemented separately by DGs and the Commission's external delegations. Although the DG External Relations (RELEX) built a new unit to coordinate the information and communication activities of the DGs, they still did not have a coherent message or grand strategy of public diplomacy in the absence of an institution specializing in foreign affairs or a department which dealt specifically with public diplomacy issues. Also, the cultural and educational programs deployed by the DG EAC rarely gained the role they deserved in EU public diplomacy. In short, EU public diplomacy lacked strategic design and resource integration.

However, the public diplomacy practice of the DGs and the European Commission's external delegations in the pre-Lisbon era does provide useful experience for future actions following the Treaty of Lisbon and offers scholars invaluable materials for the study of the development of EU public diplomacy. After the Treaty of Lisbon came into force, the EEAS does not change the essence of public diplomacy but helps integrate resources at the EU level and tries to make it more effective, which can be seen from the establishment of the EEAS and the changes of EC delegation to EU delegation.

3.2.1 The EEAS and EU Public Diplomacy

The EEAS, which serves as the EU's diplomatic service, is a new creation of the Lisbon Treaty. Literature about its precursor can be found as long ago as the EPC of 1970, and then the Constitutional Treaty was raised in a call for a new debate on the future of Europe in December 2001 which came to an end after the failure of referenda in France and the Netherlands. It finally returned to the agenda after the ratification of the Lisbon Treaty in 2009.

The EEAS can be viewed as one of the most innovative creations of the Lisbon Treaty in that this institution brings the hope of acting coherently in external activities after nearly half a century of development. Based on a series of former attempts, the Lisbon Treaty finally took a new step forward with its innovative design. Given that the EU's effectiveness depends on its institutional capacity to make collective decision and one prerequisite of its success is that of having a coherent approach to global challenges, although we still cannot evaluate the effect of these new creations after the Lisbon Treaty, from a lesser ambitious point of view, the EEAS at least provides the rest of the world with a clearer external representation and a more explicit image of the EU.[30, 31] And Cross even argues that the EEAS can shape perceptions of Europe as an international actor if it is coherent and effective.[32] Since public diplomacy also calls for a coherent message and an identifiable image of the EU. Correspondingly, the EEAS can also bring about some changes to EU public diplomacy.

The EEAS explains its public diplomacy activities towards industrialized countries and areas, but the EEAS as an institution of foreign affairs and the newly created position of the HR/VP first and foremost, embody the image of the EU in external relations because they "provide the potential leadership of the EU's visibility and weight on the global scene,"[33] which exactly meets the requirement of public diplomacy. In its official statement, the central administration of the EEAS includes information and public diplomacy, although the unit of public diplomacy has been put into the service of the FPI which is a department of the European Commission and reports directly to the HR/VP. Besides, the EEAS brings a coordinative role in the EU's external activities since it "puts an end to the formal split of the EU's external relations between two different pillars (the CFSP and the Community aspects)."[34]

Thus, the EEAS, as some scholar have argued, theoretically connects public diplomacy activities which were conducted by the European Commission and its delegations around the world on the one hand and by the Council General Secretariat on the other hand.[35] Through the structure of the EEAS, it brings the European Council, the European Commission, and member states representatives under one umbrella, which establishes a supranational institution in external policy and helps coordinate their action.[36]

Nevertheless, the DGs of the European Commission have the function of presenting a coherent and favorable image of the EU and promoting it as a normative power to a global audience, but their actions may or may not be carried out under the name of public diplomacy. The new DG Development and Cooperation claims that it is the only interlocutor for the EEAS,[37] but it "remains, therefore, an open question as to whether DG Trade and DG Development and Cooperation will take kindly to being coordinated via the EEAS in terms of public diplomacy,"[38] which still leaves structural deficiency in coordinating EU public diplomacy.

3.2.3 EU Delegations and EU Public Diplomacy

The EU delegations to third countries and international organizations are an integral part of the EEAS, which is why academic articles prefer to regard the EEAS, including the EU delegations, as a whole in their discussion of EU public diplomacy.[39] External delegations have always been key actors of EU public diplomacy before and after the Lisbon Treaty. However, the Lisbon Treaty officially upgrades these European Commission delegations into fully-fledged "European Union Delegations" with their status is officially recognized.[40] The significance of this upgrade lies in the potential for a strengthened link between the policy and delivery levels,[41] in that they were previously coordinated by the Information and Communication unit of DG RELAX but are now responsible for the EEAS and HR/VP.

Nevertheless, discussing the role of EU delegations from the EEAS in EU public diplomacy has two reasons. (1) The EEAS as a new creation of the Lisbon Treaty starts playing a coordinating role in EU external relations, but the external delegations have been equipped with new functions under the administration of the EEAS though they were hierarchically part of Commission structure.[42] (2) In practice, EU delegations are the real entities which coordinate and implement EU public diplomacy in the receiving countries. In the meantime, press releases, cooperating with local media and civil society in host countries, cultural promotion activities, and researching EU-host country relations, may or may not come directly under the remit of official public diplomacy, but they do serve the objectives of EU public diplomacy. Thus, EU delegations have to be treated separately in analyzing its public diplomacy to their countries.

Based on the Council Decision, the EEAS shall be placed under the authority of the High Representative of the Union for Foreign Affairs and Security Policy, and the EEAS shall be made up of a central administration and of the Union delegation to third countries and to international organizations.[43] While the transformation is as such not revolutionary, it is worthwhile to note that EU delegations represent all sorts of EU policies and expand their competence from areas of the European Commission's trade and aid policy to a wide range of Union programs and projects.[44] So far, the EU is represented through 139 EU delegations and offices around the world.[45]

As the "eyes" and "ears" of the EU, EU delegations in receiving countries or host organizations form the front line in explaining and implementing EU policies, observing foreign policy perceptions of the EU, and taking responsibility for disseminating EU information including the background, content, and updates of EU delegations to host administrators and governments along with cooperating with local media, business groups, academic circles, and civil society,[46, 47] which provides a solid ground for the making of EU public diplomacy. However, there activities, as the basic part of EU public diplomacy, are quite arresting, and that's why some scholars also accuse EU public diplomacy of only concentrating on information dissemination.[48] Moreover, EU delegations also assist or coordinate trade and aid activities and cultural and educational programs in the countries to which they are accredited, even though these projects may not be directly connected to foreign policy.

Nevertheless, it much be reiterated that the term "public diplomacy" is not popular in EU external communication. It is hard to find this term after checking the websites of EU delegations to third countries or offices in areas which are in the list of EU public diplomacy. Among the seven countries and three areas where the EU launched the EU Centre Programme as EU public diplomacy, the delegation to the US is the first one to establish a section of press and public diplomacy even before the Lisbon Treaty, followed by the delegation to New Zealand. The Union's delegations to Australia and Singapore, and offices in Hong Kong and Macau, only have a section known as "Political, Press and Information," while the delegation to Canada has a section called "Political and Public Affairs." Russia, South Korea, as well as Taiwan have a section of "Press and Information."[49] Therefore, the term "public diplomacy" is used in a narrow sense, and information dissemination still dominates EU public diplomacy in the daily activities of Union's delegations.

In conclusion, public diplomacy is an indispensable tool for the EU in its progress towards becoming an influential global actor. Foreign policy and external relations as one aspect of the EU's political integration have moved into a new phase following the Treaty of Lisbon, and public diplomacy is one instrument that deserves more attention in both political and academic circles. In the pre-Lisbon era, EU public diplomacy was implemented by different actors. The European Council, the European Parliament and the European Commission had either symbolic or substantive roles in communicating the EU to a world audience. DGs in the European Commission disseminated messages about the EU's development policies, enlargement policies, humanitarian aid policies, and cultural and educational policies under the coordination of the Information Committee in the DG RELEX. The EU's external delegations as a representative of the European Commission worked in host countries and explained EU policies to local citizens through press releases and cooperating with NGOs, and represented the EU as a whole in practice. The Treaty of Lisbon made some changes to EU external relations and more specifically to EU public diplomacy: it created the EEAS and HR/VP to make EU foreign policy more visible; it changed the European Commission delegations to EU delegations, which means that the delegations can officially represent the EU in the host countries; and it clearly identifies the role of public diplomacy in cooperating with industrialized countries.

Nevertheless, after noting the achievements of the Lisbon Treaty's institutional changes and the potential effect on EU foreign policy and public diplomacy, there remain unsolved problems in EU public diplomacy. The first one is how to coordinate the external communication activities among DGs which are involved in external relations under the EEAS; the second one is whether and how other educational programs work beyond the EU Centres Programme coordinated by the FPI. As mentioned before, the limited coverage of the EU Centres Programme derives from the budgetary constraints and the EU does have some other educational programs launched by different institutions. Given that this research aims to talk about academic programs and their effectiveness in EU public diplomacy, we will give more emphasis to educational programs, with a focus on the Jean Monnet Programme in particular.

3.3 EU PUBLIC DIPLOMACY PRACTICE

EU public diplomacy practice has been dispersed across different areas of external relations since the external activities of development aid, trade, cultural, and educational exchange all serve the aims of public diplomacy from the perspective of increasing the attractiveness of the EU. As already indicated, international public opinion analysis, information activities, and cultural and educational programs will be the main focus of public diplomacy in our discussion. However, except for some short-term cultural events, the EU has not officially implemented any long-term cultural programs. Therefore, it is important to analyse EU public diplomacy practices with a particular focus on information activities (EU delegations to non-EU states) and educational programs (Erasmus and Erasmus Mundus programs) before discussing the advantages of the Jean Monnet Programme and its contribution to EU public diplomacy.

3.3.1 Information Activities

Information diffusion as an integral part of public diplomacy is difficult to be isolated from other public diplomacy activities since all the relevant programs which might take the form of development aid, cooperation, cultural events, or educational exchange have an information component. Specifically for the EU, cultural programs like the promotional activities during the fiftieth anniversary celebration around the world and educational programs such as Erasmus Mundus as well as the Jean Monnet Programme that will be analyzed later, all include communication of information and knowledge. Nevertheless, cultural and educational programs aim to exert a long-term effect rather than mere short-term information diffusion. Consequently, information diffusion in this context will discuss the function of EU delegations to third countries.

Empirical studies concerning the work of EU delegations have been conducted in order to address the function of the European Union delegations as information sources in host countries.[50, 51, 52] First, the studies found that informing the citizens in host countries is a priority for the EU. The EU's delegations release official statements, use Eurobulletins, Newsletters, EU Co-operation News, and publish mass-media statements of Heads of Delegation to communicate the EU's policy and EU news to host countries.[53] Moreover, these delegations have specific strategies towards specific countries: to increase the cooperation and visibility of the EU;[54] or to help host countries improve their living standards and become prospective member states.[55] Secondly, these delegations promote the exchange of information. As well as a one-way information flow from the EU to host countries through the delegations, one of their responsibilities is providing information to EU headquarters in Brussels for the preparation of policy proposals.[56] Thirdly, these delegations are gradually beginning to play a role in both the internal coordination of EU foreign policy and external representation towards host countries,[57] through making local citizens think about Europe and realize the relevance of Europe in their lives.[58] Thus maintaining a two-way information flow occupies a large part of the delegation's daily work, and EU delegations in third countries have also started acting as diplomatic representatives around the world.

The way EU delegations are perceived in host countries can also reveal something about the role they play in EU public diplomacy. Some scholars have analyzed the external perception of EU delegations in ten Asia-Pacific locations based on ground-breaking projects deployed by professional research institutes. During the process of data collection, the interviewees were categorized into three target groups—political elites, civil society elites, and business elites and they were asked whether the EU had a delegation in their country and how they thought the delegation might be of use to them as individuals and also to their organizations.[59]

In light of the data collected in the fieldwork, some of the political elites who knew of the existence of EU delegations in their countries highlighted the cultural and educational outreach activities of the delegations, while the political elites felt that the delegation was an "information source." The civil society elites emphasized the public diplomacy efforts of the delegations through the circulation of regular newsletters and their potential for promoting two-way communication and collaboration between the delegations and locals. Although Asia-Pacific business elites generally had negative feelings about the delegations, some of them still recognised their efforts in providing key information through their websites and e-newsletters. Most of the elites of the three target groups who had positive perceptions of the EU delegations in their home countries were less well informed, which meant they had no idea or not much information about the activities of the delegations' in their countries.[60] Even though EU delegations represent the EU as a whole to third countries, the research results mentioned above show that its function of information provision attracts more attention than other activities.

It is true that delegations are an integral part of the EU's diplomatic corps which have the task of telling the EU's story with one voice, but they still face some structural problems which could hinder their role from being completely fulfilled. One the one hand, all Heads of EU delegations wear two hats and have to be accountable to two institutions because only part of the European Commission has been integrated into the EEAS. As a result, they have to differentiate policy areas under different budgets. On the other hand, even though they may come from a national diplomatic service, they can only speak and act for the EEAS as a whole.[61] In this sense, it is impossible to expect too much from the EU delegations considering the internal structural problems.

However, EU delegations can still have an effect in EU public diplomacy. Bjola and Jiang think that establishing an official account on social media helps the EU communicate knowledge and information to the general public and finds that the general public is attracted by the cultural diversity of the EU.[62] According to other research that uses discourse analysis, the officials and diplomats of the EU have credibility as an information source for the mass media.[63] ICTs offer a way to generate two-way communication between communicator and audience, but this is not reflected in EU public diplomacy practice because the inquiries raised by followers in social media are not answered by the local delegations—who are the owners of the social media accounts.[64] Therefore the delegations can be used as a source of specific information for local decision and policy makers, or to be more specific, as a credible and efficient information resource on the EU in general, and a resource on EU-host country relations with updated statistics in specific cases,[65] but creating a dialogue between the EU delegation and locals requires more work.

In sum, although they cannot fully take responsibility for representing the EU as a whole to third parties or speak with one voice, the EU delegations, as a vital part of the EU diplomatic corps, can still make contributions to EU public diplomacy since its function of information diffusion is already recognized. Cultural and educational programs also carry information, but the EU delegations are the official representative of the EU and cannot be replaced by other institutions or individuals in providing accurate and timely information. The variety of information sources available in the social media era carries both information and misinformation at the same time, but one-way message communication is still important at critical moments and for a day-to-day explanation about policy.[66] During this process, governments try to leverage the new technologies to serve and communicate with the citizens.[67] After all, as an official source of information, governments do have advantages in providing information, particularly in relation to information about national security and the national interest.

However, information diffusion from official sources works mainly in a short term, so the EU still needs cultural and educational programs to propagate its soft power resources. This is why the Jean Monnet Programme, as one of the EU's educational programs, deserves scholarly attention.

3.3.2 Cultural Programmes

Scholars carrying out public diplomacy research and official experts who are in charge of the public diplomacy programs of their own countries believe that cultural and educational programs constitute an integral part of public diplomacy for long-term relationship building. For its part the EU emphasizes the effect of using educational and cultural programs in letting the world know about the EU but it rarely mentions these programs in official statements as public diplomacy. Also, as previously stated, cultural and educational programs always have the function of information dissemination in communicating the EU to a world audience. But cultural and educational programs focus on projecting a favorable image as well as long-term relationship building, and of course, information is always delivered by the transmitters of culture and in the process of teaching and learning.

More importantly for the EU, educational and cultural programs and the relevant cooperative policies towards third countries need to avoid the failing of "one size fits all." Culture and education always have historical and geographic features, and whether these programs can flourish in target countries depends on the attraction and localization of the programs and their designers. The educational programs sponsored by the EU in third countries have been in place for quite a long time, but their effect varies from country to country. The duplication of the successful higher education cooperation program with China in India experienced a major setback[68] because the public focus of EU-sponsored programs contradicts with private universities in India,[69] and the well-known Erasmus Mundus Programme also ran into trouble in some Southeast Asian countries.[70] Therefore, evaluating the success of cultural and educational programs has to pay more attention to the reasons why it achieves its objectives rather than just focusing on encouraging results.

The discussion about the EU's cultural diplomacy or transnational cultural exchange must always take place within the framework of the evolution of the European Union, implying that cultural diplomacy is used to accelerate the integration process and create an image of the cultural diversity of the EU to publics in third countries. The EU is well known for its cultural diversity and European values are also represented by their cultural products, but EU member states are reluctant to delegate any competencies in the field of culture to the European level.[71] Thus, the official encouragement of culture and cultural programs in public diplomacy is relatively recent at the level of the EU.

Even so, the EU does endeavor to use cultural events to broadcast the image of the EU. For instance, during the fiftieth anniversary of the EU, its celebration activities were held in different countries through various kinds of cultural events including school quizzes, theater, drawing competitions, and so on.[72] Besides, from even just a glance at the websites of the EU's delegations to member states or third countries, we can easily tell that cultural events are included in their routine activities including exhibitions, European cultural week, and small quizzes about European cultural and cultural celebrities with prizes distributed through the online platform,[73] and these activities are definitely beneficial for communicating knowledge as well as the norms of the EU to publics in informal and interesting ways.[74]

Nevertheless, although the EU already has some external cultural activities that have been implemented in third countries as mentioned above, these cultural events have not been organized systematically and cultural programs still have not gained the status they should have in EU external relations in comparison with information activities and educational exchange programs. The EU is aware of this deficiency regarding the strategic use of culture, so the EU parliament adopted a resolution on the cultural dimensions of EU external activity, which called for the development of a visible common EU strategy on culture in EU external relations. Moreover, the European Commission supported a three-year research program with a budget of 5 million

Euros in order to prepare a future policy design.[75] The reports and discussion papers of this initiative indicate that cultural relations have a huge potential for enhancing European influence and attraction and that maintaining a better European cultural relationship with the rest of the world is better for all involved, but to date the EU has no grand strategy on cultural relations. Therefore, political will and commitment of high-level leaders are urgently needed along with relevant pilot projects and sufficient budget for the cultural relations strategy.[76] Cooperation and coordination among cultural relations agencies, EU institutions, as well as cultural civil society is a necessity.[77] Considering that the EU member states have a long history of wielding cultural tools, particularly in their global strategy of promoting language education by establishing new branches of language teaching institutes around the world, to exert their influence, it seems that the EU has an opportunity to integrate its cultural resources at the level of the EU and its member states with the purpose of implementing the EU's soft strategy.

Whether or not the concept of cultural diplomacy varies because of different research focuses, cultural diplomacy belongs to public diplomacy while cultural programs serve as one of public diplomacy's instruments. Cultural diplomacy between the EU and third countries reaffirms the notion of the EU as an exclusive club and a distinctive culture/civilization, and conducting EU cultural diplomacy through relevant programs will eventually enhance the universal value of European culture.[78] Although cultural activities within EU public diplomacy are still fragmented without any specific programmes that can be studied for their effect in the long run, the EU has realised its shortcomings in external cultural activities and has already worked on the preparatory action for launching cultural events in the future.

3.3.3 Educational Programs

With regard to the role of educational programs in EU public diplomacy, as far back as the mid-1960s, researchers of European integration were already urging their colleagues to concentrate on the contribution of the international population movement to European integration.[79] Behind this lay the popular assumption that the objectives of public diplomacy can be realized through personal contact with foreign publics at both the internal (facilitate political integration) and the external level (improve international relations).[80]

Educational exchange programs as an important activity of public diplomacy have been extensively discussed by many scholars,[81, 82, 83] and some of them even argue that there has to be a specific brand of diplomacy named "Education Diplomacy."[84] However, whether they are called educational exchange programs or education diplomacy, the essence of the activities has never changed. It is the practice of using education as an approach to facilitate the achievement of the foreign policy goals of reshaping perception and cultivating goodwill, thus improving international relations, which, in his paper, includes official dialogue, student and academic exchange, collaborative research projects, joint institutes, scholarship programs, language teaching as well as professional training activities.[85]

In terms of the educational programs within the public diplomacy unit of the EEAS, public diplomacy practice towards industrialized countries is implemented through establishing EU centers, public policy think tanks, and research institutes in order to increase the visibility and enhance the positive image of the EU, which are all part of the educational programs. EU centers, for instance, are established in the universities of the target countries to promote EU studies, increase the knowledge of EU in foreign students, establish a network for information and education activities, and raise the awareness of the EU in foreign publics.[86] At the time of writing, 165 centers have been established with other activities of the Jean Monnet Programme, which cover 72 countries on the five continents.[87]

The label of "Erasmus" for the higher education mobility program was first adopted in 1987, and aimed at the mobility of undergraduates and staff. The abbreviation "ERASMUS" stands for "European community Action Scheme for the Mobility of University Students."[88] The early practice of the Erasmus Programme is largely based on the idea of bringing college students together across Europe to form or enhance a sense of European identity among the participants.[89] The Erasmus Programme was incorporated into the Socrates Programme—a new program established in 1994 and executed until 1999 when another program was established and it was placed under the Lifelong Learning Programme 2007–2013,[90] and then was integrated into Erasmus Plus/Erasmus for All after 2014, which means that the label of "Erasmus programme" officially ended in 1994 albeit its action is still present today.

In 2003, another program, named the Erasmus Mundus Programme was officially launched with a general objective of "enhancing the quality of European higher education and promoting dialogue and understanding between people and cultures through cooperation with third countries,"[91] with its first phase running from 2004–2008 and the second phase from 2009–2013. Since 2014, the Erasmus Mundus Programme has been integrated into the Erasmus Plus Programme, meaning that the Erasmus Mundus Programme is replaced by the Action of Learning Mobility of Individuals under the Erasmus Plus Programme.[92] After being put into action in 2004, the most important part of the Erasmus Mundus Programme was the complex package of mobility. In 2006, the management had been taken over by the EACEA.[93] In fact, during two phases of practice, the Erasmus Mundus included two main actions: the first one was to create an innovative higher education program and deliver high-quality graduates, and the second one was to support scholar and student exchanges in partner universities between the EU and third countries by establishing partnerships with third country higher education institutions and providing scholarships for mobility.

The Erasmus Programme was aimed at promoting mobility among European citizens, while another program, also under the label of "Erasmus" was Erasmus Mundus with its aims clearly identified on its website: it is a cooperation and mobility program in the field of higher education that aims to augment the quality of European higher education and to promote dialogue and understanding between peoples and cultures through cooperation with third countries. Also, it makes contributions to the development of international cooperation capacity and the human resources of higher education institutions in third countries by increasing mobility between the European Union and these countries.[94]

Along with the well-known Erasmus Mundus Programme, which also targets students from non-EU member states, the Jean Monnet Programme endeavors to promote European Integration Studies in and outside the EU. Rather than recruiting and educating foreign students in EU member states, the Jean Monnet Programme belongs to EU external public diplomacy but only supports scholarly research and teaching on the EU and European integration, which will be discussed in the next chapter with a focus on its special features in EU public diplomacy.

Since 2014, the Erasmus Plus has incorporated seven programs including a lifelong learning program. From 2014–2020, this new program includes international mobility, joint degrees, and international cooperation partnership, integrates different programs that were implemented over the long term and put an end to the current situation of having numerous external educational programs. From the standpoint of the EU, this new program which was implemented with huge investments at the EU level for the internationalization strategy of both the EU and its member states, aims to make the EU's actions more visible, coherent, and attractive.[95]

Although it is too early to say whether this resource integration is revolutionary, it did show that the EU tries to make its educational policy more effective within and outside of the EU. This point can be proved by the clause of the Commission file that establishes "Erasmus for all" in which the EU enhances the international dimension of education, training, and youth by increasing the attractiveness of EU higher education institutions and supports the Union's external activities.[96] In this sense, education is not just a tool for the formation of an EU identity within its member states, but also needs to be promoted to the rest of the world in order to increase the attraction of the EU as a destination for education.

Another phenomenon which is also worth noting is that, although DG-EAC is the leading department of the European Commission in coordinating and managing educational programs, the educational programs of the EU, in practice, can be supported by different institutions. For instance, the EU-China Higher Education Cooperation Programme (HECP) and EU-China European Studies Centres Programme (ESCP) which were designed specifically for China were carried out in the policy area of development rather than culture and education;[97] the EU Centres programs which are within the framework of public diplomacy were sponsored by two EU external action instruments: the Instrument for Cooperation with Industrialized and other high-income countries and territories and the European Neighborhood Partnership Instrument;[98] three actions of Erasmus Mundus Programme from 2009–2013 were supervised by different departments—DG-EAC, DG-Development and Cooperation, the FPI—in European Commission according to the specific content of those actions.[99] However, this book will incorporate them in the system of educational cooperation when talking about the EU's educational exchange practice.

The EU has numerous educational programs aimed at EU and non-EU students, and this attracts the attention of scholars who evaluate the effect of these programs, particularly the Erasmus and Erasmus Mundus Programme. There is no need to re-address the effect of research on these two programs. Yet, research findings attest that these programs have a "ceiling effect"—with no marked change in students' perceptions of the EU because they already had sufficient background knowledge of the EU before participating in these programs; and their changed perceptions were based on personal experience rather than increased knowledge. However, professors sponsored by the Jean Monnet Programme teach students who have little background knowledge of the EU and this program does not support direct student mobilization, meaning that it may have a different influence compared with other programs.

3.4 THE THEORETICAL AND INSTITUTIONAL PROBLEMS OF EU PUBLIC DIPLOMACY

As argued by Jan Melissen, the diversity of EU experience in public diplomacy provides a valuable resource for other parts of the whole world and other regions consisting of a mix of democratic and semi-authoritarian or authoritarian states could never achieve what Europe has.[100] However, at the

EU level, public diplomacy helping the EU improve its global visibility and create a favorable environment for its foreign policy still encounter problems.

From a theoretical perspective, either public diplomacy or soft power has been problematic in the EU's context. As a matter of fact, since the EU is still afraid of confusing public diplomacy with propaganda, "public diplomacy" is still used in a narrow sense and information activities continue to dominate official discourse. Although information activities occupy an important role in public diplomacy practice, they are not in themselves sufficient. Rather, the EU needs to incorporate both short and medium-long term components together. In so doing, it requires new approaches to public diplomacy and professional communications structures, with appropriate human and financial resources provision, so as to avoid turning public diplomacy into an "empty shell."[101] EU delegations play an important role in coordinating and implementing EU public diplomacy in the receiving countries, but the relevant departments in these delegations have been rarely named after "public diplomacy." As afore-mentioned, information or press office is preferred in practice.

The EU's record of building and making soft power count towards a more effective foreign policy will cause mixed results: it, on the one hand, drives up internal and external expectations towards the EU, while on the other hand, it widens the capability-expectations gap in times of crisis. Thus, it has been argued that the capability-expectations gap of the EU in terms of its role on the world stage can be bridged by its soft power but is in itself very dam-aging to the EU's soft power from the external perspective.[102] However, from a practical perspective, EU soft power works when shaping the discourse and setting examples instead of focusing on the diffusion of its core norms.[103]

Worse still, EU soft power is currently in crisis. Scholarly debate over the EU as a "soft" or "civilian" or "normative" power has been lasting for years, but the recent setbacks including refugee crisis, rising populist, and Brexit have incurred serious costs on the EU's global image and its greatest assets in foreign policy—soft power.[104] Originally, the EU has been seen as something in abundance with soft power featured by its good reputation that no other region on the world can offer, but it is losing its positive radiance and magnetism as the support for the so-called "Brexit" becomes the symbol for the fear and rampant populism across the European Continent.[105] Because of its weakened soft power and lost ability in shaping global agenda and the preferences of other countries, it becomes even harder for the EU to promote its norms globally.

In fact, no matter whether portraying the EU as a civilian power or norma-tive power, the messages and discourses of EU public diplomacy are firstly directed for identity production internally. In fact, the failure of EU public diplomacy in addressing neighboring and global problems is resulted from keeping its eyes on the internal audiences, albeit it is still trying to direct its discourses towards the external world.[106] However, these messages or discourses gradually fail to capture the enormous importance of the EU with a number of rising problems starting from the financial crisis to a rising populism, eventually leading to a disconnection between EU official discourses and the daily life of its citizens.[107] Besides, by including "EU norms" and Copenhagen criteria in bilateral agreements as conditionality for a closer relationship with the Union, it placed itself in a superior level without listening to others or engaging in meaningful dialogue.[108] Put differently, the changing "interpolar" world of networks and interconnections requires international actors including the EU to be equipped with new skills to succeed in diplomacy both traditional and public. In this sense, it needs to conduct a dialogue-based monologue, to initiate and maintain a "true" dialogue and strike meaningful long-lasting collaborations in order to make the EU's messages be heard.[109]

In terms of institutional problems, with the entry into force of the EEAS, the EU has a single face after the appointment of the HR/VP, but a clear understanding of what the EU is to be communicated for effective public diplomacy is still not certain. In other words, the EU needs to communicate to the world about its global role. However, the only message that the EU might communicate to the world audiences "is one of confusion, the inability to address internal challenges accompanied by mounting doubt about the model of regional integration that the EU extols externally."[110]

EU public diplomacy is currently in a dilemma between centralization and decentralization. The EEAS and the appointment of the HR/VP showed the attempts in centralizing public diplomacy at the Union level, requiring more work to coordinate public diplomacy practice from the EEAS, the DGS of Trade, Education and Culture, Communication, Development and Cooperation and other relevant institutions. Albeit so, centralization should go beyond the institutional aspects to include the presence of clear, convincing, coherent, and mutually reinforcing messages to communicate externally.[111] However, the challenges for EU public diplomacy are that it lacks a compelling sense of global role that would form the core message for its public diplomacy engagement.[112] Thus, without a clear message that can be sent to the world audience because of the internal and external problems faced by the EU, decentralization characterized by the involvement of member states' public diplomacy and EU delegations' information activities in third parties play an important role in EU public diplomacy. Under this circumstance, EU public diplomacy would go "local" with the danger of causing more inconsistencies, which would further erode the EU's identity and weaken its narratives and the legitimacy of EU public diplomacy.[113] Moreover, when dealing with the EU's relationship with neighboring countries through public diplomacy, the

EU failed to deliver a coherent message in terms of its normative standings because of the contradicting messages between the EU's words and deeds and between the EU and its member states.[114]

When it comes to the effect of EU public diplomacy on its image projection in China, Chinese perceptions of Europe has been positive enough in general, particularly in the aspects of cultural issues and regional integration practices.[115] However, the EU's norm diffusion in China can cause frictions in bilateral relationship. Although an increasing awareness of, and positive perceptions towards, certain norms of the EU do not automatically lead to the adaptation of adoption of these norms in the target locations. Rather, it will serve as the prerequisite for a possible adaption and/or adoption process.[116] More importantly, cultural filters of the norm receiving countries will determine the result of norm diffusion to some extent, as it shapes the receivers' expectations and responses in terms of the EU's normative messages and image.[117] In fact, such perception gaps in respect to sovereignty, human rights, democracy, and liberty between the EU and China can breed misunderstandings in bilateral relationship, since these concepts can be interpreted and applied in very different senses by different societies.[118]

China's ascent and active participation in regional and global organizations shows that its political objectives and norms still deviate substantially from those claimed and insisted by the EU, and that there are no signs of convergence in a near future.[119] To further enhance EU-China strategic partnership against this backdrop, both sides need to realize that "future imperfect" will be a new normal for their long-term relationship, as they must go beyond embracing a mutual charm offensive that celebrates the "shared values" of "ancient civilisations" to appreciate the important differences within and between Europe and China.[120] In most cases, by shaping public preference to and perceptions of the EU through public diplomacy, it will inherently translate or percolate upwards to the official or policy level despite being time-consuming, which might be even complicated in a relatively closed political system like China.[121] Therefore, whether talking about EU public diplomacy in general or its practice towards China in particular, both theoretical and institutional problems need to be addressed.

Admittedly, it might not be correct to claim that the EU no longer has soft power, since the massive migration pressure is, paradoxically, reflected the EU's attractiveness based on its liberalism and multilateralism, particularly in comparison with a gradually more conservative America.[122] However, either by silencing the internal problems or by positioning the EU on the top of a temporal hierarchy, the messages and discourses of EU public diplomacy is becoming hard to be disseminated for the EU and to be received for third parties. Thus, facing internal and external challenges, the EU has to admit its deficiencies in both soft and hard power before working on its internal reform and repairing its external credibility.

This chapter systematically indicated the changing EU public diplomacy before and after the Treaty of Lisbon and gives a big picture of public diplomacy in EU external relations. It also analyses the practice of EU public diplomacy—the information activities of EU delegations in third countries and cultural/educational programmes.

All in all, as an important point in the development trajectory of the EU, the Treaty of Lisbon endeavors to enable the EU to act more coherently with the creation of the EEAS, the position of HR/VP, as well as the EU delegations which have replaced the European Commission's delegations. Although EU public diplomacy implemented through other approaches has already addressed both descriptive knowledge and normative knowledge of the EU, how the knowledge of EU norms has been disseminated in higher education institution regulated by Chinese government still needs further analysis. In comparison with the practice of EU public diplomacy analyzed in this chapter, the comparative advantages of the Jean Monnet Programme and how it works in the Chinese context will be discussed in more detail with the case study of its implementation in China in the following chapters.

NOTES

1. Bretherton, C. and Vogler, J. (2005), *The European Union as a Global Actor,* London: Routledge: 2.

2. Schmitter, P. C. (2001), *What Is There to Legitimize in the European Union . . . and How Might This be Accomplished*, Institute for Advanced Studies working paper, No.75: 1.

3. De Zwaan, J.W., Nelissen, F. A., Jans, J. H. and Blockmans, S. (2004), *The European Union: An Ongoing Process of Integration*, The Hague: T.M.C. Asser Press.

4. Eriksen, E. O. and Fossum, J. E. (2000), *Democracy in the European Union,* Preface, London: Routledge: 11.

5. Keukeleire, S. and Delreux, T. (2014), *The Foreign Policy of the European Union, 2nd Edition*, Hampshire: Palgrave Macmillan: 38–47.

6. Hill, C. and Smith, M. (2011), "International Relations and the European Union: Themes and Issues," in Hill, C. and Smith, M. (eds.), *International Relations and European Union (2nd edition)*, the New York: Oxford University press: 8–15.

7. Smith, M. (2007), "The European Union and International Order: European and Global Dimensions," *European Foreign Affairs Review*, 12(4): 441.

8. Hill, C. and Smith, M. (2011), "International Relations and the European Union: Themes and Issues," in Hill, C. and Smith, M. (eds.), *International Relations and European Union (2nd edition)*, the New York: Oxford University Press: 15.

9. Orbie, J. (2009), "A Civilian Power in the World? Instruments and Objectives in European Union External Policies," in Orbie, J. (ed.), *Europe's Global Role*, Surrey: Ashgate Publishing Limited: 1–33.

10. Nunes, I. F. (2011), "Civilian, Normative, and Ethical Power Europe: Role Claims and EU Discourses," *European Foreign Affairs Review* 16(1): 1–20.

11. Manners, I. (2002), "Normative Power Europe: A Contradiction in Terms?" *Journal of Common Market Studies*, 40(2): 238.

12. Nunes, I. F. (2011), "Civilian, Normative, and Ethical Power Europe: Role Claims and EU Discourses," *European Foreign Affairs Review* 16(1): 5–7.

13. Murray, P. (2009), "Model Europe? Reflections on the EU as a Model of Regional Integration," in Pompeo Della Posta, Milica Uvalic and Amy Verdun (eds.), *Globalization, Development and Integration*. Hampshire: Palgrave: 275.

14. Oberthür, S. (2009), "The Role of the EU in Global Environmental and Climate Governance," in Telò, M. (ed.), *The European Union and Global Governance*, London: Routledge: 192.

15. Bindi, F. (2012), "European Union Foreign Policy: A Historical Overview," in Federiga Bindi and Irina Angelescu, (eds.), *The Foreign Policy of the European Union*, Washington D.C. Brookings Institution Press: 24–27.

16. Keukeleire, S. and MacNaughtan, J. (2008), *The Foreign Policy of the European Union*, Hampshire: Palgrave Macmillan: 45–51.

17. Ibid: 54

18. Moravcsik, A. (2009), "Europe: The Quiet Superpower," *French Politics*, Vol.7: 405.

19. Ibid: 410.

20. Lynch, D. (2005), *Communicating Europe to the World: What Public Diplomacy for the EU?* EPC Working Paper, No. 21: 22–23.

21. De Magalhaes, J. C. (1988), *The Pure Concept of Diplomacy*, (translated by Bernardo Futscher Pereira), New York and London: Greenwood Press: 11–12.

22. EEAS, (2014), *Foreign Policy*, available at: http://www.eeas.europa.eu/policies/index_en.htm, [accessed May 4, 2014].

23. Ibid.

24. From the websites of EU's delegations to third countries including news reports and their activities in host countries, the EU's public diplomacy is widely implemented around the world by the EU institutions or the EU's delegations even though it is under the name of public diplomacy.

25. Duke, S. and Courtier, A. (2011), *The EU's External Public Diplomacy and the EEAS—Cosmetic Exercise or Intended Change?* Available at: http://dseu.lboro.ac.uk/publications/policypapers.html [accessed Aug. 12, 2013].

26. Lynch, D. (2005), *Communicating Europe to the World: What Public Diplomacy for the EU?* EPC Working Paper, No. 21: 19.

27. Duke, S. (2013), "European External Action Service and Public Diplomacy," in Mai'a K. Davis Cross & Melissen, J. (eds.). *European Public Diplomacy: Soft Power at Work*, Hampshire: Palgrave Macmillan: 116.

28. Michalski, A. (2005), "The EU as a Soft Power: The Force of Persuasion," in Melissen, J. (ed.), *The New Public Diplomacy: Soft Power in International Relations*, New York: Palgrave Macmillan: 126.

29. Lynch, D. (2005), *Communicating Europe to the World: What Public Diplomacy for the EU?* EPC Working Paper, No. 21: 26.

30. Edwards, G. (2013), "The EU's Foreign Policy and the Search for Effect," *International Relations*, 27(3): 278.

31. Lloveras-Soler, J. M. (2011), *The New EU Diplomacy: Learning to Add Value*, European University Institute working paper, http://cadmus.eui.eu/bitstream/handle/1814/15639/RSCAS_2011_05.pdf?sequence=1, [accessed April 9, 2014]: 1.

32. Cross, Mai'a K. D. (2011), "Building a European Diplomacy: Recruitment and Training to the EEAS," *European Foreign Affairs Review*, 16(4): 448.

33. Duke, S. and Courtier, A. (2011), *The EU's External Public Diplomacy and the EEAS—Cosmetic Exercise or Intended Change?* Available at: http://dseu.lboro.ac.uk/publications/policypapers.html [accessed Aug. 12, 2013]: 5.

34. Courtier, A. (2011), "The Challenge of Public Diplomacy for The European External Action Service," In European Institute of Public Administration (ed.), *EIPA-scope*, 30th Anniversary Special Issue: 70.

35. Duke, S. and Courtier, A. (2011), *The EU's External Public Diplomacy and the EEAS—Cosmetic Exercise or Intended Change?* Available at: http://dseu.lboro.ac.uk/publications/policypapers.html [accessed Aug. 12, 2013]: 5.

36. Özoğuz-Bolgi, S. (2013), "Is the EU Becoming a Global Power after the Treaty of Lisbon," in Boening, A. Kremer, J-F, and Van Loon, A. (eds.), *Global Power Europe*, Vol. 1, Springer-Verlag Berlin Heidelberg: 11.

37. EuropeAid, (2013), *About the EuropeAid*, available at: http://ec.europa.eu/europeaid/who/about/index_en.htm, [accessed Nov. 21, 2013].

38. Duke, S. (2013), "European External Action Service and Public Diplomacy," in Mai'a K. Davis Cross & Melissen, J. (eds.). *European Public Diplomacy: Soft Power at Work*, Hampshire: Palgrave Macmillan: 123.

39. Ibid: 113.

40. Austermann, F. (2014), *European Union Delegations in EU Foreign Policy: A Diplomatic Service of Different Speeds*, Hampshire and New York: Palgrave Macmillan: 5.

41. Duke, S. (2011), "Consistency, Coherence and European Union External Action: The Path to Lisbon and Beyond," in Koutrakos, P. (ed.), *European Foreign Policy: Legal and Political Perspectives*, Glos and Northampton: Edward Elgar Publishing Limited: 48.

42. Moran, J. and Ponz Canto, F. (2004), *Taking Europe to the World—50 Years of the European Commission's External Service*, EEAS, http://www.eeas.europa.eu/delegations/docs/50_years_brochure_en.pdf, [accessed Jan. 12, 2014]: 6.

43. Vanhoonacker, S. and Reslow, H. (2010), "The European External Action Service: Living Forwards by Understanding Backwards," *European Foreign Affairs Review*, 15(1): 13.

44. Wouters, J. and Duquet, S. (2011), *The EU, EEAS and Union Delegations and International Diplomatic Law: New Horizons*, Katholieke University Leuven working paper: 7; 12.

45. EEAS, (2014), Website of EU delegations, available at: http://www.eeas.eu ropa.eu/delegations/index_en.htm, [accessed Mar. 24, 2014].

46. Moran, J. and Ponz Canto, F. (2004), *Taking Europe to the World—50 Years of the European Commission's External Service*, EEAS, http://www.eeas.europa.eu/ delegations/docs/50_years_brochure_en.pdf, [accessed Jan. 12, 2014]: 6; 9.

47. EU insight, (2010), *Engaging the World: The EU's Public Diplomacy*, http://www.eurunion.org/eu/images/stories/euinsightpubdipl-7-10.pdf, [accessed Nov. 11, 2014].

48. Lynch, D. (2005), *Communicating Europe to the World: What Public Diplomacy for the EU?* EPC Working Paper, No. 21: 31.

49. EEAS, (2014), General introduction of the EU delegations, available at: http://www.eeas.europa.eu/delegations/index_en.htm, [accessed Mar. 24, 2014]; Foreign Policy of cooperating with industrialized countries, available at: http://www.eeas.europa.eu/ici/publicdiplomacy/index_en.htm, [accessed Mar. 21, 2014].

50. Bjola, C. and Jiang, L. (2015), "Social Media and Public Diplomacy," in Bjola C. and Holmes, M. (eds.), *Digital Diplomacy: Theory and Practice*, London and New York: Routledge: 71–88.

51. Vlasenko, A. (2013), *EU Public Diplomacy Effects on Ukrainian Attitudes towards the EU*, Department of Political Science, Lund University, available at: http://lup.lub.lu.se/luur/download?func=downloadFile&recordOId=3798270&file OId=3798564, [accessed April 6, 2013]: 23–30.

52. Chaban, N., Kelly, S. and Bain, J. (2009), "European Commission Delegations and EU Public Policy: Stakeholders' Perceptions from the Asia-Pacific," *European Foreign Affairs Review*, 14(2): 271–288.

53. Robberecht, J. (2013), *The European Union External Action in Times of Crisis and Change: Public Diplomacy and Discourse*, European Policy Brief, available at: http://www2.warwick.ac.uk/fac/soc/csgr/green/papers/policybriefs/eu20agora20pol icy20brief20-20eu20external20action20-public20diplomacy20and20discourse.pdf, [accessed June 24, 2015]: 2.

54. China.com, (2012), *The Wisdom of Public Diplomacy: The Dialogue Among Chinese, American and European Scholars*, available at: http://www.china.com.cn/ international/txt/2012-09/11/content_26492930.htm, [accessed Sept. 3, 2013].

55. Vlasenko, A. (2013), *EU Public Diplomacy Effects on Ukrainian Attitudes towards the EU*, Department of Political Science, Lund University, available at: http://lup.lub.lu.se/luur/download?func=downloadFile&recordOId=3798270&file OId=3798564, [accessed April 6, 2013]: 29–30.

56. Carta, C. (2013), "The EU in Geneva: The Diplomatic Representation of a System of Governance," *Journal of Contemporary European Research*, 9(3): 415.

57. Austermann, F. (2012), "Towards One Voice in Beijing? The Role of the EU's Diplomatic Representation in China Over Time," *Journal of European Integration History*, 18(1): 100.

58. China.com, (2012), *The Wisdom of Public Diplomacy: The Dialogue Among Chinese, American and European Scholars*, available at: http://www.china.com.cn/ international/txt/2012-09/11/content_26492930.htm, [accessed Sept. 3, 2013].

59. Chaban, N., Kelly, S. and Bain, J. (2009), "European Commission Delegations and EU Public Policy: Stakeholders' Perceptions from the Asia-Pacific," *European Foreign Affairs Review*, 14(2): 280.

60. Ibid: 280–286

61. Austermann, F. (2012), "Towards One Voice in Beijing? The Role of the EU's Diplomatic Representation in China Over Time," *Journal of European Integration History*, 18(1): 102.

62. Bjola, C. and Jiang, L. (2015), "Social Media and Public Diplomacy," in Bjola C. and Holmes, M. (eds.), *Digital Diplomacy: Theory and Practice*, London and New York: Routledge: 20.

63. Ma, X. (2012), *Beyond the Economic Ties: EU in the Chinese Media*, Centre of Public Diplomacy, University of South California, available at: http://uscpublicdiplo macy.org/sites/uscpublicdiplomacy.org/files/legacy/pdfs/XinruMaBestPaper2012. pdf, [accessed July 9, 2014]: 25.

64. Bjola, C. and Jiang, L. (2015), "Social Media and Public Diplomacy," in Bjola C. and Holmes, M. (eds.), *Digital Diplomacy: Theory and Practice*, London and New York: Routledge: 27.

65. Chaban, N., Kelly, S. and Bain, J. (2009), "European Commission Delegations and EU Public Policy: Stakeholders' Perceptions from the Asia-Pacific," *European Foreign Affairs Review*, 14(2): 287.

66. Cowan, G. and Arsenault, A. (2008), "Moving from Monologue to Dialogue to Collaboration: The Three Layers of Public Diplomacy," *Annals of the American Academy of Political and Social Science*, 616(1): 18.

67. Kavanaugh, A. L., Fox, E. A, Sheetz, S. D. (2012), "Social Media Use by Government: From the Routine to the Critical," *Government Information Quarterly*, 29(4): 480.

68. Interview with Professor A in Beijing, Dec. 11, 2013.

69. Choudaha, R. and Orosz, K. (2011), *Emerging Models of Indian-European Higher Education Collaborations*, available at: http://wenr.wes.org/2011/09/emerg ing-models-of-indian-european-higher-education-collaborations/, [accessed April 26, 2016].

70. Jones, W. J. (2009–2010), "European Union Soft Power: Cultural Diplomacy & Higher Education in Southeast Asia," *Silpakorn University International Journal*, Vol. 9–10: 65.

71. Reiterer, M. (2014), "The Role of Culture in EU-China Relations," *European Foreign Affairs Review*, 19(3/1), Special Issue: 135–136.

72. European Commission, (2007), *A Glance at EU Public Diplomacy at Work*, http://europa.eu/50/around_world/images/2007_50th_anniv_broch_en.pdf, [accessed April 2, 2015].

73. The news reports about exhibitions can be found on the websites of the EU's delegations to Croatia, China, the US, France; and the examples of small quiz can be

found on the official Micro blog of the EU's delegation to China (Chinese Weibo, equals to the Twitter in western countries).

74. Azpíroz, M. L. (2015), *Soft Power and Public Diplomacy: The Case of the European Union in Brazil*, CPD perspectives on public diplomacy, Centre on Public Diplomacy, University of Southern California: 18–19.

75. Preparatory Action on Culture in the EU's External Relations, (2014), *Introduction of the Action*, available at: http://cultureinexternalrelations.eu/about/, [accessed Sept. 14, 2014], *Main outcomes*, available at: http://cultureinexternalrelations.eu/main-outcomes/, [accessed Sept. 14, 2014].

76. Ibid.

77. European Commission, (2014), *Maximising the Impact of Cultural Diplomacy in EU Foreign Policy*, available at: http://europa.eu/rapid/press-release_IP-14-382_en.htm, [accessed Sept. 14, 2014].

78. Bátora, J. (2011), "Exclusion and Transversalism: Culture in the EU's External Relations," in Bátora, J. and Mokre, M. (eds*.), Cultural and External Relations: European and Beyond*, Aldershot: Ashgate: 90.

79. Lijphart, A. (1964), "Tourist Traffic and International Potential," *Journal of Common Market Studies*, 2(3): 260.

80. Sigalas, E. (2009), *Does ERASMUS Student Mobility Promote a European Identity?* Webpapers on Constitutionalism and Governance beyond the State, Institute for European Integration Research, Vienna, No. 2: 1.

81. Nye. J. (2005), "Soft Power and Higher Education," in *The Internet and the University: Forum 2004*, online publication, available at: http://net.educause.edu/forum/iuf04.asp?bhcp=1, [accessed 27-05-2014]: 43.

82. Lynch, D. (2005), *Communicating Europe to the World: What Public Diplomacy for the EU?* EPC Working Paper, No. 21: 5.

83. Cull, N. J. (2008), "Public Diplomacy: Taxonomies and Histories," *Annals of the American Academy of Political and Social Science*, 616(1): 33.

84. Hong, N.Y. (2014), "EU-China Education Diplomacy: An Effective Soft Power Strategy?" *European Foreign Affairs Review*, 19 (3/1), Special Issue: 156.

85. Ibid.

86. EU Centres-EEAS (2014), *Introduction*, available at: http://www.eeas.europa.eu/eu-centres/index_en.htm, [accessed March 21, 2014].

87. EACEA (2014), *Information about the Jean Monnet Programme from 2007–2013*, available at: http://eacea.ec.europa.eu/llp/jean_monnet/jean_monnet_en.php, [accessed Sept. 29, 2014].

88. Blakemore, M., Verhaeghe, S., Izaki, F., Fothergill, R., and Mozuraityte, N. (2012), *Erasmus Mundus: Clustering Erasmus Mundus Joint Programmes and Attractiveness*, Survey Report, available at: http://eacea.ec.europa.eu/erasmus_mundus/clusters/documents/sustainability/surveyreport_sust_recog.pdf, [accessed Sept. 17, 2014]: 6.

89. Mitchell, K. (2015), "Rethinking the 'Erasmus Effect' of European Identity," *Journal of Common Market Studies*, 53(2): 330.

90. Beerkens, M. and Vossensteyn, H. (2011), "The Effect of the ERASMUS Programme on European Higher Education: The Visible Hand of Europe," in Enders, J.,

de Boer, H. F. and Westerheijden, D.F. (eds.), *Reform of Higher Education in Europe*, Rotterdam: Sense Publisher: 46.

91. EACEA (2013), *About Erasmus Mundus 2009–2013*, available at: http://eacea. ec.europa.eu/erasmus_mundus/programme/about_erasmus_mundus_en.php#info, [accessed Sept. 17, 2014].

92. EACEA (2014), *Erasmus Mundus*, available at: http://eacea.ec.europa.eu/ erasmus_mundus/programme/about_erasmus_mundus_en.php, [accessed Mar. 24, 2014]; *Programme Guide of Erasmus Mundus of 2009–2013*, available at: http://eacea. ec.europa.eu/erasmus_mundus/programme/documents/2014/em_programmeguide _nov2013_en.pdf, [accessed Sept. 22, 2014].

93. Blakemore, M., Verhaeghe, S., Izaki, F., Fothergill, R., and Mozuraityte, N. (2012), *Erasmus Mundus: Clustering Erasmus Mundus Joint Programmes and Attractiveness*, Survey Report, available at: http://eacea.ec.europa.eu/erasmus_mundus/ clusters/documents/sustainability/surveyreport_sust_recog.pdf, [accessed Sept. 17, 2014]: 6.

94. EACEA (2014), *Information about the Jean Monnet Programme from 2007– 2013*, available at: http://eacea.ec.europa.eu/llp/jean_monnet/jean_monnet_en.php, [accessed Sept. 29, 2014].

95. European Commission (2013), *European Higher Education in the World, Communication from the Commission to the European Parliament, the Council, The European Economic and Social Committee and the Committee of the Region*, COM (2013) 499 final, 7th September 2013, Brussels: 10.

96. European Commission (2011), *Regulation of the European Parliament and of the Council, Establishing "Erasmus for All," the Union Programme for Education, Training, Youth and Sport*, COM (2011) 788 Final, Brussels, Nov. 23, 2011, Chapter 2, Article 5:18.

97. Interview with Professor A in Beijing, Dec. 11, 2013.

98. EEAS (2012), *Centre Profiles*, Networking Conference of EU Centres World Meeting, Brussels, 22–24 October, available at: http://www.eeas.europa.eu/ eu-centres/eu-centres_brochure_2012_en.pdf, [Sept. 22, 2014]: 1.

99. EACEA (2014), *Erasmus Plus Programme Guide*, available at: http:// ec.europa.eu/programmes/erasmus-plus/documents/erasmus-plus-programme-guide _en.pdf, [accessed Mar. 14, 2015]: 4.

100. Melissen, J. (2013), "Conclusion and Recommendations on Public Diplomacy in Europe," in Mai'a K. Davis Cross & Jan Melissen (eds.), *European Public Diplomacy: Soft Power at Work*, Basingstoke: Palgrave Macmillan, 206.

101. Courtier, A. (2011) "The Challenge of Public Diplomacy for the European External Action Service," *EIPAscope*: 71.

102. Nielsen, K. L. (2013), "EU Soft Power and the Capability-Expectations Gap," *Journal of Contemporary European Research*, 9(5): 737.

103. Persson, A. (2017), "Shaping Discourse and Setting Examples: Normative Power Europe Can Work in the Israeli-Palestinian Conflict," *JCMS: Journal of Common Market Studies*, 55(6): 1426.

104. Kugiel, P. (2017), "End of European Soft Power? Implications for EU Foreign Policy," *The Polish Quarterly of International Affairs*, 26(1): 69.

105. Sommerfeldt, N. and Zschapitz, H. (2016), "The End of European 'Soft Power,'" available at: https://gulfnews.com/opinion/op-eds/the-end-of-european-soft-power-1.1850842, [accessed Mar. 24, 2019].

106. Samei, M. F. A. (2015), "The European Union's Public Diplomacy Towards the Arab Spring: The Case of Egypt," *The Hague Journal of Diplomacy*, 10(2): 137–138.

107. Sandrin, P. O. and Hoffmann, A. R. (2018), "Silences and Hierarchies in European Union Public Diplomacy," *Revista Brasileira de Política Internacional*, 61(1): 8.

108. Ibid: 10.

109. Chaban, N. and Vernygora, V. (2013), "The EU in the Eyes of Ukrainian General Public: Potential for EU Public Diplomacy," *Baltic Journal of European Studies*, 3(2): 90.

110. Duke, S. (2013), "The European External Action Service and Public Diplomacy," in Cross, M. K. D. and Melissen, J. (eds.), *European Public Diplomacy: Soft Power at World*, New York: Palgrave Macmillan: 132.

111. Ibid: 132.

112. Duke, S. (2013), *The European External Action Service and the Quest for an Effective Public Diplomacy*, Analysis No. 216, December, available at: https://www.ispionline.it/sites/default/files/pubblicazioni/analysis_216_2013.pdf, [accessed Mar. 24, 2019].

113. Duke, S. (2013), "The European External Action Service and Public Diplomacy," in Cross, M. K. D. and Melissen, J. (eds.), *European Public Diplomacy: Soft Power at World*, New York: Palgrave Macmillan: 133.

114. Samei, M. F. A. (2015), "The European Union's Public Diplomacy Towards the Arab Spring: The Case of Egypt," *The Hague Journal of Diplomacy*, 10(2): 113.

115. Scott, D. (2014), "Trust, Structure and Track-2 Dialogue in the EU-China Relationship: Resetting and Resettling a 'Strategic Partnership,'" *Asia Europe Journal*, 12(1–2): 24.

116. Chaban, N., Kelly, S. and Holland, M. (2015), "Perceptions of 'Normative Power Europe' in the Shadow of the Eurozone Debt Crisis," in Björkdahl, A., Chaban, N., Leslie, J. and Masselot, A. (eds.), *Importing EU Norms: Conceptual Framework and Empirical Findings*, Switzerland: Springer International Publishing: 61.

117. Ibid: 71.

118. Pan, Z. (2010), "Managing the Conceptual Gap on Sovereignty in China-EU Relations," *Asia Europe Journal*, 8(2): 227.

119. Holslag, J. (2010), "The Strategic Dissonance between Europe and China," *The Chinese Journal of International Politics*, 3(2): 344.

120. Callahan, W. A. (2007), "Future Imperfect: The European Union's Encounter with China (and the United States)," *Journal of Strategic Studies*, 30(4–5): 781.

121. Scott, D. (2014), "Trust, Structure and Track-2 Dialogue in the EU-China Relationship: Resetting and Resettling a 'Strategic Partnership,'" *Asia Europe Journal*, 12(1–2): 32.

122. Kugiel, P. (2017), "End of European Soft Power? Implications for EU Foreign Policy," *The Polish Quarterly of International Affairs*, 26 (1): 70–71.

Chapter Four

The Jean Monnet Programme
Practical Contributions

In the first two chapters, the historical development of the Jean Monnet Programme and the concepts of public diplomacy and soft power were introduced in details. After looking at the historical development of the Jean Monnet Programme based on the interviews with EU officials in Brussels and China as well as official archives of the EU, we proceed to the relationship between this program and public diplomacy in concert with the empirical data collected in China by interviewing Chinese professors.

Due to the originality of this research and limited research output about the Jean Monnet Programme, this chapter relies primarily on empirical data. This chapter will move on to discuss the Jean Monnet Programme's contributions to EU public diplomacy and then proceed to look at the Jean Monnet Programme and EU soft power.

4.1 THE JEAN MONNET PROGRAMME
AND EU PUBLIC DIPLOMACY

In the field of public diplomacy research, there is an increasing trend in designing and evaluating educational programs. Educational programs have always had a special role to play in public diplomacy and Mitchell even calls these "the third dimension in international relations."[1] The US government initiated the use of educational programs, as well as transnational information transmission in the military and economic program into the "United States Programmes for National Defense."[2] In fact, in the competition with the Soviet Union during the Cold War, "educational exchange" acted as a vital means for communicating a favorable image of the US, symbolized by its material abundance and democracy.[3] These programs were focused on short-term effects but more long-term programs are now becoming appealing to public diplomacy researchers.

On a broader scale, the Jean Monnet Programme belongs to "educational programmes" but slightly differs from "educational exchange programs." Therefore, the connection between the Jean Monnet Programme and public diplomacy can be implied from its similarity to educational programs and its differences from educational exchange programs, which will be testified in the empirical chapters based on the interviews.

4.1.1 The Jean Monnet Programme as EU Public Diplomacy

Public diplomacy includes information activities, research, and analysis as well as cultural and educational activities. Information activities seem passive since they are mainly used as real-time messages intended to eliminate rumour and misunderstandings. Cultural and educational programs are more proactive in communicating the EU to a world audience. Also, educational programs always have the function of information dissemination in telling the EU's story through teaching and learning.

As already indicated in the above, designing educational programs and evaluating their effects have become an increasing trend in public diplomacy because of its special role in realizing the objectives of public diplomacy, which can be easily located in the public diplomacy practice of the US and the EU. However, the educational program in the field of public diplomacy was and continues to be implemented under the name of "educational exchange" or "international educational exchange."[4] In other words, the effect of educational programs gives emphasis to "exchange." Therefore, what is the power of "exchange" in educational programs and even in public diplomacy? Furthermore, what is the relationship between the educational exchange program and the Jean Monnet Programme that is discussed in this research?

Moreover, understanding the function of the Jean Monnet Programme in the field of public diplomacy is one of the purposes of this research, which concerns why the Jean Monnet Programme can be studied from the perspective of public diplomacy. Besides, it also aims to discover the special characteristics of the Jean Monnet Programme in realizing the objectives of the EU's endeavor to communicate itself to the outside world. In other words, the contribution of this program to EU public diplomacy is one of the key elements of this research and also closely related to the concern of this research about why and how the Jean Monnet Programme works in the EU's public diplomacy.

When it comes to educational programs as an important part of public diplomacy, their long-term effect is usually emphasized by scholars but they also have a short-term influence in practice. The influence between the students involved in international educational exchange programs and the culture of host countries is reciprocal, but the impact foreign students make on host countries is much weaker than the impact host countries make on the students: these foreign students can have influence after returning to their home country.[5] Also, there is a general conclusion about the effect of public diplomacy that the more a country is accurately understood by other countries on the world stage, the better the message that can be broadcast and interpreted in other nations.[6] In this sense, the educational exchange program can facilitate a series of positive effects, including increasing knowledge about the host country, enhanced international perception, improved communication, and intercultural learning skills, as well as the most important changes— a greater reluctance to persist with the distortions and inaccurate stereotypes of other countries and cultures.[7]

Differing from other educational exchange programs such as the Erasmus Mundus Programme, which encourages direct student exchange between third countries and EU member states,[8] the Jean Monnet Programme only supports scholars and experts from both EU member states and non-European countries to do research on European integration in their own countries.[9] Being an educational program that does not support a direct student or scholar exchange does not reduce the effect of the Jean Monnet Programme in EU public diplomacy. During the process of supporting scholars outside the EU to do EU studies, even without the mobility of students and staff, the flow of ideas matters, along with a better grasp of how the flow of ideas makes people think and act.[10] Since international education can be conceptualized as activities and programs that encourage the flow of ideas and people across cultural and territorial boundaries,[11] this means that both exchanges of ideas and individual immigration are important aspects of this transnational mobility. Therefore, the Jean Monnet Programme as a program to support European integration and EU studies belongs to international education cooperation.

Irrespective of the comparative advantages of the Jean Monnet Programme discussed in the next section, the Jean Monnet Programme, based on the definition of public diplomacy in chapter 2, can be studied as EU public diplomacy for the following reasons.

First, public diplomacy programs are designed by international actors and targeted at foreign publics. As mentioned before, EU public diplomacy possesses internal and external aspects because of its characteristic of being a supranational organization, rendering its public diplomacy practice different from that of other international actors. In this sense, the Jean Monnet Programme helps the formation of a European identity internally by bringing the European project to its citizens and it externally communicates the EU's story to foreign publics outside the EU, albeit it was originally designed for bringing European projects to its internal citizens.

Second, the Jean Monnet Programme possesses the features of an information activity. From the EU documents, promoting excellence in teaching and research activities in European integration worldwide among specialist academics, learners, and citizens through the creation of Jean Monnet Chairs and other academic activities, as well as by providing aid for other knowledge-building activities in higher education institutions is the first aim of the Jean Monnet Programme.[12] During this process, both descriptive and normative knowledge of the EU has been disseminated to college students through Chinese professors.

Furthermore, the information diffusion of the Jean Monnet Programme makes it effective in communicating the image of itself that the EU wants to promote to the world audience. The success of the educational exchange programs based on the simple assumption that face-to-face interaction can break through national stereotypes or help forge a mutual identity.[13] Specifically for the EU, recruiting students from non-EU member states to study in Europe means that they communicate with EU citizens directly and acquire the knowledge of the countries in which they are staying rather than the EU as a whole, which means that transnational individual exchanges might give the students some personal experience of individual European countries but does not offer them systematic knowledge of the EU as an institution of regional integration. It might therefore be dangerous to promote the research results of the public diplomacy of nation states to the EU as a whole without analyzing the specific situation of the EU. Although there is a lack of accurate knowledge about the EU, the general image of the EU in China is still quite good in comparison with the US.[14]

Third, in practice, the academic activities sponsored by the Jean Monnet Programme are more extensive than those listed in the introduction. On being awarded the Jean Monnet Center of Excellence, the center usually receives more funding from both the EU and the host university to recruit new staff specializing in European studies, open new academic programs for masters and PhD students, organize regional and international conferences, publish monographs and conduct public opinion surveys in the host university and even in the host country, which in turn become the basis for determining whether it can keep the honor in the next period.[15] In other words, the process of academic research and classroom education reflects how the EU's public diplomacy operates through this program.

Last, the Jean Monnet Programme promotes communication and knowledge exchange between experts in EU member states and outside the EU on European integration and EU studies, and its direct influence even extends beyond higher education to secondary and primary schools. The Jean Monnet project, as a new action of the Jean Monnet Programme within the Erasmus Plus, also supports professors in colleges who train teachers from primary and secondary schools in the knowledge of the EU and these trained teachers will in turn teach their students. As the 2014 results showed, three projects were granted to Sichuan University in China, Zagreb University in Croatia, and the University of Alicante in Spain which started delivering knowledge about the EU to young students in primary or secondary schools, with the support of the Jean Monnet Programme.[16] Both promoting knowledge exchange and extending its influence to students in primary and secondary schools around the world shows that the Jean Monnet Programme is a facet of EU public diplomacy.

The new Erasmus Plus (incorporating the Jean Monnet Programme and other educational programmes) was successfully launched in the year 2014 with a huge budget.[17] The specific actions it supports include studying the EU from a new perspective and with new methodologies so as to make it more attractive and appropriate to the various target populations; promoting reflection and discussion on EU issues; and information and knowledge dissemination.[18] Information dissemination plays a significant role in the Jean Monnet Programme.

It is encouraging that the EU centers, which were established as one of the EU public diplomacy programs for cooperating with industrialized countries, will be merged into the Jean Monnet Programme in the near future.[19] The EU centre, a public diplomacy program, has been integrated into the Jean Monnet Programme which was originally not labeled as a public diplomacy program but helped communicate the EU to the outside world, which also illustrates the role of the Jean Monnet Programme as being EU public diplomacy in practice.

Meanwhile, the predicted direct and indirect beneficiaries of this program are students, policy-makers, professionals, civil society, and the public at large rather than the narrow group of research institutions and academics.[20] These new changes make this program more public diplomacy-oriented, and also provide us with some new specific objectives: research innovation, boosting knowledge about the EU and information dissemination.

As mentioned before, both the report of the EU's delegation to the US and the speech addressed by Odile Quintin, the Director of DG EAC, emphasized the role of the Jean Monnet Programme in EU public diplomacy. Also, according to the concept of EU public diplomacy and other relevant EU official documents, the Jean Monnet Programme cannot be overlooked since it plays a vital role in EU external communication. More importantly, the above analysis reveals the function of the Jean Monnet Programme as EU public diplomacy practice. Therefore, the Jean Monnet Programme can be viewed as EU public diplomacy.

4.1.2 The Particularities of the Jean Monnet Programme in EU Public Diplomacy

As discussed in chapter 2 in details, public diplomacy has three approaches responsible for different objectives. International actors try to coordinate different public diplomacy programs of their own in order to make them serve the general objectives of foreign policies. However, each program has its own specific objectives and advantages. In the case of the Jean Monnet Programme, communicating the significance and success of European integration is the first and foremost aim, albeit EU public diplomacy has its long-term ambitions including the promotion of EU norms and the EU's role at the world stage.

The Jean Monnet Programme encourages and sponsors scholars and experts from non-EU states to do research on subjects related to European integration and teaches college students at different levels about European studies. The students who participate in the teaching modules sponsored by this program may or may not have personal living or studying experience in EU member states, but here they can receive correct information about Europe and European integration.

As mentioned beforehand, public diplomacy can be implemented directly or indirectly. In practice, within the target countries, Rasmussen views civil society as the intermediary of public diplomacy[21] and Seib regards renowned foreign journalists in target countries as the intermediaries for communicators.[22] Outside of the target countries, a country that has been successfully launched a public diplomacy program can be a model for other countries that intend to become new targets. In this research, public diplomacy through intermediary is a two steps procedure: from the communicator to the intermediary and from the intermediary to the target audience.

As already mentioned, the intermediary plays a special role in the process of public diplomacy: it does not change the operation of public diplomacy itself but divides the process of public diplomacy into two phases—the messages of EU public diplomacy travel from the EU to the intermediaries and then from the intermediaries to the end recipients. Chinese professors who serve as the intermediaries of EU public diplomacy do research on the EU, which is the first step of knowledge transfer; these professors then teach college students which achieve the second phase—knowledge transfer from intermediaries to its end recipients—college student in this study. A detailed analysis, in concert with first-hand empirical data, will be conducted to understand the EU's knowledge dissemination in Chinese universities in chapters 6–7.

The EU aims to entice third country students to study in Europe for the fulfillment of its interests as the first strand of EU policy, but it is impossible to bring all students to the EU. Therefore, exporting the educational model of the EU has become the second strand of EU policy and in fact, the EU has implemented the export of a specific EU tertiary education program via the use of foreign lecturers.[23] In this sense, it can be understood why and how public diplomacy through intermediary is being executed in the area of higher education.

In terms of the scholars sponsored by the Jean Monnet Programme, particularly the professors and those who run the Jean Monnet Modules as the intermediaries of EU public diplomacy, they are teaching and doing research in China, which is closer to the second situation. The funding for research on the EU is based on the receivers'—mainly the professors'—research achievement and academic reputation. The Jean Monnet Programme, which has the aim of increasing knowledge of the EU, seems more concerned about accurate knowledge and information because it is intended to communicate the EU and provide intellectual support for European integration. In fact, the Jean Monnet Programme is able to cross cultural barriers and make the EU's message more acceptable because the professors sponsored by this program, who serve as the intermediaries of EU public diplomacy, already display a preference towards the EU while they also have influence in target countries based on their academic reputation.

Since public diplomacy aims to influence the perceptions of the foreign communicator, the more people who are reached by public diplomacy programs, the more effective it becomes. In the case of the EU, the Jean Monnet Programme involves a greater number of participants around the world than the Erasmus Mundus Programme. In fact, although Europe attracts most international student (around 38 percent) followed by North America (about 23 percent), 72 percent of foreign students enrolled in EU21 countries come from another EU21 country.[24] Since some scholars think that applicants for the educational exchange programs run by the EU already have a good impression of the EU, it makes the effect of the public diplomacy program relatively insignificant.[25] Hence, courses on European studies towards students who cannot visit EU member states directly may extend its influence.

Because of cultural differences between EU and non-EU member states, changing perceptions of the EU by means of credible foreign professors reflects Wiessala's statement about the role of scholars in bridging the gaps between different cultures and the evolving concept of "education as foreign policy,"[26] and also proves that public diplomacy is by its very nature an activity of spanning borders that are both physical and psychological.[27] Some long-standing historical stereotypes or misunderstandings between EU and non-EU member states can be overcome by educational exchange since it is a dynamic and constructive agent of bilateral dialogue.[28] In the case of the Jean Monnet Programme in non-EU member states, the scholars and experts who obtain financial support effectively serve as intermediaries for EU public diplomacy in non-EU countries, whether as professors who deliver knowledge about the EU to students; commentators in the mass media, who help set the framework and agenda for public discussion; or think tanks which provide intellectual support for European integration. Thus, these professors have the capacity to teach and communicate the EU to students and publics in non-EU member states based on their academic reputation and they also have the advantage of being credible—telling the EU's story by scholars in host countries.

4.1.3 The Contributions of the Jean Monnet Programme to EU Public Diplomacy

In light of the general criteria for evaluating public diplomacy discussed in the chapter on the concept of public diplomacy and soft power, these principles are partly reflected in the implementation of the Jean Monnet Programme, largely because the role professors play as intermediaries of EU public diplomacy. More importantly, the Jean Monnet Programme, as a practice which partially meets the requirements of public diplomacy, can be studied through its special advantages and contribution to EU public diplomacy since it improves the efficiency of EU public diplomacy from different aspects.

Table 4.1.   General criteria for evaluating public diplomacy

(1)	listening is a start;
(2)	credibility is a basic requirement;
(3)	public diplomacy should go local;
(4)	public diplomacy aims to influence external perceptions;
(5)	public diplomacy must be connected with policy

Source: Author's own, based on the analysis in chapter 2 and section 4.1.

Among them, some of these criteria—listening as a start, going local, credibility is a requisite—can be reflected in the process of program design and implementation and the rest—changed perceptions—needs to examine the real influence on the target group.

First, listening is a start. The implementation of the Jean Monnet Programme in China is based on the achievement of previous educational exchange programs originally designed for China, and it matches the need for learning about the EU in China. In addition, this program also has to "promote policy debate and exchanges between the academic world and policymakers on Union policy priorities,"[29] reflecting the rule that public diplomacy should connect with policy. Besides, compared with the Jean Monnet Programme before its integration into the "Erasmus for All," the new program has shifted from supporting "European integration studies" to "EU studies" and covers wider target populations beyond academics, which is manifested in the feedback mechanisms that allow the EU to redirect the program towards the interests of the audience.

Second, credibility is a basic requirement. As a geographical and economic giant, the EU has made remarkable contributions to different aspects of international society. Along with these reasons, knowing what the EU is and what it does drives the people who are interested in it to seek and update information. Before the social media era, mass media was the dominant information source[30] since it was viewed as being a credible, timely, and valuable information provider,[31] and even as the best and the only source of information on political realities.[32] The ever-changing information and communication technologies not only offer the common people more information sources with greater amounts of information but also increase the difficulty of differentiating truth from falsehood. Therefore, assessing the credibility of information sources has an impact on information seeking and acceptance.[33] With the financial support of the Jean Monnet Programme, professors who do research related to the EU and teach college students are a reliable information source for their students.

Third, public diplomacy should "go local." The Jean Monnet Centres of Excellence are established in different universities both within and outside of the capital city of each country, and the Jean Monnet professors, who have also been selected by the EU according to their research achievements are spread across different areas. In China, academic projects sponsored in China cover ten universities in seven cities, which extend its influence to western and southern China by supporting European studies in these areas.[34] Not only college students are educated, but also some sectors of the local economy, such as trade with the EU, benefit from these European studies,[35] and Sichuan University as one of the best universities in Southwestern China has an active role in the local economic development and external cooperation.[36] In this regard, the Jean Monnet Programme goes local and extends its influence beyond the capital cities. Public diplomacy diplomats have realized the importance of extending public diplomacy beyond the capital city of target countries and have called for public diplomacy resource alignment between capital and non-capital cities.[37, 38] In this way the program can have more output with less input since it can cover a large number of foreign students by supporting their teachers' research. Going local also means that public diplomacy programs need to be adapted to the environment in which they are practiced, which can also be understood from the way it operates in China. Through the Jean Monnet Programme, some sensitive EU norms can still be delivered as the normative knowledge of the EU to college students in higher education institutions strictly regulated by the Chinese government, which will be discussed in chapter 7.

Also, the advantage of taking this program beyond the official documents of EU public diplomacy can be also used to increase the trust in research on the public diplomacy effect of this program. First, "sometimes the most credible voice is not one's own"[39] and that is why the Jean Monnet professors or other scholars sponsored by this program directly or indirectly are viewed as being authoritative and credible sources of information, which is good for public diplomacy. Second, high visibility does not necessarily lead to a positive image,[40] hence, the low visibility of sponsors behind public diplomacy programs can have greater output. In order to discover the empirical proof of this, the student interviewees were asked to answer whether they knew of the Jean Monnet Programme and what they thought about the knowledge delivered by the professors sponsored by the EU. The interview results will be presented in chapter 6.

Therefore, EU public diplomacy through the Jean Monnet Programme is a successful aspect of public diplomacy practice through its implementation in China and adds further useful experience to the EU's traditional information-oriented external communication strategy.

4.2 THE JEAN MONNET PROGRAMME AND EU SOFT POWER

Whether public diplomacy is studied from a communication-based approach or an international relations approach, soft power is the most common term used in public diplomacy studies. As some scholars have argued, "soft power may not be considered that hip by the latest generation of IR theoreticians in this fashion-conscious field of study, but . . . it by no means lost its practical relevance."[41] Therefore, this part will look at the relationship between the Jean Monnet Programme and EU soft power.

4.2.1 The Content of EU Soft Power

With regard to EU public diplomacy, soft power would appear to be still relevant because the EU is more closely associated with soft power than hard power[42] and public diplomacy is one of the key tools of soft power.[43] The concept of soft power will be further discussed along with its relations to public diplomacy in the next chapter. Here we shall concentrate on the source of the EU's soft power before moving on to talk about how the EU's soft power resources can be translated into actual external influence by means of public diplomacy. The core content of the EU's soft power resources is the diversity of European cultures and the identity of the EU as a model of regional integration, EU norms, as well as its institutional innovations.[44]

Cultural diversity and European identity. The motto of the EU, "united in diversity," reflects how Europeans have come together to work for peace and prosperity.[45] From a historical perspective, cultural interaction and diplomacy did not gain prominence in the EU because they had been viewed in the past as non-essential. However, as Europe prospered and became wealthier, the luxury of culture was more widely available to larger numbers of the European population. Cultural agencies which aimed to promote a country's languages and cultures to the outside world, such as Alliance Francaise and its equivalents were established.[46] Since then, culture and cultural interaction have become widespread.

In contemporary international relations, the EU's soft power resources come from both its member states and the EU itself, as follows: the time-honored history and the role of the EU in the world, the cultural achievements of EU member states including arts, literature, diversity of language, and education, the successful process of European integration, its peaceful approach to solving internal and external conflict, as well as the norms the EU has and tries to promote to the outside world such as democracy, protection of human rights, respect for the rule of law as well as the humanitarian and development aid it provides to developing countries and regions.[47]

Furthermore, in itself the EU provides a successful model for regional integration,[48] and it is also deeply involved in global governance related to climate change and economic regulation. However, despite the economic prosperity and sustainable peace across the European continent, the EU, which possesses a big market and is a leading development aid donor, also faces challenges of living up to its commitment "to shoulder its responsibilities in the governance of globalization" through "seeking to set globalisation within a moral framework . . . to anchor it in solidarity and sustainable development," implying the role of the EU in a globalized world.[49]

Communicating the EU to the outside world with an emphasis on its cultural diversity and achievements of regional integration aims to influence the foreign perceptions of the EU and project a favorable image of the EU, which will eventually benefit the objectives of the EU's foreign policies. Based on a broad definition of soft power, it can be said to contain external perceptions or international image.[50] External perceptions of the impact of the EU not only influence its role in the world, but also shape the construction of its internal identity, which further impacts on its image and effectiveness.

There is no denying that the current Eurozone crises may reduce the image of the EU's single monetary system, but member states are cooperating in eliminating the negative impression this has generated. Some scholars believe that the effective use of soft power attracts new members.[51] As a model of regional integration and as an unprecedented supranational organization, the EU's success causes the surrounding non-members states to wish to participate in the project of European integration. Based on this promising foundation, the EU's "soft power that derives from its readiness will offer a seat at the decision-making table."[52] Thus, in every sense, projecting the EU as a global actor due to its history, development, and achievements of European integration is the most important work taken by EU public diplomacy.

EU norms. European integration is based on a series of founding norms, so EU norms come as the second most important part of EU soft power resources. Although "Normative Power Europe" is an important self-perception of the EU, its significance varies due to geographical differences.[53] For the countries which hope to maintain closer connections with the EU or join EU family, the EU is perceived as a normative power; but the importance of EU norms, or at least EU norms, are not shared by the rest of the world. Plus, due to the weak commitment to its normative agenda, it has been argued that the EU is better to implement defensive normativity—getting its own house in order than in criticizing others.[54] Since a normative power is uncertain in different areas and soft power concerns how the image of the EU in the eyes of others, this research puts EU norms as the second important part of EU soft power resources.

Manners observes nine core norms of the EU which include peace, liberty, democracy, the rule of law, respect for human rights and good governance, social solidarity, anti-discrimination, and sustainable development.[55] The EU promotes its constitutive principles as action and policies in world politics, relying more on persuasion, engagement, and dialogue than illegitimate force.[56] Although some scholars consider that the idea of the EU as a normative power is utopian,[57] the EU is nonetheless still regarded as having a strong and long-established normative identity[58] even if at times its external actions do not demonstrate a coherent normative behavior.[59] Manners and other scholars emphasize the aspect of normative power in EU public diplomacy since they believe that the operation of value interpreters and translators in third countries is crucial for foreign publics to understand the EU.[60]

The EU is also regarded as a civilian power. The roots of European cooperation go back to the immediate aftermath of the Second World War, and the desire to prevent the death and destruction of war ever occurring again. The Cold War split Europe into East and West for forty years and the Council of Europe was created by West European nations in 1940 as the first step towards European cooperation, but six countries went further than this by promising each other through various bilateral and multilateral agreements that they would not attack one another in order to ensure the continuation of peaceful diplomacy and cultural interactions between their peoples.[61] Uddin believes that those endeavors constitute the bedrock of EU diplomacy and soft power.[62]

In fact, "civilian power Europe" has a longer history than "normative power Europe." The expression "civilian power Europe" was first used by Francois Duchene in the early 1970s in *Europe's Role in World Peace* and *The European Community and the Uncertainties of Interdependence* respectively. He affirms that "Europe can be exemplary of the influence wielded by a powerful co-operative formed to exert essentially civilian forms of power,"[63] and, "the European Community must be a force for the international diffusion of civilian and democratic standards,"[64] but he did not elaborate further on this notion. In Orbie's words, "the vagueness of Duchene's notion allows for different interpretations by policy makers and academics."[65]

Because of the ambiguity of the concept, to call the EU a civilian power has raised some scholarly debate, particularly following the creation of the CFSP and the ESDP. Karen Smith argues that the spectrum of instruments of foreign policy in international relations ranges from the civilian power to military power at the other extreme and the idea of civilian power Europe is dead because the EU now has military instruments.[66] However, she slightly revises her argument later and laments the fact that the only force that the EU can wield is for peacekeeping or training missions and not for coercion.[67] But some EU policy-makers believe that the idea of military means can be embedded in a civilian power context.[68] Yet it appears that European foreign and security policy still remains a purely national and inter-governmental exercise. Therefore, the EU is still principally a "civilian power" because of its use of the leverage of access to or exclusion from its large domestic market, alongside its dominant position in economic standard-setting and regulatory design.[69]

The debate on whether the EU is still a civilian power has not yet reached a certain conclusion since both views continue to be firmly held. Besides, soft power and normative power are two distinct terms. Soft power can be used for good or bad purposes and serves the objectives of foreign policy, but normative power is a theoretical term requiring an understanding of social diffusion and normative practice.[70] However, the continuing debate does not hinder us from associating the EU with soft power. Whether civilian or normative, the two together come close to Nye's conception of soft power as "the ability to get others to want what you want."[71] Also, civilian power and normative power overlap with Nye's soft power when they are used as power of attraction, and both civilian power and normative power serve to boost the EU's soft power.[72]

Institutional innovations of the EU. Every leap forward in the development of the EU brings about changes in its institutional design, and these institutions can also be viewed as being part of the EU's soft power. The Treaty of Lisbon has created the EEAS and the post of High Representative of the Union for Foreign Affairs and Security/Vice-President of the European Commission, both of these aim to bring about a more effective horizontal coordination in the EU's external activities and public diplomacy through important organizational innovations.[73] The European Council has been institutionalized and the role of the previously rotating Presidency of the European Council is subsumed in a fixed-term and full-time President, as indicated in Article 9B of the Lisbon Treaty. Thus, there are at least two new "faces" representing the EU: the HR/VP and the President of the European Council.[74] Furthermore, the administration of the delegations around the world has been transferred from the European Commission to the EEAS, which is the EU's diplomatic service. All these institutional innovations demonstrate the endeavors of the EU to project a single face to a world audience and communicate a coherent message.[75] Considering the scholarly concerns about the EU risking the loss of its soft power because of its institutional complexity, making these new institutions understood by others will be helpful in augmenting the EU's soft power.

Public diplomacy is an instrument for wielding soft power resources to engage foreign publics and translate these resources into actual external influences. The relationship between public diplomacy and soft power in general has been discussed in chapter 2, and the relationship between the Jean Monnet Programme and soft power (how soft power resources are wielded in the Jean Monnet Programme) will be analyzed in the following three sections.

4.2.2 The Jean Monnet Programme and the Formation of European Identity

As discussed above, EU public diplomacy consists of internal and external aspects: the internal one is to build a European identity for a deepened integration, and the external one is to communicate the EU to the outside world to increase its global influence. More importantly, these two aspects interlink and interact on each other—a deepening European identity will increase the visibility of the EU on the world stage, and an increasing external image will in turn help enhance the internal building of European identity. Arguably, the EU has been established on a shared foundation including its norms, values, and principles within the constraints of its institutional and political institutions, but the EU's external activities have been hampered by its comparative inability to persuade both domestic and international audiences in terms of its nature and its vision of the world order.[76] What's worse, as showed by the refugee crisis and Brexit referendum, a European identity is still incomplete.

When studying the EU, the concepts of "European identity" and "European citizenship" sometimes are used interchangeably. However, as argued by Brewer and other scholars, social identity as the perception of self as part of a larger group or social collective which provides a link between the individual and the group(s) to which he or she belongs.[77, 78] The concept of "European identity" means the traits (real or ideal) that characterize a certain individual as being "European" and the concept of "European citizenship" more narrowly define the legal status of belonging to the European polity through citizenship of one of its member states.[79] In the case of the EU, the EU's soft power to some extent comes from its motto of "unity in diversity" and European identity as mentioned before, but it seems to be more challenging to accommodate both "diversity and multiple citizenships" and "a European identity" because recognising multiple identities within a single supranational political entity can be a destablizing factor.[80]

According to scholarly research, the future of the EU will be determined partially by the degree to which the citizens in the member states started to see themselves as citizens of the EU, as integration will gradually lead to a convergence of beliefs, values, and aspirations that would unite the populations of the EU.[81] As an elite project, a historical evolvement from the ECSC to the EEC to the EU at its current form had been largely influenced by elites' decisions, but the EU's leaders realized the importance of European citizens in enhancing the integration process. Thus, the establishment of Jean Monnet Programme, at the very beginning, was to bring the European project to its citizens.

In fact, quite a few researchers examined the effect of educational and educational exchange programs such as Erasmus Programme and Erasmus Mundus Programme on the formation of European identity besides the Jean Monnet Programme. By looking at specific educational exchange programs, Kuhn emphasizes that the impact of cross-border student exchange on the social construction of European identity, which is an aspect of EU public diplomacy in that it increases knowledge of the EU and a sense of identity among citizens.[82] However, Sigalas's research argues that there no significant connection between transnational student mobility and the formation of

European identity,[83] which is further proved by Mitchell who believes that the Erasmus Programme cannot lead to a widespread formation of European identity, albeit she does think that "Erasmus study led to a significant degree of attitudinal change among the participants of this study because it made students more interested in various aspects of Europe and led them to feel more Europe."[84] Even so, it seems that those participants who are involved in transnational educational programs already have a favorable impression of the EU and therefore their overseas experience cannot make a big difference because of the "celling effect," indicating that less educated individuals might respond well to cross-border exchange programs.[85]

The Erasmus Mundus Programme, another educational exchange program, is designed to promote the mobilization of internal student and attract external students to study in EU member states and specifically aims to strengthen the partnership between European and Asian higher educational institutions. The Erasmus Programme has been a more attractive subject of study for analyzing the effect of educational programs on European identity. It is easy to confuse the "Erasmus Programme" with the "Erasmus Mundus Programme," since both bear the name of "Erasmus" and both operate in the field of higher education. The former is aimed at Europeans while the latter focuses on students and scholars from non-EU countries. The Erasmus Programme and the Erasmus Mundus Programmes may target different groups, yet both of them endeavor to inform the public about the EU, which explains why public diplomacy researchers prefer using them as case studies of EU public diplomacy. However, because of its limited coverage of students involved in the Erasmus Mundus Programme, there has been little research on this program.

Whatever the case, they are able to draw conclusions that were both different and contradictory, implying that in researching EU public diplomacy programs and its effect on European identity, the result is not as evident as expected. Therefore, two cognitive mechanisms including "exposure to Europe-related information" and "Europe-related experiences and opportunities for citizens to gain such experiences" have been emphasized in the process of European identity formation.[86] Accordingly, a higher level of knowledge of the EU will lead to higher levels of European identity, meaning that the populations will identify more strongly with the community of European citizens as they gain more knowledge about the goal and function of the EU.[87] Although Verhaegen and Hooghe think that it is an economic utilitarian (the benefits they can get from European integration) and a political trust that explains a stronger European identity, they never dismiss the relationship between an increasing knowledge of the EU and a stronger European identity.[88]

The Jean Monnet Programme increases European consciousness internally, leading to the formation of a European identity,[89] which is echoed by

Field who agrees with the impact of the European integration curriculum on "Europeanisation."[90] And externally, it enhances the students' perception of the actorness of the EU at world stage by projecting the EU as an example of regional integration. A further feature of the EU's cultural diversity is its language pluralism, which is well preserved because the sponsored courses are allowed to teach in the official member state language.[91] All this reflects the influence of the Jean Monnet Programme on EU soft power inside the EU.

European identity goes beyond a legal entitlement by emphasizing a feeling with a multicultural and multilingual community with a common project for the future,[92] so educational and educational exchange programs have been used to fill the gap between European citizenship and European identity. All these aspects pertinent to the EU have been covered by the Jean Monnet Programme through teaching and research. More importantly, Duke thinks that the internal construction of European identity and narrative through internal public diplomacy activities are employed externally,[93] meaning that the complex relations are thought as "a self-reaffirming process" between "what is portrayed and practiced internally and what is then exported externally as the Union's power and attraction."[94]

4.2.3 The Jean Monnet Programme and the EU's Norm Diffusion

As discussed above, the Jean Monnet Programme takes responsibilities of communicating the regional integration of Europe and EU norms towards third parties. In this sense, evaluating the relationship of the Jean Monnet Programme and EU soft power needs to look at the role of "European integration" in EU soft power resources and how it has been promoted to Chinese college students.

Soft power in the context of the EU has been mentioned in the second chapter and how it is related to public diplomacy was discussed in the previous section. Public diplomacy serves as an instrument of soft power by converting soft power resources into real external influence by telling the story of the EU. Here we will find out how the educational programs, particularly the Jean Monnet Programme, communicate the EU's soft power resources and also exert its soft power. Before doing so, we will answer whether and how educational programs help the projection of soft power and then address what constitutes the EU's soft power resources.

The question of whether educational programs can be discussed within the framework of soft power has been the subject of recent scholarly debate. Knight thinks that the concept of soft power has its limits when talking about the influence of international education. According to him higher education "has been drawn to [it] like bees to honey," but this connection obviously misunderstands the essence of power. As he argues, the basic notion of power is that of gaining dominance whether by hard, soft or smart power, but trans-national educational programs have no relation to any kind of dominance.[95] On the contrary, the transformation of diplomacy with new actors becoming involved in the diplomatic process creates an expanded concept of diplomacy, which is more applicable to higher education as an approach to mutual in-terests, international engagement, or more precisely, knowledge diplomacy, and eventually benefits all players. Knight's conclusion that the notion of soft power and higher education are incompatible has not received scholarly recog-nition. Kirkland says that using education to boost the interests of a country is not a new phenomenon since "many of the historical motives have been a great deal more sinister than anything we see in the modern notion of soft power."[96]

In fact, higher education can be connected to soft power for two reasons: one is to promote a common understanding and language that other forms of diplomacy are unable to communicate, implying that higher education has an advantage in establishing a knowledge community. The other one is that higher education generally affects people at a critical time of their life—in-tellectually and socially. Besides, Peterson also realizes that the parameters of diplomacy have expanded to include the concept of public diplomacy, covering a wide range of activities and actions that promote social, cultural, and educational relations among nations, and nations on the world stage seek to exert "soft power" through public diplomacy programs and initiatives.[97] Albeit academic terms like "public diplomacy" and "soft power" are still new, governments have understood these concepts through employing and achieving the aims of higher education.

The EU has been using higher education as a form of soft power for a long time. On the one hand, higher education is part of soft power for each country since it is widely acknowledged that the benefits of higher education go far beyond the mere socio-economic progress of the diploma-holders. Highly-educated citizens are crucial for states to achieve social, political, and economic development.[98] On the other hand, their highly developed higher education attracts overseas students to study in the host countries. Tomusk even comments that education has been used throughout history as a weapon to conquer the hearts and minds of adversaries, and to corrupt the youth with other gods, ideals, heroes, and ethics.[99] However, this statement bears the marks of propaganda or psychological war. Put in a neutral way, higher education can influence the perceptions of foreign students who are the future leaders of business, politics, and civil society, either by recruiting foreign stu-dents to study in host countries or promoting knowledge or education systems in foreign countries through international higher education cooperation.

For the EU, higher education, particularly cross-border academic programs such as Erasmus Mundus, Marie Curie,[100] and Tempus[101] are viewed as a means of promoting mutual understanding and cooperation through research and knowledge transfer.[102] The EU has accumulated extensive experience in public diplomacy through educational programs and research exchange, first among its member states and then with third countries around the world. These programs have raised the profile of the EU as a supranational organization, and the classroom teaching of EU courses and research have provided generations of students with the experience of studying in EU countries.[103]

Nye, who coined the term "soft power," also admits the role of higher education in wielding soft power resources through studying the American higher education, since "millions of people who have studied in the United States over the years constitute a remarkable reservoir of goodwill for our country."[104] According to Nye, the successful experience of US higher education is instructive for its European friends, who have been increasing their endeavors to recruit foreign students in their schools and universities.[105] A recent report from the European Commission's *European Higher Education in the World*, indicates that the global networks of graduates from the EU educational exchange programs can be used as a valuable tool of its soft power, to affect and engage new audiences and advance the interests of EU member states or the EU as a whole.[106]

The EU's soft power resources consist of cultural diversity and European identity, EU norms, as well as its institutional innovations. Nye's definition of soft power concludes that it is attractive instead of coercive power, while Tulmets further explains that the EU's soft power refers to a combination of policy discourses on the attractive power of European values and norms, and of a philosophy based on partnership, differentiation and participation.[107] Thanks to its emphasis on its founding norms, the EU is viewed as a normative power by others.[108] The EU's contributions to the resolution of conflicts between hostile countries and long-lasting peace and prosperity on the European continent through an economic approach cause it to be viewed as a civilian power. With its experience of regional integration, the EU wishes to be seen as an important global player.[109]

In defining the EU's role on the world stage, Article 10A of the Treaty of Lisbon states that: "the Union's actions on the international scene shall be guided by the principles which have inspired its creation, development and enlargement, and which it seeks to advance in the wider world. These principles include democracy, the rule of law, the universality and individuality of human rights and fundamental freedom, respect for human dignity, the principles of equality and solidarity, and respect for the principles of the United Nations Charters and international law."

Whether civilian or normative power, the two taken together come close to Nye's conception of soft power as "the ability to get others to want what you want."[110] Of course, coming close to Nye's definition of soft power does not mean that they completely equal it in all respects. Both civilian and normative power can be used to induce, but also to coerce.[111] When the EU uses conditionality to spread its norms by making its trade contracts or aid agreements conditional on the respect of democratic principles and protection of human rights, the EU communicates the appropriateness of these norms, which is the regulation set by the EU.[112] However, the EU uses sanctions or other negative tools to coerce other countries to respect the relevant rules if the EU disapproves of their activities or policies, and thus they are not soft power in the sense Nye intended.

Nevertheless, how the EU norms have been disseminated and localized in the Chinese context beyond the discussion of this research. As argued by some scholars, the promotion of EU norms as EU soft power resources needs to consider the appropriateness of these norms in the different contexts of recipient countries and restructure these norms due to the cultural characteristics of recipient countries.[113, 114, 115] Thus, the research cannot study whether these EU norms have successfully rooted in the Chinese context through the educational process, but it can tell how these norms as the guidance of EU internal and external behaviors have been manifested in practice by looking at the classroom teaching of EU norms in Chinese higher education institutions.

The EU norms as EU soft power resources cannot be easily realized through educational process, but they have been delivered to Chinese students—the audience of EU public diplomacy in the case of the Jean Monnet Programme—through classroom teaching, which help Chinese students understand the role of the EU at world stage. In this sense, as an integral part of knowledge dissemination regarding the EU, the information of EU norms as a prerequisite that helps convert EU soft power resources into external influence.

The Jean Monnet Programme was originally designed for promoting worldwide research and study on European integration, whose main purpose was information dissemination of European integration and EU studies. This program, like other public diplomacy programs, does not produce soft power directly but translates the EU's soft power resources into real effect during the process of knowledge transmission and relationship building. Therefore, research on the EU's international role always stresses the importance of soft power resources, including the cultural diversity and identity formation, EU's founding norms, as well as its institutional innovations, but the EU concentrates more on how to project a favorable external image and promote its norms while interacting with other international actors.[116]

When the Jean Monnet professors teach college students in their home countries, their knowledge about Europe and the EU is delivered to students who may or may not have opportunities to visit the EU member states or who are not majoring in European studies. The funding invested in the research projects and courses related to European integration studies or EU studies might, for some researchers, be an important support and motivation to carry on their research and teaching. Some scholars think that, for geopolitical reasons, applying for government funding for European studies in China is not as easy as for American or Japanese studies,[117] in that China as an East Asia country paid more attention to the research on Asian area and an important player beyond Asia—the US.[118]

Research and teaching on European integration for foreign scholars in their home countries is a means of wielding soft power resources because they are embedded in this program and will reach college students and foreign publics. For the EU, through exporting its model of regionalism and multilateralism, encouraging regional identity formation, enhancing cultural interaction, promoting the common norms of the region, and furthermore, shaping the forms and direction of Asian regionalism, the EU can use its soft power resources to exert real effect.[119] Obviously, during this process, understanding is just the beginning. On top of mutual understanding, the image of itself that the EU wants to promote can also be communicated to students and publics more widely.

As indicated in the concept of public diplomacy, the EU's public diplomacy is intended to produce real external influence by communicating and promoting its soft power resources. In other words, public diplomacy is used as one of the foreign policy instruments that make soft power resources work. In fact, public diplomacy activities do not engender soft power directly. Rather, they promote mutual understanding, nurture a favorable image and build a long-term relationship between two countries involved in the communication process. In doing so, public diplomacy practice provides a first but important step in translating soft power resource into real international influence.[120] The Jean Monnet Programme is one such tool.

4.2.4 The Jean Monnet Programme Yields Soft Influence

As discussed above, the EU's soft power resources are reflected in various public diplomacy programs including the Jean Monnet Programme and communicated by implementing this program around the world. We shall now discuss whether the Jean Monnet Programme translates EU soft power resources into real influence.

The influence of one country's soft power derives from its capacity to translate potential soft power resources into the behavior of attraction.[121] According to Nye, it is easy to answer the question about the essence of soft power: nature or nurture? Soft power is nurtured intentionally by countries instead of being naturally possessed. Based on an analysis of American soft power, Nye concludes that the sources of a country's soft power largely depend on three basic elements: its culture, its political values, and its foreign policies, but as already discussed, the content and meaning of soft power can change according to the specific situation of different players in the world. Thus, the EU's soft power has its own content.

With regard to the real impact of the EU's soft power in international relations, setting a model of regional integration is one of the most attractive features that the EU makes. Although it has been an explosion of various forms of regionalism, the most pervasive example has been the widening and deepening of the EU.[122] Besides, the founding rules which underpin the EU and European regional integration not only reflect the image of the EU but also exert soft power through storytelling,[123] which can be understood as how storytelling in EU public diplomacy can be used to enhance its influence on the world stage and foster goodwill towards the EU. However, almost two and a half decades after Maastricht, and one after Lisbon, the EU remains an international actor trying to assert its presence to the world audience.[124] Since the EU needs public diplomacy to enhance it world image of international actors, promoting the Jean Monnet Programme around the world allows foreign scholars to tell the EU's story in their home countries, which helps translate the EU's soft power into real external influence.

The soft power resources of the EU, including the EU's cultural diversity and European identity, its founding norms, as well as the institutional innovations of the EU were discussed previously. Although the EU norms have always emphasized by academics because of the self-portrayal of Normative Power Europe, the Jean Monnet Programme as EU public diplomacy gives more attentions to the role of EU as an example of regionalism. In fact, the role of the EU as a model of regional integration has been delivered in classroom teaching through the Jean Monnet Programme, and EU norms which underpin European integration have also been embedded in the course content sponsored by this program. Meanwhile, it helps the formation of European identity internally. Although this research stresses how EU soft power resources have been communicated and translated into real external influence through the Jean Monnet Programme, its cultural diversity and European identity that were formed through internal public diplomacy are eventually exported externally.[125]

Chinese European studies started with introducing European development experience to China, and had the basic precondition that the European experience was useful and attractive to China. The growth of Chinese European studies can be partially attributed to the strengthening of EU-China relations and the lessons to be learned from the European experience for China's development is a starting point for Chinese European studies. From the 1980s, Chinese scholars and government officials tried to draw lessons from the European experience of regional policy in its search for effective solutions to the economic disparity between different regions in China. Also, other aspects of the EU, including foreign policy and external relations, its approaches in dealing with neighboring countries, its multilateralist approach to global and regional security, were all studied by Chinese scholars.[126]

Scholars argue that conceptual gaps on soft power do exist between the EU and China, as China stresses cultural soft power while the EU is viewed as a regional soft power because of its attraction to neighboring countries. However, the EU also aims to communicate its soft power resources through exporting regionalism,[127] which may cause some policy conflicts because of different understandings of this concept.[128] Even so, both the EU and China use soft power to explain their development paths,[129] making this term explainable based on mutual understanding of the cultural and historical backgrounds. In other words, improving knowledge and appreciation of each other's culture and society will bring conceptual gaps.[130] In this sense, public diplomacy, or the Jean Monnet Programme explains soft power resources first and converts them into external influence.

Considering that the founding rules of the EU constitute a key part of EU soft power, it is worth discussing further how this aspect of EU soft power works. Crookes, who echoes Small's opinion, also mentions that the "values gap" between the EU and China is at the heart of prevalent tensions in bilateral relations, which means that the EU's endeavors in projecting its normative power in China generate resentment instead of increasing the EU's external attractiveness.[131, 132] Put differently, Chinese appreciation of the EU as a global normative power varies in different dimensions.[133] Thus, EU norms can be promoted through mutual interests based cooperative programs.[134] Delivering these founding rules through classroom teaching will not engender soft power for the EU directly, but it helps people know what the EU stands for and how these norms have been reflected in its internal and external behaviors, which is the preliminary requirement of accepting and localizing EU norms in the Chinese context.

Manners and Whitman believe that EU public diplomacy requires an active form of engagement in order to ensure that the audience is aware of the EU's aspirations, which can be achieved by broadcasting the dialectic.[135] This has also been discussed by Wallström—of being ("what we are and what we stand for") and becoming ("what we do or want to do").[136] They use the EU centers, launched by the unit of public diplomacy at the EU level, as the overseas institutes of European studies to explain how these rules have been communicated and also point out that the satellite university campuses that are established by EU member states in third countries can also be used to communicate the EU and those EU rules that are beneficial for both the EU and the host society.[137] Since the Jean Monnet Programme was also implemented by supporting European studies, and the EU centers will be incorporated into the Jean Monnet Programme in the near future, it can be concluded that the Jean Monnet Programme wields soft power by communicating the EU's founding rules, creating consensus, and sharing ideas, besides broadcasting a favorable international image.

In this sense, the Jean Monnet Programme that yields soft power can be explained from two aspects: one is that the Jean Monnet Programme, by researching and teaching European integration, increases the attractiveness of the EU as an example of regional integration from economic cooperation to political cooperation. The other is that, by teaching EU norms as the underpinning basis of European integration, the Jean Monnet Programme enlightens further generation—college students in this case to know what the EU stands for and how these EU norms have guided and have been reflected in the EU's internal and external behaviors, which provides an intellectual preparation for the EU's long-term norm promotion. In other words, the EU's descriptive knowledge dissemination aims to increase the college students' understandings of the EU while normative knowledge dissemination helps the EU enhance its soft influence in a long term.

It can be concluded that the Jean Monnet Programme as EU public diplomacy practice towards target countries, wields soft power through translating its soft power resources into real external influence. During this process, the increased accurate understanding of the EU and the lessons that can be drawn from the EU for China's development are the most important aspect of an understanding of its attractiveness and influence. This will be more fully explained with the empirical data from China and discussed in chapters 6 and 7.

As Nye also says, "predictions of European decline rely on an out-dated understanding of power. On all issues that require power over others, Europe has impressive capacity."[138] The idea of a war between EU member states seems impossible, and the development of the EU greatly enhances Europe's attractiveness and its soft power.[139] That's why some scholars insist that soft power has by no means lost its practical relevance, particularly in explaining the EU.[140]

Through looking at the origins and development of the Jean Monnet Programme and its role in EU public diplomacy practice, it can be concluded that it can not only be viewed as an EU public diplomacy practice but also make contributions to the EU's practice per se. For one thing, it meets the general criteria of public diplomacy based on its specific objectives and the practices in different countries. For another, it has its own comparative advantages in communicating the EU to a world audience. Thus, the question regarding why the Jean Monnet Programme can be studied from the perspective of public diplomacy has been answered.

Since EU public diplomacy serves the aim of promoting the EU's soft power, the Jean Monnet Programme is intended to encourage European integration research and EU studies in both member and non-member states, and exemplifies the EU's endeavors in promoting foreign understanding of the integration process and the EU as a whole. More importantly, the EU's descriptive knowledge dissemination aims to increase the college students' understandings of the EU while normative knowledge dissemination helps the EU enhance its soft influence in a long term. Although public diplomacy does not produce soft power directly, it works by increasing mutual understanding between the EU and third parties and projecting a favorable image of the EU can translate the soft power resources of the EU into real effect. How the Jean Monnet Programme has been implemented and why it works in China will be discussed with empirical data in the following three chapters.

NOTES

1. Mitchell, J. M. (1986), *International Cultural Relations*, London: Allen & Unwin: 1.

2. United States Advisory Commission on Information, (1952), *Sixth Semi-annual Report of United States Advisory Commission on Information*, available at: http://www.state.gov/documents/organization/175481.pdf, [accessed July 6, 2015]: 20.

3. Bu, L. (1999), "Educational Exchange and Cultural Diplomacy in the Cold War," *Journal of American Studies*, 33(3): 394.

4. Lima Jr., A. F. (2007), "The Role of International Educational Exchanges in Public Diplomacy," *Place Branding and Public Diplomacy*, 3(3): 237.

5. Marshall, T. (1970) "The Strategy of International Exchange," in Eide, I. (ed.), *Students as Links between Cultures*, Universitetsforlaget, Oslo, Norway: 19–20.

6. Lima Jr., A. F. (2007), "The Role of International Educational Exchanges in Public Diplomacy," *Place Branding and Public Diplomacy*, 3(3): 240.

7. Bachner, D. and Zeutschel, U. (2009), "Long-term Effects of International Educational Youth Exchange," *International Education*, 20(1): 45.

8. La Porte, T. (2011), *The Power of the European Union in Global Governance: A Proposal for a New Public Diplomacy*, Los Angeles: Figueroa Press: 24.

9. EACEA, (2014), *Erasmus Plus: Actions,* available at: http://eacea.ec.europa.eu/erasmus-plus/actions_en#, [accessed Sept. 17, 2014].

10. Ronfeldt, D. and Arquila, J. (2009), "Noopolitik: A New Paradigm for Public Diplomacy," in Snow, N. and Taylor, P. M., (eds.), *Routledge Handbook of Public Diplomacy*, New York: Routledge: 362.

11. Sowa, P. A. (2002) "How Valuable Are Student Exchange Programmes?" *New Directions for Higher Education*, No.117: 63.

12. European Commission (2011), *Regulation of the European Parliament and of the Council, Establishing "Erasmus for All," the Union Programme for Education, Training, Youth and Sport*, COM (2011) 788 Final, Brussels, Nov. 23, 2011: 21.

13. Bellamy, C. and Weinberg, A. (2008), "Educational and Cultural Exchange to Restore America's Image," *The Washington Quarterly*, 31(3): 59.

14. Morini, M. Peruzzi, R. and Poletti, A. (2010), "Eastern Giants: The EU in the Eyes of Russia and China," in Lucarelli, S. and Fioramonti, L. (eds.), *External Perceptions of the European Union as a Global Actor*, Hoboken: Taylor and Francis: 33.

15. Interview with Professor B in Beijing, Dec. 11, 2013; Interview with Professor F in Shanghai, Dec. 22, 2013.

16. EACEA (2014), *Selection Results—Jean Monnet Networks and Jean Monnet Projects*, available at: https://eacea.ec.europa.eu/sites/eacea-site/files/documents/eac-s11-13_policy-debate-with-academic-world_en.pdf, [accessed Sept. 1, 2015].

17. EACEA (2014), *Erasmus Plus Programme Guide*, available at: http://ec.europa.eu/programmes/erasmus-plus/documents/erasmus-plus-programme-guide_en.pdf, [accessed Mar. 14, 2015].

18. Ibid.

19. Interviews with Vito Borrelli and Renato Girelli in Brussels, Feb. 6, 2015.

20. EACEA (2014), *Erasmus Plus: Actions,* available at: http://eacea.ec.europa.eu/erasmus-plus/actions_en#, [accessed Sept. 17, 2014].

21. Rasmussen, S. B. (2010), "The Messages and Practices of the European Union's Public Diplomacy," *The Hague Journal of Diplomacy*, 5(3): 218.

22. Seib, P. (2012), *Real-time Diplomacy: Politics and Power in the Social Media Era*, New York: Palgrave Macmillan: 116.

23. Jones, W. J. (2009–2010), "European Union Soft Power: Cultural Diplomacy & Higher Education in Southeast Asia," *Silpakorn University International Journal*, Vol.9–10: 53.

24. De Wit, H., (2012), "Student Mobility between Europe and the Rest of the World: Trends, Issues and Challenges," in Curaj, A., et al. (eds.), *European Higher Education at the Crossroads: Between the Bologna Process and National Reforms*, Dordrecht, Heidelberg and New York, London: Springer: 433.

25. Kuhn, T. (2012), "Why Educational Programmes Miss Their Mark: Cross-border Mobility, Education and European Identity," *Journal of Common Market Studies*, 50(6): 994.

26. Wiessala, G. (2013), "Social-Cultural and Educational Cooperation between the EU and Asia," in Christiansen, T. Kirchner, E. and Murray, P. B. (eds.), *The Palgrave Handbook of EU-Asia Relations*, Hampshire: Palgrave Macmillan: 221.

27. Fisher, A. (2013), *Collaborative Public Diplomacy: How Transnational Networks Influenced American Studies in Europe*, New York: Palgrave Macmillan: 10.

28. Wiessala, G. (2013), "Social-Cultural and Educational Cooperation between the EU and Asia," in Christiansen, T. Kirchner, E. and Murray, P. B. (eds.), *The Palgrave Handbook of EU-Asia Relations*, Hampshire: Palgrave Macmillan: 212.

29. European Commission (2011), *Regulation of the European Parliament and of the Council, Establishing "Erasmus for All," the Union Programme for Education, Training, Youth and Sport*, COM (2011) 788 Final, Brussels, Nov. 23, 2011: 21.

30. Murch, A. W. (1971), "Public Concern for Environmental Pollution," *The Public Opinion Quarterly*, 35(1): 101.

31. Heath, R. L., Liao, S. and Douglas, W. (1995), "Effects of Perceived Economic Harms and Benefits on Issues Involvement, Use of Information Source, and Actions: A Study in Risk Communication," *Journal of Public Relations Research*, 7(2): 102–103.

32. McCombs, M. and Shaw, D. L. (1972), "The Agenda-Setting Function of Mass Media," *The Public Opinion Quarterly*, 36(2): 185.

33. Westerman, D., Spence, P. R. and Der Heide, B. V. (2014), "Social Media as Information Source: Recency of Updates and Credibility of Information," *Journal of Computer-Mediated Communication*, 19(2): 172.

34. Interview in Brussels with Vito Borrelli, Feb. 6, 2015.

35. Interview in Chengdu with Professor H, Sichuan, Dec. 17, 2013.

36. EUPIC—The EU Project Innovation Centre (2013), *EU-China B&T Cooperation Fair VIII*, available at: http://www.eu-china.org.cn/download/file.html?id=10, [accessed April 26, 2016].

37. Wallström, M. (2008), *Public Diplomacy and its Role in the EU's External Relations*, Mortara Center for International Studies, Georgetown University, available at: http://europa.eu/rapid/press-release_SPEECH-08-494_en.pdf, [accessed April 3, 2015]: 3.

38. Cabral, R., Engelke, P., Brown, K. and Wedner, A. T. (2014), *Diplomacy for a Diffuse World*, Issue Brief, Atlantic Council: Brent Scowcroft Centre on International Security, available at: http://www.atlanticcouncil.org/images/publications/Diplo macy_for_a_Diffuse_World.pdf, [accessed April 3, 2015]: 6.

39. Cull, N. J. (2010), "Public Diplomacy: Seven Lessons for its Future from its Past," *Place Branding and Public Diplomacy*, Vol. 6: 14.

40. Manheim, J. B. (1994), *Strategic Public Diplomacy and American Foreign Policy: The Evolution of Influence*, New York: Oxford University Press: 126–47.

41. Cross, Mai'a K. D. and Melissen, J. (2013), "Introduction," in Mai'a K. Davis Cross & Jan Melissen (eds.), *European Public Diplomacy: Soft Power at Work*, Hampshire: Palgrave Macmillan: 18.

42. Azpíroz, M. L. (2015), *Soft Power and Public Diplomacy: The Case of the European Union in Brazil*, CPD perspectives on public diplomacy, Centre on Public Diplomacy, University of Southern California: 6.

43. Nye, J. (2010), *The Future of Power*, New York: Public Affairs: 100.

44. Azpíroz, M. L. (2015), *Soft Power and Public Diplomacy: The Case of the European Union in Brazil*, CPD perspectives on public diplomacy, Centre on Public Diplomacy, University of Southern California: 6.

45. Ibid.

46. Uddin, Z. (2011), "Soft and Normative Power: The Power of Attraction in International Politics," *E-International Relations*, 1st Oct., available at: http://www.e-ir. info/2011/10/01/soft-and-normative-power-the-power-of-attraction-in-international -politics/, [accessed May 20, 2014].

47. Azpíroz, M. L. (2015), *Soft Power and Public Diplomacy: The Case of the European Union in Brazil*, CPD perspectives on public diplomacy, Centre on Public Diplomacy, University of Southern California: 6–7.

48. Cameron, F. (2005), *The EU Model of Integration—Relevance Elsewhere?* Jean Monnet/Robert Schuman Paper Series, 5(37), Miami European Union Centre, available at: http://aei.pitt.edu/8166/1/Cameronfinal.pdf, [accessed June 16, 2015]: 1.

49. Peters, M. A. (2007), "Europa, Europeanisation, and Europe: Constituting New Europeans," in Kuhn, M. (ed.), *Who is the European?—A New Global Player*, New York: Peter Lang Publishing: 75.

50. Fan, Y. (2008), "Soft Power: Power of Attraction or Confusion?" *Place Branding and Public Diplomacy*, 4(2): 147.

51. Wagner, J. (2014), "The Effectiveness of Hard & Soft Power in Contemporary International Relations," *E-International Relations*, 14th May, available at: http://www.e-ir.info/2014/05/14/the-effectiveness-of-soft-hard-power-in-contemporary-international-relations/, [accessed May 21, 2014].

52. Cooper, R. (2004), "Hard Power, Soft Power and the Goals of Diplomacy," in: D. Held & M. Koenig-Archibugi, (eds.), *American Power in the 21st Century*. Cambridge: Polity Press: 179–180.

53. Larsen, H. (2014), "The EU as a Normative Power and the Research on External Perceptions: The Missing Links," *Journal of Common Market Studies*, 52(4): 906.

54. Mattlin, M. (2012), "Dead on Arrival: Normative EU Policy towards China," *Asia Europe Journal*, 10(2): 182.

55. Manners, I. (2002), "Normative Power Europe: A Contradiction in Terms?" *Journal of Common Market Studies*, 40(2): 242.

56. Manners, I. (2008), "The Normative Ethics of the European Union," *International Affairs*, 84(1): 77.

57. Scheipers, S. and Sicurelli, D. (2007), "Normative Power Europe: A Credible Utopia?" *Journal of Common Market Studies*, 45(2): 436.

58. Youngs, R. (2004), "Normative Dynamics and Strategic Interests in the EU's External Identity," *Journal of Common Market Studies*, 42(2): 416.

59. Tocci, N. (2008), "The European Union as a Normative Foreign Policy Actor," in Tocci, N. (ed.), *Who is a Normative Foreign Policy Actor? The European Union and its Global Partners*, Brussels: Centre for European Policy Studies: 26.

60. Manners, I. and Whitman, R. (2013), "Normative Power and Future of EU Public Diplomacy," in Mai'a K. Davis Cross & Melissen, J. (eds.), *European Public Diplomacy: Soft Power at Work*, Hampshire: Palgrave Macmillan: 195.

61. European Union (2014), *A Peaceful Europe—The Beginning of Cooperation*, available at: http://europa.eu/about-eu/eu-history/1945-1959/index_en.htm, [accessed May 20, 2014].

62. Uddin, Z. (2011), "Soft and Normative Power: The Power of Attraction in International Politics," *E-International Relations*, 1st Oct., available at: http://www.e-ir.info/2011/10/01/soft-and-normative-power-the-power-of-attraction-in-international-politics/, [accessed May 20, 2014].

63. Duchene, F. (1972), "Europe's Role in World Peace," in Mayne, R. (ed.), *Europe Tomorrow: Sixteen Europeans Look Ahead*, London: Fontana/Collins: 47.

64. Duchene, F. (1973), "The European Community and the Uncertainties of Interdependence," in Kohnstamm, M. and Hager, W. (eds.), *A Nation Writ Large? Foreign-Policy Problems before the European Community*, London and Basingstoke: The Macmillan Press LTD: 20.

65. Orbie, J. (2006), "Civilian Power Europe: Review of the Original and Current Debates," *Cooperation and Conflict*, 41(1): 124.

66. Smith, K. E. (2005), *Beyond the Civilian Power Debate*, London: LSE Research online, available at: http://eprints.lse.ac.uk/812/1/BeyondPDF.pdf, [accessed June 7, 2014]: 77.

67. Smith, K. E. (2014), "Is the European Union's Soft Power in Decline?" *Current History*, March: 104–105.

68. Orbie, J. (2009), "A Civilian Power in the World? Instruments and Objectives in European Union External Policies," in Orbie, J. (ed.), *Europe's Global Role*, Surrey: Ashgate Publishing Limited: 14.

69. Niblett, R. (2013), *Strategic Europe: Still a Civilian Power*, Carnegie Europe, available at: http://carnegieeurope.eu/publications/?fa=45665&reloadFlag=1, [accessed June 10, 2014].

70. Diez, T. and Manners, I. (2007), "Reflecting on Normative Power Europe," in Berenskoetter, F. and Williams, M. J. (eds.), *Power in World Politics*, New York: Routledge: 179.

71. Hill, C. (2010), "Cheque and Balances: The European Union's Soft Power Strategy," in I. Parmar and M. Cox, (eds.), *Soft Power and US Foreign Policy: Theoretical, Historical and Contemporary Perspectives*, London: Routledge: 184.

72. Smith, K. E. (2014), "Is the European Union's Soft Power in Decline?" *Current History*, March: 180.

73. Azpíroz, M. L. (2015), *Soft Power and Public Diplomacy: The Case of the European Union in Brazil*, CPD perspectives on public diplomacy, Centre on Public Diplomacy, University of Southern California: 7.

74. Chopin, T. and Lefebvre, M. (2010), "Three Phone Numbers for Europe: Will the Lisbon Treaty Make the European Union More Effective Abroad?" *US-Europe Analysis Series,* Number 43, Centre on the United States and Europe at Brookings: 2.

75. Duke, S. (2013), *The European External Action Service and Public Diplomacy*, Discussion Papers in Diplomacy, No. 127, Netherlands Institute of International Relations, The Hague: 25.

76. Michalski, A. (2005), "The EU as a Soft Power: The Force of Persuasion," in Melissen, J. (ed.), *The New Public Diplomacy: Soft Power in International Relations*, Basingstoke: Palgrave Macmillan: 125.

77. Brewer, M. B. (2001), "The Many Faces of Social Identity: Implications for Political Psychology," *Political Psychology*, 22(1): 115–125.

78. Hogg, M. A. and Abrams, D. (1988), *Social Identification: A Social Psychology of Intergroup Relations and Group Process*, New York: Routledge.

79. Ammaturo, F. R. (2018), "Europe and Whiteness: Challenges to European Identity and European Citizenship in Light of Brexit and the 'Refugees/Migrants Crisis,'" *European Journal of Social Theory*: 5. DOI:10.1177/1368431018783318.

80. Martinelli, A. (2017), "The European Identity," *Glocalism: Journal of Culture, Politics and Innovation*, 23. DOI: 10.12893/gjcpi.2017.2.11.

81. Fligstein, N., Polyakova, A., and Sandholtz, W. (2012), "European Identity, Nationalism and European Identity," *JCMS: Journal of Common Market Studies*, 50(1): 107.

82. Kuhn, T. (2012), "Why Educational Programmes Miss Their Mark: Cross-border Mobility, Education and European Identity," *Journal of Common Market Studies*, 50(6): 994–1010.

83. Sigalas, E. (2009), *Does ERASMUS Student Mobility Promote a European Identity?* Webpapers on Constitutionalism and Governance beyond the State, Institute for European Integration Research, Vienna, No. 2.

84. Mitchell, K. (2015), "Rethinking the 'Erasmus Effect' of European Identity," *Journal of Common Market Studies*, 53(2): 331.

85. Kuhn, T. (2012), "Why Educational Programmes Miss Their Mark: Cross-border Mobility, Education and European Identity," *Journal of Common Market Studies*, 50(6): 994.

86. Bergbauer, S. (2018), *Explaining European Identity Formation: Citizens' Attachment from Maastricht Treaty to Crisis*, Switzerland: Springer Nature, 27.

87. Philippou, S., Keating, A., and Ortloff, D. H. (2009), "Citizenship Education Curricula: Comparing the Multiple Meanings of Supra-national Citizenship in Europe and Beyond," *Journal of Curriculum Studies*, 41(2): 291–299.

88. Verhaegen, S., and Hooghe, M. (2015), "Does more Knowledge about the European Union Lead to a Stronger European Identity? A Comparative Analysis among Adolescents in 21 European Member States," *Innovation: The European Journal of Social Science Research*, 28(2): 127.

89. Shore, C. (2000), *Building Europe: The Cultural Politics of European Integration*, London and New York: Routledge: 28.

90. Field, H. (2001), *European Integration Curricula and "Europeanisation": Alternative Approaches and Critical Appreciation*, paper presented to the ECSA Seventh Biennial International Conference, May 31–June 2, 2001, Madison: Wisconsin: 1.

91. Baroncelli, S. (2014), "Linguistic Pluralism in European Studies," in Baroncelli, S., et al. (eds.), *Teaching and Learning the European Union*, New York and London: Springer: 144.

92. Osler, A., and Starkey, H. (1999), "Rights, Identities and Inclusion: European Action Programmes as Political Education," *Oxford Review of Education*, 25(1–2): 202.

93. Duke, S. (2013), *The European External Action Service and Public Diplomacy*, Discussion Papers in Diplomacy, No. 127, Netherlands Institute of International Relations, The Hague: 3.

94. Duke, S. (2013), *The European External Action Service and the Quest for an Effective Public Diplomacy*, Analysis No. 216, December. Available at http://www.ispionline.it/sites/default/files/pubblicazioni/analysis_216_2013.pdf, [accessed Aug. 16, 2015]: 7.

95. Knight, J. (2014), *The Limits of Soft Power in Higher Education*, University World News, 31st Jan., available at: http://www.universityworldnews.com/article.php?story=20140129134636725, [accessed May 31, 2014]

96. Kirkland, J. (2014), *Soft Power in Higher Education: Friend or Foe?* The Association of Commonwealth Universities, available at: https://www.acu.ac.uk/news-events/blog/soft-power-higher-education, [accessed May 31, 2014].

97. Peterson, P. M. (2013), *Global Higher Education as a Reflection of International Relations*, European Association for International Education Conference, 12th Sept., Istanbul.

98. Chapman, D. W. (2009), "Education Reform and Capacity Development in Higher Education," in Hirosato, Y. and Kitamura, Y. (eds.), *The Political Economy of Educational Reforms and Capacity Development in Southeast Asia Education in the Asia-Pacific Region: Issues, Concerns and Prospects,* Vol. 13, London: Springer: 104.

99. Tomusk, V. (2007), "Pizza Bolognese a la Russe: The Promise and Peril of the Bologna Process in Russia," in Tomusk, V. (ed.), *Creating the European Area of Higher Education: Voices from the Periphery*, Dordrecht: Springer: 229.

100. Marie Sklodowska-Curie actions support researchers at all stages of their careers, irrespective of nationality. Researchers including industrial doctorates working across all disciplines are eligible for funding.

101. Tempus is the European Union's program which supports the modernization of higher education in the Partner Countries of Eastern Europe, Central Asia, the Western Balkans, and the Mediterranean region, mainly through university cooperation projects.

102. Polglase, G. (2013), "Higher Education as Soft Power in the Eastern Partnership: The Case of Belarus," *Eastern Journal of European Studies*, 4(2): 111.

103. Michalski, A. (2012), "China and the EU: Conceptual Gaps in Soft Power," in Pan, Z. (ed.), *Conceptual Gaps in China-EU Relations*, Hampshire and New York: Palgrave Macmillan: 72.

104. NAFSA: Association of International Educators (2003), *In America's Interest: Welcoming International Students*, available at: http://www.nafsa.org/Resource_Library_Assets/Public_Policy/In_America_s_Interest__Welcoming_International_Students/, [accessed May 27, 2014]: 5.

105. Nye, J. (2004), *Soft Power: The Means to Success in World Politics*, New York: Public Affairs: 43.

106. European Commission (2013), *European Higher Education in the World, Communication from the Commission to the European Parliament, the Council, The European Economic and Social Committee and the Committee of the Region*, COM (2013) 499 final, 7th September 2013, Brussels.

107. Tulmets, E. (2007), "Can the Discourse on 'Soft Power' Help the EU to Bridge its Capability-Expectation Gap?" *European Political Economy Review*, No.7: 216–217.

108. Versluys, H. (2009), "European Union Humanitarian Aid: Lifesaver or Political Tool?" In Jan Orbie, (ed.) *Europe's Global Role: External Policies of the European Union*, Hampshire: Ashgate Publishing Limited: 112.

109. EEAS (2014), *Foreign Policy*, available at: http://www.eeas.europa.eu/poli cies/index_en.htm, [accessed May 4, 2014].

110. Hill, C. (2010), "Cheque and Balances: The European Union's Soft Power Strategy," in Parmar, I. and Cox, M. (eds.), *Soft Power and US Foreign Policy: Theoretical, Historical and Contemporary Perspectives*, London: Routledge: 184.

111. Smith, K. E. (2014), "Is the European Union's Soft Power in Decline?" *Current History*, March: 105.

112. Antoniades, A., O'Loughlin, B. and Miskimmon, A. (2010), *Great Power Politics and Strategic Narratives*, March, Working Paper, No. 7, The Centre for Global Political Economy of Sussex: 14.

113. Gilardi, F. (2012), "Transnational Diffusion: Norms, Ideas, and Polices," in Carlsnaes, W. Risse, T. and Simmons, B. (eds.), *Handbook of International Relations, 2nd edition*, Thousand Oaks: Sage Publication: 22.

114. Peerenboom, R. (2002*), China's Long March toward Rule of Law*, Cambridge: Cambridge University Press: 6.

115. Mattlin, M. (2012), "Dead on Arrival: Normative EU Policy towards China," *Asia Europe Journal*, 10(2): 181.

116. Antoniades, A., O'Loughlin, B. and Miskimmon, A. (2010), *Great Power Politics and Strategic Narratives*, March, Working Paper, No. 7, The Centre for Global Political Economy of Sussex: 14.

117. Interview with Professor H in Chengdu, Dec. 17, 2013.

118. Tang, S., Zhang, J. and Cao, X. (2005), "Zhongguo De Diqu Yanjiu: Chengjiu, Chaju He Qidai," *Shijie Jingji Yu Zhengzhi*, (Area Studies in China: Achievements, Deficiencies, and Prospects, *World Economics and Politics*), No. 11: 10.

119. Chen, Z. and Song, L. (2012), "The Conceptual Gap in Soft Power between China and Europe and its Impact on Bilateral Relations," in Pan, Z. (ed.), *Conceptual Gaps in China-EU Relations*, Hampshire and New York: Palgrave Macmillan: 53.

120. Vuving, A. L. (2009), *How Soft Power Works* Paper presented at the panel "Soft Power and Smart Power," American Political Science Associate Annual Meeting, 3rd Sept., Toronto: 13.

121. Nye, J. (2010), *The Future of Power*, New York: Public Affairs: 84.

122. De Lombaerde, P., Söderbaum, F., Van Langehove, L., and Baert, F. (2010), "The Problem of Comparison in Comparative Regionalism," *Review of International Studies*, 36(3): 732.

123. Pamment, J. (2014), "Strategic Narratives in US Public Diplomacy: A Critical Geopolitics," *Popular Communication*, 12(1): 50.

124. Barrinha, A. (2016), "Progressive Realism and the EU's International Actorness: Towards a Grand Strategy?" *Journal of European Integration*, 38(4): 441.

125. Duke, S. (2013), *The European External Action Service and the Quest for an Effective Public Diplomacy*, Analysis No. 216, December. Available at http://www. ispionline.it/sites/default/files/pubblicazioni/analysis_216_2013.pdf, [accessed Aug. 16, 2015]: 7.

126. Song, X. (2010), "European 'Models' and Their Implications to China: Internal and External Perspectives," *Review of International Studies*, 36(03): 765–774.

127. Chen, Z. and Song, L. (2012), "The Conceptual Gap in Soft Power between China and Europe and its Impact on Bilateral Relations," in Pan, Z. (ed.), *Conceptual Gaps in China-EU Relations*, Hampshire and New York: Palgrave Macmillan: 52–53.

128. Ibid: 57

129. Michalski, A. (2012), "China and the EU: Conceptual Gaps in Soft Power," in Pan, Z. (ed.), *Conceptual Gaps in China-EU Relations*, Hampshire and New York: Palgrave Macmillan: 77.

130. Ibid.

131. Crookes, Paul C. I. (2014), "EU Soft Power with China: Technical Assistance in the Field of Intellectual Property Rights," *European Foreign Affairs Review*, 19 (3/1), Special Issues: 83.

132. Small, A. (2011), "Cooperation between China and the EU in the UN Security Council (1)," in *EU-China: Close Cooperation on the Multilateral Agenda*, EU-China Policy Dialogues Support Facility, July: 44–48.

133. Chen, Z. (2012), "Europe as a Global Player: A View from China," *Perspectives*, 20(2): 8.

134. Crookes, Paul C. I. (2014), "EU Soft Power with China: Technical Assistance in the Field of Intellectual Property Rights," *European Foreign Affairs Review*, 19 (3/1), Special Issues: 84.

135. Manners, I. and Whitman, R. (2013), "Normative Power and Future of EU Public Diplomacy," in Mai'a K. Davis Cross & Melissen, J. (eds.), *European Public Diplomacy: Soft Power at Work*, Hampshire: Palgrave Macmillan: 195–196.

136. Wallström, M. (2008), *Public Diplomacy and its Role in the EU's External Relations*, Mortara Center for International Studies, Georgetown University, available at: http://europa.eu/rapid/press-release_SPEECH-08-494_en.pdf, [accessed 03-04-2015]: 3.

137. Manners, I. and Whitman, R. (2013), "Normative Power and Future of EU Public Diplomacy," in Mai'a K. Davis Cross & Melissen, J. (eds.), *European Public Diplomacy: Soft Power at Work*, Hampshire: Palgrave Macmillan: 194.

138. Nye, J. (2010), *The Future of Power*, New York: Public Affairs: 163.

139. Nye, J. (2011), *Why Europe Is and Will Remain, Powerful?* Utopian.org. available at: http://www.the-utopian.org/post/2424081389/why-europe-is-and-will -remain-powerful, [accessed May 11, 2015].

140. Cross, Mai'a K. D. and Melissen, J. (2013), "Introduction," in Mai'a K. Davis Cross & Jan Melissen (eds.), *European Public Diplomacy: Soft Power at Work*, Hampshire: Palgrave Macmillan: xviii.

Chapter Five

The Jean Monnet Programme in China

Following our attempts to understand the relationship between the Jean Monnet Programme and public diplomacy as well as its contribution to the EU's descriptive and normative knowledge dissemination, this chapter presents the Jean Monnet Programme as EU public diplomacy practice in the target countries. This research takes its practice in China as a case, so its implementation in China will be discussed based on interviews with Chinese professors and EU officials in Beijing and Brussels since these two groups know well of the implementation of the Jean Monnet Programme from the perspectives of implementers and participants. Interviewing people from these two groups will help map the development path of this program in China, and the data collected from each of them complement each other by looking at the implementation of this program from different standpoints.

The Jean Monnet Programme was officially extended to non-EU states in 2001, and China was one of the first countries to be included in the program. Even before the official worldwide extension, the Jean Monnet Programme had already been deployed in Poland and Hungary in 1993 and the Czech Republic in 1997 before these countries became EU member states.[1] Although there is a clear qualitative difference between China and those candidate countries that aimed to eventually become member states of the EU, contact with the units in charge of the Jean Monnet Programme in those candidate countries provided examples for the administrative units to deal with new countries covered by the program outside of the EU. In its first three years (1990–1993), over 3000 applications had been received.[2] By 2011, over 3,000 projects had been implemented in 72 countries, which meant that the worldwide extension had already gained some experience.[3]

The Jean Monnet Programme aimed initially to bring the European project to EU citizens through an academic approach. Yet, the success of the Jean

Monnet Action in member states of the European Community in its first few years attracted more countries that had not yet gained formal membership. In 1993, financial support was extended to applicants from Poland and Hungary, and to the Czech Republic in 1997, when Leo Tindemans became the new president of the European University Council for the Jean Monnet Action. These three countries were candidate states of the European Community at that time.[4] More importantly, after getting into contact with the University Information Unit before officially joining the European Union, the professors in Hungary not only got financial support from the Jean Monnet Action for their research and studies about the European project, but it also helped them become involved in the process that led to Hungary joining the EU in 2004. Professor Péter Balázs, who was working in Hungary, agreed in an interview that "the Jean Monnet Programme played an invaluable role in this, albeit in a manner that is difficult to quantify."[5]

Di Fonzo, a former project manager of the Jean Monnet Programme, noted that promoting the Jean Monnet Programme to non-EU member states had already been set in motion before the official decision was made.

> The Jean Monnet Programme had been successfully implemented in Poland, Hungary and the Czech Republic before these countries joined the EU family, which meant the programme managers at that time had been thinking of promoting this programme to non-EU member states. However, the new target groups required changed budget and relevant decisions from the Parliament. Suddenly, in 2001, a new budget about the Jean Monnet Programme with enlarged target groups had been raised and approved eventually.[6]

Although promoting the Jean Monnet Programme to non-EU member states in 2001 was largely dependent on the visionary EU leaders who were in power, some other factors might also have accelerated this process. William Fingleton, Press Officer in the Delegation of the EU to China, stated that the EU's global strategy, which was released around 2001 required the EU to start communicating the EU to the outside world, which then resulted in the promotion of the Jean Monnet Programme in China.[7] In fact, the policy documents mentioned by Fingleton included a Commission proposal released in 2001 which contained a strategic framework for EU-Asia relations and stressed the core objectives of "strengthening the EU's political and economic presence across the region, and raising this to a level commensurate with the growing global weight of an enlarged EU," as well as a policy paper dealing specifically with China in 2003.[8, 9] Therefore, the promotion of the Jean Monnet Programme can be attributed to a small group of leaders and also the EU's requirement of enhancing its global presence.

It is unreasonable to discuss the effect of the Jean Monnet Programme by separating it from other relevant academic programs or isolating it from the academic environment of European studies in China. Although launching this program in China emanated from the EU's requirement of increasing the knowledge of the EU by boosting teaching and research activities worldwide and promoting European integration with intellectual support, the development of this program was deeply rooted in the academic sphere of China and China's internal motivation of learning from advanced western countries.

5.1 THE CHINESE CONTEXT FOR EUROPEAN STUDIES

The Jean Monnet Programme started its practice in EU member states over 25 years ago and has been implemented in China for over 15 years, but the Chinese context within which this program has been practiced in qualitatively different from EU member states or even other non-EU member states covered by this program beyond EU borders. The Jean Monnet Programme as an educational program in China aims to support Chinese professors to do research on and deliver knowledge of the EU to college students, which helps the EU enhance its soft power in China.

According to the introduction of the Jean Monnet Programme, researching and teaching the integration process of Europe from economic, political, and social aspects, is one of the most important objectives of this program. Put differently, knowledge dissemination is the first and foremost concern of this program. During this process, EU norms as an integral part of the knowledge and information regarding the EU have also been delivered through the teaching and learning process.[10] Thus, in this research, the EU's knowledge dissemination in China includes descriptive and normative knowledge dissemination. The descriptive knowledge of the EU referring to the facts of the EU such as its history, development, and current status has been taught and researched in higher education institutions since China keeps drawing different lessons from the EU, which will be testified by the interview results analyzed in chapters 6 and 7. The EU's normative knowledge dissemination in China might tell a different reality considering China has a different understanding of EU norms and does not agree with the "universality of values."

As previously mentioned, EU norms that are also termed as "Western values" in China, constitute an integral part of EU soft power, which are also needed to be addressed as normative knowledge of the EU in classroom teaching. However, the EU's norm diffusion to China has not been regarded as a successfully story.[11] The 1648 Peace of Westphalia established the idea that sovereign states are the only legitimate actors of international politics, and on top of that, states are equal and free to choose its own social, political, and economic system which should not be interfered by other countries. The liberalism has been further developed in the twentieth century under the leadership of the US by introducing a notion of moral universalism, based on the liberal values of democracy and human rights.[12] The relationship between China and the norms will lead to two assumptions: one is that China will accept economic and political norms based on liberalism and eventually becomes a part of the system; the other is that China will turn to be a radically different kind of superpower than any that we have witnessed so far through bringing a different ideological system, so China will rely on notions of Chinese essentialism instead of accepting the idea of the "universality of norms."[13] Based on these two different assumptions, China might replace the existing liberal world order if the former one stands, but China might prefer coexistence of different values if the latter one is tenable.

Moreover, China is always cautious about the EU's attempts in diffusing its norms to China, since stressing the universality of norms in international politics has been used as "weapons" for the intended social or regime changes by Western countries around the world. As argued by some scholars, the "China-EU relationship conflicts in ideology and values still remain" and that the EU's norm diffusion activities could be an "attempt to Westernize and disintegrate China," calling for China's "counter-measures."[14, 15] China has not adopted the European norms such as freedom, democracy and human rights simply by arguing that these norms are not entirely applicable to the Chinese reality. Although it is argued that EU norm (also Western norms or universal values) are just the values of Western capitalism,[16] China does not intend to reform the existing international order with new norms as an alternative. In other words, China stresses variety of norms in international politics and believes that each country should follow their own development path, meaning that the EU and China can co-exist by admitting and respecting each other's normative standings.

Following different understandings of universal norms between the EU and China, citizenship education emphasized by the Chinese government also challenges the EU's norm diffusion. As a common convention in all countries, citizenship education serves as a tool preparing the citizens for the political and social life of a country, which matters even more since citizenship education plays an important role in sustaining regime legitimacy in the Chinese context. Therefore, the Chinese government always highlights official guidance on school education under the name of "ideological and political education [sixiang zhengzhi jiaoyu]." The Chinese Communist Party—the ruling party of China—portrays these Western values as unsuitable for China and claims that western ideas and values are "dangerous," "subversive" and a threat to Chinese's social stability,[17] particularly for young students as showed in the Tiananmen Square Issue of 1989.[18]

Thus, in December 2013, an official document has been circulated among high-ranking party cadres warning of negative impacts of Western norms within Chinese society. The document listed "seven perils" considered by the Chinese high-level officials as present threats to its authority, so it cannot be discussed in Chinese colleges based on a set of instructions in this document (known as "Seven Speak-Nots").[19] However, since this document was never made public, there were different versions of the so-called "Seven Speak-Nots." Veg indicates that the "Seven Speak-Nots" includes constitutional democracy, universal values, civil society, market liberalism, media independence, criticizing errors in the history of the Party ("historical nihilism"), and questioning the policy of opening up and reform and the socialist nature of the regime;[20] while Godement states that the "Seven Speak-Nots" consists of "universal values, freedom of the press, civil society, civil rights, mistakes made in the history of the Chinese Communist Party, the bourgeois elites, the independence of the judiciary,"[21] which is the same as the content of a news report appeared in *New York Times*.[22]

News reports about the "Seven Speak-Nots" appeared in Western media attracted public discussion since these regulations may silence the liberal voices,[23] but no academic publication regarding these new regulations has been published since it may take a while to discuss its influence. Irrespective of different versions of the "Seven Speak-Nots," "universal values" as one of the seven things that cannot be talked about in higher education institutions in China seems contradictory to the EU's normative knowledge dissemination in Chinese classroom.[24] As Chinese students disagreed with the professors who criticized the practice of EU norms or Western values in China[25] and foreign professors also stated that they can talk about universal norms in Chinese universities,[26] how governmental regulations, particularly the "Seven Speak-Nots" influence the EU's normative knowledge dissemination needs more analysis.

In this sense, understanding the Chinese context for the implementation of the Jean Monnet Programme needs to address two aspects: one is that the EU's knowledge dissemination, particularly the EU's normative knowledge dissemination, is the first step of norm diffusion; the other is that these norms emphasized by the EU engender different understandings in the context of China, and that may contradict classroom teaching of EU norms, albeit upholding the norm and emphasising the role of norms in China's transition to an open society is a priority of the EU's China policy.[27] As one associate professor said, teaching European integration cannot skip the knowledge of EU norms,[28] so the EU's knowledge dissemination, including the EU's descriptive and normative knowledge, will be studied with empirical data in chapters 6 and 7 respectively, in order to fully address the Chinese context for the implementation of the Jean Monnet Programme.

5.2 EU PUBLIC DIPLOMACY IN CHINA AND EU-CHINA EDUCATION COOPERATION

In terms of the actors of EU public diplomacy to China, the European Union's Delegation is a major player in EU public diplomacy.[29, 30] Before the Treaty of Lisbon came into force, most Commission Delegations were mere information offices or agencies of the EU carrying out some EU programs in the host countries. However, over the past decades, particularly in the post-Lisbon era, the Delegation of the EU has taken over a growing number of classical diplomatic tasks.[31] According to Fingleton, the delegation of the EU works for the implementation of EU programmes in China by cooperating with the Chinese governments at different levels and the embassies of EU member states.[32] The increasing importance of the EU's delegation to China reflects the widening and deepening of EU integration for diplomatic representation on the one hand while on the other hand it addresses Jean Monnet's claim that Europe needs to create an identity for itself overseas.[33]

When it comes to the role of the Delegation of the EU to China, in a conference on "*the Wisdom of Public Diplomacy: the dialogue among Chinese, American and European scholars*," William Fingleton, the Press Officer of the Delegation of the EU to China, stated that the EU's public diplomacy to China is conducted through four approaches: cooperation, sharing, participation, and communication. According to Fingleton, the public diplomacy practice of the EU's Delegation to China aims to get people to think about Europe and to realize the relevance of Europe in their lives.[34] Additionally, EU public diplomacy carried out by the Delegation of the EU to China involves daily communication in terms of press conferences that explain EU policies and rapid response to misinformation or crises; strategic communication on broader issues such as climate change, trade policy; people-to-people diplomacy through scholarships, cultural exchange, and training.[35]

Besides, based on a study on Chinese media outlets (*CCTV1, People's Daily, China Daily and International Finance News*), the Chinese mass media is a vital channel for Chinese people to learn about the EU since it has provided extensive coverage of European integration and development, high-level meetings, and development of bilateral relationships[36] and according to Li's 2006 finding, most of the reports under examination are objective and mild in tone, helping Chinese people develop clear perceptions of the EU.[37]

Based on the research conducted in China, the news coverage about the EU in the Chinese media including newspapers and TV news (the reports about the EU in newspapers are more extensive than that in TV news) is mainly neutral and stresses the role of the EU in the world due to its achievements of regional integration rather than its internal issues.[38] It is consistent with scholarly research that China is probably the most supportive "great power" on the European integration.[39]

However, the news reports about the EU in the Chinese mass media may also be affected by international relations and Chinese external relations. For instance, according to Ma, EU news in the Chinese media is marginalized because EU-China relations are still constrained and overshadowed by US-China relations.[40] Moreover, the representation of the EU in Chinese newspapers is localized and fits in with Chinese "domestic discourse,"[41] meaning that EU-China relations have an impact on the news reports of the EU in the Chinese mass media. Besides, Chinese college students do not use Chinese mass media as their main information sources of the EU.[42]

Nevertheless, it does not mean that the messages of the EU have been manipulated or interpreted by Chinese media to make it consistent with the official discourse of the EU. In fact, the EU has never lost its control over information dissemination of the EU in its public diplomacy practice. The official website of the Delegation of the EU to China, its official Weibo account and the interviews with EU officials working in China released in the Chinese media provide other ways for the EU to engage Chinese students and public directly. Besides, cultural and educational events highlighted in EU Weibo account help Chinese students and the Chinese public gain information of the EU beyond government controlled approaches. All these factors explain that the messages of the EU can be disseminated through both Chinese and EU approaches, which will be further explored in chapter 6.

Besides identifying the main sources of information about the EU for the Chinese Public, discussing the public diplomacy function of the Jean Monnet Programme in China cannot be isolated from the environment in which it is practiced, so we will briefly review the development of European studies as a research area and academic subject in China.

Before this program was officially implemented in China in 2001, European studies had been carried out by Chinese scholars in different institutions, but studying Europe has internal reasons. Song Xinning and Dai Bingran, the only two Jean Monnet Chairs "Ad Personam" in China, work at Renmin University of China and Fudan University respectively. In fact, Dai produced the first translation of European Community Treaties in Chinese and some important books on EU-China relations[43] and was the only person awarded the Jean Monnet Prize in Asia in 2008.[44] Song is the founding director of the Jean Monnet Centre of Excellence at Renmin University of China.[45]

Song and Dai divide the development history of European studies in China into four phases but with some slight differences. These four phases are the 1950s–1960s, the 1970s to 1980s, the 1990s, and the 2000s according to Song[46] while Dai considers them to be the 1950s–1960s; 1960s–1970s, 1970s–1990s, and the late 1990s to the present.[47] However, these two opinions arise largely from personal preference and experience rather than any difference in background knowledge.

Both Song and Dai agree that the first phase was the 1950s–1960s. During this period, Chinese scholars viewed western European countries as a part of the Imperial camp led by the US and there was little serious research on European integration.[48, 49] However, lack of public attention did not mean that there were no European studies at all because closed-circulation and classified studies were carried out within the Communist Party, government and the organs of the intelligence service. Two important research institutions, the Chinese Institute of International Studies (CIIS) in Beijing and the Shanghai Institute for International Studies (SIIS) were established with some pioneer research on the "capitalist world," which benefited the government and started to circulate among university scholars in the early 1960s.[50]

According to Dai, the second phase was from 1960s to 1970s because academic—as distinct from "governmental"—studies of Europe began in this period, followed by the decision of the high-level leaders in Beijing that Peking University and Renmin University of China in Beijing and Fudan University in Shanghai were instructed to do research on "the developing world," "the socialist world," and "the capitalist world" respectively.[51] Since academic research on Europe officially started, albeit under government instruction, 1960–1970 can be considered as an independent period. However, the early years of the period were interrupted by the "Cultural Revolution."

This situation changed in the third phase of the 1970s and 1980s after Richard Nixon's visit to China in 1972 and the establishment of formal diplomatic relations between China and Western European countries, and the first research institution was established at Fudan University in 1977. A book, entitled *the Western European Common Market*, was produced by a group of scholars from Fudan University and was probably the first academic work on the European Community in China.[52] During this period, due to China's reform and opening-up policy, western European countries were regarded as examples for China's economic and political reform. In other words, studying individual European countries and their implications for Chinese development occupied the mainstream of European studies. More importantly, a series of teaching programs on European studies were launched in Chinese universities although European studies was then taught in different disciplines rather than as an independent subject.[53]

In the fourth phase of the 1990s China's European studies flourished due to several reasons: the EU's sanctions including an arms embargo toward China after the 1989 Tiananmen event made Chinese scholars realize the strength of EU collective action; the process of European integration progressed quickly after the Maastricht and Amsterdam Treaties; and the EU's first China strategy set out by the European Commission in 1995 offered a new direction for EU-China relations after 1989. With the coming of the twenty-first century, European studies in China highlighted EU-China relations and comparative regional integration studies, which meant that China's European studies came closer to EU studies.[54] Zhou Hong, Director of the Institute of European studies at Chinese Academy of Social Science, regarded European studies as being an academic discipline that has been developing very fast after the establishment of the European Union in 1992. With its enlarging geographical area and increasing international reputation, the EU is not far from China and the Chinese people,[55] requiring more research and understanding of the EU. The history of European studies in China tells us that they are rooted in the requirement of learning from the development experience of advanced countries, which in turn makes the EU's public diplomacy program under the guise of promoting European studies worldwide more easily localized in China.

Based on China's desire to learn from advanced countries and the EU's willingness to promote European studies to the outside world, the EU's international education cooperation with China has been in progress for around twenty years. The first program was the EU-China HECP of 1998–2001 (HECP), which was followed by the EU-China ESCP, 2004–2007. Those two programs laid a solid foundation for contemporary EU studies in China. The EU-China HECP was then the largest foreign aid to higher education in China (nearly a million Euros) because it supported research and mobility from more than 50 universities and helped increase the number of established European studies centers to 14 nationwide. The ESCP, which increased its total investment to over a million Euros, concentrated on the 14 existing centers and started two new ones.[56]

From the documents produced by EuropeAid, there were various achievements in China during the implementation of EU-China ESCP, including two new centers, four teaching programs, 50 Chinese scholars' fieldwork in Europe, 122 European scholars' courses and speeches in China. Seventeen monographs and 60 articles were published, and 10 international conferences and 17 workshops involving more than 700 participants were held by EU-China ESCP grantees.[57] Two of the Jean Monnet professors in Mainland China who were also sponsored by these programs stated that most of the scholars who started researching Europe and European integration during these twenty years had benefited from the programs which had a remarkable influence on the disciplinary development of European studies in China.[58] In 2012, the EU-China High Level People-to-People Dialogue (HPPD) was launched in Brussels EU Commissioner Androulla Vassiliou and China's State Councillor Liu Yandong, which represented a "third pillar" in the relations between the two partners, building on the two previous ones—the High Level Strategic Dialogue ("first pillar") and the High Level Economic and Trade Dialogue ("second pillar").

As a result of the first round of the HPPD, a series of follow-up actions in education, language, culture, and youth issues were agreed by leaders from both sides, and the EU-China Higher Education Platform for Cooperation and Exchange (HEPCE) was launched as a priority by the EU and China to promote future cooperation in the area of education.[59] From the review of Chinese European studies and the brief history of EU-China higher education cooperation, it is easy to tell that the achievements of European studies in China and EU-China higher education can be attributed to the needs and motivations of both sides.

The implementation of the Jean Monnet Programme started after the EU-China HECP but before the EU-China ESCP, and, benefiting from the first program, two Chinese academics became Jean Monnet professors after the Jean Monnet Programme was extended to non-EU countries in 2001.[60] After the EU-China ESCP, the Jean Monnet Programme was the only academic program that sponsored European studies in China, which, as one director indicated, was an indispensable motivation for China's European studies,[61] considering the competitiveness of applying for governmental funding for EU studies in China.[62] As of 2014, there are two Jean Monnet Chairs "Ad Personam," fifteen Jean Monnet Chairs, three Jean Monnet Centres, eleven Modules as well as other relevant activities being carried out in mainland China.[63] Although the previous two programs were implemented within the framework of EuropeAid by the DG Development and Cooperation in European Commission while the Jean Monnet Programme was deployed and carried out the DG EAC, they all supported European studies in China and the latter was developed on the basis of the previous two programs. In other words, the three programs supporting Chinese European studies had an inheritance relationship.

The fieldwork which was used to collect data about the status of Jean Monnet Centres, classroom teaching, hosting academic conferences, and the students' feedback was conducted in three Jean Monnet Centres of Excellence in China.

5.3 THE IMPLEMENTATION OF THE JEAN MONNET PROGRAMME IN CHINA

Since the EACEA started taking charge of the Jean Monnet Programme, most historical archives and documents about this program and its practice in China can be found in its publications. To date, over 40 projects including Jean Monnet Centres of Excellence, Jean Monnet Chairs "Ad Personam," Jean Monnet Chairs, and Jean Monnet Modules and several other academic activities have been sponsored by the Jean Monnet Programme in mainland China. According to Vito Borrelli,

> China is by far the most active Asian country in the field of European Integration studies in the context of the Jean Monnet Activities and the growing interest of Chinese institutions in this field of study is reflected in the steep increase of applications over recent years.
>
> Under the 2014 call for proposals, 5 projects were selected from a total of seven applications submitted, representing a 71% success rate in the current selection year and continuing a trend established over recent years (application selected between 2008–2013 totalling 21 out of 41 submitted).[64]

However, because of their different backgrounds, these three centers have distinct characteristics.

1). The Centre for European Studies at Renmin University of China (RUC) was officially established in 1994 under the name of Centre for European Community Document and Research from 1994 to 1996. It was selected as one of the partner institutes in China supported by the EU-China HECP and undertook 116 projects including academic research, scholarly exchange, academic conferences and curriculum development. It was also selected as one of the target institutes sponsored by EU-China ESCP. This university-based research center houses top scholars working in different areas of European studies and provides high-level research output, but since it was affiliated with the Department of International Studies before it became a university-based center with an annual budget and separate office facilities, the Centre for European Studies at RUC specialises in EU politics and foreign policy. This Centre was officially named as "the Jean Monnet Centre of Excellence" by the DG EAC of the European Commission in 2005, and was one of ten Jean Monnet Centres in non-EU member states.[65]

The Jean Monnet Centre of Excellence at RUC has three approaches to training including curriculum setting in different disciplines, international student exchange, and training European students. Based on official data of 2012 released on its website, this center trained college students at the undergraduate, postgraduate, and PhD levels from different schools. At the School of International Studies, this center helped train 24 undergraduate students, 35 postgraduate students, and 18 PhD students. It offers courses given by professors from the School of International Studies, including *Theory and Practice of Regional Integration, Comparative Regional Integration, Frontier of International Issues, Germany and European Integration, Germany and France in the Context of European Integration*, etc. Also, professors from the School of Economics and Law offer courses such as *Studies on Regional Economy, the History of Western Economic Thought, International Law, Anglo-American Law, Roman law*, and so on.

In terms of international student exchange, the center also endeavors to sponsor Chinese students to study in European universities as well as recruit European students to be trained at RUC. In 2012, 17 students at different levels from the School of International Studies were sent to European universities while 39 European students started their study and research at RUC and 5 graduated. International student exchange helps Chinese students broaden their horizon and get to know international rules, and it also assists future generations from the EU to know China better.[66]

2). The Centre for European Studies at Fudan University (FDU) dates back to the Department of European Community Research which was the first research institute for European Studies in China affiliated to Fudan's Institute of World Economy, and the Centre was finally established in 1993 with its current name and structure, under the aegis of the School of Economics at FDU.[67] FDU has a long history of European studies. An institute was created in 1964 to carry out studies on developed economies with a focus on western European countries and was renamed "the Institute of World Economy" in the 1970s. Almost simultaneously, a European Community Research Office was set up alongside other research offices on the German, French, and UK economies. Therefore, the Centre for European studies is better known for its research on the European economy and monetary system albeit it also attracts many scholars from other schools at FDU.[68] This Centre also obtained financial support from the previous two programs and was selected as "the Jean Monnet Centre of Excellence" by the DG EAC in 2005.

Although the center at FDU is based at the School of Economics, it also brings professors of different subjects together and conducts a series of interdisciplinary research programs. Since the 1970s, its predecessor has been undertaking research projects, publishing research achievements, and offering postgraduate teaching programmes and editing the Journal of European Integration Studies. More importantly, it initiated direct contact with European Community institutions in the late 1970s and the European Commission established its first European Documentation Centre (EDC) in China at FDU. Currently, this center offers BA, MA, and PhD courses, including *European*

Economic and Political Integration, EU Politics and Foreign Relations, European Monetary Integration and Euro, the Single European Market, EU's Trade Politics and External Trade Relations, Social Security and Social Policy in EU and Its Member States, Introduction to International Politics and Economics, etc. New courses are being developed and will be available to students, including *Seminar on European Union Enlargement, Foreign Relationship of the European Union, European Social Security System, European National Economy and Contemporary Germany Economy.*[69]

The center at FDU also lists the monographs and translation works of the resident researchers. Although it seems that the list has not been updated for a while, their publications cover a wide range of topics related to EU studies, such as *Common Security Policies of the EU and its Coordination with the US, States and Supra-states—Comparative Study of European Integration Theory, International Trade and International Finance.*[70]

3). The Centre for European studies at Sichuan University (SCU) is the youngest "Jean Monnet Centre of Excellence" in China, awarded by the DG EAC in 2011. Differing from the other two centres, the European Studies centre at SCU is affiliated with the School of Foreign Languages and Cultures, and therefore, European studies at SCU concentrates on interdisciplinary and multi-area research with a focus on literature, culture, and religion. Since it has become one of the Jean Monnet Centres of Excellence, the European Studies center at SCU has undertaken two research projects from the DG EAC: *Diversity in Unity: European Integration and European Social Development*; and *On European Cultural Diversity in the Context of European Integration: History, Culture and Ideology in European Identification.* It also offers compulsory and elective courses to college students from different levels, such as *History of European Thought, European Cultures and European Integration, European Identification and European Integration,* as well as *European Economic Integration.*[71] It is insufficient to study European integration and the European Union without paying enough attention to its political and economic aspects, but the exchange of scholars, academic conferences, and young scholar training supplement this deficiency.[72] According to the news reports released on the website of the Jean Monnet Centre of Excellence at SCU, student and scholar exchange between SCU and universities in China and abroad are quite frequent.

As the only three Jean Monnet centers in Mainland China with 15 Jean Monnet Chairs in total, understanding its history and its research areas is a prerequisite for conducting fieldwork and analyzing the data. To summarize, according to the Jean Monnet Programme selection results (2008–2012) and the interview with Vito Borrelli, combined with the project directory, Chinese scholars and research centers that have obtained funding under this program for their research on European integration and other topics related to European study are shown in the following tables.

Table 5.1. Chinese Universities covered by the Jean Monnet Programme

China University of Political Science and Law, Beijing

Fudan University, Shanghai

Guangdong University of Foreign Studies, Guangzhou

Macau University

Nankai University, Tianjin

Renmin University of China, Beijing

Sichuan University, Chengdu

Tongji University, Shanghai

Tsinghua University, Beijing

Wuhan University, Wuhan

Source: Author's own, based on the Jean Monnet Project selection results.[1]

1. EACEA, (2014), *Selection Results—Jean Monnet Networks and Jean Monnet Projects*, available at: https://eacea.ec.europa.eu/sites/eacea-site/files/documents/eac-s11-13_policy-debate-with-academic-world_en.pdf, [accessed Sept. 1, 2015].

As already mentioned above, the fieldwork on the implementation of the Jean Monnet Programme in China was conducted at RUC, FDU, and SCU because they have the Jean Monnet Centres and have also been granted 25 out of 37 projects in China. Wuhan University (WHU) undertook three projects and Nankai University (Nankai) had two projects, China University of Political Science and Law (CUPL), Guangdong University of Foreign Studies (GDUFS), Tongji University (Tongji), University of Macau (UMAC), Tsinghua University (Tsinghua) had only one module or one Jean Monnet Chair holder. Even so, this does not mean that these universities are not important in EU studies in China. Thus, a brief introduction to the status quo of the European centers in other universities in mainland China covered by this program will help us understand the context of Chinese European studies.

Established in 2014, the Centre of European Studies at CUPL is brand new, but European studies in the university started long before 2014. As a matter of fact, the China-EU School of Law, which is the only law school training professionals of Chinese, European, and international law, was set up in CUPL in 2008. Besides, Zhang Baosheng, the honorary Director of the Centre of European studies at CUPL, was also the first and only scholar sponsored by the Jean Monnet Programme there.[73]

Sponsored by the EU-China HECP and ESCP, the Centre for European Studies at Nankai was established in 1997, but European studies at Nankai started in 1975 when the Agricultural Department undertook a project on EU's *"Common Agricultural Policy."* It has over 40 full-time or part-time Chinese and foreign scholars and its research activities have involved scholars from the Schools of Economics, International Business, Law and Politics and History, meaning that European studies at Nankai is also an interdisciplinary research area.[74]

The European Studies Centre at WHU was set up in 1996 and covered by EU-China HECP. Students at different levels are trained by the Schools of Economics and Management, Law, Foreign Language and Literature, Political Science, and Public Administration. It has around 50 full-time or part-time researchers and the research of this center focuses on the innovations of small- and medium-sized enterprises in the EU, EU currency and finance; EU environmental and sustainable development policy and law.[75]

The Center for European Studies at GDUFS was established in 1997 and started recruiting masters students in European studies. It has five subordinate research sections (EU Economy and Trade Studies, EU Law and Diplomacy Studies, European Cultural Studies, EU Enterprise Management Studies, European Higher Education Studies) and nearly 30 full-time or part-time researchers. The center opened 6 public elective courses for college students including *Political and Economic Studies of European Countries, Contemporary History of Europe, Contemporary International Relations, Process of European Integration and European Cultures*, with over 2000 students registered for these courses.[76]

The European Study Centre at Tongji was established in 2009 and carried out research on EU institutions and governance, EU Common Foreign and Security Policies, Central and East Europe, China-Europe relationship, US-Europe relationship. Although this center is still quite young, it plays a role in coordinating different institutes related to European studies in Tongji. Tongji has the first German Studies Centre in China set up in 1985 and famous for its research on the economy, politics, culture, public opinion, society, and foreign policy of Germany and its role in and impact on European integration and the future of the EU.[77, 78]

The Jean Monnet Chair was only awarded to one professor of politics, but the Centre of China-EU Relations at Tsinghua conducted a series of projects addressing China-EU relations. Tsinghua held five international conferences and five seminars on China-EU relations and opened courses on *China-EU Relations* at postgraduate level under the Tsinghua-Groningen Cooperation Project; it conducted research projects on *China-EU-African Relations* and *Cultural Values of China and the EU: Similarities and Differences* with Tsinghua-Carnegie Centre; it undertook the Asia-Europe Foundation's projects on the *EU and European in the Eyes of Asia* and *Asia in the Eyes of the EU* as well as Tsinghua's self-funded project on *China in the Eyes of the EU*.[79]

The Jean Monnet Activities have also awarded two grants to the Chinese Society for EU studies and the national European Community Studies Association (ECSA). In looking at European studies centers in other universities covered by the Jean Monnet Programme, it is worth noting three key points: first, six centers (RUC, FDU, SCU, WHU, Nankai, and GDUFS) were set up in the 1990s during the China-EU HECP, and the establishment of these centers benefited directly from this program. Although some universities only have one Jean Monnet Chair holder or Jean Monnet Module, their centres for European studies have plenty of researchers and European studies is conducted by scholars from different disciplines. Third, college students at different levels are well trained in different schools, providing reserve forces for European studies in China.

Table 5.2. Activities in China sponsored by the Jean Monnet Programme from 2001–2014

Jean Monnet Modules	Jean Monnet Chairs	Jean Monnet Chairs "Ad Personam"	Jean Monnet Centres	Activities in Support of National ECSA Networks	Multilateral Research Groups	Jean Monnet Projects
11	15	2	3	2	1	1

Source: Author's own, based on the Jean Monnet Project selection results.[1]

1. EACEA, (2014), *Selection Results—Jean Monnet Networks and Jean Monnet Projects*, available at: https://eacea.ec.europa.eu/sites/eacea-site/files/documents/eac-s11-13_policy-debate-with-academic -world_en.pdf, [accessed Sept. 1, 2015].

According to table 5.2, it is stressing that 15 Jean Monnet Chairs are scholars holding full-time teaching posts in the field of EU studies, two of which were awarded the Jean Monnet Chair "Ad Personam" title in recognition of their high-level EU specialization and international renown.

Three Jean Monnet Centres of Excellence: at Fudan University (awarded in 2004 and led by Professor Bingran Dai), at Sichuan University (awarded in 2011 and led by professor Jian Shi), and at Renmin University of China (awarded in 2005 to Professor Xinning Song and renewed in 2013 with the contract on-going).

One multilateral Research Group awarded in 2008 to Renmin University of China under the coordination of Professor Xinning Song on "*Comparative Regional Integration: the European Integration Process and its Implication for East Asia*," comprising a consortium of six partner institutions in Belgium, China (coordinator), Germany, Italy, Poland, and the UK and involv-

Table 5.3. Chinese scholars' research topics or academic activities sponsored by the Jean Monnet Programme

Action Name	Institute and Funding time	Title
Jean Monnet Centre of Excellence	Fudan University, Shanghai, Prof. Bingran Dai (Director), 2004	EU Interdisciplinary Studies
	Renmin University of China, Beijing, Prof. Xinning Song (Director), 2005	EU Interdisciplinary Studies
	Sichuan University, Chengdu, Prof. Jian Shi (Director), 2011	Diversity in Unity: European Integration and European Social Development
Jean Monnet Chair "Ad Personam"	Prof. Xinning Song, Renmin University of China, 2010	Renovation of the Postgraduate Teaching Programme on European Integration at Fudan University
	Prof. Bingran Dai, Fudan University, 2010	Political Economy of European Integration
Jean Monnet Chair	Prof. Bingran Dai, Fudan University, 2001	European Economic Integration
	Prof. Xinning Song, Renmin University of China, 2001	European Political Integration
	Prof. Lingliang Zeng, Wuhan University, 2001	EU Legal Studies
	Prof. Zhigang Luo, Wuhan University, 2002	EU Political Integration
	Prof. Paulo CANELAS DE CASTRO, University of Macau, 2007	European Union Law—Facing the Constitutional and Governance Challenges in the Era of Globalisation
	Prof. Jian Shi, Sichuan University, 2008	On European Cultural Diversity in the Context of European Integration: History, Culture and Ideology in European Identification
	Prof. Zhimin Chen, Fudan University, 2009	European Integration and European Foreign Relations
	Prof. Xiaojin Zhang, Tsinghua University, 2011	EU Political and Administrative Studies

(continued)

Table 5.3. *(continued)*

Action Name	Institute and Funding time	Title
	Prof. Chun Ding, Fudan University, 2012	European Economic Integration and Social Affairs in the Era of Globalization
	Prof. Weiping Huang, Renmin University of China, 2012	European Economic and Monetary Union and Global Economic Governance
	Prof. Yamei Wang, Sichuan University, 2012	The EU Regional Policy and its Implication to China
	Prof. Jiadong Tong, Nankai University, 2012	The Process of European Integration and its Driving Force
	Prof. Zhicheng Wu, Nankai University, 2014	European Governance in the Process of European Integration
	Prof. Lei Rao, Sichuan University, 2014	Study on EU Environmental Policy with Economics
	Prof. Xiang Deng, Sichuan University, 2014	The EU Environmental Policy and its Implication for China
Module	Fudan University, Prof. Ronghua Hu, 2004	EU Legal Studies
	Fudan University, Prof. Zhimin Chen, 2005	European Union's Common Foreign Policy
	Renmin University of China, Prof. Xiaojin Zhang, 2009	European Security Strategy: Implication to the EU as a Global Player
	Fudan University, Prof. Chun Ding, 2010	EU Harmonization in the Field of Employment and Social Affairs
	Tsinghua University, Prof. Qiang Li, 2010	Comparative Regional Integration: EU and East Asia
	China University of Political Science and Law, Prof. Baosheng Zhang, 2011	Harmonisation of European Law in European Integration and its Impact in East Asia

	Guangdong University of Foreign Studies, Prof. Xiaohai Wang, 2011	Cultural Studies of European Integration
	Sichuan University, Prof. Lei Rao, 2011	Climate Policy under the Background of European Integration
	Renmin University, Prof. Gang Peng, 2013	The EU Development Policy and its Implication to the EU as a Global Player
	Tongji University, Prof. Ye Yang, 2013	European Integration: Experiences, Practices and Policies
	Wuhan University, Prof. Shuangwu Yan, 2014	The EU's Trade Policy and its Role in the World
Activities in support of National ECSA Network	Chinese Society of EU studies, Prof. Bingran Dai, 2006	National ECSA Network Activities
	Chinese Society of EU studies, Prof. Bingran Dai, 2012	National Network of EU studies in China
Multilateral Research Group	Renmin University of China, Prof. Xinning Song, 2008	Comparative Regional Integration: The European Integration Process and its Implication to East Asia
Jean Monnet Projects	Sichuan University, Prof. Jian Shi, 2014	Training Young Teachers and Promoting the EU's Visibility in West China

Source: Author's own, based on the Jean Monnet Project selection results.[1]
1. Ibid.

ing 5 Jean Monnet Chairs, resulting in a major scientific publication of the research results.

One Jean Monnet Project, a new action type introduced under the Erasmus Plus Jean Monnet Activities in 2014 and awarded to Sichuan University under the coordination of Professor Jian Shi on the theme of *"Teaching Young Teachers and Promoting the EU's Visibility in West China,"* aims to take EU studies into the classrooms of primary and secondary schools in the region.

Through looking at the Chinese context within which the Jean Monnet Programme has been implemented and the research topics and research centers sponsored by this program, we can tell that they not only cover most aspects of the European Union but also promote the innovation of European studies from a Chinese perspective. Although the coverage of this program in China is still small compared with its large geographical area and huge population, its effect in promoting the development of Chinese–European integration and EU studies as well as training reserve professionals in relevant areas is significant.

More importantly, these research results, disseminated through classroom teaching, public lectures, professional monographs, and mass media broadcasting, will play an important role in educating Chinese students, and even the public, about the EU. The European or EU research centers in different universities have numerous research results, teaching experience in training postgraduate and PhD students, publishing experience, and experience in hosting conferences about EU studies, when they are awarded the title of "Jean Monnet Centre of Excellence," and these students and academic publications also act as a channel for transmitting knowledge of the EU in China. In other words, the Jean Monnet Programme serves as a channel for public diplomacy and a global think-tank for the EU, which will be proved with empirical data in the following two chapters.

NOTES

1. European Union (2014), *Thinking about Europe: Jean Monnet Support to European Studies*, Luxembourg: Publications Office of the European Union: 24

2. Calligaro, O. (2013), *Negotiating Europe: EU Promotion of Europeanness Since the 1950s*, New York: Palgrave Macmillan: 35.

3. EACEA (2014), *Information about the Jean Monnet Programme from 2007–2013*, available at: http://eacea.ec.europa.eu/llp/jean_monnet/jean_monnet_en.php, [accessed Sept. 29, 2014].

4. European Union (2014), *Thinking about Europe: Jean Monnet Support to European Studies*, Luxembourg: Publications Office of the European Union: 24–25.

5. Ibid: 31.

6. Interview in Brussels with Luciano Di Fonzo, Feb. 17, 2015.

7. Interview with William Fingleton in Beijing, Dec. 11, 2014.

8. European Commission, (2001), *European and Asia: A Strategic Framework for Enhanced Partnership,* COM (2001) 469: 3.

9. Weissmann, M. (2013), *A European Strategy towards East Asia: Moving from Good Institutions to Action,* the Swedish Institute of International Affairs, UI Occasional Paper, No. 19: 5.

10. Interview with Professor C in Beijing, March 29, 2016.

11. Michalski, A. and Pan, Z. (2017), *Unlikely Partners? China, The European Union and the Forging of a Strategic Partnership,* Singapore: Palgrave Macmillan: 71.

12. Ikenberry, G. J. (2011), "The Future of the Liberal World Order: Internationalism after America," *Foreign Affairs,* 90(3): 58–58.

13. Dams, T., and Van Der Putten, F. P. (2015), *China and Liberal Values in International Relations: Opposing the Promotion of Democracy, Human Rights and Liberal Market Economy,* Working Report, The Hague: Netherland Institute of International Relations, "Clingendael": 11.

14. Scott, D. (2007), "China and the EU: A Strategic Axis for the Twenty-First Century," *International Relations,* 21(1): 28.

15. Huo, Z. (2005), "Lun Zhongou Zhanlue Guanxi (On China-EU Strategic Relationship)," *Guoji wenti yanjiu [International Studies]:* 4.

16. Qi, J. (2011), "The Debate Over 'Universal Values' in China," *Journal of Contemporary China,* 20(72): 888.

17. Maher, R. (2016), "The Elusive EU-China Strategic Partnership," *International Affairs,* 92(4): 963.

18. Qi, J. (2011), "The Debate Over 'Universal Values' in China," *Journal of Contemporary China,* 20(72): 884–885.

19. Maher, R. (2016), "The Elusive EU-China Strategic Partnership," *International Affairs,* 92(4): 963.

20. Veg, S. (2014), "China's Political Spectrum under Xi Jinping," *The Diplomat,* available at: http://thediplomat.com/2014/08/chinas-political-spectrum-under-xi-ji nping/, [accessed May 25, 2016].

21. Godement, F. (2013), "Law and Power in Xi's China," *China Analysis,* European Council of Foreign Relations, available at: http://www.ecfr.eu/page/-/China _Analysis_Law_and_Power_in_Xis_China_December2013.pdf, [accessed May 25, 2016]: 5.

22. Piao, V. (2014), "3 Universities Pledge to Uphold Party Ideals on Campus," *The New York Times,* available at: http://cn.nytimes.com/china/20140904/c04campus/dual/, [accessed May 25, 2016].

23. Veg, S. (2014), "China's Political Spectrum under Xi Jinping," *The Diplomat,* available at: http://thediplomat.com/2014/08/chinas-political-spectrum-under-xi-jin ping/, [accessed May 25, 2016].

24. Li, R. (2013b), "Seven Subjects Off Limits for Teaching, Chinese Universities Told," *South China Morning Post,* available at: http://www.scmp.com/news/china/

article/1234453/seven-subjects-limits-teaching-chinese-universities-told, [accessed June 7, 2016].

25. People.com.cn (2014), "Laoshi, Qing Buyao Zheyang Jiang Zhongguo (Teacher, Please Do Not Teach China in This Way)," available at: http://edu.people.com.cn/n/2014/1114/c1006-26025286.html, [accessed May 13, 2016].

26. Bell, D. (2015), "Teaching 'Western Values' in China," *The New York Times*, available at: http://www.nytimes.com/2015/04/17/opinion/teaching-western-values-in-china.html?_r=0, [accessed May 13, 2016].

27. Delegation of the EU to China (2015), *The European Union and China: A Maturing Partnership*, available at: http://eeas.europa.eu/delegations/china/eu_china/political_relations/index_en.htm, [accessed March 31, 2015].

28. Interview with Professor J in Chengdu, March 14, 2016.

29. Twigg, S. (2005), "Preface," in De Gouveia, P. F. and Plumridge, H., (eds.), *European Infopolitik: Developing EU Public Diplomacy Strategy*, London: Foreign Policy Center: 7.

30. Rasmussen, S. B. (2012), "Current Challenge to European Union Public Diplomacy," *Public Diplomacy Magazine*, University of Southern California, available at: http://publicdiplomacymagazine.com/current-challenges-to-european-union-public-diplomacy/, [accessed Nov. 22, 2014].

31. Austermann, F. (2012), "Towards One Voice in Beijing? The Role of the EU's Diplomatic Representation in China Over Time," *Journal of European Integration History*, 18(1): 84.

32. Interview with William Fingleton in Beijing, Dec. 11, 2014.

33. Moran J. and Ponz Canto, F. (2004), *Taking Europe to the World—50 Years of the European Commission's External Service*, available at: http://www.eeas.europa.eu/delegations/docs/50_years_brochure_en.pdf, [accessed 12-01-2014]: 11.

34. Fingleton, W. (2012), *The Influence of Public Diplomacy on EU-China Relations*, speech at conference of the the the conference of "the Wisdom of Public Diplomacy: the dialogue among Chinese, American and European scholars" was held on 19th May 2012 in Beijing, by Netherland Institute of International Relation "Clingeneal" and The Charhar Institute, a Chinese non-governmental think-tank for international relations and diplomacy, available at: http://www.charhar.org.cn/newsinfo.aspx?newsid=4629, [accessed Sept. 2, 2015].

35. Ibid.

36. Chan, K. (2010), "The Image, Visibility and the Prospects of Soft Power of the EU in Asia: The Case of China," *Asia Europe Journal*, 8(2): 136.

37. Li, X. (2007), "Chinese Television Coverage and Chinese Perceptions of Sino-EU Relations," in Kerr D, and Liu, F. (eds.), *The International Politics of EU-China Relations*, Oxford: Oxford University Press: 116.

38. Morini, M. Peruzzi, R. and Poletti, A. (2010), "Eastern Giants: The EU in the Eyes of Russia and China," in Lucarelli, S. and Fioramonti, L. (eds.), *External Perceptions of the European Union as a Global Actor*, Hoboken: Taylor and Francis: 42.

39. Wang, Y. (2012), "The Identity Dilemmas of EU Normative Power: Observations from Chinese Traditional Culture," paper presented at the seminar "International Society and the Rising Power," 2nd, Nov. King's College London, the UK.

40. Ma, X. (2012), *Beyond the Economic Ties: EU in the Chinese Media*, Centre of Public Diplomacy, University of South California, available at: http://uscpublicdiplo macy.org/sites/uscpublicdiplomacy.org/files/legacy/pdfs/XinruMaBestPaper2012. pdf, [accessed July 9, 2014]: 24.

41. Peruzzi, R. P., A. and Zhang, S. (2007), "China's View of Europe: A Maturing Partnership," *European Foreign Affairs Review*, 12(3): 327.

42. See section 7.2, the second-round interview with college students showed different choices of information sources of the EU.

43. DG-EAC (2008), *The European Union and the World: European Success Story*, Luxembourg: Office for Official Publications of the European Communities, available at: http://unipd-centrodirittiumani.it/public/docs/success2008_en.pdf, [accessed Sept. 2, 2015]: 6.

44. Interview with Professor F in Shanghai, Dec. 23, 2013.

45. Centre for European Studies at Renmin University of China (2014), http://www.cesruc.org/, [accessed June 15, 2015].

46. Song, X. (2010), "European 'Models' and Their Implications to China: Internal and External Perspectives," *Review of International Studies*, 36(03): 755–775.

47. Dai, B. (2008), "European Studies in China," in Shambaugh, D., Sandschneider E. and Zhou H. (eds.), *China-Europe Relations: Perceptions, Polices and Prospects*, London and New York: Routledge: 105–126.

48. Ibid.

49. Song, X. (2010), "European 'Models' and Their Implications to China: Internal and External Perspectives," *Review of International Studies*, 36(03): 756.

50. Dai, B. (2008), "European Studies in China," in Shambaugh, D., Sandschneider E. and Zhou H. (eds.), *China-Europe Relations: Perceptions, Polices and Prospects*, London and New York: Routledge: 106.

51. Ibid.

52. Ibid.

53. Ibid: 107

54. Song, X. (2010), "European 'Models' and Their Implications to China: Internal and External Perspectives," *Review of International Studies*, 36(03): 755–775.

55. Zhou, H. (2011), *The Past, Present and Future: the Institute of European Studies of Chinese Academy of Social Science*, available at: http://ies.cass.cn/Article/gybs/sq30/201104/3816.asp, [accessed June 12, 2015].

56. Dai, B. (2008), "European Studies in China," in Shambaugh, D., Sandschneider E. and Zhou H. (eds.), *China-Europe Relations: Perceptions, Polices and Prospects*, London and New York: Routledge: 108.

57. EuropeAid (2008), *EU-China European Studies Centres Programme*, available at: http://ec.europa.eu/europeaid/documents/case-studies/china_higher-educ ation_en.pdf, [accessed July 7, 2014].

58. Interviews with Professor A and B in Beijing, Dec. 11, 2013.

59. EU-China Policy Dialogue Support Facility II (2013), 1st Meeting of EU-China Higher Education Platform for Cooperation and Exchange (HEPCE), April, 2013. Available at: http://www.eu-chinapdsf.org/EN/Activity.asp?ActivityId=292& ActivityStatus=1, [accessed Aug. 2, 2014].

60. Interviews with Professor A and B in Beijing, Dec. 11, 2013.

61. Interview with Professor H in Chengdu, Dec. 17, 2013.

62. Tang, S., Zhang, J. and Cao, X. (2005), "Zhongguo De Diqu Yanjiu: Chengjiu, Chaju He Qidai (Area Studies in China: Achievements, Deficiencies, and Prospects)," *Shijie Jingji Yu Zhengzhi*, (*World Economics and Politics*), No. 11: 10.

63. The data is from the European Commission's publication about the selection results of the Jean Monnet Programme as well as the interview with Vito Borrelli, Head of Sector Jean Monnet and China desk on Feb. 6, 2015, in Brussels.

64. Interview with Vito Borrelli in Brussels, Feb. 6, 2015.

65. Centre for European Studies at Renmin University of China (2014), http://www.cesruc.org/, [accessed June 15, 2015].

66. Ibid.

67. Centre for European Studies at Fudan University (2014), http://www.cesfd.org.cn/index.htm, [accessed June 15, 2015].

68. Interview with Professor H in Chengdu, Dec. 17, 2013.

69. Centre for European Studies at Fudan University (2014), http://www.cesfd.org.cn/index.htm, [accessed June 15, 2015].

70. Ibid.

71. Centre for European Studies at Sichuan University (2014), http://ces.scu.edu.cn/Index.html, [accessed June 15, 2015].

72. Interview with Professor H in Chengdu, Dec. 17, 2013.

73. Centre of European Studies at CUPL (2014), available at: http://www.cupl.edu.cn/html/7189.html, [accessed June 15, 2015].

74. Centre for European Studies at Nankai (2015), available at: http://eucentre.nankai.edu.cn/noscript/eucentre/index.htm, [accessed June 15, 2015].

75. European Studies Centre at WHU (2015), available at: http://wuesc.whu.edu.cn/about.aspx?id=42, [accessed June 15, 2015].

76. Centre for European Studies at GDUFS (2015), available at: http://www1.gdufs.edu.cn/esc/newslist.asp?treeid=%D6%D0%D0%C4%B8%C5%BF%F6, [accessed June 15, 2015].

77. European Study Centre at Tongji (2015), available at: http://spsir.tongji.edu.cn/content.aspx?info_lb=103&flag=92, [accessed June 15, 2015].

78. German Study Centre at Tongji, (2015), available at: http://german-studies-online.tongji.edu.cn/37/list.htm, [accessed June 15, 2015].

79. Centre of China-EU Relations at Tsinghua, available at: http://www.imir.tsinghua.edu.cn/publish/iis/7221/index.html, [accessed June 15, 2015].

Chapter Six

The EU's Descriptive Knowledge Dissemination through the Jean Monnet Programme

The professors sponsored by the Jean Monnet Programme are actually serving as the intermediaries of EU public diplomacy in Chinese universities. Through teaching process and promoting their research output, college students as the elites of the next generation are informed by accurate and up-to-date knowledge of the EU, not to mention their potential influence on the general public more broadly through the mass media and public lectures. However, due to the ideological differences between China and the EU, the implementation of the Jean Monnet Programme might meet some resistance from Chinese governmental regulations.

Thus, the EU's knowledge dissemination in China includes descriptive and normative knowledge dissemination. The descriptive knowledge of the EU refers to the facts of the EU such as its history, development, and current status, which has been taught and researched in higher education institutions since China keeps drawing different lessons from the EU, so the effect of the EU's descriptive knowledge dissemination will be analyzed in this chapter. However, as discussed in chapter 5, there might be a paradox between the importance of EU norms in understanding the EU and the Chinese context that does not accept the concept of "universal values," whether and how the EU's normative knowledge dissemination has been carried out in the Chinese context will be discussed in the next chapter.

Based on the analysis of data from seven-month data collection period through interviewing the participants of this programme in China (December 2013–February 2014; December 2014–January 2015 and March 2016–April 2016), this chapter focuses on the EU's descriptive knowledge dissemination through the Jean Monnet Programme. As indicated in chapters 1 and 4, European experience including its development models, regional policies, and integration process has been introduced and learnt proactively by Chinese scholars, so no seemingly evident contradiction between the EU and China in the area of descriptive knowledge.[1]

6.1 THE PROFESSORS OF EUROPEAN STUDIES AND THE EU'S KNOWLEDGE DISSEMINATION

As indicated in the previous chapters, the most important contribution of the Jean Monnet Programme to EU public diplomacy has been the creation of the intermediaries in the host countries. Although the concept of public diplomacy by intermediary has not been widely discussed and universally accepted, its practice in public diplomacy has already attracted scholarly attention. According to the discussion in the introduction and its application to EU public diplomacy in chapters 2 and 3, the intermediary of public diplomacy can be civil society, mass media, and even influential individuals inside the target countries, and, a country other than the target country can be an intermediary of public diplomacy for the implementer. Inside the target country, the credibility and legitimacy of the intermediary are the most important while outside the target country, the intermediary is supposed to serve as a successful model to attract the target country and influence its behaviors.[2, 3]

Nevertheless, since "proxy" can be manipulated by public diplomacy implementers in international relations though Danielsen thinks that "proxy" and "intermediary" are the same concept,[4, 5] this research views the professors of European studies in China as the intermediaries instead of proxies of EU public diplomacy to show the independence of academics and academic activities. The Jean Monnet Programme requires project applicants to teach and research the EU in their home countries for knowledge dissemination, innovation, and exchange with evaluations on the project implementation, but this program does not monitor the content or focuses of the applicants' research or teaching. Thus, intermediary rather than proxy will be a better term to define the role of professors in their home countries. Thus, the communication process of EU public diplomacy in the case of the Jean Monnet Programme consists of two phases: the messages first travel from the communicator to the intermediary and then from the intermediary to the end recipients (college students in this case).

6.1.1 Professor Interviewees and Interview Questions

Albeit this section is dedicated to analyzing the responses of professor interviewees, some interview results from Chinese college students, news reports, and academic publications will be cross-referenced for triangulation purposes, which is also the case with the analysis on interviews in the next chapter. To be specific, in the case of the Jean Monnet Programme to China, the reasons why certain Chinese professors serve as the intermediaries of EU public diplomacy have to do with their academic achievement and their credibility in knowledge delivery. According to the selection criteria of the Jean Monnet Programme, as well as the interviews with Chinese professors,

> Although there is no specific requirement indicated about the publications and relevant academic activities for applying for the title of Jean Monnet Chair, it usually requires the applicants to list their publications related to European integration studies in the past few years according to those professors who successfully had been awarded this position. In other words, they already have research achievement in relevant fields. After being awarded this position, Chair holders have to teach at least 90 hours per year.[6]

It is almost the same with the applicants of the Jean Monnet Modules. In fact, the leader of a Jean Monnet Module who was interviewed said that he had been teaching development economics with the development policy of the EU as a part of his courses for over 30 years. Because of his research and teaching experience, he was awarded funding from the Jean Monnet Module in 2013.[7] In this sense, all the Jean Monnet Programme funding holders already have solid knowledge and rich research output in EU studies since it is the prerequisite for obtaining the funding.[8]

During the first round interview, which took place in China from December 2013 to February 2014 and from December 2014 to January 2015, three Jean Monnet Centres—located at Renmin University of China, Beijing; Fudan University, Shanghai, and Sichuan University, Chengdu—were visited. Face-to-face and telephone interviews were used in order to establish the teachers' assessment of the implementation of the Jean Monnet Programme at their universities and how students' attitudes towards the EU had changed as a result of attending courses on European studies. Professors interviewed were running courses sponsored by the Jean Monnet Programme and teaching students at different levels; thus they have personal experience and opinions about the potential impact of their activities on students' perceptions of the EU.

Table 6.1. Information of the professor interviewees

	Professors	Description
Renmin Univ.	4	1 Jean Monnet Chair "Ad Personam," 1 Jean Monnet Chair, 1 Director of the Jean Monnet Centre, 1 leader of a Jean Monnet Module
Fudan Univ.	3	1 Jean Monnet Chair "Ad Personam," 1 Jean Monnet Chair (also Director of Jean Monnet Centre), 1 assistant professor who worked in the Jean Monnet Centre
Sichuan Univ.	4	1 Jean Monnet Chair, 1 Director of Jean Monnet Centre, 2 assistant professors who worked in the Jean Monnet Centre

Source: Author's own, based on the information about professor interviewees.

Before proceeding to talk about the interview questions and data collection from the fieldwork in China, it is necessary to talk about the number of interviewees in the fieldwork and its representativeness in qualitative studies since this relates closely to the research results. Considering that the Jean Monnet Programme had been in operation in China for 13 years prior to the fieldwork, there were thousands of college students following the first two Jean Monnet Chairs being awarded to Chinese professors by the European Commission. Thus the most ideal and reliable data would be from the interviews with all the college students who participated in those courses. Obviously this is not practical and so the question arise of how to deal with the relations between the small sample (abbreviated as "Small-N" study in Statistics) and their representativeness. Two standard alternatives are explained by Mario Louis Small, based on the research of Weiss: one is sampling of range, a longstanding technique that could yield better and more reliable data based on the interests of the researcher;[9] while the other is snow-ball sampling, the well-known practice of asking the interviewees to recommend others.[10]

In regard to the technique of sampling of range, since time and financial constraints prevented the author of this research from interviewing all the participants of the Jean Monnet Programme in China, the research used this technique and identified three sub-categories (undergraduate, masters, and PhD students) of the target group (college students) and interviewed a given number of people in each category. Although the problems of bias and representativeness remain from the standpoint of statistics, it can identify the attitude change of different sub-groups in a more appropriate way.

When it comes to the technique of snow-ball sampling, researchers might still argue that some interviewees recommended by others could comprise a social network. In other words, people recommend interviewees from their own social network, which might introduce bias into the research even though it increases the number of respondents.[11] However, the "bias" cannot be a standard or evaluation of the research. In fact, although the interview questions were designed long before the interview, the face-to-face interview was not a simple repetition but was continually adjusted and re-evaluated. For example, while interviewing professors, with regard to the question "do you think the Jean Monnet Programme has any impact on your research," the first respondent might answer the question with his personal experience of support for the publication of his monograph, and so the next respondent would be asked whether the program had an impact on her publications or other aspects of her research. Finally, with the increasing number of interviewees, each new one contributed very little new information about the relations between the Jean Monnet Programme and the interviewees' own research. Furthermore, this research does not aim to and cannot herein jump to any general conclusions about the influence of the Jean Monnet Programme on students' perceptions of the EU, but it can only try to summarize its potential influence on college students (student interviewees) and give a phenomena analysis based on the interview. In sum, large-sample surveys are valuable, but small-sample interviews can still make a contribution to knowledge. Therefore, the number of interviewees in the field-based research about the effect of this programme in China attained saturation.

According to the general criteria for assessing public diplomacy in chapter 2, and combined with the specific objectives of the Jean Monnet Programme under the "Erasmus Plus" in particular in chapters 1 and 3, the professors were required to answer the following questions.

Table 6.2.   Interview questions for Chinese professors in the first round interview

Demographic questions:	
A1	Gender: male/female
A2	Teaching level: undergraduate/master/PhD
A3	How many years have you been teaching?
Warming-up questions:	
A4	What course do you teach?
A5	How many years do you teach this/these courses?
Leading questions:	
A6	How many courses do you teach and what is their content?
A7	Do you think the Jean Monnet Programme has impacted on your research, and how?
A8	Do you think this research has impacted on the content of your teaching, and how?
A9	Do you agree that the students' view of the EU has changed as a result of their increased knowledge?
A10	Do you think that your view of the EU has improved after performing research on European studies?

The interview questions include three parts: demographic questions, warming-up questions, and leading questions. Demographic questions are used to get the basic information of interviewees, which are followed by "warming-up" questions as a transition into the interview itself that make the interviewees feel related and be involved in the interviews.[12] The third part consists of direct/probing/leading questions which are to elicit direct responses to questions what have just been said and draw out a more completed narrative respectively.[13] This three-section structure of interview questions will be followed throughout the interview process.

Among the leading questions, questions A6 and A7 were used to assess one of the objectives of the Jean Monnet Programme—information and knowledge dissemination; A8 were aimed at partially evaluating the influence of the program on knowledge innovation; A9 and A10 were intended to estimate changes in perceptions before and after taking the relevant courses.

6.1.2 The Influence of the Jean Monnet Programme on Teaching and Research

Of the eleven professors, two Jean Monnet Chairs "Ad Personam," three Jean Monnet Chairs, three directors (one from each center, one of whom is also a Jean Monnet Chair), one leader of a Jean Monnet Module and three assistant professors who were working in the Jean Monnet Centres were interviewed. These professor interviewees include 7 male professors and 4 female professors, and among them, two professors at FDU and SCU started their career in the late 1970s, and five professors at RUC, FDU and RUC and one associate professor at RUC started teaching in International Relations, World Economics and with a particular focus on European integration in 1980s, and three assistant professors joined the faculties at FDU and SCU in the late 2000s (one of them was promoted to associate professor shortly after the first round interview and was re-approached during the second round interview).

The Jean Monnet Chair holders are professors who delivered classroom teaching about European integration studies. The "Ad Personam" is awarded to Jean Monnet Chairs who deliver high-quality European integration studies and/or individuals who have a particular knowledge of European integration. Both the Jean Monnet Chairs and the Jean Monnet Chair "Ad Personam" have rich experience in classroom teaching and in-depth research on EU studies, and more importantly, they participate in the process of knowledge transmission and have a direct understanding of the effect of courses related to European studies on Chinese students' perceptions of the EU. However, after being integrated into the Erasmus Plus, the Action of Jean Monnet Chair "Ad Personam" as one of the Actions of Jean Monnet Programme no longer exists.

As already indicated in chapter 1, the Jean Monnet Chair "Ad Personam" is awarded to professors who have held a teaching post and have made significant contributions to European integration studies in their own countries.[14] After being integrated into the Erasmus Plus, the Erasmus Plus Jean Monnet Programme no longer has the action of Jean Monnet Chair "Ad Personam" because of some changes to program design, but the Jean Monnet Chair "Ad Personam" as one position in the past still implies that the position holder has rich knowledge and makes important contributions to European integration studies. As the only two Jean Monnet Chairs "Ad Personam," they not only had abundant experience in teaching and researching but also had a good knowledge of the development history of China's European studies, while three directors of Jean Monnet Centres of Excellence offered details about the development history, structure, and status of the centers. Those three assistant professors who were teaching courses related to European studies when the fieldwork was conducted offered their opinions about European studies in Chinese universities. Face-to-face interviews help us obtain the information about China's European studies and their influence on Chinese students' perceptions of the EU from the viewpoints of the professors.

According to the interviews, eight professors, including Jean Monnet Chairs "Ad Personam," Jean Monnet Chairs, Centre directors and a leader of the Jean Monnet Module, taught at least two courses to both undergraduate and postgraduate students: these courses included *European integration; European economic integration; Comparative regional integration and its implication to China; European social policy; The EU's development policy*; and its welfare system. In chapter 5, the titles of the Jean Monnet projects in China were listed. It can tell from the sponsored topics that Chinese professors who do research on European integration studies or EU studies emphasise the experience of the EU and its implications for East Asia and China. According to one professor at RUC,

No matter whether the EU supports European integration studies in China or not, Chinese professors would have to do their research on the EU because China can learn a lot from the development experience of the EU. Certainly, with the financial support from the EU, we can do our research better.[15]

European studies in China has experienced from government initiated research on capitalism camp in early 1950s,[16] to autonomous scholarly research on development models of EU member states and regional policy of the EU in 1980s,[17] which was ahead of the sponsored research on European integration by the EU started in 1990s. In this sense, European integration studies in China had been largely originated from the internal requirement of learning European experience. Regarding the importance of European integration studies in China, one professor specializing in international development and trade research at RUC, added,

> The EU has a long history of actively communicating itself to the public in other countries by supporting foreign scholars to study and do research in EU member states. I studied and did research in some EU countries before and had a good impression about EU, so I always have positive comments while teaching the students in my courses. I think the strategy of communicating the EU by supporting foreign scholars to open courses about European studies in target countries is successful.[18]

Based on the selection criteria of the Jean Monnet Action, the Jean Monnet Chair has to deliver at least 90 hours of teaching per semester and each Jean Monnet Module lasts at least 40 hours per semester. Both the Jean Monnet Chair and the Jean Monnet Module are closely related to knowledge delivery in the classroom. As Jones argues, a direct connection between the educational program and cross-fertilization of cultures, minds, further decision makers is still present, albeit the budget distributed to each target country is limited.[19] One professor at RUC has been running a three-year Jean Monnet Module for undergraduate and postgraduate students at RUC since 2013. The module is called "*The EU's development policy and its implication to the EU as a global player*" but is taught as a part of his postgraduate module of "Development Economics." In this course, the EU's development policy including economic integration, economic development, and its implications to developing countries have been taught and discussed, and according to one professor at RUC, this first report has already been submitted for evaluation. With regard to the title—"development policy" instead of "development economics," he explained that,

> As a matter of fact, opening a new course would experience an evaluation procedure by the academic committee, therefore, the Jean Monnet Module has been integrated into the course of Development Economics that I have been lecturing for many years. Although this course has been running for several years with the content of European practice, the development policy of the EU as an integral part has been further strengthened with the support of the Jean Monnet Programme. The budget offered by this programme can be used to hire more research students for document collection and invite experts to give lectures, which definitely improves the efficiency of classroom education. [20]

As also indicated by students interviewees during two round interviews, professors doing European studies in China preferred explaining international issues by referring to the case of the EU in classroom teaching,[21] which, from the perspective of college students, partially illustrated how the knowledge of the EU had been disseminated through the teaching process. In fact, this professor's explanation directly illustrates how the funding works in disseminating information about the EU in college courses. Moreover, the three centers in China have hosted 9 Jean Monnet Chairs so far, and this is a large number in comparison with the total number of Jean Monnet Chairs in China but still small relative to the college students who can be covered by these Chairs. However, these three centres also host professors and researchers doing European studies other than the Jean Monnet Chairs.

According to the interview with Chinese professors, besides the courses run by Jean Monnet professors, all three Jean Monnet Centres host professors who have not been awarded the honor of Jean Monnet Chair but who also teach courses related to European studies. As was indicated in the brief introduction to these centres, courses at the undergraduate and postgraduate levels on different topics were started by professors in each center and new courses were continuously being designed with the aim of understanding new issues of the EU as they arise. Among the professors who were interviewed, one assistant professor, who was educated in France, taught undergraduates who major or minor in international relations about European integration and France at FDU; one assistant professor, who was educated in Belgium, was teaching undergraduate students and also doing her PhD at the same time at SCU. She changed her research and teaching interests from literature translation to European studies after having worked in the Jean Monnet Centre of Excellence for two years. She was responsible for organizing EU themed public lectures for undergraduate and postgraduate students. Following her own experience of studying overseas at the University of Leuven, Belgium, she believed that she can teach her students with what she saw and heard in EU countries and make her course more appealing.[22] According to student interviewees, professors at their university had overseas study experience, which not only made them provide more vivid anecdotes of the EU for students but also let them possess a more critical view of EU norms during classroom teaching.[23] Another assistant professor at SCU, who did his research in Belgium, organized and taught part of the course called "*Twelve Lectures in European Studies*" to around 100 students, all of whom had no prior background in international or European studies.

Besides classroom teaching, seven out of eleven professor interviewees were doctoral supervisors who advised both PhD and masters students and four of them supervised masters students doing research on Europe and European countries. Of those seven doctoral supervisors, three of them were researching political aspects of the EU, including European politics, foreign policy, and politics of the EU member states, three were looking at economic integration, such as agricultural policy, development policy, and trade policy, and one did research on European literature and cultures, with a focus on the impact of cultural exchange on the formation of European identity. This also reflects the status of European studies in China.

Moreover, according to the interviews with those professors who supervised PhD students, most of their PhD graduates obtained positions in distinguished Chinese universities and continued their research and teaching, while some of their current PhD students were part-time students who also worked in local universities and taught EU-related courses. Through interviewing the professors in the Jean Monnet centres about the courses they taught in their universities, the way how the information about the EU had been communicated in the educational process can be partly understood, since these courses cover almost every aspect of the EU and were open to a large group of students. Although European studies is now included in academic subjects such as international economics and international politics, and most higher education institutions have relevant courses or programs that are closely related to European studies, examining these three centers is still meaningful since they have the specific intention of training professionals in European studies in China.

All professors believed that this program had an impact on their research. Three of them thought that the funding had been helpful for publishing their findings and attending academic events in other universities. Two interviewees believed that EU funding affected their research topics since they could not continue their research without this financial support. It is worth keeping in mind that, for geopolitical reasons, European studies is not as easy as Japanese or American studies in getting financial support from the Chinese government or non-governmental institutes,[24] which is consistent with the research result on the status of area studies in China.[25] For Chinese academics, researching Sino-Japan relations and Sino-US relations is much easier to find funding for, since these two bilateral relationships are significant for contemporary China (the military presence of the US in East Asia and the US—Japan alliance have great influence on China's regional policy and the US's "return to Asia" strategy as well as the revisions to the Japanese Constitution make research in these areas important and indispensable).[26] William Fingleton also mentions that,

> You can tell from the words used in diplomatic documents that Chinese officials regard that China-U.S. relations are urgent while China-EU relations are important, [so it is easy to understand that Chinese professors doing research on China-U.S. relations can get more government funding].[27]

On the China's policy paper on the EU, the EU is regarded as China's important strategic partner[28] while the both China and US agree that it is important and urgent to enhance bilateral cooperation and control differences,[29] which has been reflected in research on area studies in China. Therefore, the support Chinese professors receive to do research and open courses on European integration and EU studies allows them to continue their research without any distraction. Besides the financial support to individuals such as Jean Monnet Professors and the successful applicants at Jean Monnet Modules, the Jean Monnet Programme also helps the Jean Monnet centres host academic conferences as well as establish academic associations between different centres within China and abroad, enhancing academic exchange and knowledge delivery.

However, supporting Chinese professors to do research on the EU also enhances EU studies in China. One professor said that there was no restricted area in Chinese European studies: there are no geopolitical conflicts or highly sensitive political issues,[30] and academic research conducted by famous Chinese scholars on conceptual gaps on global governance, human rights, and democracy has been published in Chinese and English.[31, 32, 33] Coincidentally, Professor Dai was nominated a Jean Monnet Professor in 2001 and renewed as Jean Monnet Professor "Ad Personam" in 2010 because of his contribution to EU studies in China, and was also the only winner of a Jean Monnet Prize in 2008, which was also the only prize granted to an Asian professor.[34]

One director said that the Jean Monnet Programme encouraged Chinese scholars to study the EU after two previous programs ended, and also mentioned that, after attending the Jean Monnet Conference of 2013 in Brussels, she knew that the EU had redesigned the Jean Monnet Programme with a huge budget after it was being integrated into the new program "Erasmus Plus."[35] Through comparing the funding criteria of the Jean Monnet Programme before and after being emerging into Erasmus Plus Programme, the grant for Jean Monnet Module was rose from 21,000 to 30,000 Euros and the grant for Jean Monnet Chair from 45,000 to 50,000 Euros.[36, 37] Besides, one assistant professor felt that his university had become an important center for European studies in China, thanks to the support of the Jean Monnet Programme. Two assistant professors at SCU mentioned that they had more opportunities to communicate with distinguished professors because the Centre for European Studies at SCU now held more national and international conferences after it was selected as the Jean Monnet Centre of Excellence. Given that SCU is located in southwest China, the Centre for European Studies at SCU creates more opportunities for professors in this area to exchange opinions and research achievements with their peers,[38] and regular academic exchange activities have been maintained in the forms of invited talks, student exchange, scholar exchange, or joint academic exchange with European universities.[39]

However, one professor also stated that the program only covered a small group of scholars and universities in China in comparison with two previous educational programs, making its impact limited. In short, the funding from the Jean Monnet Programme was important for professors who were doing European studies in China, but the number of projects it sponsored was still quite small. China has been one of the most active East Asian countries in applying for funding from the Jean Monnet Programme and has also been awarded grants for many research projects, but its coverage in China is still limited considering that China is geographically huge.[40] This is echoed by Marcin Grabiec, who is the first secretary and education and culture counsellor in the Delegation of the EU to China. He thought the Jean Monnet Programme was one of, but not the only, EU public diplomacy programs implemented in China and the success of EU public diplomacy depended on the coordination of different programs.[41]

On the relationship between research and teaching, three professors and two assistant professors commented that their research had enriched the content of their teaching. Since teaching is a two-way process, most of the interviewees mentioned the time-honored proverb, "teaching others teaches yourself (jiao xue xiang zhang),"[42] which precisely described the way academic research sponsored by the EU had an influence on and also had been influenced by classroom teaching. As mentioned before, student interviewees did realize that professors preferred citing the case of the EU in their courses even if the courses were not about the EU.[43] The research findings improved their knowledge of the EU, which in turn enabled their students to be better informed; while questions raised by students during the teaching process had also enabled them to consider their research from different perspectives.

One of the Jean Monnet Professors who was researching regional policy of the EU in China said that she worked as an advisor to some students' research projects sponsored by the college innovation fund on regional policies, and she learnt a lot while supervising those young researchers because she started paying attention to new areas and topics that had not researched before. Besides, she also encouraged the junior and senior students who registered for her courses to apply for the national innovation fund for college students with the questions and topics they had raised during the courses.[44] According to selection results of National Innovation Fund 2012–2015 released on the website of Ministry of Education, China, two projects related to the research on the EU at SCU were sponsored in 2012 and over 30 projects about the EU from 25 Chinese universities were sponsored from 2012 to 2015.[45]

One of the assistant professors stated that he had no comprehensive study on the EU before finishing his PhD thesis about European identity and Turkey's accession to the EU, but the new elective course to undergraduate students led by him required him to look systematically at different aspects of the EU, including politics, economy, culture, education, and religion. Although he needed to organize professors specializing in different areas of European studies at his university rather than deliver the course himself, he still had to know it in order to structure the course well. According to him, he would never have had the chance to study the EU comprehensively if he had not organized the course.[46]

Irrespective of specific projects that were sponsored by the Jean Monnet Programme, either under the action of Jean Monnet Chairs or the action of Jean Monnet Modules, those projects can eventually be helpful for the students. Although some actions of the Jean Monnet Programme were not designed specifically to support classroom education through opening more Jean Monnet Modules at the undergraduate and postgraduate levels, the interview results tell us that the academic research and classroom education are closely linked and college students can benefit from the research by attending lectures and seminars hosted by Jean Monnet professors or refer to academic publications. In this sense, the Jean Monnet Programme can actually affect the spread of knowledge in China.

Another aspect that is worthy of discussion with regard to the Jean Monnet Programme is inviting professors from foreign universities to give lectures or teach college students and establishing networks for European studies in universities at home and abroad. During the period 2007–2013, besides supporting Jean Monnet Professors, Jean Monnet Modules and Jean Monnet Centres, the Action One of the Jean Monnet Programme also sponsored multilateral research groups and associations of professors and scholars related to European integration.[47] Renmin University of China and Fudan University have led the multilateral research group and association of professors and scholars respectively.[48] Besides, the director of the Jean Monnet Centre at SCU said that they hosted several international conferences about the EU and also invited foreign professors to give lectures and teach college students after being sponsored by this programme,[49] which was reflected in the student interviews from SCU, since they also said that they attended lectures about the European debt crisis, EU-China relations and other issues related to the EU.[50]

Although the Jean Monnet Programme is not an educational exchange program because it only supports scholarly research and classroom teaching in home countries rather than encouraging direct student exchange from non-EU member states to EU member states, it still possesses some features of transnational mobility. At the core of the research on international educational mobility or exchange programs is a simple but powerful finding: a country's people are its greatest asset for promoting its noblest values to the world in that face-to-face interactions break through national stereotypes.[51] The Chinese Jean Monnet professors are obliged to teach Chinese college students, but the Jean Monnet professor from another country, especially an EU member state, can play a different role. For college students who have no opportunity to study abroad during their college study, face-to-face communication with professors doing research on the EU from EU member states can help them understand the EU not only from the research output of these professors but also from the personal stories of these professors as EU citizens. Thus, the small scale academic exchange in the Jean Monnet Programme and its effect can enhance the effectiveness of public diplomacy to a certain extent.

As well as changes in attitude among the students that will be analyzed below based on the interview data from college students and will serve to triangulate professor interview data, professors also gave their own evaluation of these changes in attitude. All the professor interviewees insisted that the students' knowledge had increased after attending relevant courses; two professors and two assistant professors considered that their students now have a positive attitude to the EU as a result. One assistant professor gave lectures to students who were studying international relations as a minor discipline: according to this professor, classroom teaching was the main channel for those students to obtain accurate knowledge about the EU in order to finish their assignments and exams; while another assistant professor organized and taught elective courses to students who had no background in international relations and he thought that the course helped students from areas such as Physics, Chemistry, and Engineering to broaden their horizons. Besides attending lectures and seminars, students from these majors may be stimulated to seek out more information about the EU out of their own interest.

Since most college students concentrate on their own subjects, enrolling in EU related courses helps them enrich their knowledge and get extra credit.[52] One professor, who had been doing research on European integration studies and teaching college students for around 40 years, thought that Chinese students' awareness of the EU was much deeper than European students' knowledge about China. He also stated that Chinese students' and the general public's interest in the EU had been growing in recent years, which can be seen in the increasing number of news reports about the EU and China-EU relations,[53] and was also indicated in scholarly research about the EU in the eyes of the Chinese press.[54]

With regard to the impact on the professors' perceptions of the EU after carrying out EU-related research, interestingly, only three professors answered that they had chosen their topic because of their interest in the EU but most of their students believed their teachers definitely had a preference for or positive attitude towards it. However, with the increase in funding from both the EU and the Chinese government, many more young scholars were trained in the academic field of EU studies and national, regional, and even international conferences were held in Chinese universities, which led to the establishment of the academic network in East Asia.[55] With the increasing amount and velocity of information dissemination and knowledge exchange, young scholars were gradually becoming interested in and were attracted to EU studies. Some assistant professors and PhD students admitted that they changed their research topics after face-to-face interaction with Chinese or foreign scholars doing EU research. [56] In order to clarify the discussion in this chapter, a summary of the answers of professor interviewees is presented below.

The data presented in this chapter from interviews with Chinese professors, combined with the analysis on the Jean Monnet Programme and Chinese college students, has answered one of the research questions raised in this research—how does the Jean Monnet Programme work in China?

At first glance, the Jean Monnet Programme as an educational and academic program appears only to offer a small grant for financial support (as indicated in Erasmus Plus Programme Guide, 30,000 Euros for a Jean Monnet Module lasting for three years and 50, 000 Euro for a Jean Monnet Chair lasting for three years, though the total budget for the Jean Monnet Programme appears to be large).[57] However, it supports the research and teaching of Chinese professors from different aspects.

Firstly, the Jean Monnet Programme can support information dissemination through establishing EU-related courses in China. The Jean Monnet Module is specifically designed for professor applicants to set up new courses in their host institutions, usually higher education institutions. In some cases, the original parts of their courses that deal with the EU can be strengthened with the funding even though they are not new. According to the interviews, the funding can be used to increase academic publications, invite external professors and experts, and hire teaching assistants from among the senior research students, which improves the effect of classroom knowledge delivery. The funding works well in a market-oriented educational environment in China and overseas.

Secondly, the Jean Monnet Programme can increase knowledge innovation by supporting academic research in China. The research topics of Chinese professors cover a wide range from the experience of European integration, the problems it faces, to its future and its implication to the EU as a global player and for China as a developing country which is drawing experience of the EU. This improves knowledge innovation by studying the EU from a comparative perspective and benefits Chinese students who want to learn about the EU in the classroom. Besides, knowledge innovation, through supporting Chinese professors' research on the EU, publishing the research results in this field and

Table 6.3. A summary of the answers of professor interviewees

A6	How many courses do you teach and what is their content?	Eight professors lectured at least two courses to both undergraduate and postgraduate students; one assistant professor lectured two undergraduate courses while another two assistant professors lectured one elective course to undergraduate students. These professors also delivered lectures to local Party schools and other universities, in China and overseas.
		These courses included *European integration; European economic integration; Comparative regional integration and its implication to China; European social policy; The EU's development policy*; and its welfare system.
A7	Do you think the Jean Monnet Programme has impacted on your research, and how?	Three of the professor interviewees thought that the funding had been helpful for publishing their findings and attending more academic events in other universities. Two believed that EU funding determined their research topics, as they could not continue their research without financial support.
		One director said that the Jean Monnet Programme encouraged Chinese scholars to study the EU after EU-China HECP and ESCP. Two assistant professors mentioned that they had more opportunities to communicate with distinguished professors because more conferences were held in their university.
A8	Do you think this research has impacted on the content of your teaching, and how?	Three professors and two assistant professors commented that their research had enriched the content of teaching.
		One assistant professor, who led an elective course for undergraduate students, thought that he started looking at the EU more comprehensively after lecturing that module.
A9	Do you agree that the students' view of the EU has changed as a result of their increased knowledge?	All the professor interviewees insisted that the students' knowledge had increased after attending relevant courses; two professors and two assistant professors considered their students to now have a positive attitude towards the EU as a result.
A10	Do you think that your view of the EU has improved after performing research on European studies?	Three professors said that they had chosen their topics because of their interest in the EU when asked about the motivations of doing research on the EU, but most of their students believed their teachers definitely had a preference for or positive attitudes towards it.

promoting the exchange of knowledge and ideas among Chinese and foreign scholars, broadens their views with regard to EU related issues.

Thirdly, the Jean Monnet Programme can support knowledge exchange by promoting academic interaction between experts from different institutions in both the EU and China. Three Jean Monnet Centres of Excellence in China host national and international research conferences every year and scholars from Chinese universities and overseas research institutions are invited to discuss current issues facing the EU as well as deliver papers to their peers, all of which promotes knowledge exchange. These conferences are mostly open to college students. One professor at FDU said that their center held two or three conferences every year for the staff working in the centre to share their research progress.[58] A director of the Jean Monnet Centre at SCU said that two Chairs from China and Europe respectively were selected at the annual conference on EU studies held in their center, with the purpose of stressing the importance of knowledge exchange.[59] Based on the news reports of the Jean Monnet Centres in China, academic conferences about the current issues of the EU have been held regularly at different universities at inter-school, regional, national, and international levels in China.[60, 61, 62]

In general, we can see that professors believed the Jean Monnet Programme affected their teaching and research through providing necessary funding and encouraging more scholarly exchange, and it also influenced college students' knowledge of the EU, and furthermore, impacted on their perceptions of the EU to a certain extent. Since college students have been the main target group since the inception of the Jean Monnet Programme what has been the influence of the programme on the future generation, or more specific, Chinese college students?

6.2 COLLEGE STUDENTS AND THEIR PERCEPTIONS OF THE EU

6.2.1 Interview Questions for College Students

Due to the differences between different study levels, the analysis below will be divided into two parts: the first concentrates on data analysis in general in order to understand the knowledge dissemination and changed perceptions; while the latter focuses on PhD students who were doing research on the EU because they would possibly become new intermediaries in telling the EU story.

Eighty-seven students from different levels covered by the Jean Monnet Programme at three different universities were interviewed. The students were selected from different levels according to the numbers enrolled in the different courses, which can be used for vertical comparison to understand the impact of knowledge dissemination on college students at different levels.

The horizontal comparison had also been made between the three different universities to look at geographical differences.

Table 6.4.   Interview questions for Chinese students in the first round interview

Demographic questions:	
B1	Gender: male/female
B2	Studying level: undergraduate/master/PhD
B3	Age.
Warming-up question:	
B4	What are you studying?
Leading questions:	
B5	How many courses related to European studies have you attended so far, and what have you learnt from these courses?
B6	Do you think that your knowledge about the EU has increased after attending these courses?
B7	Do you think that you have sufficient knowledge about the EU?
B8	Do you think that your perception has changed after attending these courses, and, if so, can you describe your perception of the EU before and after attending these courses?
B9	Do you find yourself looking for more information about the EU after attending these courses, and how?
B10	Do you know the Jean Monnet Programme?
B11	Do you think it can influence your perception of the EU if the research is sponsored by the EU?
B12	What is your PhD research topic?
B13	What are the main sources for you to get the information about the EU?

6.2.2 Chinese College Students' Knowledge and Perceptions of the EU

Before proceeding to the analysis on the answers to leading questions, a summary of demographic questions is provided.

Table 6.5.   The number of student interviewees in each studying level in the first round interview

	PhD students	Postgrad. taught	Undergraduate
RUC	2	10	18
FDU	3	9	14
SCU	5	10	16

Table 6.6. The demographic information of student interviewees in the first round interview

	Undergraduate students		Master students		PhD students	
	M	F	M	F	M	F
RUC	8	10	6	4	1	1
FDU	7	7	5	4	1	2
SCU	6	10	3	7	2	3

Since all the compulsory courses of the undergraduate programs opened in the second and third year of undergraduate study in Chinese universities, all the interviewees from the undergraduate level were in their second or third year of university study.

All student interviewees at RUC were doing International Politics at School of International Studies. Among them, 10 undergraduate students were at their second year study while 9 at the third year, so they aged 18–21; all 9 postgraduate student interviewees were at their second year study and aged 23–25, and 2 PhD students were at first and third year respectively and aged 24–28. Of 26 student interviewees at FDU, 13 undergraduate students were doing International Politics at School of International Relations and Public Affairs and 1 was doing Architecture and minoring in Foreign Affair; all 9 postgraduate students were doing International Politics and aged 23–26; 3 PhD students included two second year and one third year students who were doing International Politics and Foreign Affairs respectively and aged 25–28. At SCU, since the course related to the EU at undergraduate level in this research was an elective course, student interviewees at second year of undergraduate study were majoring in History (2), Physics (5), Mathematics (2), English (3), Chemistry (1), Electric Engineering (2), and Computer Science (1), and they aged 19–22. All postgraduate students included 10 masters students, 3 second year PhD and 2 third year PhD, were doing European Culture studies at School of Foreign Languages and Cultures, and they aged 20–30.

All the undergraduate students attending the interview at SCU had no background knowledge of international studies or European studies except for one elective course they attended in the fall semester of 2013–2014 and finished on 5th December 2013—one week before the fieldwork was conducted. The masters students involved in the interview who came from RUC and FDU had attended the courses run by Jean Monnet professors in their universities, while those from SCU were majoring in literature with a special focus on European culture, since the Centre of European studies is based in the School of Foreign Languages and Cultures at SCU and its masters program in international politics in the School of Marxism has a small enrollment. However, the masters students from SCU had attended courses such as *European Identity and European Integration* and *The Cultural Basis of European Integration*, and most of them admitted that they attended the seminars, public lectures, and international conferences about the EU, Eurozone crisis, and EU-China relations in their university. All the PhD students were supervised by the Jean Monnet professors in China and majored in European studies (PhD interviewees at SCU included part-time students.

From five leading questions for college students above, questions B5, B6, and B7 were used to assess one of the objectives of the Jean Monnet Programme—information/knowledge dissemination; B8 and B9 were to estimate the changed perceptions before and after taking the relevant courses; B10 and B11 were used to assess the relationship between credibility of information source and communication effect; and B12 and B13 were designed for PhD students' knowledge of current research on the EU in China.

First, the student interviewees were asked to answer how many courses related to European studies they have attended and what they have learnt from these courses. Although in the previous chapter, the courses established in three centers and taught by the professor interviewees were mentioned, it is still necessary to ensure what courses the student interviewees attended because their knowledge of the EU may not come solely from the courses mentioned before. Based on this question, this research aimed to identify the sources of information about the EU.

Second year student interviewees at RUC had not attended the compulsory courses in international relations. Therefore, their knowledge about the EU and EU member states came mainly from two courses: *History of Contemporary International Relations* and *Comparative Political Institutions*. The former course stressed regional integration in Western Europe after the Second World War while the latter covered the political institutions of different western countries located in Europe. It is worth mentioning that some students said that *History of Contemporary International Relation* was taught by one professor, who was also the director of the Jean Monnet Centre at RUC.

I attend the course named History of Contemporary International Relations in the second half of my first year at RUC and the course instructor taught us this course. I knew she was educated in Germany for several years and she was conducting research on the history of European integration and the role of Germany in this process. What she taught was not only from the textbook but also from her personal studying and living experience in Germany, which made her course very attractive and rewarding. She told us the characteristics of Germany and Germans and the way Germany dealt with the international relations of Europe after the Second World War and linked it with the role of Germany in the EU at

Table 6.7. **Modules of European studies**

School	Level of study	Course title
RUC	Undergraduate	History of Contemporary International Relations (Europe after Second World War)
		Comparative Political Institutions (Political Institutions of EU member states)
		European Security and Defence Policy
	Master taught	The Theory and Practice of Regional Integration
		Comparative Regional Integration
FDU	Undergraduate	History of Contemporary International Relations (Europe after Second World War)
		European Politics and Diplomacy
		French Studies
		European Economic Integration
	Master taught	European Political and Economic Integration
		European Politics and Diplomacy
		German Studies
		Introduction to EU-China Relations
SCU	Undergraduate	Twelve Lectures on European Studies
	Master taught	European Cultures and European Integration
		History of European Thought

the current stage. Although so far my knowledge about the EU is mainly from her course, I think I will select another course named European Integration Research in my junior year.[63]

Most of the student interviewees from RUC who were junior year students attended the courses on *European Integration Research* and *Comparative Regional Integration Research*, both of which were beneficial for the students' knowledge of the history and status of European integration and the specific features of regional integration in Europe in comparison with regional integration in other areas. Moreover, four second year undergraduate students also mentioned that they selected the course on *European Security and Defence Policy* given by professors from Belgium during the RUC Summer School.

In FDU, there was a similar situation in that the history of Western European countries after the Second World War as a part of the course on *History of Contemporary International Relations* was one of the main sources for the first and second year college students. The course on *European Politics and Diplomacy* was also open to undergraduate students in the second half of their junior year for students majoring in international relations. One student who went to Hong Kong University for one semester exchange studied the *French Studies* course. Also, two students in the first half of their junior year said that the course on *Chinese Diplomacy* lectured by Professor Chen, who is a Jean Monnet professor at FDU, composed rich content on EU-China relations. They said:

> Although the course was about Chinese foreign policy and the history of Chinese external relations, that course also talked about EU-China relations and Professor Chen sometimes liked to use the case of the EU in explaining issues related to that course because he is an expert in European studies. Therefore, actually, we can learn the knowledge of the EU almost from all the courses given by Professor Chen.[64]

For postgraduate students at FDU, the courses included *European Politics and Diplomacy, European Economic and Political Integration, German Studies*, and *EU-China Relations* were available for them as either compulsory or elective courses. Considering that the interviewees at FDU were from the discipline of international relations, a greater number of courses related to EU studies were set up by professors from the School of Economics home to the Jean Monnet Centre of Excellence, albeit the interview did not cover students from that school.

In SCU, since all the undergraduate student interviewees attended the course entitled *Twelve Lectures on European Studies,* the table 6.7 also listed this course. For graduate students, the courses included *the History of European Thought* and *European Cultures and European Integration* and were given by Professor Jian Shi, who is a Jean Monnet Professor at SCU.

The table 6.7 did not indicate the course title for PhD students in three universities because most of the PhD student interviewees said that they attended the courses related to European studies during the period of their undergraduate and postgraduate studies, which meant the courses listed above had already covered the courses taken by PhD students. For them, the PhD courses they attended were mainly on research design and research methodology, and the PhDs who transferred from other disciplines would be asked to take the undergraduate and postgraduate courses before they officially started their research.

Second, personal opinions about whether their knowledge of the EU has increased after attending these courses were collected. As one of the criteria for assessing the public diplomacy program, increasing the knowledge of the communicator is the primary aim of transnational communication, which is applicable to the Jean Monnet Programme. Of the 87 college students interviewed, 86 acknowledged that their knowledge of the EU had increased after attending relevant courses.

Table 6.8.   The ratio of knowledge increase after taking EU-related courses

Do you think that your knowledge about the EU has increased after attending these courses?

YES	86	98.9%
NO	1	1.1%

The students interviewed had a clear picture of EU institutions, important treaties, member states, its role in international relations, and the reasons for and results of issues such as the European debt crisis, or the EU's role in global environmental governance. All the interviewees can tell the differences between the European Commission, European Council, and Council of the EU as well as their respective functions, and they can also list the 28 member states of the EU, which they would not have been able to do before attending these courses. One of the students said that he would not have known the history of the EU if he had not participated in the elective course, *Introduction to European Union.* Another student believed that most Chinese students who were doing science or economics were only interested in getting the diploma and good jobs rather than broadening their horizons. In other words, the elective courses in European studies gave college students the opportunity to learn something outside of their majors,[65] which was one of the reasons that elective courses in humanities and social science were encouraged at SCU.[66] Only one student said that she did not feel that she had learned more about the EU: she had attended a course on European history, which she already knew about from her extracurricular reading.

It would be interesting to know whether the course content or the teaching methods used can affect student perceptions of the EU.[67] In fact, this question was partly mentioned in previous sections. It is harder to obtain the governmental funding for European studies in China than for American or Japanese studies and the news reports about European issues are not considered to be as newsworthy. This can be attributed to geopolitical reasons since the US, Japan, and Taiwan are geographically closer to China and have more influence on the security and authority of China. The decrease in research on the EU and Europe and the lack of news reports about EU issues lead directly to the poor knowledge of the EU in college students and the Chinese public. However, the Jean Monnet Programme does alter the situation. On the one hand, the funding for professors and scholars creates expertise in Chinese scholars; on the other hand, in the long run, well-trained college students from reputable universities can eventually exert their influence and increase the public's knowledge about the EU when they go to work in different areas. Thus, the Jean Monnet Programme increases the opportunities for Chinese students to study and get more knowledge about the EU, which can be the first step in creating a positive view of the EU.

Based on the interview questions B1 and B2, the result—at least according to the interviewees' responses—proved that courses about European studies have a positive impact on Chinese college students' perceptions of the EU. Admittedly, we cannot isolate the effect of teaching methods used by professors, but it is still possible to conclude that these courses were useful based on the answers.

Third, the student interviewees were asked whether they had sufficient knowledge about the EU. Although it is a question requiring a "yes" or "no" answer, the interviewees gave more detailed responses that cannot be simply divided into two different groups.

In fact, according to the data collected from the fieldwork, only three PhD students from three universities thought that they had a good knowledge of the EU in specific issues compared with their peers who were not doing EU studies, but they also admitted that much work still needed to be done in other areas which were not covered by their PhD research. 7 PhD students, 13 out of 29 masters students and only 2 out of 48 undergraduate students considered that they had sufficient knowledge of the EU since they were majoring in international relations or chose an aspect of the EU as their dissertation, but they also added that this can only be assessed in comparison with students from other disciplines. Student interviewees from three universities believed that they did not have enough knowledge about the EU as it is a supranational organization which has complicated institutional design and constantly changing treaties, charts, and arrangements.

Table 6.9. The ratio of different self-evaluation of the college students' knowledge of the EU

A good knowledge of the EU	PhD	3	3.45%
	Master taught	0	0
	undergraduate	0	0
Sufficient knowledge of the EU	PhD	7	8.05%
	Master taught	13	14.94%
	undergraduate	2	2.30%
Insufficient knowledge of the EU	PhD	0	0
	Master taught	16	18.39%
	undergraduate	46	52.87%

Cultural factors must also be taken into account since Chinese students (and Chinese people in general) prefer to give modest and conservative answers in face-to-face interviews.[68] But the answers to this questions can still tell us two things: the first one is that, for Chinese students interviewed, the EU or European studies as an academic discipline is very broad and inclusive, making it hard to completely understand the EU; the second one is that, for policy makers of the EU, promoting European integration studies or EU studies still has a long way to go.

Fourth, based on students' personal opinions, it is aimed to measure whether their perceptions of the EU have been changed after attending EU-related courses. After evaluating the information dissemination in the public diplomacy program, the interview questions moved on to look at the changes in perceptions of the EU.

Table 6.10. The ratio of perception changes after taking EU-related courses

Do you think that your perception has changed after attending these courses?				
Changed	Positively	From negative to neutral	10	
		From neutral to positive	32	65.5%
		From negative to positive	9	
		From positive to neutral[1]	6	
	Negatively	/	8	9.2%
No change	Positive	/	14	
	Negative	/	7	24.1%
	Neutral	/	0	
No idea	/	/	1	1.1%

1. The remaining 6 felt that their views had changed in the opposite direction, from positive to neutral, but they also felt that their views were now more accurate than hitherto, as their previously positive stance had been based on lack of knowledge.

Apart from one South Korean student—who was more interested in the situation in the Korean peninsula, and did not have any opinion on the EU—86 interviewees responded. Twenty-one of these 86 thought that their perceptions of the EU had not been influenced noticeably by the course content; 14 of those 21 had always had confidence in the future of the EU, while 7 possessed a neutral attitude, reasoning that while its contribution was important, internal conflict cannot be ruled out.

Regarding the question on "whether your perception of the EU has changed after attending the relevant courses," 57 students believed that their views of the EU had changed positively. Among them, 51 considered that they had been influenced by what they had learnt during the courses, with their perceptions of the EU changing from negative to neutral (10), neutral to positive (32), or negative to positive (9). One junior student at FDU who attended an exchange program with an American university thought that the Jean Monnet Programme as well as European studies in her university had great influence on her peers' perceptions of the EU in that some students who also attended similar exchange programs with American partner universities changed their dissertation topics of Bachelor's Degree in American studies to European studies after participating in courses related to European studies offered by her university. Although she was doing research on Sino-US relations, she stated that European studies flourished in her university because she knew that there were numerous academic conferences, lectures given by foreign professors, student research associations, and study groups about the European Union that had taken place during the previous two years.[69] Another sophomore stated that he had previously thought that the EU was controlled by the great powers—Germany, France and the UK, but he had been taught the history of the EU and its internal negotiations with the case of the Treaty of Lisbon, and he even thought that this model could be applied to regional cooperation in East Asia.[70]

The table 6.11 summarizes the terms used by these students to describe the EU before and after attending relevant courses. Only eight students had a negative view of the EU after attending the courses because they were now aware of the internal problems within the Union. When asked for their reasons, 6 of them believed that the Eurozone crisis would finally cause the failure of the Euro without any new financial system being put in place for the EU and 4 of them also mentioned that they had not previously been aware of the amount of internal bickering between the EU and its member states and their conflicting interests. Based on those negative impressions, they predicted that the EU would enter into decline without making any further contribution to the contemporary international system.

According to the table 6.11, Chinese students' perceptions of the EU, to a certain extent, had changed after taking courses in European studies in the three universities. The EU was described using the words "Fair," "Ambiguous," "Rich," "Conservative," and "Solidarity" since the mass media, literature and artistic works are the main sources for the formation of Chinese views of the EU. In other words, their description of the EU was based on personal feelings rather than accurate knowledge. On the other hand, descriptions such as "Model of regional integration," "Global actor," "Supranational

Table 6.11. Frequency of words used to describe the EU before and after attending relevant courses

Before		After	
Far	12	Model of regional integration	21
UK, Germany, France	10	Global actor	14
Great power group	9	Complex	14
Economic prosperity	9	Diversity	13
Ambiguous	9	Supranational organisation	10
Loose cooperation	5	Conflict among member states	9
Rich	5	European debt crisis	8
Western Europe	4	Climate Change	8
Conservative	4	Destination of study	7
Solidarity	4	Specific	5
Economic crisis	4	Leader in global environment governance	4
Destination of tourism	2	Destination of tourism	4
Organisation	2	Democracy	3
Transferring of sovereignty, human rights, EEC, Anti-dumping towards Chinese exports, climate change, regional integration	Once for each	The EU troika, human rights, Schuman, international actor	Once for each

organization," and "Leader in global environmental governance" which definitely came from classroom education and seemed more academic. However, this does not mean that the Jean Monnet Programme, or public diplomacy in general, have the function of brainwashing.

In fact, the Centre for European Studies at SCU did a similar survey in five universities in Sichuan province by using questionnaires to understand undergraduate students' perceptions of the EU in Chengdu, the capital city of Sichuan province. That survey started from the basic assumption that all the undergraduate students had a higher level of general knowledge and education and paid more attention to international politics and economics than the general public, and aimed to find out the undergraduate students' understandings about the future of the EU and Sino-EU relations. They sought their opinion on the current issues relating to the EU and bilateral relations between the EU and China, which was different from this book's research into the effect of supporting European studies as the EU's public diplomacy practice. However, according to a report published in the *European Studies Forum*—an internal journal of SCU, undergraduate students became more concerned about the future of the EU and the internal negotiations among its member states in solving the current problems after the European debt crisis.[71] Thus college students may change their perceptions of the EU in two opposite directions: on the one hand, we can see that the increasing knowledge of the EU leads to a positive change in attitude, which implies that mutual understanding helps eliminate the stereotypes about the EU. On the other hand, it was still possible that the perceptions of the EU deteriorated because some of the students focused more on problems and potential hazards of the EU rather than its achievements in regional peace and prosperity, albeit this group was small.

Admittedly, the content of table 6.11 was based on the self-reflection of the interviewees, so their perception of the EU might be affected by the information from other sources besides classroom learning. However, since academic research and knowledge communication give equal attention to achievements and problems—in short, a real EU—it can be completely distinguished from brainwashing or propaganda. Telling the truth and increasing the credibility of communicators (the EU as the designer/implementer and the professors as intermediaries of EU public diplomacy) might also cause the decline of positive perceptions, yet it can harvest more in the long run since credibility matters greatly in public diplomacy.[72]

Based on the data about the changed perceptions of the EU before and after attending relevant courses, the benefits of educational programs as an instrument of public diplomacy would be better thought of as being realized in the long-term rather than the short-term because they are not useful for achieving pressing political objectives. However, educational programs may help educate foreign publics about the founding rules of the EU, which usually have a longer perspective than other programs and yield more indirect returns in forming positive attitudes towards the communicators during the educational process.[73] In the case of the Jean Monnet Programme, the EU as the implementer of the program can benefit from supporting overseas European studies and educating the younger generation in strategic partnership countries.

Fifth, the interviews examined whether college students actively looked for more knowledge about the EU. As we can see from the table 6.11, the students' attitudes towards the EU was more specific and positive as a result of attending the courses. In fact, when asked whether they were looking for more information about the EU following their courses, 77 of 87 interviewees acknowledged that they actively looked for more information as a consequence; the remainder did not feel that they wanted to know more about the

EU, because 9 of them were majoring in international politics, and had their own academic interests in the US, Japan, or Africa. Interestingly, only 17 of the undergraduate student interviewees (16 from SCU and 1 from FDU) who attended the interview had no background knowledge in international studies or political science, but all of them thought they were actively looking for more information about the EU on the Internet after attending their courses. These interviews were in fact conducted just after David Cameron's visit to Chengdu, and this official visit of the Prime Minister of the United Kingdom aroused the curiosity of interviewees at SCU because some of them who were studying engineering or physics started asking about the role of the UK in the EU and the relationship between the EU and its member states.[74]

Table 6.12. The ratio of increasing motivation for seeking further knowledge of the EU

Did college students actively look for more knowledge about the EU after attending relevant courses?		
Yes	77	88.51%
No	10	11.49%

According to the interview, at postgraduate level, 3 of 10 students in Beijing (2 to King's College London, UK and 1 to Free University of Berlin, Germany), and 4 of 9 students in Shanghai (2 to Lund University, Sweden and 2 to Sciences Po, Paris, France), had been to EU member states before through school exchange programs, although there were none in Sichuan. At the undergraduate level, all 32 students from Beijing and Shanghai had a background in international relations, but most interviewees in Sichuan were from disciplines related to science and no one was majoring or taking secondary courses in international relations or political science. When we compared the interview results across these three universities horizontally, the undergraduate students in Sichuan had been influenced more by European studies courses. As one professor noted, Sichuan University, a famous university in south-west China, does not have enough international cooperation opportunities, because it is not afforded geographical priority in the manner of Beijing or Shanghai.[75] For the students who travelled to European countries or had studied there for a while, they had direct personal experience of the EU and European countries because they had communicated with locals and benefitted from the Schengen Visa and Euros.

Both Renmin and Fudan Universities have a long history and good reputation in international studies with a well-established disciplinary system from undergraduate, masters, to PhD level while Sichuan University started recruiting undergraduate students in international politics in 2003 and postgraduate students in 2007 at the School of Marxism. European studies involves a multi-disciplinary approach through political science (including international relations and comparative politics), economics, cultural studies, language studies, history, geography, etc., but European studies is still led by economic studies (Economic integration, Economic model, Euros, and EU-China economic relations)[76] and political studies with two branches of international relations (the EU's external relations and foreign policy, the EU and its role on the world stage, its member states research, EU-China relations, European international relations theories and international relations history of Europe)[77] and politics (politics at the EU level, politics of its member states and party politics)[78] albeit there is increasing interest in law and social studies.[79] This partially explains why all the undergraduate students participating in the interviews believed that their view of the EU positively changed after knowing the EU more if they had no background knowledge of international studies or political science.

In this situation, supporting professors from non-EU member states to research and teach European studies in their home countries is important for the EU to communicate itself to a world audience. More importantly, the influence of geographical differences also tells us that public diplomacy needs to give more attention to places outside the capital. In fact, the universities in Beijing have more opportunities and funding to carry out educational exchanges such as inviting foreign professors to give lectures to college students or supporting more Chinese students to study in EU member states, because, according to one professor at SCU, the universities in Beijing have a comparative advantage in getting more resources.[80] According to the list of Higher Education Budget in 2007, Shanghai and Beijing ranked first and second respectively, and Sichuan Province ranked 29.[81] Moreover, it is much easier to invite leaders of the EU, EU member states, or diplomats from the Delegation of the EU to China to visit the universities in Beijing and address staff and students there in that all of the Embassies of the EU member states are located in Beijing.[82] Therefore, students studying in universities out of the capital city have fewer opportunities to see or communicate with leaders of the EU or EU member states compared to the students in the capital city, which means that classroom teaching is even more important for them. Accordingly, the EU needs to pay more attention to the students and others who are not studying or living in the capital city since the public diplomacy program can be more effective in these areas.

Another interesting finding comes from the vertical comparison, which pertains to the different impact of the program in the three academic levels.

Only 2 of 10 PhD students had a positive attitude towards the EU; the remainder was concerned about its internal conflicts and future. Considering the critical views of academic researchers, the responses of the PhD students were understandable. This means that the academic programs were more effective among undergraduate students than at masters and PhD levels because these programs provided basic and accurate information about the EU to undergraduate students who had no systematic knowledge of the EU or previous studying or living experience in the European countries. Nevertheless, this finding does not mean that the EU only needs to focus on college students at the lower levels without supporting PhD research on the EU, since well-trained PhD students will eventually become the intermediaries of the EU's public diplomacy in the future. In fact, of a large number of PhD students in China, the proportion of those who are interested in European studies is small. Therefore, training more PhD students specializing in European studies has a potential influence on Chinese students' perceptions of the EU.

All the student interviewees gave their opinions on the visibility of the Jean Monnet Programme and their confidence in the knowledge related to European studies delivered through Jean Monnet Programme-sponsored courses. Of the 87 interviewees, 27 did not know the Jean Monnet Programme at all; 57 only knew about it in the sense that their universities had Jean Monnet Professors or Centres, and only 3 knew that the program was implemented by the DG-EAC. However, all trusted the knowledge provided by their teachers, even though the latter are funded by the EU: the students felt that their professors were entirely ethical, though interestingly around 30 of them believed that their teachers definitely displayed a preference towards the EU. In terms of the relationship between the credibility of the sources of the information, the independence of the information sources and communication channels already connects to the high credibility of the information being delivered. Although the Jean Monnet professors and models were supported by the EU, the information about the EU taught in Chinese universities was deemed accurate and credible from the view of knowledge diffusion.

Table 6.13. **The visibility of the Jean Monnet Programme**

Do you know the Jean Monnet Programme?		
Some knowledge	3	3.45%
A little knowledge	57	65.52%
No	27	31.03%

Table 6.14.　The confidence in the knowledge delivered in the Jean Monnet Programme-sponsored courses

Do you think it can influence your perception of the EU if the research is sponsored by the EU?		
Yes	0	0
No	87	100%

Former research results and the interests in Europe are the prerequisites of getting the funding for these professors, meaning that they already know the EU well and more importantly, they display a preference for it. Besides, the reputable professors doing academic research on the EU and having a rich output in this area have to conform to research ethics. The Jean Monnet Professors and other scholars who get funding for teaching can give their students an accurate picture of the EU without any misleading ideas or bias. The credibility of information transmission is one of the important characteristics of successful public diplomacy. Therefore, professors who do research related to Europe and teach college students have become a reliable information source for their students. They can spread their ideas about the EU among the public by accepting interviews from the mass media and connecting the EU and their home countries, and also work as a think tank which provides intellectual support for European integration, which are exactly the aims for which the Jean Monnet Programme was designed.[83]

Public diplomacy is by its very nature an activity of boundary spanning—not only across geographical borders, but also across networks of communities of different ideals, customs, faiths, and political objectives which may decisively influence the outcomes of public diplomacy.[84] On the one hand, as already indicated in chapter 4, the intermediaries of public diplomacy—the Jean Monnet Professors and other experts sponsored by this program—are those who can move between networks and create a connection between particular clusters. According to research on the diffusion of American studies in Europe conducted by Fisher, it can be concluded that the key point to placing the study of America within an analysis of public diplomacy is the need for communication between the distinct communities.[85] This particular approach has the greatest potential where individuals can bridge communities and cross the cultural barriers in order to understand the meaning behind particular questions and perspectives that each community has developed. When it comes to the Jean Monnet Programme in China, what matters most is that the diffusion of European studies in China fits the trend of learning from western developed countries and Chinese professors and experts sponsored by this program naturally have the capacity of bridging these two different cultural entities through their own research, teaching, and transcultural communication ability. In this sense, these professors can be regarded as a reliable source of the EU.

On the other hand, the high visibility of public diplomacy programs does not necessarily lead to a positive image.[86] Although the professors sponsored by the Jean Monnet Programme serve as intermediaries of EU public diplomacy in China and tell the EU's story to Chinese college students, it is still an official educational and academic program. "We [Westerners] do not trust what governments say (not only Communist governments but also our own governments), so a low visibility of the sponsor behind public diplomacy projects can have more success."[87] As the interviews in China show, Chinese college students have insufficient knowledge about the Jean Monnet Programme itself, but they do trust the knowledge about the EU delivered by Chinese professors sponsored by this program. In other words, the objective of this program—knowledge dissemination—has been embedded in its implementation process. Although not enough data was obtained to evaluate the relationship between the visibility of the Jean Monnet Programme in Chinese universities and students' perception of the EU, Manheim's findings remain persuasive.

Also, the public diplomacy function of the Jean Monnet Programme can be discerned through the EU's action of promoting this program to China. According to Wilson, public diplomacy programmes can also bring other diplomatic benefits even if they do not act effectively as expected (like increasing foreign publics' knowledge of or positively changed perceptions of the communicator).[88] For example, the act of creating exchange and mobility programs for foreign publics sends signals to those publics and their governments. The history of the major scholarship programs proves that they were originally designed to signal goodwill or distract attention from potentially embarrassing policies.

All in all, based on the data from the fieldwork, the Jean Monnet Programme has an influence on college students' knowledge and perceptions of the EU, and this influence is, to a large extent, positive. In the following part, we will analyze the data from Chinese PhD students.

6.2.3 Chinese PhD Students' Research Topic Related to the EU

The analysis of the interviews recorded above has already included data from PhD students who were researching the EU, its member states, and other relevant subjects, but the PhD students as a special group of college students deserve further analysis here. Compared with the undergraduate and masters students in China, who are mainly educated in practical skills no matter what majors they are studying, most of the PhD students are trained for research work and academic positions, meaning that they will continue their research independently and start teaching college students after graduation. In this regard, training the PhD students of European studies can have more impact. Since this research focuses on the effect of the Jean Monnet Programme on Chinese students and even the public more broadly, all the interviewees from the PhD group were supervised by the Jean Monnet Professors in China.

Although the quantity of PhD students trained by a Jean Monnet Professor can be used as an indicator of this program, in that around 15 years ago, this indicator was used to research the effect of the Jean Monnet Action (carried out by a French independent company), this research studies the effect of supervisors on PhD students and their research related to the EU through looking at the process of PhD training and also the potential effect of these PhD students after obtaining their degrees and starting academic research. In other words, this research is concerned more about the quality of the PhD students of European studies.

Through talking with these PhD students—who were participating in the interview voluntarily—it is possible to figure out how these PhD students were affected by their supervisors during the process of topic selection, material collection, and thesis writing, which will also imply how those PhD students might exert their influence on their own students in the future.

With regards to the supervisors of these PhD students, first of all, they qualified as doctoral supervisors according to rigid standards and procedures, which shows that they meet the requirements in terms of degrees, academic achievement and teaching qualifications in higher education institutions. Secondly, they were selected by the implementation branch of the Jean Monnet Programme as Jean Monnet Professors based on their research output concerning European studies. Therefore, the Jean Monnet Professors in China are capable of supervising PhD students who are interested in researching the EU and relevant issues.

In terms of the influence of the Jean Monnet Professors as PhD supervisors, it can also be partially explained by the regulations for recruiting new PhD students in China. For PhD students in western countries, there is a tradition of applying for a PhD position based on personal motivations and previous academic performance, but passing entrance exams including a written exam and an oral test are the main methods for recruiting new PhD students in China. In other words, prospective PhD students in China have the right to choose supervisors according to their own research interests before attending the entrance exam but do not have to decide on their research topics. Therefore, Chinese professors have more influence on topic selection and the writing of papers.

According to the interviews, three PhD students at SCU chose their thesis topics in European studies because their supervisors were doing research on European culture and literature, but they had more space and freedom to develop their own research since their supervisors were willing to cooperate with them in investigating some new subjects. One PhD interviewee at FDU said that his supervisor decided the thesis topic for him in that his supervisor thought the comparative study of crisis management between the EU and China was a new academic field deserving of more scholarly study[89] while another PhD student at RUC believed that she focused on the cooperation on clean energy technologies between Germany and China not only because she was interested in that topic but also because she could transfer to the Free University of Berlin for fieldwork with the assistance of her supervisor.[90] One PhD student at SCU who was doing her PhD degree in literature with a focus on European culture said that she attended some lectures and seminars on European integration, European identification and Turkey's accession to the EU given by professors from the University of Leuven and Vrije University Brussels before making a decision on her PhD research topic, and she finally chose to research the issue of nationality during the process of European integration.[91] This shows that Chinese professors can influence the research topics of their PhD students in different ways.

Furthermore, the PhD students trained in the three centres also promoted the establishment of European Union research network among other research students. At SCU, the Jean Monnet Centre supported a PhD Forum to encourage communication and knowledge exchange among research students.[92] At FDU, student groups were organized to discuss EU-themed topics regularly, while the Youth Forum in Shanghai Institute for European Studies held conferences and encourages PhD students as well as young scholars to publish research papers on EU studies.[93] All of these activities benefit the training of the future generation.

When it comes to the possible influence of these PhD students, it can be identified from two aspects: one of them is based on their current research and publications since all the PhD students are required to publish at least two papers in academic journals as one of the requirements for obtaining their PhD degree. In fact, in the highly competitive academic job market for PhD graduates, most of them endeavor to publish their papers in well-known and influential journals, participate in international conferences, and present their research papers, all of which promotes academic discussion and debate about European studies in China. The other is that those PhD students who are doing research on different aspects of the EU have an influence on European studies and prospective college students. Of the 10 PhD students, three of them were part-time since two of them also worked in other universities as lecturers and one was working as a researcher in Shanghai Institute of European Studies, and the rest who were full-time PhD students intended to look for academic positions in colleges or research institutes.

According to the interview record, the PhD topics of those ten PhD students are as follows:

Cooperation between Germany and China on Clean Energy Technologies;
Cooperation between the EU and China on Climate Change;
Comparative study between the EU and China on Crisis Management;
Public Opinion and Europe's Perception of China;
The Issue of Nationality during the Process of European Integration;
The Immigration policy of the EU;
The Ideological Basis of European Integration;
The Historical Evolution of European Identity in the Official Documents of
  the EU;
Religion and European Integration;
The Historical Evolution of the Notion of Democracy

Those research themes examined the EU from the different angles of politics, economics, and culture, and among them, 4 of the topics were about EU-China relations in different issue areas; 3 of them discussed the factors influencing European integration; 2 were on regional policies of the EU and one of them gave attention to the notion of democracy—one of the important principles of the EU. From their PhD topics, we can tell that the research of PhD students in China covered the significant aspects and hotly debated issues of European integration and EU-China relations. As an innovative study, PhD students aim to make scholarly contributions to the areas they are studying. Therefore, it is not difficult to tell that all these PhD topics that have been little researched, which enriches the content of European studies in China.

When it came to the main information sources for researching the EU, all of them indicated that the official websites of the EU provided them with all the archives, official statements, speeches of the leaders, full text of the treaties, and even the treaties or official papers in progress. In fact, considering the information transparency of the EU, most of the useful documentation can be easily found in EU websites. Besides providing the basic data for scholarly research about the EU, the EU offers everyone an equal and easy opportunity to acquire accurate information about the EU, helping the EU communicate a positive image to Chinese PhD students.

Also, the research results of European professors were another crucial reference for their PhD theses. Referring to the research achievements of European professors including their journal papers, conference presentations, articles, and monographs, indicates that the Chinese students keep pace with new research development that matters for both their doctoral research and their knowledge delivery activities in the future.

Four of them mentioned that they paid attention to the news reports and professional comments on current issues of the EU in the Chinese mass media but mainly for keeping updated rather than getting information. They usually compared the news reports from both the Chinese and overseas mass media and checked the official statements of the EU if they were interested in some issues that had happened recently so as to maintain a balanced perspective.

At this stage, it can be concluded that the Jean Monnet Programme has had an impact on the research and teaching on the EU of the academics who were interviewed. In fact, since the Jean Monnet Professors as the intermediaries of EU public diplomacy mainly serve the information communication of the EU in China, interviewing them can only imply that they can play a role in telling the EU's story to college students with the necessary financial support from this program.

College students' perceptions of the EU before and after attending the relevant courses were discussed in this chapter. Most PhD students who were interviewed showed a more balanced attitude towards the EU although they had different research areas and interests. The Jean Monnet Programme has no sub-program to support PhDs in European studies, but those PhD students who studied in the Jean Monnet Centres in China benefited from other academic programs sponsored by the EU such as Erasmus Mundus. Therefore, those academic programs launched by the EU have consistently promoted research on European integration and the EU, and they try to cover scholars from different levels of higher education, and as many as possible through coordinating those programs internally.

Admittedly, the research results about descriptive knowledge dissemination in this chapter rely on the self-reflection of the student interviewees, but they are adults who may able to identify the influence of classroom teaching from other information sources. Based on the interview data, in general, a positive influence on Chinese students' descriptive knowledge and perceptions of the EU through the Jean Monnet Programme can be seen, which echoes the result of previous research that "Chinese people who know more about the EU's internal complexity, such as EU's history and the membership of the EU, are also more likely to have a positive attitude about the EU as well as EU citizens."[94] Although the interviews only included college students in three universities, its role in educating future generations of young elites has already been proved following its implementation in China to a certain extent, as this research illustrates. However, as mentioned in the introduction, China is qualitatively different from the EU member states where the Jean Monnet

Programme has been implementing for over 25 years due to the ideological differences, so it has to look at how this program has been implemented in the Chinese context. Moreover, in chapter 7, a comparative study between students who registered for EU themed courses and those who did not attend any EU-related modules will be made in order to further testify the effect of descriptive and normative knowledge dissemination through this program.

NOTES

1. Interview with Professor E in Shanghai, Dec. 23, 2013.

2. Rasmussen, S. B. (2010), "The Messages and Practices of the European Union's Public Diplomacy," *The Hague Journal of Diplomacy*, 5(3): 280.

3. Alexander, C. (2011), "Public Diplomacy and the Diplomatic Truce: Taiwan and the People's Republic of China in EI Salvador," *Public Diplomacy and Place Branding*, 7(4): 274.

4. Forster, C. and Owen, J. (2006), *Understanding Iran: A Solution to the Nuclear Crisis?* London: Foreign Policy Centre, available at: http://fpc.org.uk/fsblob/710.pdf, [accessed May 10, 2016].

5. Danielsen, H. (2009), "Making Friends at Court: Slow and Indirect Media in US Public Diplomacy in Norway, 1950–1965," *Contemporary European History*, 18(2): 184.

6. Interview with Professor H in Chengdu, Sichuan, Dec. 17, 2013.

7. Interview with Professor C in Beijing, Dec. 16, 2014.

8. Interview with Vito Borrelli in Brussels, Feb. 6, 2016.

9. Weiss, R. (1994), *Learning from Strangers*, New York: Free Press.

10. Small, M. L. (2009), "How Many Cases Do I Need? On Science and the Logic of Case Selection in Field-Based Research," *Ethnology*, 10(1): 13–14.

11. Ibid: 14.

12. Hannabuss, S. (1996), "Research Interviews," *New Library World*, 97(5): 25.

13. Qu, Q. S. and Dumay, J. (2011), "The Qualitative Research Interview," *Qualitative Research in Accounting & Management*, 8(3): 249.

14. Interviews with Vito Borrelli and Renato Girelli in Brussels, Feb. 6, 2015.

15. Interview with Professor A in Beijing, Dec. 11, 2013.

16. Dai, B. (2008), "European Studies in China," in Shambaugh, D., Sandschneider E. and Zhou H. (eds.), *China-Europe Relations: Perceptions, Polices and Prospects*, London and New York: Routledge: 106.

17. Song, X. (2008), "China's View of European Integration and Enlargement," in Shambaugh, D., Sandschneider E. and Zhou H. (eds.), *China-Europe Relations*, London and New York: Routledge: 179.

18. Interview with Professor D in Beijing, Dec. 16, 2014.

19. Jones, W. J. (2009–2010), "European Union Soft Power: Cultural Diplomacy & Higher Education in Southeast Asia," *Silpakorn University International Journal*, Vol. 9–10: 63–64.

20. Interview with Professor D in Beijing, Dec. 16, 2014.

21. Interview with college students in Beijing, Shanghai and Chengdu, Dec. 11, 2013 to Feb. 4, 2014

22. Interview with Professor K in Chengdu, Sichuan, Dec. 16, 2013.

23. Interviews with students in Chengdu, Sichuan, Mar. 31, 2016; April 2, 2016.

24. Interviews with Professor I and J in Chengdu, Sichuan, Dec. 16, 2013; Dec. 17, 2013.

25. Tang, S., Zhang, J. and Cao, X. (2005), "Zhongguo De Diqu Yanjiu: Chengjiu, Chaju He Qidai (Area Studies in China: Achievements, Deficiencies, and Prospects)," *Shijie Jingji Yu Zhengzhi* (*World Economics and Politics*), No. 11: 10

26. Edmonds, R. L. (2002), "China and Europe since 1978: An Introduction," *The China Quarterly*, Vol. 169: 2.

27. Interview with William Fingleton in Beijing, Dec. 11, 2014.

28. MFA (2014), *China's Policy Paper on the EU: Deepen the China-EU Comprehensive Strategic Partnership for Mutual Benefit and Win-win Cooperation*, available at: http://www.fmprc.gov.cn/mfa_eng/wjdt_665385/wjzcs/t1143406.shtml, [accessed April 26, 2016].

29. MFA (2016), Wang Yi Meets with Assistant to the US President for National Security Affairs Susan Rice, available at: http://www.fmprc.gov.cn/mfa_eng/zxxx_662805/t1343846.shtml, [accessed April 26, 2016].

30. Interview with Professor E in Shanghai, Dec. 23, 2013.

31. Zhang, C. (2008), "Renquanguan Chayi Ji Zhongou Guanxi (*Different Concepts of Human Rights and China-EU Relations*)," Doctoral Thesis, Beijing: Peking University.

32. Zhou, H. (2011), "Zhongou Guanxi Zhong De Renzhi Cuowei (Congitive Dissonance in China-EU Relations)," *Guoji Wenti Yanjiu* (*International Studies*), No. 5.

33. Pan, Z. (ed.), (2012), *Conceptual Gaps in China-EU Relations*, London: Palgrave Macmillan.

34. European Commission, (2008), Presentation of Jean Monnet Prize 2008, available at: http://europa.eu/rapid/press-release_IP-08-1765_en.htm, [accessed May 12, 2016].

35. Interview with Professor H in Chengdu, Sichuan, Dec. 17, 2013.

36. EACEA (2014), *Erasmus Plus Programme Guide*, available at: http://ec.europa.eu/programmes/erasmus-plus/documents/erasmus-plus-programme-guide_en.pdf, [accessed Mar. 14, 2015].

37. EACEA (2014), *Information about the Jean Monnet Programme from 2007–2013*, available at: http://eacea.ec.europa.eu/llp/jean_monnet/jean_monnet_en.php, [accessed Sept. 29, 2014].

38. Interviews with Professor H and J in Chengdu, Sichuan, Dec. 16, 2013; Dec. 17, 2013.

39. Centre for European Studies at Sichuan University (2014), http://ces.scu.edu.cn/Index.html, [accessed 15-06-2015].

40. Interview with Professor A in Beijing, Dec. 11, 2014.

41. Interview with Marcin Grabiec in Beijing, Dec. 11, 2014.

42. Interview with Professor E in Shanghai, Dec. 24, 2013.

43. Interview with college students in Beijing, Shanghai and Chengdu, Dec. 11, 2013 to Feb. 4, 2014

44. Interview with Professor H in Chengdu, Sichuan, Dec. 17, 2013.

45. Ministry of Education, China (2015), The Notification of the 2015 Project List of National College Student Innovation Fund, available at: http://www.moe.gov.cn/s78/A08/A08_gggs/A08_sjhj/201510/t20151029_216448.html, [accessed May 12, 2016].

46. Interview with Professor J in Chengdu, Sichuan, Dec. 16, 2013.

47. EACEA (2014), *Information about the Jean Monnet Programme from 2007-2013*, available at: http://eacea.ec.europa.eu/llp/jean_monnet/jean_monnet_en.php, [accessed Sept. 29, 2014]

48. Interview with Professor A in Beijing, Dec. 11, 2013; Interview with Vito Borrelli in Brussels, Feb. 6, 2015.

49. Interview with Professor H in Chengdu, Sichuan, Dec. 17, 2014.

50. Interview with students in Chengdu, Sichuan, Dec. 18, 2014; Dec. 19, 2014; Dec. 20, 2014.

51. Bellamy, C. and Weinberg, A. (2008), "Educational and Cultural Exchange to Restore America's Image," *The Washington Quarterly*, 31(3): 59.

52. Interview with student interviewees in Beijing, Dec. 14, 2013; Dec. 15, 2103.

53. Interview with Professor E in Shanghai, Dec. 23, 2014.

54. Chaban, N, and Elgström, O. (2014), "The Role of the EU in an Emerging New World Order in the Eyes of the Chinese, Indian and Russian Press," *Journal of European Integration*, 36(2): 170–188.

55. Interview with Professor E in Shanghai, Dec. 23, 2014.

56. Interviews with Professor J and K in Chengdu, Sichuan, Dec. 17, 2013; Dec. 18, 2013; Dec. 19, 2013.

57. European Union (2014), EU treaties, available at: http://europa.eu/eu-law/decision-making/treaties/index_en.htm, [accessed Mar. 24, 2015].

58. Interview with Professor E in Shanghai, Dec. 23, 2013.

59. Interview with Professor H in Chengdu, Sichuan, Dec. 17, 2013.

60. Centre for European Studies at Renmin University of China (2014), http://www.cesruc.org/, [accessed June 15, 2015]

61. Centre for European Studies at Fudan University (2014), http://www.cesfd.org.cn/index.htm, [accessed June 15, 2015].

62. Centre for European Studies at Sichuan University (2014), http://ces.scu.edu.cn/Index.html, [accessed June 15, 2015].

63. Interview in Beijing, Dec. 15, 2014.

64. Interview in Shanghai, Dec. 22, 2014, Dec. 23, 2013.

65. Interview with an undergraduate student in Chengdu, Dec. 17, 2013.

66. Interview with Professor I in Chengdu, Sichuan, March 14, 2016.

67. When the author of the book went to Brussels for a conference about EU-China relations (17th–19th June, 2014), he presented the outline of this research to the scholars participating in that conference. Some of them asked this question.

68. Chen, G. M. (1995), "Differences in Self-disclosure Patterns among Americans versus Chinese: A Comparative Study," *Journal of Cross-Cultural Psychology*, 26(1): 87–90.

69. Interview in Shanghai, Dec. 29, 2013.

70. Interview in Chengdu, Dec. 17, 2013.

71. Yi, D. Shi, J. and Li, Z. (2013), "Oumeng Fazhan De Buqueding Yu Zhongou Guanxi De Weilai (The Uncertain Trend of the EU and Future of Sino-EU Relations)," in *Ouzhou Yanjiu Luncong (European Studies Forum)*, Vol. 15: 26–29.

72. Nye, J. (2008), "Public Diplomacy and Soft Power," *Annals of the American Academy of Political and Social Science*, 616(1): 106.

73. Mulcahy, K. V. (1999), "Cultural Diplomacy and the Exchange Programme: 1938–1978," *The Journal of Arts, Management, Law, and Society*, 29(1): 12–13.

74. Interview with an undergraduate student in Chengdu, Dec. 13, 2013.

75. Interview with Professor H in Chengdu, Sichuan, Dec. 17, 2014.

76. Chen, X., Xiong, H., Qin, H., Sun, Y. (2011), *Ouzhou Jingji Yanjiu Shinian Pingshu (2001–2010) (The Review of European Economy Research [2001–2010])*, Institute of European Studies of Chinese Academy of Social Science, available at: http://ies.cass.cn/Article/cbw/ozjj/201108/4140.asp, [accessed July 29, 2014].

77. Zhang, J. (2012), *Ouzhou Guoji Guanxi Yanjiu Shinian Pingshu (2001–2010) (The Review of European International Relations Research [2001–2010])*, Institute of European Studies of Chinese Academy of Social Science, available at: http://ies.cass.cn/Article/cbw/ouwj/201108/4122.asp, [accessed July 29, 2014]

78. Wu, X., Zhao, C., Zhang, L. (2011), *Ouzhou Zhengzhi Yanjiu Shinian Pingshu (2001–2010) (The Review of European Politics Research [2001–2010])*; Institute of European Studies of Chinese Academy of Social Science, available at: http://ies.cass.cn/Article/cbw/ozzz/201108/4128.asp, [accessed July 29, 2014].

79. Dai, B. (2008), "European Studies in China," in Shambaugh, D., Sandschneider E. and Zhou H. (eds.), *China-Europe Relations: Perceptions, Polices and Prospects*, London and New York: Routledge: 108–110.

80. Interview with Professor H in Chengdu, Sichuan, Dec. 17, 2014.

81. Chen, A. and Wu, B. (2011), "The Regional Division of the Higher Education Sector in China: A Spatial Analysis," in Morgan, W. J. and Wu, B. (eds.), *Higher Education Reform in China: Beyond the Expansion*, London and New York: Routledge: 18.

82. Both Polish ambassador to China and officer in European Commission were invited to give public speeches in Renmin University of China when the author was doing his masters' degree there; Angela Merkel, the Chancellor of Germany was invited to give a speech in Tsinghua University in July 8, 2014.

83. European Commission (2011), *Regulation of the European Parliament and of the Council, Establishing "Erasmus for All," the Union Programme for Education, Training, Youth and Sport*, COM (2011) 788 Final, Brussels: 21.

84. Fisher, A. (2013), *Collaborative Public Diplomacy: How Transnational Networks Influenced American Studies in Europe*, New York: Palgrave Macmillan: 10–11.

85. Ibid: 14.

86. Manheim, J. B. (1994), *Strategic Public Diplomacy and American Foreign Policy: The Evolution of Influence*, New York: Oxford University Press: 126–47.

87. Conversation with an EU official during a roundtable discussion affiliated to Europe China Research and Advice Network (ECRAN) annual conference on 17–19 of June, 2014 in Brussels.

88. Wilson, I. (2010), *Are International Exchange and Mobility Programmes Effective Tools of Symmetric Public Diplomacy?* Aberystwyth University, available at: http://cadair.aber.ac.uk/dspace/handle/2160/7177, [accessed Sept. 18, 2014]: 2.

89. Interview with a PhD student in Shanghai, Dec. 30, 2013

90. Interview with a PhD student in Beijing, Dec. 11, 2013

91. Interview with a PhD student in Chengdu, Dec. 16, 2013.

92. Centre for European Studies at Sichuan University (2014), http://ces.scu.edu.cn/Index.html, [accessed June 15, 2015].

93. Centre for European Studies at Fudan University (2014), http://www.cesfd.org.cn/index.htm, [accessed June 15, 2015].

94. Wang, Z. and Popescu, B. G. (2011), *Understanding EU's Internal Complexities Help Increase Chinese Perception of The EU and Europe*, China Policy Center in University of Nottingham, http://www.nottingham.ac.uk/cpi/research/funded-projects/chinese-eu/consortium.aspx, [accessed Oct. 10, 2014]: 2.

Chapter Seven

The EU's Normative Knowledge Dissemination through the Jean Monnet Programme

As the previous chapter always showed, the view of the EU as a model of regional integration has gained acceptance among most college students in China based on the first round interview results. However, besides descriptive knowledge of the EU, telling the EU's story in China cannot be isolated from the normative knowledge dissemination. However, considering that the EU and China do not share a common ground in terms of the norms highlighted by the EU such as freedom, democracy, human rights, and rule of law, particularly the governmental regulations on citizenship education in higher education institution, whether classroom teaching of EU norms can still be carrying out regularly in Chinese universities needs to be addressed in this research.

Thus, besides the fieldwork in EU headquarters in Brussels and three Chinese universities in Beijing, Shanghai, and Chengdu, this project conducted another small-scale survey by re-engaging four professor interviewees and approaching 62 new student interviewees at Renmin University of China in Beijing and Sichuan University in Chengdu. The European studies centers at these two universities as only two European studies centers in China are not only awarded the Jean Monnet Centres of Excellence but also approved and supported by the Ministry of Education, P. R. China as Bases for National and Regional Studies, so how to meet the requirements of both sponsors may be reflected on how the teaching has been carried out regarding some sensitive issues. This research was carried out in March and April 2016, and a detailed analysis on the interviewees with professor and student interviewees is as follows.

As triangulation is to realize a more effective method for capturing and fixing of a social phenomenon in order to achieve a more accurate explanation and analysis,[1] archives (of official sources of the EU) and documentary evidence (the news stories from some influential media outlets such as *The New York Times, The South China Morning Post, The Financial Times*, and *The*

Reuters) will be referred. Besides, interviews with professors and students will be cross-referred for the purpose of triangulation.

7.1 CLASSROOM TEACHING OF EU NORMS

In order to understand whether/how governmental regulations regarding citizenship education in China have an impact on classroom teaching of universal norms in general or EU norms in particular, the second round interview re-approached four professors at RUC and SCU, including one Jean Monnet Chair and one Jean Monnet Module leader at RUC and one Jean Monnet Chair and one Associate Professor working at SCU.

Table 7.1.   Interview questions for Chinese professors in the second round interview

Demographic questions:	
C1	Gender: male/female
C2	Teaching level: undergraduate/master/PhD
C3	How many years have you been teaching?
Warming-up questions:	
C4	What course do you teach?
C5	How many years do you teach this/these course(s)?
C6	Why do you teach this/these course(s)? Did you take this position because of personal interests, departmental need or university demand?
Leading questions:	
C7	When you deliver classroom teaching, are EU norms included your teaching content?
C8	Which norm(s) are discussed/delivered in your module(s)? Why this (these) norm(s)?
C9	Why do you choose this (these) norm(s) to be taught/discussed in your modules?
C10	When you teach or conduct research in Chinese universities, do you think that you can teach or research independently based on academic principles without being influenced by political factors?
C11	Do you know the government instructions known as "Seven Speak-Nots" regulating higher education?
C12	After this regulation came into force, do you make any necessary changes to your modules design/content?

Leading questions:	
C13	After this regulation came into force, do you make any necessary changes to discussions in your classroom?
C14	Do you think that your module content has been changed because of governmental regulations in terms of citizenship education?
C15	Do you need to get an approval for your modules from any governmental departments? If yes, how does this process work?

7.1.1 Interview Questions for Professor Interviewees

As mentioned in the previous section, interview questions for different groups will consist of three parts: demographic questions for basic information of the interviewees; warming-up questions used to make the interviewees feel relaxed; and leading questions used to get direct responses from the interviewees.

7.1.2 Analysis on the Interviews with Chinese Professors

All four professor interviewees including three male professors and one female professor were interviewed in the first round interview, and they were re-approached during this interview and asked to give their answers regarding the questions above. And among them, two professors at RUC had lectured on courses at the undergraduate and postgraduate levels for around 30 years, and one professor at SCU started teaching *Economy of Foreign Countries and Regions* since 1984, while one associate professor doing European identity formation during European integration for his PhD degree at SCU started teaching at the Jean Monnet Centre of Excellence after 2011. All these three professors have rich experience in curricular development, research project application, student supervision, and academic publication in China, and the associate professor who has been working in the Jean Monnet Centre of Excellence at SCU has his career across the launch of new governmental regulations. Thus, their answers would enlighten us whether and how the governmental regulations have an impact on academic activities of higher education institutions.

All these three professors have been teaching *World Economy*, and all of them started lecturing on this course at RUC and SCU in the early 1980s. One professor at RUC also taught *International Trade Negotiation* and *International Marketing*, while the other professor at RUC taught *International Economics* and *Project Management*. One professor at SCU lectured on *Money and Banking*, and *Economy of Foreign Countries and Regions*, and one associate professor lectured on *Twelve Lectures on European Studies* during 2012–2015. As all four professor interviewees said, they chose to teach these courses because of their own research interests.

Three professors teach international economics with a special focus on European economic integration, but their courses are not designed specifically for EU norms which are covered by these courses during the teaching process. However, it is because of the course design and content requirements instead of any governmental regulations. As one professor at RUC mentioned, the modules sponsored by the Jean Monnet Programme had a general requirement—information dissemination of European integration, so the knowledge regarding the EU including its history and current status should be fully addressed. Every year, he had to submit an annual report about the course content to a unit of the EU in charge of the Jean Monnet Programme, and the assessment process was very strict.[2] He also added that the module was taught by a group of professors, they can choose any aspect they specialized in albeit the course content cannot be deviated from European integration.[3] As showed in the Programme Guidance of the Jean Monnet Programme, the projects will be evaluated from five aspects including outputs, methods, experiences, policy implications, and European cooperation, requiring knowledge dissemination "within a certain field and topic," knowledge innovation, cross-border academic exchange and feedback for the adjustment to the further practice of this program.[4]

Considering that EU-China economic relations play a great part in international economy research since both the EU and China are economic giants in the world and economic situation of the EU and China's economic development attract world attention, all Chinese professors who teach *International Economics* or *World Economy* have to mention the EU-China economic relations. During the interviews with these three professors, two professors said they can talk about the debates on China's market economy status and having different opinions was totally acceptable. One professor said that he did not think China officially entered the phase of market economy when he taught one module because the problems faced by China including food security and stock market manifested that planned economy rather than market economy influenced China's economic performance. Although the liberal market economy is not one of EU norms indicated by Manners,[5] it is still a hot issue in EU-China relations and the debates on China's market economy status can be fully discussed without being interrupted by any governmental policies.

Besides, the rule of law is an EU norm being discussed in these economic courses. As one professor said, talking about EU-China economic relations will unavoidably cover the role of WTO in solving the trade disputes such as anti-dumping between the EU and China. In this sense, international economic law and the rule of law will be discussed in the course content.[6] One associate professor said that all the EU norms cannot be avoided when teaching the political aspects of the EU and according to his teaching and research experience, all these norms can be taught in the Chinese classrooms of higher education institutions.[7] Altbach thinks that restriction on academic freedom is an integral part of university life in China, particularly in social sciences that are considered politically and ideologically sensitive.[8] However, according to the interviews with students, professors can still be able to discuss EU norms without surveillance in the classroom,[9] which at least implies that normative knowledge dissemination has not been disrupted during classroom teaching process.

As the course leader of *Twelve Lectures on European Studies,* one associate professor organised a group of professors at SCU to teach different sessions of the module consisting of EU economic integration, cultural diversity, religions, politics, foreign policy, education policy, enlargement, and humanitarian aid. This course as a public elective course opened for the undergraduate students at SCU, which approximately covered 100 students each year. He said he can teach the knowledge of EU norms in this course, and the course content of the concept of "Normative Power Europe" and some EU norms including human rights, democracy and liberty can be detailed discussed. On the one hand, the course content would be determined by the research interests of each professor because they had their own research agendas. On the other hand, some students who were interested in EU norms would ask questions about these norms, particularly liberty, human rights, and democracy, and the course leaders would also have to answer their students' questions.

> Since Chinese students have more opportunities to access the information of the EU as well as the information that might not be released on the Chinese mass media, their questions can address any informational knowledge or criticism on China. Under this circumstance, we will answer their questions based on our research achievements.[10]

However, he also added that we [course leaders] would give a correct guidance to the students' reflective thinking on EU norms.[11] As Wang argues, because "the EU's normative power originates from European civilisation, it is difficult to cross civilisations and to impact on other than Europe's own, rather homogenous, civilization," which is almost a consensus regarding Western norms among Chinese academics.[12] However, the students stated that they did use foreign media reports, EU official news releases as well as academic publications as their information sources of the EU,[13] so the governmental regulations did not seem to exert a perceived influence on students' knowledge of EU norms.

Because of the interviewees who can be approached this time mainly focused on economic integration and social issues during European integration, the norms covered by their modules were only closely related to the content they taught. Moreover, according to the professor interviewees, their research and teaching can elaborate on these EU norms if necessary. Since the interviews with professors and students took place at the same period, two professor interviewees were asked whether they felt that their publications had been influenced because one student said professors can talk about Western values in the classroom but not in their publications. One professor at RUC insisted that he did not think his publications had been affected by presenting some recent newspaper commentaries and a journal article to the interviewer[14] while anther professor at the same university said that there might be some revision comments based on the editors' understanding, but he had the freedom to accept or not.[15] By checking the titles of publications in academic journals in Chinese Academic Journal Full-text Database, from January 2014 to May 2016, over 1,000 papers about human rights, 7,600 about democracy and 11,000 about the rule of law had been published.[16] However, the top 10 oft-cited papers in each category stressed the Chinese path, Chinese characteristics or the particularity of the Chinese context without making any comparison with international understanding of these norms. In this sense, students' views about their professors' publications might be correct to some extent.

When it comes to the visibility of governmental regulations including "Seven Speak-Nots" in higher education institutions, three professor interviewees said they had never heard of these regulations. One professor said there were some regulations in dealing with cooperation with foreign universities as she once served as the secretary in charge of external relations for her university for several years, but she did not think there were any perceived regulations on classroom teaching.[17] One professor at RUC said he started researching and teaching international economics in 1985, but no one had ever said that he cannot lecture on some content in his classroom.[18] He might make some changes to the course content because of knowledge updates since the economic reality of the world continued to change, but these changes were made based on his research and understanding rather than any governmental regulations or administrative orders.[19] Even so, academic freedom has always been one of the concerns that impede the progress of Chinese universities.[20] Yet, some leading Chinese universities had never ceased their endeavors in pursuing academic freedom by influencing policy environment and public policy.[21]

One professor at RUC said he heard about the "Seven Speak-Nots," but he believed that it aimed to regulate the course content to satisfy the requirement of knowledge dissemination emphasized by students rather than any governmental policy. He added that a great number of professors started doing research through interdisciplinary approaches, which should be a good thing. However, their research capability in other disciplines might not be strong enough, making the course content irrelevant to course objectives but simply based on some anecdotes sometimes. Based on his experience, it was not the governmental regulations that required some adjustments to course content, but students who paid for their higher education and wanted to get objective knowledge asked to make the course content more knowledge-oriented. Based on the anonymous online replies from over 300 college students, a survey result about the course content regarding contemporary China was released on *Liaoning Daily* in October 2014 which generated nationwide discussion in China. It found that college students were not agreed with some professors who turned the classroom into a place to express his anger to the government,[22] which might be one of the reasons that governmental regulations had to be released. Yet, Chinese professors did not feel pressured to change their way of teaching due to the survey result.[23]

On the contrary, although the Great Famine remained a taboo in China as claimed by Western scholars or Western mainstream media,[24, 25] one professor at RUC also said that some controversial issues in Chinese politics such as the exact number of victims of the natural disasters of the late 1950s and 1960s can be discussed academically. He had presented his research regarding this topic based on the documents released in China and the US, which had never been questioned by any governmental department,[26] albeit no news reports can be found regarding his lectures. Besides, the Ministry of Education and other relevant governmental departments encouraged the high-level talent attracting ("yin-zhi"), so a great number of Western experts in social science and humanities started their career, either full-time or part-time, in Chinese universities. Under these policies, the Chinese government and educational departments evaluated these professors based on their academic qualifications and research influence rather than their political belief. In this sense, teaching and research in higher education institutions in China are, at least in the field of EU studies, based on academic principles rather than any political regulations. One professor at RUC cited the summer school as a case to further his opinion on the academic freedom in China.

> Summer school at the RUC is very popular and some famous Western professors are invited to teach summer school courses every year. I do not think they have been restricted to talk about any norms about the EU.[27]

However, he also added that there was no boundary of academic research but should be some rules on classroom teaching. Classroom teaching is to disseminate knowledge and raise critical thinking, so the knowledge that each course includes should be accurately delivered to the students through teaching and discussion process.

In terms of the influence of "Seven Speak-Nots" on course design, course content and classroom discussion, no one thought there was any perceived governmental influence on these aspects. One professor at RUC said that he had been teaching for over 30 years but no one had ever asked him to make any changes to the course content because it was not consistent with the objectives of China's citizenship education, and he would do the changes to the course design or course content only if the knowledge he delivered was out of time.[28] However, some Chinese academics did express their concerns about the effect of ideological crackdown on academic freedom in the long run,[29] albeit the governmental control might not be in effect in a short term.

One associate professor at SCU said some content of the EU-China relations that seemed sensitive in politics can actually be talked in the classroom, and the lecturers may also be asked by the students regarding these sensitive issues even if these topics had not been addressed. Put differently, the course content was not a simple decision of the lecturers themselves but based on the preference and feedback of college students. Since the student evaluation on teachers' performance will have an impact on the promotion of universities' teachers,[30] university teachers have to compromise between students' requirements and governmental regulations if there are any. One professor at SCU thought there were not too many sensitive topics in the areas of European economic integration or international economics since these areas were mainly established by empirical and statistical data, so she did not think she would meet any ideological problems in teaching the EU.[31] At least in the classroom, the student interviewees also agreed that EU norms can be taught without any restrictions,[32] so did some foreign professors worked in China.[33]

With regard to the classroom discussion, the students would have their own preferred discussion topics related to the courses, so the course leaders had to respond to their questions including some sensitive topics as already mentioned before. However, the most important thing was that academic integrity and freedom, at least in the courses outside schools of Marxism, had been maintained after the release of "Seven Speak-Nots" in 2013, according to the interviewees.

In terms of the submission of new course plans, no professor mentioned that he/she had to submit any plan to the governmental departments or needed to get approval for their new course syllabuses. One professor at SCU said her university encouraged professors to open new courses, particularly public elective courses, to students at different levels, in that her university wanted students to learn knowledge of different disciplines to open their eyes.[34] She also added that all the applicants who wanted to open new courses only needed to submit course syllabuses to the school office in charge of course arrangement, and the school office usually just paid attention to how many prospective students may register for the new courses.[35] One associate professor expressed the same ideas about new course plan submission at SCU, and he also stated that no courses with the words of "foreign" or "Western" in the course titles had not been approved by the school office according to his colleagues' and his own experiences.[36] At the RUC, one professor added that the Jean Monnet Module as a part of *Development Economics*, a course that he had been teaching for over ten years in order to avoid the application procedure of opening a new course, but he believed that it was not difficult to apply for a new module if he wanted.[37] Besides, all these two professor interviewees at RUC said applying for opening new courses would not be a problem, because new modules that would be opened every year solely depended on the research interests of the new faculties joined in the university.

Some argue that curricula are still set with reference to the governmental regulations regarding ideological education.[38] In China, governmental regulations on higher education institutions have been reflected on the governmental approval for new degree programs. However, higher education institutions have the autonomy in textbook editing and selection as well as syllabuses.[39] Although the governmental regulations on the introduction of the new degree programs will influence what course can be taught in higher education institutions, the course content can still be determined by the course leaders.

Since no academic discussion about the direct influence of "Seven Speak-Nots" on academic freedom in China until 2016—two years after it had been released, this research mainly relies on the interviews with EU officials, Chinese professor and college students. In fact, no one had ever mentioned the influence of governmental regulation on European studies in China during the interview with EU officials in Brussels and Beijing in late 2014 and early 2015. Besides, student interviewees also believed that at least during the classroom teaching process, professors in their universities can discuss EU norms or other relevant norms that might be considered politically sensitive in China. Moreover, professor interviewees covered in the second round interview also stated that they had not been affected by any governmental regulations on course design, classroom discussion, and course content. Although we cannot jump to the conclusion that academic activities have not been influenced by the instruction of "Seven Speak-Nots" or other governmental regulations, the interview data shows that normative knowledge dissemination had not been interrupted in the classroom. Besides, the EU also has its own approaches to engage Chinese students and the Chinese public directly, which will be elaborated later.

In sum, according to the interviews with Chinese professors, there was no perceived political impact of the governmental regulations on classroom teaching of the EU or EU norms, and professors sponsored by the Jean Monnet Programme can still talk about any topics of the EU based on the research findings of their own. One professor did say it was necessary to regulate the

Table 7.2.   A summary of the answers of professor interviewees regarding the teaching of EU norms

C7	When you deliver classroom teaching, are EU norms included your teaching content?	Yes. Basically, EU norms had always been covered by the courses sponsored by the Jean Monnet Programme, but different courses had different priorities.
C8	Which norm(s) are discussed/ delivered in your module(s)? Why this (these) norm(s)?	The modules related to European Economic integration paid more attention to the rule of law and China's market economy status while the modules of EU external relations concerned human rights and democracy in EU-China relations.
C9	Why do you choose this (these) norm(s) to be taught/discussed in your modules?	As mentioned above, EU norms covered by the specific modules were usually based on the content of different sessions, and the module leaders would not refer to some norms if they were irrelevant to the course content.
C10	When you teach or conduct research in Chinese universities, do you think that you can teach or research independently based on academic principles without being influenced by political factors?	Yes. Although governmental regulations about citizenship education had been released to regulate course content in higher education institutions, the professor interviewees thought they might have an impact on the courses opened by schools of Marxism. However, as it would show through the interviews with students, even professors at schools of Marxism maintained their freedom of academic discussion in the classroom to some extent.
C11	Do you know the government instructions known as "Seven Speak-Nots" regulating higher education institutions?	According to professor interviewees, 3 out of 4 did not know the "Seven Speak-Nots" regulations. Only one professor said he knew the regulations, but he thought it was necessary to regulate the course content since knowledge dissemination was still the first objective of classroom teaching.
C12–C14	After this regulation came into force, do you make any necessary changes to your modules design/content/ classroom teaching?	None of the professor interviewees thought the "Seven Speak-Nots" regulations had an impact on the course design, classroom discussion or course content. 3 out of 4 professor interviewees had been teaching in higher education institutions for over 30 years and they never made any changes to the course content or course design because of any governmental regulation, except the necessary knowledge updates based on their own research achievements.
C15	Do you need to submit your course plan to any government departments for their approval? If so, how this process works in your university?	All the professor interviewees said they did not need to submit course plans to governmental departments for their approval. They needed to submit course syllabuses to school departments in charge of course management, but these departments only evaluated the possibility of student registration. According to their experience, new course plans always got approval.

course content since knowledge dissemination in the classroom should be focused on the specific objectives of different courses instead of random criticism on governmental policies or political issues, but the visibility of governmental regulations, particularly the "Seven Speak-Nots" was low in academic circle based on the interviews. In the following section, it moves to look at how students see the classroom content of EU studies and EU norms in the Chinese context.

7.2 CLASSROOM LEARNING OF EU NORMS

Since this interview aims to find out whether EU norms can be disseminated in the Chinese context and whether there are obvious differences in college students' knowledge of the EU between students who enrolled in modules of EU studies/supervised by Jean Monnet Professors (Experimental group) and those who did not enrol in the modules of EU studies/ were not supervised by Jean Monnet Professors (Control group), student interviewees of each level include two categories with "E" indicating those covered by this program and "C" indicating those who were not covered by it.

"Experimental group" and "control group" as academic concepts are employed here to explain the differences between these two groups, but this interview is not an experiment in a social setting. Both "experimental group" and "control group" are concepts used in psychological experiment in natural (field) or laboratory settings, which aims to address whether significant differences have been made by the experimental stimulus or not in this specific stance by comparing the results of the experimental group with that of the control group.[40] In laboratory settings, more sources of error (extraneous variable) can be isolated from the experiments, so solid conclusions regarding the interventions as the real reasons for the results can be reached. Nevertheless, laboratory settings are not something the subjects encounter in real life, making the experiment results less likely to be generalized.[41] On the contrary, field experiments allow researchers to observe how people react to an experimental treatment or independent variable in natural settings and other real-world interactions.[42]

In this case of the implementation of the Jean Monnet Programme in the context of China, attending the Jean Monnet Modules/being supervised by the Jean Monnet Professors can be viewed as an experimental treatment (independent variable), so it seems that dividing student interviewees into two different groups meets the requirement of experiment in a field setting in this case. However, external factors that cannot be isolated from field experiments in a social setting may also influence the knowledge dissemination. Thus, studying the effect of the EU's knowledge dissemination in the Chinese context with two groups for comparison is not a field experiment.

However, dividing student interviewees in this interview into two groups including "experimental" and "control" groups is not meaningless. Registered for the EU-themed modules or supervised by Jean Monnet Professors serves as the only factor distinguishing the "experimental group" from the "control group." Based on the self-reflection of student interviewees, their answers can be generalized to some extent.

Table 7.3.   The number of the interviews in each category

	Undergraduate student		Master student		PhD student	
	E	C	E	C	E	C
Renmin University	9	11	5	6	1	1
Sichuan University	10	10	5	5	2	1

7.2.1 Interview Questions for College Students

These student interviewees were asked to answer the following questions:

Table 7.4.   Interview questions for Chinese students in the second round interview

Demographic questions:	
D1	Gender: male/female
D2	Studying level: undergraduate/master/PhD
D3	Age.
Warming-up questions:	
D4	What are you studying?
D5	Why are you studying this? A, school reputation; B, job expectation; C, parents' advice; D, personal interests; E, other.
D6	Which subjects do you like best in your discipline? Or which teacher do you like best?
Leading questions:	
D7	Have you studied EU norms as part of your modules or degree? If so, which eu norms have you discussed?
D8	Since the EU is regarded as a normative power, what do you think about the founding norms of the EU? Such as . . . (peace, liberty, democracy, rule of law, human rights, social solidarity, anti-discrimination, sustainable development, and good governance)?

Leading questions:	
D9	What do you think about the EU's norms taught in the classroom if any?
D10	What do you think about the EU's approach to the norm of . . . (peace, liberty, democracy, rule of law, human rights, social solidarity, anti-discrimination, sustainable development, and good governance)? Any specific examples?
D11	(Based on the answers to questions above, some follow-on questions would be raised) Because of the different understandings of these norms in the EU and China, do you think that the course content may be influenced by ideological education and the specific Chinese context? If no, why can these norms be taught in Chinese classroom albeit different understandings exist? If yes, why cannot these norms be taught in Chinese classroom? Any specific examples?
D12	Do you think you have more knowledge of the EU's norms after taking this/these course(s)? What specific aspects?
D13	Do you think you have more knowledge of the EU after taking this/these course(s)? What did they not know before? And how do they think differently now?
D14	Do you have any other approaches to access to the information of the EU besides classroom teaching? How do you think about Chinese news reports of the EU?

7.2.2 Analysis on the Interviews with Student Interviewees

As it showed in the table above, 40 undergraduate students at RUC and SCU were interviewed. Among them, the number of college students who attended the Jean Monnet Modules was 9 at RUC and 10 at SCU, while the scale of those who did not attend the EU themed courses was 11 and 10 at RUC and SCU respectively.

These student interviewees at RUC included 10 female and 10 male students who were doing Politics and Administration, International Politics or Foreign Affairs at School of International Relations home to the Jean Monnet Centre of Excellence. All these students aged 20–23 at the second or third year of college study because all compulsory courses related to their majors were taught during these two years. These undergraduate student interviewees at SCU included 13 female and 7 male students. 4 out of 20 undergraduate students who attended EU related modules as elective modules were doing Food Science and Physics, and the rest were doing English Language and Literature or Russian Language and Literature at School of Foreign Languages and Cultures which houses the Jean Monnet Centre of Excellence. All these student interviewees at SCU aged 21–24 at the third or fourth year of university study.

Eleven postgraduate students aged 22–24 at RUC included 3 female and 8 male students doing Political Theories, Chinese Politics or Foreign Affairs at School of International Studies. Two PhD students including 1 female and 1 male student were doing International Politics with a focus on EU studies at the same school. Ten postgraduate students aged 21–25 at SCU were all female doing European Culture studies, American Culture studies, or American/British Literature at School of Foreign Language and Cultures. Three PhD students including 2 female and 1 male student were doing English Language and Literature at the same school.

Table 7.5. The demographic information of student interviewees in the second round interview

	Undergraduate student				Master student				PhD student			
	E		C		E		C		E		C	
	F	M	F	M	F	M	F	M	F	M	F	M
RUC	6	3	4	7	2	3	1	5	1	0	0	1
SCU	6	4	7	3	5	0	5	0	1	1	1	0

Of 66 student interviewees, only 3 said that s/he was not very interested in what s/he studied because s/he had to compromise between dream school and dream disciplines after the national college entrance examination. The rest believed that they were interested in what they were studying for different reasons: personal interests (56); job expectation (3); school reputation (3); parents' advice (1), which were consistent with the result of a nation-wide survey regarding the major choice of Chinese students: personal interests determine major choices.[43]

With regard to their favorite subjects during their study, their answers varied. The answers of students at RUC included Chinese politics, political theories, comparative political institutions, American politics, Sino-US relations, Sino-Japanese relations, northern European countries (Demark), European member states (France, Germany or the UK), international conflicts, international history, global governance, international organizations (the UN), the EU, the ASEAN, India, etc., and most student interviewees at SCU said they were interested in translation or English literature with only one said she was interested in international tourism management, which made the interview results more persuasive considering that their knowledge of the EU was mainly from classroom teaching because their diversified study and research interests reduced the possibility of actively looking for more information about the EU except taking these modules.

By combining interview questions with the responses of interviewees, it shows a full picture of how college students view the influence of governmental regulations on classroom learning of EU norms, and the analysis on the interviews with Chinese students is as follows.

First, the dissemination of EU norms constitutes an integral part of Chinese classroom teaching. The previous interview had not addressed whether EU norms, which also were phased as Western values, had been delivered in Chinese classroom, but some new governmental regulations released in 2013 raised the scholars' curiosity since some EU norms such as "democracy," "human rights," "press freedom," "respect for civil society," and "elected constitutionalism" had been explicitly forbidden in academic discussion.[44] Given that the role of the EU as a norm promoter has been widely accepted,[45, 46, 47] discussing the EU's knowledge dissemination sponsored by the Jean Monnet Programme in the Chinese context needs to think about EU norms and their visibility in classroom teaching against the backdrop of strict governmental regulations.

As a matter of fact, a great number of international or national norms had been addressed in classroom teaching such as democracy, human rights, trade freedom, press freedom, freedom of expression, Internet freedom, constitutionalism, civil society, the rule of law, anti-corruption, market economy, etc. Daniel Bell, a professor who started teaching controversial political theories at Tsinghua University—one of the top universities in China—since 2004, said "I routinely discuss politically sensitive topics and much of what I teach would fall in the 'prohibited' category if official warnings were enforced to the letter" and "I continue to be pleasantly surprised by the amount of freedom in the classroom."[48] For all the students covered by this interview, they had learnt some or most of these norms in courses related to citizenship education such as *Introduction to the Theories of Marxism*, *Introduction to Mao Zedong Thought and the Theoretical System of Socialism with Chinese Characteristics*, and *History of Modern and Contemporary China*. The student interviewees at RUC were from School of International Studies also learnt these norms from courses including *Comparative Political Institutions*, *American Government and Politics*, *Chinese Government and Politics* and *Introduction to Politics*. For student interviewees at SCU, *American Politics and Cultures*, *Introduction to Western Cultures*, *History of Western Thoughts*, and *History of Western Philosophy* came as the first few courses where they learnt about those EU norms since most of the student interviewees covered by this interview were from School of Foreign Languages and Cultures.

According to the student interviewees from two groups at RUC, teaching and discussing the political institutions of different Western countries were, particularly the UK, the US, Germany, and France, covered by the first few modules they attended because *Comparative Political Institutions* and *History of Western Political Thoughts* were compulsory modules for all the second year undergraduate students. As being emphasized by students at SCU, the knowledge about the cultural roots or historical evolvement of democracy, human rights and the rule of law had been discussed as part of modules including *Introduction to Western Cultures* and *History of Western Thoughts* as these two courses were also compulsory courses for students at School of Foreign Languages and Cultures at SCU. One student majoring in Food Science at SCU said that he knew some Western values such as constitutionalism, the rule of law and human rights from a module titled *Constitutionalism and Human Rights*.[49] Besides this course started in 2005, other relevant courses including *Human Right Theory*, *International Human Rights Law* were taught since 2004 and masters and PhD students majoring in *Human Rights Law* were trained.[50] From the perspective of the higher education in cultivating critical thinking and self-learning,[51] delivering these courses to college students is a good start for knowledge dissemination of EU norms since students will further explore these areas by information seeking.

It is interesting that EU themed modules are not recognized by student interviewees as the main sources of their knowledge regarding EU norms, which can be explained from two aspects: one is that the modules sponsored by the Jean Monnet Programme focus on the only theme of European integration from economic, political, and social perspectives without much specific attention being given to EU norms; the other can be understood as that governmental regulations have not had any perceived influence, considering college students in China can access information of Western values from different courses and approaches as indicated above.[52] Both these two aspects will be further addressed in detail with the analysis on the answers below.

Second, the EU as a normative power has been addressed in some EU themed courses, but classroom teaching is not the only source of the EU and EU norms for college students. The question regarding the term of "Normative Power Europe" and the EU as a norm promoter had been raised to all the student interviewees. Based on the answers to the interview questions, the modules delivered by the Jean Monnet Centres of Excellence at these two universities are listed.

All 5 postgraduate interviewees covered by the Jean Monnet Modules at RUC knew well of the term of "Normative Power Europe" in that they attended the module of *Politics and Foreign Policy of the EU* taught in English by Professor Song, one of the two Jean Monnet Chairs "Ad Personam" in China. One of them cannot recall the concept of "Normative Power Europe" when being asked whether the EU founding norms had been addressed in EU themed courses, but he added that he remembered this term after the

Table 7.6.   List of EU-themed modules attended by student interviewees

School	Level of study	Course title
RUC	Undergraduate	Theories and Practice of European Integration
		Political Economy of European Union
		Theories and Practice of EU-China Relations
		Politics and Foreign Policy of Germany
	Master taught	Politics and Foreign Policy of European Union (English module)
SCU	Undergraduate	Twelve Lectures on European Studies
		European Cultures
	Master taught	European Cultures

interviewer listed some norms the EU emphasized such as democracy, human rights, and the rule of law. As these five student interviewees said, their module instructor emphasized the role of norms in EU internal and external policies. Six out of nine undergraduate students at RUC can recall the term of "Normative Power Europe" albeit only one knew its exact meaning.

Only one postgraduate student at SCU who attended the module of *European Cultures* knew the term of "Normative Power Europe," but she got the knowledge of this term from extracurricular reading rather than classroom learning. The rest at SCU knew some of EU norms when attending the module of *European Cultures*, and they said that their module instructor preferred citing the case of the EU when talking about cultural roots of some EU founding norms. Four out of 10 undergraduate student interviewees who also attended the module of *Twelve Lectures on European Studies* taught by the Jean Monnet Centre of Excellence at SCU said they were aware of the term of "Normative Power Europe," and the rest of them also knew some of EU norm after taking the course of *European Cultures*.

All these PhD students doing European studies at RUC and SCU knew the term of "Normative Power Europe" as well as its content well, and they all mentioned that these norms as the founding norms of the EU play a very important role in its internal governance and external influence. Considering these three PhD students were doing EU-China cooperation on climate change, environmental governance and the EU's immigration policy, all of them mentioned that "Normative Power Europe" as the theoretical framework was used to structure their theses.

Of all the student interviewees who never attended any modules or courses related to the EU at both undergraduate and postgraduate levels at RUC and SCU, only one student at SCU read a book about European integration and remembered that there was some analysis on EU norms. Although the rest of the interviewees had never been told that the EU was founded on and fought for these norms, they still believed that West and Northern European countries had a good record in democracy and human rights protection.

Table 7.7. Student interviewees' awareness of the term of "Normative Power Europe"

	Undergraduate				Master				PhD			
	E		C		E		C		E		C	
	YES	NO	YES	NO	YES	NO	YES	NO	YES	NO	YES	NO
RUC	6/9	3/9	0/11	11/11	5/5	0/5	0/5	5/5	1/1	0/1	0/1	1/1
SCU	4/10	6/10	1/10	9/10	1/5	4/5	0/5	5/5	2/2	0/2	0/1	1/1

Table 7.8. Student interviewees' awareness of EU norms

	Undergraduate				Master				PhD			
	E		C		E		C		E		C	
	YES	NO	YES	NO	YES	NO	YES	NO	YES	NO	YES	NO
RUC	9/9	0/9	11/11	0/11	5/5	0/5	5/5	0/5	1/1	0/1	1/1	0/1
SCU	10/10	0/10	10/10	0/10	5/5	0/5	5/5	0/5	2/2	0/2	1/1	0/1

These two tables above show the student interviewees' awareness of the term of "Normative Power Europe" and their awareness of EU norms respectively. According to the table 7.7, it can easily tell the differences in students' awareness of "Normative Power Europe" between those who attended EU themed modules and those who did not attend relevant modules at RUC, but the differences at SCU are not evident. The different student responses can be explained from two aspects. First, the Jean Monnet Programme is a program supporting EU Studies with a focus on European integration studies, so telling the theories and practice of European integration and informing young students of the history and contemporary issues of European integration are the content of this program. In this sense, EU norms relating to European integration have been covered by undergraduate and postgraduate modules at RUC.

Second, the information of "Normative Power Europe" seems more easily to be disseminated in the modules regarding high politics instead of low politics. Although neoliberalism emphasizes the changed hierarchy of issues in world politics since some issues in traditional fields of low politics such as environmental problems and epidemic gain worldwide attention,[53] the story of the EU has been talked more in courses of politics and foreign policy rather than European cultures in China. At SCU, the module of *European Cultures* taught by a Jean Monnet Professor focuses on the historical evolvement of European cultures, and it is the personal research interests of the professor that makes him preferred citing the story of the EU in his courses. Admittedly, all four students who attended the module of *"Twelve Lectures on European Studies"* knew the term of "Normative Power Europe." Comparing with the students' awareness of "Normative Power Europe" at RUC, students at SCU seemed more unfamiliar with this term.

However, when moving to see the table 7.8, all the student interviewees have some knowledge of the norms that the EU stands for, which can also be understood from two aspects. One is that the EU has more channels to engage Chinese student and the public more broadly by various approaches including official websites, social media accounts, cultural and educational events, which has been discussed in chapter 6 and will be further elaborated later. The other is that Chinese students also have more channels to access the information of the EU directly. According to the interviews with college students, except 1 student at RUC and 2 at SCU said they were not interested in the EU and did not pay any attention to the information or news reports regarding the EU, the rest of students disclosed their ways seeking information of the EU, EU-China relations or EU statements on Chinese politics.

Based on the interviews, the Chinese media was almost the last choice for Chinese students to acquire the information of the EU, no matter whether there was governmental censorship on news reports appeared in the Chinese media. International media, particularly the BBC, was the first choice for Chinese students' information of international events. Two students at RUC said they read news reports of the EU in German media since they were studying German, and one of them even elaborately explained the preferences of news reports on different German media outlets.[54] Five students admitted that they used special software to access foreign websites that were blocked in mainland China. The cross-wall software, including Virtual Private Network (VPN), allows to access the websites blocked in China, although it is suffering disruptions due to China's online censorship system.[55] For college students in China, foreign media reports are preferred when they are searching for the facts of current issues.

Social media, such as Weibo and WeChat (public accounts for information sharing) comes as the second important information source of the EU. The Internet and social media provide the Chinese public with a convenient and efficient way to get information, indicating why the social media accounts of the Delegation of the EU to China matter. Although information and misinformation co-exist in the Internet era due to the absence of "gatekeepers" in information releasing,[56] the official websites and official Weibo accounts through Internet can also eliminate the negative influence of misinformation by publishing official announcements immediately. More importantly, some social media owners usually translate the news reports of foreign media to attract more viewers to their pages and increase their followers.

Official websites of the EU are always referred as the information or data sources for college students to do academic research. Twenty-two students from two universities claimed that they visited EU websites to look for the official documents, leaders' speeches or the introduction of different institutions in the EU. This finding echoes previous interview results because college students prefer citing official information sources in academic writing to ensure the authority of the information.

Academic publications are another supplementary source for Chinese college students to access the information of the EU. However, as some students added, academic publications that emphasized academic analysis and theoretical construction always lagged behind the news reports stressing the timely information circulation, so they can be used to understand the issues of the EU in the academic circle rather than to get the facts of current issues.

It is surprising that the Chinese media comes last in college students' information sources. It seemed that the Chinese media as the information source had been mentioned as frequent as academic publications based on the interviews with two universities' students, but at least three students at SCU said that the Chinese news reports were just used as the study materials for translation.[57] One Student at RUC and one at SCU said they listened to the news reports of *CCTV—NEWS* to practice their listening skills,[58] and a survey shows that 80 percent Chinese audience of English programs produced in China aims to develop their understanding of English.[59]

As more Chinese students start pursuing their further education in overseas education institutes in EU member states, interpersonal communication also matters in information acquisition. Two students at RUC said their friends who were studying in Germany always posted news of the EU with their own comments over WeChat—an instant messaging tool, and they were informed with their friends' posts. Another student at SCU mentioned that she had personal connections with some European friends after her four-month stay in Denmark, so she can discuss some current issues of the EU over emails or other chatting tools with her friends.

Therefore, no matter how media control and Internet censorship have been carried out on the top of Chinese political agenda, information seeking activities of college students have not been interrupted in terms of its results albeit the process of information seeking in China might become complicated.[60, 61] In this sense, classroom teaching would not and will never be the only source for college students to acquire the information of the EU or EU norms. On the contrary, international media, social media, and official websites owned by the Delegation of the EU to China or the EU on the Internet can engage Chinese students and the Chinese public in general directly. However, classroom teaching has its own comparative advantage in systematically delivering the knowledge of the EU and European integration, which can be proved by the analysis in chapter 6 and will be further discussed in the following parts.

Third, democracy, human rights, and the rule of law are EU norms frequently being talked for students covered by EU themed modules.

Table 7.9. Frequency of each EU norms recalled by student interviewees who registered for EU-themed modules

	RUC	*SCU*
Democracy	11	13
Human rights	8	11
Rule of law	10	8
Peace	7	6
Sustainable development	5	3
Good governance	5	2
Liberty	2	2
Social solidarity	3	1
Anti-discrimination	1	1

Of all 32 students who attended Jean Monnet Modules or EU themed courses taught by Jean Monnet Professors from two universities, 5 postgraduate students at RUC said EU norms had been taught as a specific topic of "Normative Power Europe," which made them have a clear idea of the content to EU norms. Besides, four undergraduate students at SCU knew the norms emphasized by the EU because they registered for the module of *Twelve Lectures on European Studies* taught by a group of professors at Jean Monnet Centre of Excellence and devoted part of the content of EU norms. Democracy and human rights were two norms being addressed the most when teaching the cultural roots and historical evolvement of these two terms. Almost all the students from SCU at both postgraduate and undergraduate levels stated that how European cultures produced the special concepts of democracy and human rights in the Western world and its civilization had been taught and discussed in the module of *European Cultures*, and human rights had been addressed when their professors explained EU asylum policy dealing with the refugees of Syria. Although scholarly research argued that EU policies dealing with European refugee crisis in late 2015 had failed because of conflicting national interests of EU member states,[62] Chinese students still thought that the EU contributed a lot to human rights protection.

The students at RUC had more information of EU norms based on the interview results, but it was a bit difficult for them to recall which norms had been discussed the most during the courses they attended. As mentioned above, all five postgraduate students at RUC knew EU norms when the module leader explained the concept of "Normative Power Europe" to them, but they all mentioned that EU norms were not the main focus of the course. Five undergraduate students at RUC said they were required to do presentations at an EU-themed module taught by one professor who was serving as executive director of Jean Monnet Centre of Excellence of RUC. The course syllabus did not indicate EU norms as a specific topic, but they can choose any topic related to the EU as the topic for their presentations. Two students stated that human rights and democracy were also introduced in the framework of EU-China relations when attending EU themed courses, and added that the EU wanted to export their ideas of democracy and human rights because some EU member states did have a high standard of democracy and human rights protection. However, they also added that the EU did not take specific Chinese cultural and historical factors into consideration when they tried to evaluate Chinese democracy and human rights records with their own standards.

The rule of law had been recalled by these student interviewees as they said that a decision regarding "legal affairs" dialogue had been made in 2015 and the rule of law was gaining its priority in public administration in China. In fact, the EU's China policy does note the rule of law and respect for human rights as a basic requirement in supporting China's transition towards an open society and a decision regarding EU-China Legal Affairs Dialogue, that could serve as a new avenue to discuss the rule of law, had been made in 17th EU-China Summit in 2015,[63] and in contemporary China, strengthening the rule of law had been emphasized as the top priority of the Chinese Communist Party's Plenum, which was the first time for a Party session to center on the rule of law.[64]

Peace, sustainable development, social solidarity, and good governance had been mentioned a few times when asking students about the course content of EU norms. Sustainable development had also been recalled several times because of the EU's contributions to environmental governance, clear energy technology innovation, and climate change. Social solidarity was mentioned twice by student interviewees because their professors at SCU said the religious diversity and conflicts as barriers to European integration had to be considered by EU leaders in enhancing integration degree during the module of *History of European Thoughts*.[65]

To summarize, most of the student interviewees who attended EU themed courses claimed that some EU norms such as democracy, human rights, and the rule of law went through the content of the teaching process but had never been addressed as a separate topic. However, only one student thought more content regarding EU norms should be added to classroom teaching while the rest from two universities thought that the courses they attended had already included enough knowledge of EU norms because the courses were not about EU norms but European integration. Three students at RUC insisted that these EU norms as Western values had already been discussed in the courses of *Comparative Political Institutions* or *Introduction to Politics*, so there was no need to repeat them in a course that was supposed to tell them something different.[66]

Fourth, the rule of law and good governance are the most important EU norms in concert with the reality of the EU and China according to the student interviewees. Although democracy, human rights and the rule of law are EU norms that had been frequently talked in EU themed modules in Chinese universities, college students believe that rule of law and good governance should be the most important norms in the Chinese context.

Table 7.10. Frequency of each EU norms valued by student interviewees in the Chinese universities

	RUC	SCU
Rule of law	20	17
Good governance	16	10
Human rights	11	13
Democracy	7	10
Sustainable development	7	7
Peace	3	2
Liberty	1	1
Social solidarity	1	0
Anti-discrimination	0	0

According to the student interviewees who attended Jean Monnet Modules or courses taught by Jean Monnet Professors at RUC and SCU, the rule of law and good governance were the most important norms that the EU contributed to world politics and should be learnt by China. At least 10 students from two universities said the rule of law and good governance were the practical norms that can be implemented in the Chinese context and used to deal with the problems faced by China.

Rule of law, as one of the EU's founding norms, has been mentioned as one of the guiding principles of the EU's external action and one of them that the EU wants to promote to outside world in its relations with third parties.[67] Although the EU's official statement merely states that every action taken by the EU is founded on treaties,[68] without providing any specific definition of the rule of law in the EU's understanding, yet the demands of the rule of law, including the principle of legality and the protection of fundamental rights, are always among the EU's concerns.[69]

Chinese students stressed the significance of the rule of law that China needed to learn from the EU because they believed that governmental emphasis on the rule of law was far from enough. One the one hand, they related that China needed to improve this capacity of law enforcement, On the other hand, all the Chinese citizens, either high-profile officials or ordinary citizens, should be equal in front of the law.[70] Although both the EU and China place priority on the rule of law, their understandings of the rule of law are different. Scholarly research also attests that the rule of law implies transparency, fairness, legal certainty, independent courts, judicial review, equality, and prohibiting arbitrage of administration, from the perspective of the EU.[71] For China, the 4th Plenum of the CCP emphasized that the core role of the Constitution in strengthening the rule of law and Chinese top leaders also stressed the importance of laws and regulations in the anti-corruption campaign.[72] However, the legal system in China remains a type of rule by law instead of a form of rule of law,[73] meaning that Chinese "rule by law" links to maintain the social order and pursue public good, and is more likely, with the use of law, to restrict the liberty of people rather than to protect the liberty of people.[74]

When asked about democracy and human rights that emphasized by the EU in EU-China relations, no one thought the concepts of democracy should be used directly in the Chinese context. Over a half of student interviewees at two universities said democracy and human rights should be considered in different cultural contexts albeit they admitted that the EU was a model in democracy promotion and human rights protection.

At least 10 students agreed that the Chinese context needed a different concept of democracy because the EU's understanding of democracy cannot explain the reality of China and surely cannot solve the problems faced by the Chinese government regarding legitimacy. One student said democracy as one of the ideological weapons used by the Western countries in international politics met the requirement of increasing their international influence on the Asian area, but the Western scholars did not understand the history and culture of ancient China where contemporary China came from.[75] Human rights were regarded by the student interviewees as one of the important universal norms should be given more attention in China, but the students thought China should focus on more practical aspects of development related to human rights. One student stressed that democracy cannot promote the equality and justice, but the rule of law would make a great contribution to the social progress and political development.[76] Since the criticism on China's death penalty as a violation of human rights had been debated over years,[77] another postgraduate student used China's "death penalty" as a case to refute the criticism on China's human rights protection because she thought Chinese legal system would not guarantee an appropriate punishment to murderers without death penalty, so human rights protection needed to address the reality of China.[78]

Sustainable development had been mentioned in the framework of global environmental governance. One PhD student at RUC said the carbon tax enacted by serval European countries was a reflection of the EU's pioneering role in promoting sustainable development of the world.[79] Several students regarded that the EU actively participated in the international conferences regarding climate change such as Copenhagen and Paris conferences, and their contributions to environmental protection and promotion of sustainable development should be stressed and learnt by other countries including China.

Liberty was only mentioned once by an undergraduate student at RUC and she said China did not do well in human rights protection and respect for Internet freedom, but the government even made Chinese citizens believe that their rights were not violated. She is Han Chinese from Xinjiang province home to Uigur Community—a minority community in China, and she emphasized that she cannot access the Internet when she went back home because of information control. What even angered her was that her parents thought it was not a big deal since the government had the rights to do so, but she believed that information regulation was a violation of liberty,[80] which is also stressed by Stevenson that the Internet censorship threatens the freedom of speech in a networked world.[81]

Of 34 students who did not register for any EU themed course, good governance as one of the EU norms came first, but the answers varied. Good governance has not been discussed above because most students stressed good governance, whether they were covered by the Jean Monnet Modules or not, at RUC. Although EU norms had not been elaborated as a separate topic on the modules related to European integration, but EU norms, or more accurately, these universal norms, had been detailed taught, discussed, and even evaluated in the final exams of modules compulsory to the student interviewees at RUC such as *Comparative Political Institutions* and *Introduction to Politics*.

All five masters students who did not register for the Jean Monnet Modules at RUC said they attended at least two modules specifically related to these norms, and their professors taught these norms from different research angles.

Human rights were mentioned several times but not related to some traditional topics such as the political rights of dissenters emphasized by the Western world. Two postgraduate students at RUC and SCU respectively said "one child policy" criticised by Westerners was a violation of human rights. Luckily it was ended because of the government regulations, but it caused another question whether the current government regulations allowing to have a second child the same as the "one child policy" were simply implemented by administrative order instead of based on serious social survey or opinion poll.[82]

Social solidarity was mentioned once in that one student at RUC said that the governmental policies towards minority groups needed to be improved in order to address the problems existing in the minority areas in China.[83] Among all the interviewees at both groups of two universities, no one had ever mentioned "anti-discrimination" as an important norm for China though it is one of EU founding norms. When asked why they thought "anti-discrimination" was not important in China, most interviewees replied that they did not think China had "discrimination" problem.

All the student interviewees at RUC covered by the Jean Monnet Programme were from School of International Studies, and student interviewees who did not attend the relevant modules were also from the same school. To be more specific, all the students were covered by courses related to *Comparative Political Institutions*, *History of International Political Thoughts*, or *Chinese Politics* at this school, so they were aware of EU norms to a certain extent and commented a lot on the EU norms and their application to Chinese politics and society. When it comes to the students at SCU, all the student interviewees were from School of Foreign Languages and Cultures which is home to the Jean Monnet Centre of SCU, so their knowledge of these norms was partially from the courses regarding European history and Western political thoughts. Put differently, the degree of knowing EU norms is different between students from these two universities, so their answers seem a bit different due to their personal and studying experience. Thus, it can be told from table 7.10 that student interviewees at RUC stressed the rule of law and good governance because they attended other courses that systematically explained these two norms while student interviewees at SCU had varied attitudes towards the importance of EU norms.

Fifth, EU norms can be taught during teaching process, but the direct comparison between the EU and China has been rarely made. According to the student interviewees from two universities, only less than ten students thought that the classroom content had been affected by the governmental regulations regarding citizenship education in China, and most of the students at different levels believed that their professors can still deliver the knowledge of the EU including the EU's founding norms in the classroom.

According to the students covered by the Jean Monnet Programme, they said that EU norms went through the course content although most of them were certain that EU norms had not been addressed as a specific topic in their courses. Two student interviewees knew the governmental policies released in 2013 to regulate the classroom teaching, but they did not see any evident changes in the courses they took since their professors still talked about norms and values.

However, at least three students said their professors lectured on these norms of the EU and made an in-depth discussion about them, but they also indicated in advance that all their discussion shouldn't be recorded and be distributed beyond the classroom. Also, one student regarded that his professor can talk about these norms and make a comparison between the EU and China, but his ideas seemed more conservative in his publications than what he expressed in the classroom.[84] Although the classroom teaching had not been affected by the governmental regulations released in 2013, professors still had to adjust their research focuses when they applied for researching funding from governmental organs. As two students at RUC indicated, the professors had to survive, so they had to make their research meet the governmental regulations.[85]

Different from the mainstream opinions of most student interviewees, two students expressed their opposite comments on the classroom content of these norms. One student said she did not think it was acceptable to talk too much about these norms if their arguments were based on personal political belief instead of evidence, in that students were not mentally mature and can be easily manipulated by passionate but inaccurate words.[86] This idea was indicated above by one professor at RUC since he thought the governmental regulation was not to inhibit the academic freedom but to make sure the knowledge was delivered to students instead some anecdotes without solid evidences,[87] which was also mentioned by a nation-wide survey result that shows the students were not content with the classroom teaching of contemporary China because teachers used the teaching process to express their anger towards governments based on some anecdotes.[88]

Among all the student interviewees at RUC, one undergraduate student who registered for an EU-themed course came from Macau. He went to RUC for the undergraduate study after finishing the junior and high school in Macau. When asked whether he thought that the courses regarding his discipline (international politics) and EU studies had been influenced by the citizenship education in mainland China, he said he did not think there was any perceived influence on classroom teaching. Admittedly, in comparing with university education in Macau, he had to attend some courses taught by School of Marxism. However, the courses about citizenship education were still capable of discussing these EU norms.[89]

For all 34 student interviewees who were not covered by the Jean Monnet Programme from two universities, eight students thought that the course content had been influenced, which were all undergraduate students including 2 at RUC and 6 at SCU. However, they only mentioned that some professors who lectured on modules of School of Marxism were very conservative, and no one thought the compulsory courses of their majors had been transformed to the courses of citizenship education.

One postgraduate at RUC said they attended courses of *Chinese Politics* and *Political Theories* taught by two professors, but these two professors held opposite opinions regarding the same concepts. One professor thought China should establish its own theoretical framework based on the achievements of thirty-year reform and opening up policy to explain the Chinese reality while the other professor was more critical of Chinese democracy and disappointed with the political changes in the past few decades. However, he said two views were based on their research interests and evidence rather than simple government propaganda, so they were still informed by different views.[90]

It was interesting that all five postgraduate students at RUC who did not register for any modules related to the EU did their undergraduate study at five different Chinese universities including RUC, WHU, Nankai, Jilin University, and Zhejiang University, and one student from Jilin University said their teachers had more freedom to express their academic opinions since he thought that Jilin University located far from the capital city. Considering all these five postgraduate students agreed that the courses they attended at RUC and at the universities where they did their bachelor degrees had not been affected by the citizenship education and all these five universities are top universities in China, it can imply that professors still had some freedom in determining course content.

Most students who did not attend modules related to the EU but took the compulsory courses of citizenship education said some professors were very conservative and kept putting good words on China and bad words on Western countries, but some professors who also lectured on ideological courses were very liberal to express their academic opinions different from textbooks. Thus, when asked whether different teaching styles of their professors regarding some EU norms were because of personal characteristics instead of governmental regulations, most students answered "YES."

Most students at RUC said they believed that academic freedom was still maintained in Chinese universities and teachers would not get punished if they were doing academic research rather than political mobilization. Since most student interviewees at SCU from School of Foreign Language and Cultures, some of them said all their professors had overseas study or research experiences and they were quite westernized. Therefore, they thought their professors had not been affected by the governmental regulations.

Sixth, most student interviewees believed that their knowledge of EU norms had been reified, and they surely had more knowledge of the EU and how EU norms embedded in EU internal and external behaviors after attending EU themed courses. When asked whether their knowledge of EU norms had increased after taking modules related to the EU, only four undergraduate students registered for a module of *Theories and Practice of EU-China Relations* said they knew more about EU norms including democracy, human rights, and the rule of law in the contexts of the EU and China. It seemed that the students' knowledge of these norms had not experienced an evident increase, but according to the interviews, they surely knew how these norms embedded in EU internal and external behaviors. In other words, teaching the courses related to the EU makes these abstract and intangible norms into the information of the EU that is concrete and graphic. Most students added that the concepts of these norms or norms emphasized by the Western countries had been greatly improved after attending other courses such as *Comparative Political Institutions*, *History of Western Political Thoughts* and *Introduction to Politics*, but attending the EU themed courses made them understand how these norms worked in the EU's internal and external policies and had been reflected in its practice.

As mentioned in chapters 1 and 4, the Jean Monnet Programme supports the Jean Monnet Professors, the Jean Monnet Modules, and the establishment of the Jean Monnet Centres of Excellence as well as various research activities regarding European integration. EU norms as one of the important parts of the EU should be addressed in the classroom, but it is not the only information of European integration that needs to be mentioned in college education. As a matter of fact, different theories used to explaining regional integration, important treaties during the integration process, enlargement process as well as conflicting interests between member states and the EU are supposed to be the modules content sponsored by the Jean Monnet Programme, which have been covered in the Chinese classroom.

EU norms as the guiding principles of the EU's internal and external behaviors have been lectured on and delivered during the normative knowledge dissemination process, and students have a more specific picture of how these norms have been manifested in the EU's policies and behaviors albeit students do not think they get more information about these norms because they are more informed about these Western norms through other courses. Nevertheless, it does not mean the EU's knowledge dissemination is not successful. According to the objective of the Jean Monnet Programme, researching and teaching European integration is always its focus. How the EU and Western countries value these EU norms and how China learns from advanced countries and improves its performance in these respects have been elaborated in other courses focusing on political values. As the interview data shows above, Chinese students do know EU norms including EU norms well from different courses and approaches, so there is no need to re-emphasize these EU norms as something different since they are not central to the modules. Even so, how EU norms are embedded in EU internal and external behaviors still gain its awareness in Chinese college students after attending these courses.

Furthermore, all the student interviewees who registered for the Jean Monnet Modules or EU themed courses admitted that they had more knowledge of the EU.

Table 7.11.   The changed knowledge of the EU of different groups

University	Knowledge increase	Numbers	Ratio
RUC	YES	15	100%
	NO	0	0
	NOT SURE	0	0
SCU	YES	12	70.59%
	NO	4	23.53%
	NOT SURE	1	5.88%

For the students who did not attend any course related to the EU, only one student at RUC said he knew more of the EU since he was planning to study in Germany, so he did some research on the education, immigration, and cultural policies. The rest of the student interviewees said they did not pay attention to the EU, and some even claimed that they did not care about any information regarding the EU.

However, all the student interviewees who attended EU themed courses at RUC said they had more knowledge of the EU including its institutional structures, important phases and treaties of European integration, five times enlargement, and the EU's contributions to climate change. Some student interviewees at RUC who also registered in the module of *Theories and Practice of EU-China Relations* said they knew the important issues and conceptual gaps between the EU and China. Due to different courses attended by students at SCU, one student who registered for the module of *Twelve Lectures on European Studies* said he knew more about the educational policies and monetary policies of the EU because their professors taught these two sessions with personal experiences.[91] For most students at SCU, one professor lectured on one module of *European Cultures* for the first year postgraduate students and another module of *European Cultures and European Integration* for the second year postgraduate students, so most of the interviewees covered by this interview said they knew more about the cultural diversity of the EU and the difficulties to deal with the regional conflicts due to cultural diversity.

Seventh, according to students who accessed news from the Chinese mass media, most students believed that news reports of the EU were mainly neutral or positive. As indicated above, the Chinese media was not the main source for college students to access the information of the EU based on the interviews with student interviewees. In general, except two students stated that the news reports about the EU were negative, most students who read the news reports of the Chinese mass media and those who ever paid attention to the Chinese media thought that the Chinese news reports about the EU were mainly positive or neutral. Put differently, as Wang (2012b) indicated, China is one of the most supportive countries for the EU.

Around five students including 1 at RUC and 4 at SCU said they cannot tell whether the news reports of the EU were objective or not because of the lack of knowledge of the EU. As these students indicated, they did not have much background knowledge of the EU and the news reports in Chinese were mainly used for information updates, so they cannot point out whether these news reports objectively showed the reality of the EU.

However, there were some features regarding the news reports of the EU in the Chinese media according to the answers of student interviewees. First, compared with a large number of news reports of the US and Japan, the news reports regarding the EU were not significant in volume because China-US relations and China-Japan relations were more important for China from the perspective of geopolitics. Second, most news reports appeared on the Chinese media were about the explosive news of the EU instead of information about the routine business of the EU, so it was hard to understand the EU through the Chinese news reports. Third, the news reports of the EU in the Chinese media focused on real-time news explanation rather than comments provision. Fourth, more attention had been given to economic news instead of political news. Fifth, no sensitive news relating to the EU or EU-China relations had been covered in the Chinese media.

Although citizenship education in the Chinese context does not accept the universality of norms, the EU has never lost its autonomy in engaging Chinese students directly as already mentioned in chapter 5. The official website of the Delegation of the EU to China has both English and Chinese versions with information about the EU and EU-China relations that can be visited in mainland China, and official announcements or comments regarding China's human rights records, democracy, and the rule of law appear regularly. By filtering the posts on its official website of the Delegation of the EU to China between September 2009 and May 2016 with keywords including human rights, freedom, the rule of law, and democracy, around 560 news reports about EU-China relations, including bilateral high-level meeting, economic and trade issues, visits of EU officials, and official announcements, were posted. Among them, 37 were about China's human rights, the rule of law, and freedom of expression. All these three concepts were emphasized at the same time in each official announcement or statement because they were based on the lawsuit against human rights lawyers or political dissenters.[92]

Besides, the Delegation of the EU to China and most EU member states also have its official Weibo accounts with over 1 million followers as mentioned before, which offer them an important platform for information dissemination in China. Although there is strict Internet censorship in China,[93] all the posts of the Delegation of the EU to China regarding some sensitive issues can still be accessed. From February 18, 2011 to April 10, 2016, over 7000 posts had been released on its Weibo account, and the information varied from social, cultural and educational events or cooperation between the EU and China, to high political issues including security, terrorist attack, and sensitive political themes on EU-China relations. By researching the Weibo posts which give its focus on cultural exchange and culture events, there are around 150 posts about liberty or freedom, human rights, democracy, and the rule of law. Some of these posts may not talk about China directly, but they do show the standpoints of the EU on norms.

Among them, on June 16, October 22, 2015, and January 29, 2016, the EU released three official statements titled *EU concerns about the Human Rights situation in China*, which had appeared on the Weibo account in China. On January 8, 2016, the EEAS released a statement on *the disappearance of individuals associated with the Mighty Current publishing house in Hong Kong*, which had never been addressed by the Chinese mass media but still appeared on the Weibo account of the Delegation of the EU to China with Chinese translation. On February 5, 2016, the news titled *EU plans public consultations over China's market economy status* also appeared on its official Weibo account. Irrespective of the highly sensitive information regarding China's human rights and the rule of law, the Delegation of the EU also released the documents about the democratization of European countries in history, the current situation of different EU member states as well as the development of the EU and the problems it faces at the current stage.[94]

Besides the official website and media account of the Delegation of the EU to China, the diplomats of the EU working in China also participate in the official conferences regarding different aspects of EU-China relations and organize cultural events, which had been covered by the Chinese media. Plus, they are also invited to comment on current EU issues or EU-China relations. Furthermore, the EU also help train Chinese journalists and editors specializing EU-China relations.[95] All these approaches empower the EU to engage Chinese students and the Chinese public, informationally and politically. Thus, researching the effect of EU public diplomacy, either the programs engaging the Chinese public directly or the practice trying to employ the capacity of intermediary in public diplomacy process, still makes sense in the Chinese context since the messages have been delivered, though through different messengers.

This chapter analyzed the interviews with Chinese professors and college students in the second round interview and tried to explain whether and how the Jean Monnet Programme had been implemented in the Chinese context, and a special attention had been given to the classroom teaching of EU norms that might be contradicted some Chinese governmental regulations since some conceptual gaps regarding EU norms did exist between the EU and China.

As the analysis above shows, the knowledge of the EU, including EU norms that seem sensitive in the Chinese context, can be delivered in the Chinese classroom. Although the Chinese government has some regulations on the classroom teaching of the Western values at the higher education level, they are mainly used to guide the citizenship education courses opened by schools of Marxism in higher education institutions. Based on the interviews with Chinese professors and students, it seemed that the discussion of EU norms and dissemination of normative knowledge of the EU had not been interrupted during the teaching process in the classroom, albeit it cannot evaluate its long-term effect.

Besides, the information of the EU can be accessed by college students with the help of searching software that can easily skip the Internet censorship, and college students and the Chinese public more broadly can be engaged by the EU directly through the social media accounts of the Delegation and the EU, cultural events, public talks, or interviews with EU officials by the Chinese mass media. Thus, the Jean Monnet Programme in the Chinese context has not been hindered by any perceived political factors.

NOTES

1. Wolfram Cox, J. & Hassard, J. (2005). "Triangulation in Organizational Research: A Re-presentation," *Organization, 12*(1): 111.

2. Interview with Professor C in Beijing, March 29, 2016.

3. Ibid.

4. EACEA, (2014), *Information about the Jean Monnet Programme from 2007–2013,* available at: http://eacea.ec.europa.eu/llp/jean_monnet/jean_monnet_en.php, [accessed Sept. 29, 2014].

5. Manners, I. (2002), "Normative Power Europe: A Contradiction in Terms?" *Journal of Common Market Studies,* 40(2): 235–258. Manners, I. (2008), "The Normative Ethics of the European Union," *International Affairs,* 84(1): 65–80.

6. Interview with Professor I in Chengdu, March 14, 2016.

7. Ibid.

8. Altbach, P. G. (2001), "Academic Freedom: International Reality and Challenges," *Higher Education,* 41(1): 211.

9. Interviews with students in Beijing and Chengdu, March 16, 2016 to April 2, 2016.

10. Interview with Professor J in Chengdu, March 14, 2016.

11. Ibid.

12. Wang, Y. (2012), "The Identity Dilemmas of EU Normative Power: Observations from Chinese Traditional Culture," paper presented at the seminar "International Society and the Rising Power," 2nd, Nov. King's College London, the UK.

13. Interviews with students in Beijing and Chengdu, March 16, 2016 to April 2, 2016.

14. Interview with Professor D in Beijing, March 29, 2016.

15. Interview with Professor C in Beijing, March 29, 2016.

16. See Chinese Academic Journal Full-text Database, available at: http://oversea.cnki.net/Kns55/brief/result.aspx?dbPrefix=CJFD, accessed May 12, 2016

17. Interview with Professor I in Chengdu, March 14, 2016.

18. Interview with Professor C in Beijing, March 29, 2016.

19. Ibid.

20. Mohrman, K. (2008), "The Emerging Global Model with Chinese Characteristics," *Higher Education Policy,* Vol. 21: 29.

21. Heron, L. (2013a), "Nine Chinese Universities Sign Academic Freedom Pact," *The South China Moring Post,* available at: http://www.scmp.com/news/china/article/1331803/nine-chinese-universities-sign-academic-freedom-pact, [accessed May 26, 2016].

22. People.com.cn, (2014), "Laoshi, Qing Buyao Zheyang Jiang Zhongguo (Teacher, Please Do Not Teach China in This Way)," available at: http://edu.people.com.cn/n/2014/1114/c1006-26025286.html, [accessed 13-05-2016].

23. Li, J. (2014), "Educators Have a Duty to Teach About China's Problems: Chinese Newspapers," *The South China Moring Post,* available at: http://www.scmp.com/news/china/article/1660338/educators-have-duty-teach-about-chinas-problems-chinese-newspaper, [accessed May 27, 2016].

24. Gao, H. (2012), "After 20 Years of Silence, China Slowly Confronts the 'Great Leap Forward,'" available at: http://www.theatlantic.com/international/ar chive/2012/05/after-50-years-of-silence-china-slowly-confronts-the-great-leap-for ward/257797/, [accessed April 15, 2016].

25. Branigan, T. (2013), "China's Great Famine: The True Story," available at: http://www.theguardian.com/world/2013/jan/01/china-great-famine-book-tomb stone, [accessed April 15, 2016].

26. Interview with Professor C in Beijing, March 29, 2016.

27. Ibid.

28. Ibid.

29. Li, J. (2015), "China's Education Dilemma: Building Harvard-level Universities within a Firm Ideological Lock," *The South China Moring Post*, available at: http://www.scmp.com/news/china/policies-politics/article/1876856/chinas-education-di lemma-building-harvard-level, [accessed May 27, 2015].

30. Bie, D. and Meng, F. (2009), "On Student Evaluation of Teaching and Improvement of the Teaching Quality Assurance System at Higher Education Institutions," *Chinese Education and Society*, 42(2): 102.

31. Interview with Professor I in Chengdu, March 14, 2016.

32. Interviews in Beijing and Chengdu, March 16, 2016 to April 2, 2016.

33. Bell, D. (2015), "Teaching 'Western Values' in China," *The New York Times*, available at: http://www.nytimes.com/2015/04/17/opinion/teaching-western-values -in-china.html?_r=0, [accessed May 13, 2016].

34. Interviews in Beijing and Chengdu, March 16, 2016 to April 2, 2016.

35. Ibid.

36. Interview with Professor J in Chengdu, March 14, 2019.

37. Interview with Professor C in Beijing, March 29, 2016

38. Anderlini, J. (2015), "'Western Values' Forbidden in Chinese Universities," *The Financial Times*, available at: https://next.ft.com/content/95f3f866-a87e-11e4-bd17 -00144feab7de#axzz45G6UbTay, [accessed April 9, 2016].

39. Yang, X. (2014), "Xueke Zhuanye Shezhi Zhengzhi Xuxiang Gaoxiao Rangdu Quanli (The Government Needs to Give Higher Education Institutions Autonomy in Setting Degree Programmes)," *people.com.cn*, available at: http://edu.people.com. cn/n/2014/0225/c1006-24453298.html, [accessed May 13, 2016].

40. Campbell, Donald T. (1957), "Factors Relevant to the Validity of Experiments in Social Setting," *Psychological Bulletin*, 54(4): 257.

41. Abbott, M. L., and McKinney, J. (2013), *Understanding and Applying Research Design*, Hoboken, NJ: John Wiley & Sons: 262.

42. Ibid: 261

43. Fan, M., and Chen, X. (2009), "Zhongguo Daxuesheng Zhuanye Xuanze Diaocha Zhi Jiben Fenxi (A Survey on the Major Choice of Chinese Undergraduates)," *Daxue Jiaoyu Kexue (University Education Science)*, No. 3: 92.

44. Anderlini, J. (2015), "'Western Values' Forbidden in Chinese Universities," *The Financial Times*, available at: https://next.ft.com/content/95f3f866-a87e-11e4-bd17 -00144feab7de#axzz45G6UbTay, [accessed April 9, 2016].

45. Herlin-Karnell, E. (2012), "The EU as a Promoter of Values and the European Global Project," *German Law Journal*, 13(11): 1225.

46. Poletti, A., and Sicurelli, D. (2012), "The EU as Promoter of Environmental Norms in the Doha Round," *West Europe Politics*, 35(4): 911.

47. Sicurelli, D. (2015), "The EU as a Norm Promoter Through Trade: The Perceptions of Vietnamese Elites," *Asia Europe Journal*, 13(1): 23.

48. Bell, D. (2015), "Teaching 'Western Values' in China," *The New York Times*, available at: http://www.nytimes.com/2015/04/17/opinion/teaching-western-values-in-china.html?_r=0, [accessed May 13, 2016].

49. Telephone interview in Chengdu, March 25, 2016.

50. Humanrights.cn, (2014), "Sichuan Daxue Renquan Falv Yanjiu Zhongxin (Research Centre of Human Rights Law at Sichuan University)," available at: http://ww.humanrights.cn/html/2014/5_0703/1218_3.html, [accessed May 14, 2016].

51. Pithers, R. T. and Soden, R. (2000), "Critical Thinking in Education: A Review," *Educational Research*, 42(3): 240.

52. Bell, D. (2015), "Teaching 'Western Values' in China," *The New York Times*, available at: http://www.nytimes.com/2015/04/17/opinion/teaching-western-values-in-china.html?_r=0, [accessed May 13, 2016].

53. Keohane, R. and Nye, J. (2011), *Power and Interdependence, 4th edition*, New York: Longman: 19.

54. Interview in Beijing, March 20, 2016.

55. Carsten, P. Rajagopalan, M. and Wee, S. l. (2015), "In China, VPN Internet Access Tools Suffer Further Disruptions," *The Reuters*, available at: http://www.reuters.com/article/us-china-internet-vpn-idUSKBN0KW0WS20150123, [accessed May 27, 2016].

56. Tsatsou, P. (2014), *Internet Studies: Past, Present and Future Directions*, Burlington, VT and Surrey: Ashgate: 88.

57. Telephone interview, April 1, 2016.

58. Interview in Beijing, March 21, 2016; Telephone interview, April 1, 2016.

59. Rawnsley, G. (2012), "Approaches to Soft Power and Public Diplomacy in China and Taiwan," *The Journal of International Communication*, 18(2): 132.

60. Hassid, J. and Sun, W. (2015), "Stability Maintenance and Chinese Media: Beyond Political Communication?" *Journal of Current Chinese Affairs*, 44(2): 9.

61. Wang, D. and Mark, G. (2015), "Internet Censorship in China: Examining User Awareness and Attitudes," *ACM Transaction on Computer-Human Interaction (TOCHI)*, 22(6), Article no. 31: 2.

62. Lehne, S. (2016), *How the Refugee Crisis will Reshape the EU*, Carnegie Europe, available at: http://carnegieeurope.eu/2016/02/04/how-refugee-crisis-will-reshape-eu/itj7, [accessed 11-04-2016].

63. Delegation of the EU to China (2015), The European Union and China: A Maturing Partnership, available at: http://eeas.europa.eu/delegations/china/eu_china/political_relations/index_en.htm, [accessed March 31, 2015].

64. Keck, Z. (2014), "The 4th Plenum: Rule of Law with Chinese Characteristics," *The Diplomat*, available at: http://thediplomat.com/2014/10/4th-plenum-rule-of-law-with-chinese-characteristics/, [accessed Feb. 27, 2016].

65. Telephone interviews, March 22, 2016.

66. Interviews in Beijing, March 15, 2016; March 16, 2016.

67. Pech, L. (2009), "The Rule of Law as a Constitutional Principle of the European Union," *Jean Monnet Working Paper 04/09*, NYU School of law: 9–22.

68. European Union (2014), EU treaties, available at: http://europa.eu/eu-law/decision-making/treaties/index_en.htm, [accessed March 24, 2015].

69. Pech, L. (2009), "The Rule of Law as a Constitutional Principle of the European Union," *Jean Monnet Working Paper 04/09*, NYU School of law: 69.

70. Interviews in Beijing, March 15, 2016; March 16, 2016.

71. Hartmann, B. (2015), Speech delivered at the routable discussion on China and the Rule of Law, Madariaga Foundation, Brussels, Belgium, 4th Feb 2015.

72. Chen, D. (2015), "China's Anti-Corruption Campaign Enters Phase Two," *The Diplomat*, available at: http://thediplomat.com/2015/07/chinas-anti-corruption-campaign-enters-phase-two/, [accessed Feb. 27, 2016].

73. Peerenboom, R. (2002*), China's Long March toward Rule of Law*, Cambridge: Cambridge University Press: 8.

74. Van Der Mensbrugghe, F. (2015), Speech delivered at the routable discussion on China and the Rule of Law, Madariaga Foundation, Brussels, Belgium, 4th Feb 2015.

75. Interview in Beijing, March 15, 2016.

76. Interview in Beijing, March 16, 2016.

77. Monthy, J. T. (1998), "Internal Perspective on Chinese Human Rights Reform: The Death Penalty in the PRC," *Texas International Law Journal*, 33(1): 192.

78. Interview in Beijing, March 16, 2016.

79. Interview in Beijing, March 20, 2016.

80. Telephone interview, March 20, 2016.

81. Stevenson, C. (2007), "Breaching the Great Firewall: China's Internet Censorship and the Quest for Freedom of Expression in a Connected World," *Boston College International and Comparative Law Review*, 30(1): 531.

82. Telephone interview, March 23, 2016.

83. Telephone interview, April 1, 2016.

84. Interview in Beijing, March 17, 2016.

85. Interviews in Beijing, March 15, 2016; March 17, 2016.

86. Telephone interview, April 1, 2016.

87. Interview with Professor C, March 29. 2016.

88. People.com.cn (2014), "Laoshi, Qing Buyao Zheyang Jiang Zhongguo (Teacher, Please Do Not Teach China in This Way)," available at: http://edu.people.com.cn/n/2014/1114/c1006-26025286.html, [accessed 13-05-2016].

89. Interview in Beijing, March 15, 2016.

90. Ibid.

91. Interview in Chengdu, March 21, 2016.

92. Delegation of the EU to China, (2016a), News, available at: http://eeas.europa.eu/delegations/china/press_corner/all_news/index_zh.htm, [accessed April 10, 2016].

93. King, G., Pan, J. and Roberts, M. E. (2013), "How Censorship in China Allows Government Criticism but Silences Collective Expression," *American Political Science Review*, 107(2): 326.

94. Information regarding the Weibo posts of the EU can be found: http://www. weibo.com/euinchina?is_all=1, [accessed April 10, 2016].

95. Delegation of the EU to China (2016), Professional training for Chinese journalists and editors, available at: http://eeas.europa.eu/delegations/china/press_corner/ all_news/news/2016/20160401_en.htm, [accessed April 10, 2016].

Chapter Eight

Research Findings and Policy Implications

Public diplomacy matters greatly in the information era. Each global actor must deploy it effectively in pursuit of their interests. In the case of the EU, public diplomacy is required to communicate efficiently and help create a favorable international environment for its policy implementation. The EU's experience of information dissemination in public diplomacy has been widely discussed, in combination with the abundant cultural activities carried out by EU delegations in host countries. However, as a target group, students require specific plans and in this case, the responsibility is shouldered by the Jean Monnet Programme. The program has been under-researched, although scholars have called for research to be carried out on how identity creation and ideology transfer are at work in the context of EU studies centers and Jean Monnet Chairs.[1] Therefore, this book takes the implementation of the Jean Monnet programme in China as a case to study EU public diplomacy.

8.1 RESEARCH FINDINGS

Based on a review of the existing research output on public diplomacy and EU public diplomacy, this book defines public diplomacy as a communication process. To be more specific, it is a communication process deployed and carried out by international players including governments of nation states, international governmental organizations, non-governmental organizations, and even terrorist groups, through various direct or indirect informational, educational, and cultural activities to engage and influence foreign publics, in order to improve the foreign public opinion environment, enhance mutual understanding and serve the interests, namely soft power, of its communicator(s), or sometimes the interests of all participants in the process—a "win-win" situation.

More importantly, reviewing public diplomacy literature also provides us with five general criteria to assess public diplomacy practice: 1) listening is a start; 2) credibility is a basic requirement; 3) public diplomacy should go local; 4) public diplomacy aims to influence external perceptions; 5) public diplomacy must be connected with policy.

Soft power is one of the oft-cited concepts in studying public diplomacy. Although different disciplines have made contributions to public diplomacy research, the term "soft power" which is used to explain the effect of public diplomacy has never been out of fashion. Soft power is, in short, attraction and influence based on culture, political values, and foreign policy, defined by Joseph Nye.[2] However, the wide use of soft power makes it a catch-all term, which enriches the content of soft power on the one hand but on the other hand increases the difficulty of understanding this term and may threaten its explanatory power.[3]

Scholarly research also identifies that soft power needs to be explained and re-conceptualized according to different contexts, so understanding the EU's soft power needs to consider more factors, such as the internal and external behaviors of the EU, its notion of European history, culture, and lifestyle, as well as the deep-seated values of European societies. Therefore, the EU's soft power resources, including the EU's founding principles, regional integration experience and its role in global governance, can be transferred to the EU's soft power and external influence in reality through utilizing public diplomacy.

Even so, choosing an appropriate approach for public diplomacy towards target groups, by using information activities, educational programs or cultural events independently or coordinately, can be more productive. In fact, the implementation of the Jean Monnet Programme as a case can explain why and how an educational program works.

According to the analysis of the data obtained from interviewing EU officials, Chinese professors and college students who were and are involved in the Jean Monnet Programme, it can tell us that this program works since it realises the general objectives of a public diplomacy program summarized above as well as the specific objectives indicated in the program guide.

This book has identified that in China, the Jean Monnet Programme does help the EU disseminate information and project a positive image to future generations based on data from three Chinese universities, which has partly answered the question of whether teaching and research activities affect the perceptions of the EU in third countries and moreover, has provided lessons for the EU's future public diplomacy practice.

Table 8.1. The criteria of public diplomacy and its application to the Jean Monnet Programme

Types of objectives	Objectives	Yes/No/Not applicable
General objectives	listening is a start	Yes
	credibility is a basic requirement	Yes
	public diplomacy should go local	Yes
	public diplomacy aims to influence external perceptions	Yes
	public diplomacy must be connected with policy	Not applicable
Specific objectives	Knowledge dissemination	Yes
	Knowledge innovation	Yes
	Cross-fertilization	Not applicable

In terms of the lessons learnt from the Jean Monnet Programme conducted by the EU towards China, a basic idea is that a public diplomacy program has to consider cultural differences. Based on its implementation in China, promoting European integration and EU studies in China meets the requirements of both sides: the EU wants to raise its visibility in China while China wants to learn from EU experiences in various areas. This book studies the effect of the Jean Monnet Programme in China at a micro-level, which cannot show the full content and process of EU public diplomacy. However, it does offer implications for the EU in deploying other public diplomacy programs in that complying with the general criteria of public diplomacy by supporting the Chinese scholars to do research on the EU can be useful. Since two criteria of evaluating the Jean Monnet Programme, "public diplomacy must be connected with policy" concerned with the influence of the programs on the EU's policy from the point of view of the EU's policymakers and "cross-fertilization" required by this program after joining Erasmus Plus, are not applicable here, the rest of the criteria for evaluating a public diplomacy program, including four general principles and two specific objectives, are reflected in the implementation of the Jean Monnet Programme in China.

Information dissemination and innovation: the program aims to disseminate knowledge of the EU to future generations through classroom education. During this process, not only was the image of the EU enhanced among these students, but to some extent, information was also broadcast to the public through mass media, and may have also helped provide intellectual support. It is worth noting that, for geopolitical reasons, European studies does not receive enough financial support from the Chinese government that Japanese or American studies do. Therefore, supporting Chinese professors to initiate more courses on European studies is helpful for college students to learn and understand the EU and its role in the world. Besides supporting Chinese professors to study the EU from different perspectives, it also helps knowledge innovation.

Listening is a start: The implementation of the Jean Monnet Programme is based on the successful experiences of former educational exchange programs originally designed for China. Compared with the Jean Monnet Programme before its integration into the "Erasmus Plus," the new program has moved from supporting "European integration studies" to "EU studies" and covers a wider target population beyond academics and using the feedback mechanisms will allow the EU to redirect the program towards what interests the audience.

Credibility is a basic requirement: Based on the interview data, we cannot estimate whether the low visibility of the sponsor behind the program increases the credibility of knowledge about the EU, but as intermediaries of EU public diplomacy, Chinese academics do enhance the confidence of their students regarding information related to the EU. As Cull noted, "sometimes the most credible voice is not one's own,"[4] which is why the Jean Monnet professors or other scholars sponsored by this program, whether directly or indirectly, are viewed as authoritative and credible sources of information. Besides, high visibility does not necessarily lead to a positive image;[5] and thus the low visibility of the sponsors behind a public diplomacy project can have more output. In Seib's words a perceived lack of "foreignness" is an asset in public diplomacy.[6] Although not enough data was obtained to evaluate the relationship between the visibility of the Jean Monnet Programme and students' perceptions of the EU, Manheim's findings remain persuasive.

Public diplomacy should go local: Because of cultural differences between the EU and China, the changed perceptions of the EU are based on the credibility of Chinese professors in knowledge delivery. In the case of the Jean Monnet Programme in China, those scholars and experts who obtain financial support effectively serve as intermediaries for EU public diplomacy in non-EU countries, whether as professors who deliver knowledge about the EU to students; commentators in the mass media, who help set the framework and agenda for public discussion; or through think tanks, providing intellectual support for European integration. Thus, these professors have the capacity of teaching and communicating the EU to Chinese students and the Chinese public based on their academic reputation and they also have the advantage of credibility—telling the EU's story by Chinese in China. However, the EU's attempt to emulate its success in Indian education experienced a major reverse. Given the importance of cultural background, we cannot leap to the conclusion that the Jean Monnet Programme will also succeed in other countries. Again, this reflects the simple, vital point that public diplomacy starts from listening.[7]

Public diplomacy influences external perceptions in target countries: as discussed in the previous section, the data from fieldwork offers a positive conclusion. However, the study of social science always carries with it certain exceptions. Other factors including news reports and EU-China relations which might impact the attitude of Chinese students towards the EU cannot be isolated, but professors' positive comments on the EU are still preferred. In any case, all the interviewees are college students, fully able to differentiate between various sources of information and influence. Thus to a large extent, the interview result is still valid.

According to the data from two rounds interviews, Chinese students' perceptions of the EU become more specific after attending the Jean Monnet Modules or courses taught by the Jean Monnet professors (the first round interview), and students' knew more of the EU from different perspectives in comparison with students who did not attend any EU themed course (the second round interview). More importantly, by conducting second round interview at RUC and SCU, this research also finds that EU studies, or more particularly the implementation of Jean Monnet Programme in China, has not been evidently affected by governmental regulations regarding citizenship education. Although China did release some governmental guidance on higher education institutions, all the professor and student interviewees did not think that their classroom teaching or learning process had been influenced by governmental regulations.

The Jean Monnet Programme has covered 10 higher education institutions in China by establishing the Jean Monnet Centres, awarding the Jean Monnet Chairs and opening the Jean Monnet Modules, but this book only covered three higher institutions due to time and financial constraints. In other words, considering that the Jean Monnet Programme has been implemented in China through different activities besides establishing research centres, more data from other Chinese universities which only have chairs, like Nankai University in Tianjin, or modules like Tongji University in Shanghai, and some comparisons between them and the centers might achieve more persuasive conclusions about the effect of this program. Furthermore, the interviews in Brussels did not cover EU foreign policy-makers, so whether EU public diplomacy program has been integrated into the general goals of EU foreign policy cannot be answered here. However, the fieldwork covers the professors and students involved in the only three Jean Monnet Programme of Chinese universities, so the data from the interviews with college students at different study levels from three Chinese universities can still be significant in researching the effect of this program in China.

8.2 POLICY IMPLICATIONS

By drawing on the case of the Jean Monnet Programme in China, this book analyzes EU public diplomacy and its impact on its soft power projection. Although conceptual gaps on soft power will cause policy conflicts regarding value differences, improving knowledge and appreciation of each other's culture and society will bridge conceptual gaps.[8] Put differently, public diplomacy or the Jean Monnet Programme explains soft power resources first and converts them into external influence. Therefore, facing with the internal and external pressure, the EU needs public diplomacy, with a particular focus on educational programs to increase its presence and visibility in different sovereign states, and more importantly, maintain a favorable international environment for their policy implementation around the world.

First, implementing educational programs helps image projection for international actors on the world stage. As the case study showed, the Jean Monnet Programme helps project a favorable image of the EU to the Chinese students. Since the EU's soft power resources including its cultural diversity and European identity, EU norms as well as its institutional innovations, projecting a positive international image of the EU needs to make the outside world understand what the EU is and what the EU stands for. Considering both Chinese professors and students covered by this program display a preference towards the EU, it shows the capacity of storytelling in fostering goodwill towards the EU. Besides, Chinese European studies started from learning European experience for China's development in the 1980s and nowadays it still emphasizes the EU's experience for governance in China, showing the attractiveness of the EU to China in one aspect.

Second, information transmission and knowledge innovation constitute an integral part of public diplomacy programs. It has been argued that the information of the EU on mass media may not be a complete reflection of the EU's reality due to the direct or indirect government censorship,[9, 10] so it is hard for the Chinese public to obtain information about the EU. Thus, classroom teaching is one of the most important channels for the Chinese students to gain the accurate and systematic information of the EU. Furthermore, the Jean Monnet Programme not only sponsors research and teaching on EU studies but also aims to promote knowledge innovation of EU studies at universities around the world. Both information transmission and knowledge innovation sponsored by the EU through the Jean Monnet Programme help the actorness of the EU be rooted in college study and research and enhance the EU's image in promoting knowledge innovation, which cannot be isolated from the EU's soft power. Therefore, through educational programs,

EU public diplomacy can also realize the purpose of information transmission and knowledge innovation at the same time.

Third, promoting educational exchange between the EU and China shows the robustness of bilateral relations. China is one of the first few non-EU states covered by the Jean Monnet Programme, which manifests the importance of China in EU-China relations and also shows the kindness of the EU to China with research and teaching support. Meanwhile, EU studies in China is shadowed by American and Japanese studies due to geographical reasons, so supporting Chinese scholars to research and teach the EU in Chinese universities will surely increase a good impression on the EU through a soft way. Moreover, viewing the EU as a "destination of study" and "destination of tourism" reflects its influence and high-level achievements in higher education and its attractiveness as a destination for tourists. According to the interviews, serval students had studied in EU member states or had been planning to study and make a short visit there. The attraction of the EU and EU higher education also reflects its soft influence on the decisions of students' further education or tourism destinations. As the interview data shows, courses on European integration or EU studies are, first and foremost, cultivating students' interest in the EU, which in turn encourages the students to look for more information on their own.

Last but not the least, educational programs stress a long-term effect on soft power. On the one hand, the EU norms have gone through the teaching process in concert with the specific events, making these intangible EU norms which had been learnt as "Western values" in general from other courses more concrete in the context of the EU and EU-China relations. Although it cannot directly exert an impact on Chinese politics and society, an informed intellectual community in the long run may exert their influence on policy process of different fields since these students are studying in some well-known Chinese universities and would stand a good chance of being future policy makers. On the other hand, the cultural filters defined by external perceptions of the EU which drive categorizations and images serve as one of the key pre-conditions for EU influence shaping receivers' expectations and responses.[11] Knowledge dissemination that helps the formation of the Chinese perceptions of the EU is the main objective of the Jean Monnet Programme and has been studied in book, but norm diffusion as a process which is beyond the scope of this book may also gain more acceptances in the Chinese context due to the educational programs.

All in all, as the only academic study on the effect of the Jean Monnet Programme from the perspective of public diplomacy to date—based on empirical fieldwork and direct contact with professors and college students covered by this program—this book has hinted at the potential of the EU's educational programs in different cultural contexts. Again, this book studies the effect of the Jean Monnet Programme in China at a micro-level by locating it within the context of EU public diplomacy, so it does provide lessons for the EU when they deploy other public diplomacy programs. More importantly, it has been argued that the EU must replace offensive norm promotion (coercing others to accept) by defensive norm diffusion (setting examples for others to follow),[12] as setting example through mutual exchange will avoid norm conflicts and promote understandings. While considerable further research on the impact of EU public diplomacy—such as comparative studies looking at the success or otherwise of Jean Monnet Programmes in different countries, or at different public diplomacy programs in one country—is plainly merited, it is hoped that the findings of this book represent at least an encouraging start.

NOTES

1. Wiessala, G. (2013), "Social-Cultural and Educational Cooperation between the EU and Asia," in Christiansen, T. Kirchner, E. and Murray, P. B. (eds.), *The Palgrave Handbook of EU-Asia Relations*, Hampshire: Palgrave Macmillan: 213

2. Nye, J. (2004), *Soft Power: The Means to Success in World Politics*, New York: Public Affairs: 5.

3. Roselle, L., Miskimmon A., O'Loughlin, B. (2014), "Strategic Narrative: A New Means to Understand Soft Power," *Media, War & Conflict*, 7(1): 70.

4. Cull, N. J. (2010), "Public Diplomacy: Seven Lessons for its Future from its Past," *Place Branding and Public Diplomacy*, Vol.6: 14.

5. Manheim, J. B. (1994), *Strategic Public Diplomacy and American Foreign Policy: The Evolution of Influence*, New York: Oxford University Press: 126–47.

6. Seib, P. (2013), *Public Diplomacy and the Media in the Middle East*, CPD perspectives on public diplomacy, Centre on Public Diplomacy, University of Southern California: 8

7. Cull, N. J. (2010), "Public Diplomacy: Seven Lessons for its Future from its Past," *Place Branding and Public Diplomacy*, Vol. 6: 12.

8. Michalski, A. (2012), "China and the EU: Conceptual Gaps in Soft Power," in Pan, Z. (ed.), *Conceptual Gaps in China-EU Relations*, Hampshire and New York: Palgrave Macmillan: 77.

9. Schilling, E. (2012), *When the Rising Dragon Sees Fading Stars: China's View of the European Union*, CEPS Special Report, No. 73, Centre for European Policy Studies: 2.

10. Ma, X. (2012), *Beyond the Economic Ties: EU in the Chinese Media*, Centre of Public Diplomacy, University of South California, available at: http://uscpublicdiplo macy.org/sites/uscpublicdiplomacy.org/files/legacy/pdfs/XinruMaBestPaper2012. pdf, [accessed July 9, 2014]: 24.

11. Chaban, N. Kelly, S. and Holland, M. (2015), "Perception of 'Normative Power Europe' in the Shadow of the Eurozone Debt Crisis," in Björkdahl, A., Chaban, N., Leslie, J. and Masselot, A. (eds.), *Importing EU Norms: Conceptual Framework and Empirical Findings*, New York and London: Springer: 69.

12. Mattlin, M. (2012), "Dead on Arrival: Normative EU Policy Towards China," *Asia Europe Journal*, 10(1–2): 196.

Bibliography

Abbott, M. L., and McKinney, J. (2013), *Understanding and Applying Research Design*, Hoboken, NJ: John Wiley & Sons.

Akami, T. (2008), "The Emergence of International Public Opinion and the Origins of Public Diplomacy in Japan in the Inter-War Period," *The Hague Journal of Diplomacy*, No.3: 99–128

Alexander M.G. Levin, S. and Henry, P.J. (2005), "Image Theory, Social Identity, and Social Dominance: Structural Characteristics and Individual Motives Underlying International Image," *Political Psychology*, 26(1): 27–45.

Alexander, C. (2011), "Public Diplomacy and the Diplomatic Truce: Taiwan and the People's Republic of China in EI Salvador," *Place Branding and Public Diplomacy*, 7(4): 271–288.

Alexander, C. (2011), *China, Costa Rica, and the Race for U.N. Security General*, Centre on Public Diplomacy, University of South California, available at: http://uscpublicdiplomacy.org/blog/china_costa_rica_and_the_race_for_un_secretary_general, [accessed June 5, 2014].

Altbach, P. G. (2001), "Academic Freedom: International Reality and Challenges," *Higher Education*, 41(1): 205–219.

Ammaturo, F. R. (2018), "Europe and Whiteness: Challenges to European Identity and European Citizenship in Light of Brexit and the 'Refugees/Migrants Crisis,'" *European Journal of Social Theory*: 5. DOI:10.1177/1368431018783318.

Anderlini, J. (2015), "'Western Values' Forbidden in Chinese Universities," *The Financial Times*, available at: https://next.ft.com/content/95f3f866-a87e-11e4-bd17-00144feab7de#axzz45G6UbTay, [accessed April 9, 2016].

Anholt, S. (2006), "Public Diplomacy and Place Branding: Where's the Link?" *Place Branding*, Vol. 2: 217–275.

Antoniades, A., O'Loughlin, B. and Miskimmon, A. (2010), *Great Power Politics and Strategic Narratives*, March, Working Paper, No. 7, The Centre for Global Political Economy of Sussex.

255

Arquila, J. and Ronfeldt, D. (1999), *The Emergence of Noopolitik: Toward an American Information Strategy*, Santa Monica, CA: Rand.

Austermann, F. (2012), "Towards One Voice in Beijing? The Role of the EU's Diplomatic Representation in China Over Time," *Journal of European Integration History*, 18(1): 83–102.

Austermann, F. (2014), *European Union Delegations in EU Foreign Policy: A Diplomatic Service of Different Speeds*, Hampshire and New York: Palgrave Macmillan.

Azpíroz, M. L. (2015), *Soft Power and Public Diplomacy: The Case of the European Union in Brazil*, CPD perspectives on public diplomacy, Centre on Public Diplomacy, University of Southern California.

Bachner, D. and Zeutschel, U. (2009), "Long-term Effects of International Educational Youth Exchange," *International Education*, 20(1): 45–58.

Banks, D. (2011), "The Questions of Cultural Diplomacy," *Theatre Topics*, 21(2): 109–123.

Baroncelli, S. (2014), "Linguistic Pluralism in European Studies," in Baroncelli, S., et al. (eds.), *Teaching and Learning the European Union*, New York and London: Springer: 133–156.

Barrinha, A. (2016), "Progressive Realism and the EU's International Actorness: Towards a Grand Strategy?" *Journal of European Integration*, 38(4): 441–454.

Barroso, J. M. (2011), "Europe at the Crossroads—What I Think," in European Union, (ed.), *20 Years of Support for European Integration Studies*, Luxembourg: Publications Office of the European Union: 6–13

Bátora, J. (2005), *Public Diplomacy in Small and Medium-Sized States: Norway and Canada*, Discussion papers in diplomacy, Netherland Institute of International Relations, "Clingendael."

Bátora, J. (2011), "Exclusion and Transversalism: Culture in the EU's External Relations," in Bátora, J. and Mokre, M. (eds.), *Cultural and External Relations: European and Beyond*, Aldershot: Ashgate: 81–98.

Beerkens, M. and Vossensteyn, H. (2011), "The Effect of the ERASMUS Programme on European Higher Education: The Visible Hand of Europe," in Enders, J., de Boer, H. F. and Westerheijden, D.F. (eds.), *Reform of Higher Education in Europe*, Rotterdam: Sense Publisher: 45–62.

Bell, D. (2015), "Teaching 'Western Values' in China," *The New York Times*, available at: http://www.nytimes.com/2015/04/17/opinion/teaching-western-values-in-china.html?_r=0, [accessed May 13, 2016].

Bellamy, C. and Weinberg, A. (2008), "Educational and Cultural Exchange to Restore America's Image," *The Washington Quarterly*, 31(3): 55–68.

Beneyto, J. M. (2011), "The Future of the Jean Monnet Programme and of European Integration Studies," in European Union, (ed.), *20 Years of Support for European Integration Studies*, Luxembourg: Publications Office of the European Union: 318–327.

Bergbauer, S. (2018), *Explaining European Identity Formation: Citizens' Attachment from Maastricht Treaty to Crisis*, Switzerland: Springer Nature.

Bie, D. and Meng, F. (2009), "On Student Evaluation of Teaching and Improvement of the Teaching Quality Assurance System at Higher Education Institutions," *Chinese Education and Society*, 42(2): 100–105.

Bindi, F. (2012), "European Union Foreign Policy: A Historical Overview," in Federiga Bindi and Irina Angelescu, (eds.), *The Foreign Policy of the European Union*, Washington, DC. Brookings Institution Press: 11–39.

Bjola, C. and Jiang, L. (2015), "Social Media and Public Diplomacy," in Bjola C. and Holmes, M. (eds.), *Digital Diplomacy: Theory and Practice*, London and New York: Routledge: 71–88

Blakemore, M., Verhaeghe, S., Izaki, F., Fothergill, R., and Mozuraityte, N. (2012), *Erasmus Mundus: Clustering Erasmus Mundus Joint Programmes and Attractiveness*, Survey Report, available at: http://eacea.ec.europa.eu/erasmus_mundus/clusters/documents/sustainability/surveyreport_sust_recog.pdf, [accessed Sept. 17, 2014].

Bound, K. Briggs, R. Holden, J. and Jones, S. (2007), *Cultural Diplomacy*, London: Demos, available at: http://www.demos.co.uk/files/Cultural%20diplomacy%20-%20web.pdf, [accessed Nov. 11, 2013].

Branigan, T. (2013), "China's Great Famine: The True Story," available at: http://www.theguardian.com/world/2013/jan/01/china-great-famine-book-tombstone, [accessed April 15, 2016].

Bretherton, C. and Vogler, J. (2005), *The European Union as a Global Actor*, London: Routledge.

Brewer, M. B. (2001), "The Many Faces of Social Identity: Implications for Political Psychology," *Political Psychology*, 22(1): 115–125.

Broś, N. (2017), "Public Diplomacy and Cooperation with Non-Governmental Organisations in the Liberal Perspective of International Relations," *Journal of Education, Culture and Society,* No.1: 11–22.

Brown, R. (2004), "Information Technology and the Transformation of Diplomacy," *Knowledge, Technology & Policy*, 18(2): 14–29.

Bu, L. (1999), "Educational Exchange and Cultural Diplomacy in the Cold War," *Journal of American Studies*, 33(3): 393–415.

Burman, A. (2007), *The State of the American Empire: How the USA Shapes the World*, Oxon and New York, Earthscan.

Cabral, R., Engelke, P., Brown, K. and Wedner, A. T. (2014), *Diplomacy for a Diffuse World*, Issue Brief, Atlantic Council: Brent Scowcroft Centre on International Security, available at: http://www.atlanticcouncil.org/images/publications/Diplomacy_for_a_Diffuse_World.pdf, [accessed April 3, 2015].

Callahan, W. A. (2007), "Future Imperfect: The European Union's Encounter with China (and the United States)," *Journal of Strategic Studies*, 30(4–5): 777–807.

Calligaro, O. (2013), *Negotiating Europe: EU Promotion of Europeanness since the 1950s*, New York: Palgrave Macmillan.

Cameron, F. (2005), *The EU Model of Integration—Relevance Elsewhere?* Jean Monnet/Robert Schuman Paper Series, 5(37), Miami European Union Centre, available at: http://aei.pitt.edu/8166/1/Cameronfinal.pdf, [accessed June 16, 2015].

Campbell, D. T. (1957), "Factors Relevant to the Validity of Experiments in Social Setting," *Psychological Bulletin*, 54(4): 297–312.

Carsten, P. Rajagopalan, M. and Wee, S. l. (2015), "In China, VPN Internet Access Tools Suffer Further Disruptions," *The Reuters*, available at: http://www.reuters.com/article/us-china-internet-vpn-idUSKBN0KW0WS20150123, [accessed May 27, 2016].

Carta, C. (2013), "The EU in Geneva: The Diplomatic Representation of a System of Governance," *Journal of Contemporary European Research*, 9(3): 406–423.

Chaban, N, and Elgström, O. (2014), "The Role of the EU in an Emerging New World Order in the Eyes of the Chinese, Indian and Russian Press," *Journal of European Integration*, 36(2): 170–188.

Chaban, N. and Vernygora, V. (2013), "The EU in the Eyes of Ukrainian General Public: Potential for EU Public Diplomacy," *Baltic Journal of European Studies*, 3(2): 68–95.

Chaban, N. Kelly, S. and Bain, J. (2009), "European Commission Delegations and EU Public Policy: Stakeholders' Perceptions from the Asia-Pacific," *European Foreign Affairs Review*, 14(2): 271–288

Chaban, N., Kelly, S. and Holland, M. (2015), "Perceptions of 'Normative Power Europe' in the Shadow of the Eurozone Debt Crisis," in Björkdahl, A., Chaban, N., Leslie, J. and Masselot, A. (eds.), *Importing EU Norms: Conceptual Framework and Empirical Findings*, Switzerland: Springer International Publishing: 57–78.

Chan, K. (2010), "The Image, Visibility and the Prospects of Soft Power of the EU in Asia: The Case of China," *Asia Europe Journal*, 8(2): 133–147.

Chapman, D. W. (2009), "Education Reform and Capacity Development in Higher Education," in Hirosato, Y. and Kitamura, Y. (eds.), *The Political Economy of Educational Reforms and Capacity Development in Southeast Asia Education in the Asia-Pacific Region: Issues, Concerns and Prospects*, Vol. 13, London: Springer: 91–109.

Chen, A. and Wu, B. (2011), "The Regional Division of the Higher Education Sector in China: A Spatial Analysis," in Morgan, W. J. and Wu, B. (eds.), *Higher Education Reform in China: Beyond the Expansion*, London and New York: Routledge: 13–29.

Chen, D. (2015), "China's Anti-Corruption Campaign Enters Phase Two," *The Diplomat*, available at: http://thediplomat.com/2015/07/chinas-anti-corruption-campaign-enters-phase-two/, [accessed Feb. 27, 2016].

Chen, G. M. (1995), "Differences in Self-disclosure Patterns among Americans versus Chinese: A Comparative Study," *Journal of Cross-Cultural Psychology*, 26(1): 84–91.

Chen, X., Xiong, H., Qin, H., Sun, Y. (2011), *Ouzhou Jingji Yanjiu Shinian Pingshu (2001–2010) (The Review of European Economy Research [2001–2010])*, Institute of European Studies of Chinese Academy of Social Science, available at: http://ies.cass.cn/Article/cbw/ozjj/201108/4140.asp, [accessed July 29, 2014].

Chen, Z. (2012), "Europe as a Global Player: A View from China," *Perspectives*, 20(2): 7–29.

Chen, Z. (2016), "China, the European Union and the Fragile World Order," *JCMS: Journal of Common Market Studies*, 54(4): 775–792.

Chen, Z. and Song, L. (2012), "The Conceptual Gap in Soft Power between China and Europe and its Impact on Bilateral Relations," in Pan, Z. (ed.), *Conceptual Gaps in China-EU Relations*, Hampshire and New York: Palgrave Macmillan: 50–64.

Cheng, C. (1991), *New Dimensions of Confucian and Neo-Confucian Philosophy*, NY: Albany: State University of New York Press.

Cheng, Y. C. (2001), *Paradigm Shift in Higher Education: Globalization, Localization, and Individualization*, presented at the conference of Innovation in African Higher Education, Ford Foundation, Nairobi, Kenya, Oct. 1st to 3rd: 10

China.com, (2012), *The Wisdom of Public Diplomacy: The Dialogue among Chinese, American and European Scholars*, available at: http://www.china.com.cn/international/txt/2012-09/11/content_26492930.htm, [accessed Sept. 3, 2013]

Chopin, T. and Lefebvre, M. (2010), "Three Phone Numbers for Europe: Will the Lisbon Treaty Make the European Union More Effective Abroad?" *US-Europe Analysis Series,* Number 43, Centre on the United States and Europe at Brookings.

Choudaha, R. and Orosz, K. (2011), *Emerging Models of Indian- European Higher Education Collaborations*, available at: http://wenr.wes.org/2011/09/emerging-models-of-indian-european-higher-education-collaborations/, [accessed April 26, 2016].

Cini, M. and Borragán, N., (eds.), (2009), *European Union Politics (3rd edition),* New York: Oxford University.

Cohen, Y. (1986). *Media Diplomacy: The Foreign Office in the Mass Communications Age*, London: Frank Cass.

Cooper, R. (2004), "Hard Power, Soft Power and the Goals of Diplomacy," in: D. Held & M. Koenig-Archibugi, (eds.), *American Power in the 21st Century*. Cambridge: Polity Press: 167–180.

Copeland, D. (2011), "The Seven Paradoxes of Public Diplomacy," in Fisher, A. and Lucas, S. (eds.), *Trials of Engagement: The Future of US Public Diplomacy*, Leiden: Martinus Nijhoff Publishers: 183–200.

Council on Foreign Relations, (2001), *Improving the U.S. Public Diplomacy Campaign in the War against Terrorism*, Task Force Report No. 38.

Courtier, A. (2011), "The Challenge of Public Diplomacy for The European External Action Service," In European Institute of Public Administration (ed.), *EIPAscope*, 30th Anniversary Special Issue: 69–73.

Cowan, G. and Arsenault, A. (2008), "Moving from Monologue to Dialogue to Collaboration: The Three Layers of Public Diplomacy," *Annals of the American Academy of Political and Social Science*, 616(1): 10–30.

Crookes, Paul C. I. (2014), "EU Soft Power with China: Technical Assistance in the Field of Intellectual Property Rights," *European Foreign Affairs Review*, 19 (3/1), Special Issues: 77–96.

Cross, Mai'a K. D. (2011), "Building a European Diplomacy: Recruitment and Training to the EEAS," *European Foreign Affairs Review*, 16(4): 447–464.

Cross, Mai'a K. D. (2013), "Conceptualising European Public Diplomacy," in Mai'a K. Davis Cross & Jan Melissen (eds.), *European Public Diplomacy: Soft Power at Work*, Hampshire: Palgrave Macmillan: 1–11.

Cross, Mai'a K. D. and Melissen, J. (2013), "Introduction," in Mai'a K. Davis Cross & Jan Melissen (eds.), *European Public Diplomacy: Soft Power at Work*, Hampshire: Palgrave Macmillan.

Cull, N. J. (2008), "Public Diplomacy: Taxonomies and Histories," *Annals of the American Academy of Political and Social Science*, 616(1): 31–54.

Cull, N. J. (2010), "Public Diplomacy: Seven Lessons for its Future from its Past," *Place Branding and Public Diplomacy*, Vol.6: 11–17.

Cull, N. J. (2013), "Roof for a House Divided: How U.S. Propaganda Evolved into Public Diplomacy," in Auerbach, J. and Casteronovo, R. (eds.), *The Oxford Handbook of Propaganda Studies*, New York: Oxford University Press: 131–146.

Cull, N. J., D. Culbert, and D. Welch. (2003). *Propaganda and Mass Persuasion: A Historical Encyclopaedia, 1500 to the Present*. Santa Barbara, CA: ABC-CLIO.

Cummings Milton C. 2003, Cultural Diplomacy and the United States Government: A Survey, Washington. DC: Center for Arts and Culture, cited from Center for Arts and Culture, 2004, Cultural Diplomacy: Recommendations and Research, Washington. DC.

Dai, B. (2008), "European Studies in China," in Shambaugh, D., Sandschneider E. and Zhou H. (eds.), *China-Europe Relations: Perceptions, Polices and Prospects*, London and New York: Routledge: 105–126.

Dams, T. and Van Der Putten, F. P. (2015), *China and Liberal Values in International Relations, Clingendael Report*, Netherlands Institute of International Relations "Clingendael."

Danielsen, H. (2009), "Making Friends at Court: Slow and Indirect Media in US Public Diplomacy in Norway, 1950–1965," *Contemporary European History*, 18(2): 179–198.

De Gouveia, P. F. and Plumridge, H. (2005), *European Infopolitik: Developing EU Public Diplomacy Strategy*, London: Foreign Policy Center, available at: fpc.org. uk/fsblob/657.pdf. [Accessed Dec. 12, 2012].

De Lombaerde, P., Söderbaum, F., Van Langehove, L., and Baert, F. (2010), "The Problem of Comparison in Comparative Regionalism," *Review of International Studies*, 36(3): 731–753.

De Magalhaes, J. C. (1988), *The Pure Concept of Diplomacy*, (translated by Bernardo Futscher Pereira), New York and London: Greenwood Press.

De Wit, H., (2012), "Student Mobility between Europe and the Rest of the World: Trends, Issues and Challenges," in Curaj, A., et al. (eds.), *European Higher Education at the Crossroads: Between the Bologna Process and National Reforms*, Dordrecht, Heidelberg and New York · London: Springer: 431–439.

De Zwaan, J.W., Nelissen, F. A., Jans, J.H. and Blockmans, S. (2004), *The European Union: An Ongoing Process of Integration*, The Hague: T.M.C. Asser Press.

Delegation of the EU to China, (2015), *The European Union and China: A Maturing Partnership*, available at: http://eeas.europa.eu/delegations/china/eu_china/politi cal_relations/index_en.htm, [accessed March 31, 2015]

Delegation of the EU to China, (2016), *News*, available at: http://eeas.europa.eu/
delegations/china/press_corner/all_news/index_zh.htm, [accessed April 10, 2016].

Delegation of the EU to China, (2016), *Professional Training for Chinese Journalists and Editors*, available at: http://eeas.europa.eu/delegations/china/press_corner/
all_news/news/2016/20160401_en.htm, [accessed April 10, 2016].

Deng, K. G. (2010), "Globalisation, China's Recent Miracle Growth and Its Limits," in Deng, K. G. (ed.), *Globalization—Today, Tomorrow*, Available at: http://
www.intechopen.com/books/globalization--today--tomorrow/globalisation-china-s
-recent-miracle-growth-and-its-limits-, [accessed Aug. 6, 2014].

DG-EAC, (2008), *The European Union and the World: European Success Story*,
Luxembourg: Office for Official Publications of the European Communities, available at: http://unipd-centrodirittiumani.it/public/docs/success2008_en.pdf, [ac-
cessed Sept. 2, 2015].

DG Research and Innovation, (2014), *A Global Actor in Search of A Strategy: European Union Foreign Policy between Multilateralism and Bilateralism*, available
at: https://ec.europa.eu/research/social-sciences/pdf/policy_reviews/kina26572enc.
pdf, [accessed April 19, 2016].

Dibble, V. K. and Pekowsky, B. (1973), "What Is and What Ought to Be: A Comparison of Certain Characteristics of the Ideological and Legal Styles of Thoughts,"
American Journal of Sociology, 79(3): 511–549.

Diez, T. and Manners, I. (2007), "Reflecting on Normative Power Europe," in Berenskoetter, F. and Williams, M. J. (eds.), *Power in World Politics*, New York:
Routledge: 173–188.

Ding, S. (2010), "Analysing Rising Power from the Perspective of Soft Power: a new
look at China's rise to the status quo power," *Journal of Contemporary China*,
19(64): 255–272.

Dinnie, K. (2008), *Nation Branding: Concepts, Issues, Practice*, Oxford: Butterworth-Heinemann.

Duchene, F. (1972), "Europe's Role in World Peace," in Mayne, R. (ed.), *Europe
Tomorrow: Sixteen Europeans Look Ahead*, London: Fontana/Collins: 32–47.

Duchene, F. (1973), "The European Community and the Uncertainties of Interdepen-
dence," in Kohnstamm, M. and Hager, W. (eds.), *A Nation Writ Large? Foreign-
Policy Problems before the European Community*, London and Basingstoke: The
Macmillan Press LTD: 1–21.

Duke, S. (2011), "Consistency, Coherence and European Union External Action: The
Path to Lisbon and Beyond," in Koutrakos, P. (ed.), *European Foreign Policy:
Legal and Political Perspectives*, Glos and Northampton: Edward Elgar Publishing
Limited: 15–54.

Duke, S. (2013), "The European External Action Service and Public Diplomacy," in
Cross, M. K. D. and Melissen, J. (eds.), *European Public Diplomacy: Soft Power
at World*, New York: Palgrave Macmillan: 113–136.

Duke, S. (2013), "The European External Action Service and the Quest for an Effective Public Diplomacy," Analysis No. 216, December, available at: https://www.
ispionline.it/sites/default/files/pubblicazioni/analysis_216_2013.pdf, [accessed
Mar. 24, 2019].

Duke, S. (2013), *The European External Action Service and Public Diplomacy*, Discussion Papers in Diplomacy, No. 127, Netherlands Institute of International Relations, "Clingendael."

Duke, S. and Courtier, A. (2011), *The EU's External Public Diplomacy and the EEAS—Cosmetic Exercise or Intended Change?* Available at: http://dseu.lboro. ac.uk/publications/policypapers.html [accessed Aug. 12, 2013]

EACEA (2013), *About Erasmus Mundus 2009-2013*, available at: http://eacea. ec.europa.eu/erasmus_mundus/programme/about_erasmus_mundus_en.php#info, [accessed Sept. 17, 2014]

EACEA (2014), *Erasmus Mundus*, available at: http://eacea.ec.europa.eu/erasmus_ mundus/programme/about_erasmus_mundus_en.php, [accessed Mar. 24, 2014]; *Programme Guide of Erasmus Mundus of 2009-2013*, available at: http://eacea. ec.europa.eu/erasmus_mundus/programme/documents/2014/em_programmeguide _nov2013_en.pdf, [accessed Sept. 22, 2014]

EACEA (2014), *Erasmus Plus Programme Guide*, available at: http://ec.europa. eu/programmes/erasmus-plus/documents/erasmus-plus-programme-guide_en.pdf, [accessed Mar. 14, 2015].

EACEA (2014), *Erasmus Plus: Actions,* available at: http://eacea.ec.europa.eu/ erasmus-plus/actions_en#, [accessed Sept. 17, 2014]

EACEA (2014), *Information about the Jean Monnet Programme from 2007–2013*, available at: http://eacea.ec.europa.eu/llp/jean_monnet/jean_monnet_en.php, [accessed Sept. 29, 2014]

EACEA (2014), *Selection Results – Jean Monnet Networks and Jean Monnet Projects*, available at: https://eacea.ec.europa.eu/sites/eacea-site/files/documents/eac -s11-13_policy-debate-with-academic-world_en.pdf, [accessed Sept. 1, 2015]

ECOTEC Research and Consulting (1999), *External Evaluation Report of the Jean Monnet Action*, available at: http://ec.europa.eu/dgs/education_culture/evalreports/ education/1999/jeanmonnet/JMintrep_fr.pdf, [accessed Oct. 20, 2014].

Edmonds, R. L. (2002), "China and Europe Since 1978: An Introduction," *The China Quarterly*, Vol.169: 1–9.

Edward Murrow Center (1965) *What is Public Diplomacy?* http://fletcher.tufts.edu/ Murrow/Diplomacy, [accessed Oct. 10, 2013].

Edwards, G. (2013), "The EU's Foreign Policy and the Search for Effect," *International Relations*, 27(3): 276–291.

EEAS (2012), *Centre Profiles*, Networking Conference of EU Centres World Meeting, Brussels, 22–24 October, available at: http://www.eeas.europa.eu/eu-cen tres/eu-centres_brochure_2012_en.pdf, [Sept. 22, 2014].

EEAS (2014), *Foreign Policy*, available at: http://www.eeas.europa.eu/policies/in dex_en.htm, [accessed May 4, 2014].

EEAS (2014), General introduction of the EU delegations, available at: http://www. eeas.europa.eu/delegations/index_en.htm, [accessed Mar. 24, 2014]; Foreign Policy of cooperating with industrialised countries, available at: http://www.eeas. europa.eu/ici/publicdiplomacy/index_en.htm, [accessed Mar. 21, 2014]

EEAS (2014), *Organisation Charts*, available at: http://eeas.europa.eu/back ground/docs/organisation_en.pdf, [accessed Mar. 12, 2015]; EEAS, (2014), website of EU delegations, available at: http://www.eeas.europa.eu/delegations/index_en.htm, [accessed Mar. 24, 2014]; general introduction of the EU delegations, available at: http://www.eeas.europa.eu/delegations/index_en.htm, [accessed Mar. 24, 2014]; Foreign Policy of cooperating with industrialised countries, available at: http://www.eeas.europa.eu/ici/publicdiplomacy/index_en.htm, [accessed Mar. 21, 2014].

EEAS (2014), Website of EU delegations, available at: http://www.eeas.europa.eu/delegations/index_en.htm, [accessed Mar. 24, 2014].

EEAS (2015), *EU-China 2020 Strategic Agenda for Cooperation*, available at: http://www.eeas.europa.eu/china/docs/20131123_agenda_2020__en.pdf, [accessed Mar. 29, 2015].

Emmons, D. C. (1972), "Normative Knowledge," *The Journal of Value Inquiry*, 6(4): 294–303.

Eriksen, E. O. and Fossum J. E. (2000), *Democracy in the European Union*, Preface, London: Routledge: 11

EU Centres- EEAS, (2014), *Introduction*, available at: http://www.eeas.europa.eu/eu-centres/index_en.htm, [accessed March 21, 2014].

EU insight, (2010), *Engaging the World: The EU's Public Diplomacy*, http://www.eu-runion.org/eu/images/stories/euinsightpubdipl-7-10.pdf, [accessed Nov. 11, 2014]

EU-China Policy Dialogue Support Facility II, (2013), 1st Meeting of EU-China Higher Education Platform for Cooperation and Exchange (HEPCE), April, 2013. Available at: http://www.eu-chinapdsf.org/EN/Activity.asp?ActivityId=292&ActivityStatus=1, [accessed Aug. 2, 2014].

EUPIC—The EU Project Innovation Centre, (2013), *EU-China B&T Cooperation Fair VIII*, available at: http://www.eu-china.org.cn/download/file.html?id=10, [accessed April 26, 2016].

Europa.eu (2014), *Enhancing the Asian Strategy*, available at: http://europa.eu/legislation_summaries/external_relations/relations_with_third_countries/asia/r14202_en.htm, [accessed Nov. 3, 2014].

EuropeAid (2008), *EU-China European Studies Centres Programme*, available at: http://ec.europa.eu/europeaid/documents/case-studies/china_higher-education_en.pdf, [accessed July 7, 2014].

EuropeAid (2013), *About the EuropeAid*, available at: http://ec.europa.eu/europeaid/who/about/index_en.htm, [accessed Nov. 21, 2013].

European Commission (1995), *A Long-term Policy for EU–China Relations*, COM (1995) 279 final.

European Commission (1998), *Building a Comprehensive Partnership with China*, COM (1998) 181 final.

European Commission (2001), *EU Strategy towards China: Implementation of the 1998 Communication and Future Steps for a More Effective EU Policy*, COM (2001) 265 final.

European Commission (2003), *A Maturing Partnership—Shared Interests and Challenges in EU-China Relations*, COM (2003) 533 final.

European Commission (2006), *Commission Working Document, Accompanying COM(2006) 631 Final: Closer Partners, Growing Responsibilities, A Policy Paper* on *EU-China Trade and Investment: Competition and Partnership*, COM (2006) 632 final.

European Commission (2006), *EU-China: Closer Partners, Growing Responsibilities*, COM (2006) 631 final:9

European Commission (2011), *Regulation of the European Parliament and of the Council, Establishing "Erasmus for All," The Union Programme for Education, Training, Youth and Sport*, COM (2011) 788 Final, Brussels, Nov. 23, 2011, Chapter 2, Article 5.

European Commission (2013), *European Higher Education in the World, Communication from the Commission to the European Parliament, the Council, The European Economic and Social Committee and the Committee of the Region*, COM (2013) 499 final, 7th September 2013, Brussels.

European Commission (1995), *A Long Term Policy for China-Europe Relations, Communication of the Commission*, COM (1995) 279/final, available at: http://eeas.europa.eu/china/docs/com95_279_en.pdf, [accessed Mar. 23, 2015].

European Commission (2001), *European and Asia: A Strategic Framework for Enhanced Partnership*, COM (2001) 469.

European Commission (2007), *A Glance at EU Public Diplomacy at Work*, http://europa.eu/50/around_world/images/2007_50th_anniv_broch_en.pdf, [accessed April 2, 2015].

European Commission (2008), Presentation of Jean Monnet Prize 2008, available at: http://europa.eu/rapid/press-release_IP-08-1765_en.htm, [accessed May 12, 2016].

European Commission (2014), *Maximising the Impact of Cultural Diplomacy in EU Foreign Policy*, available at: http://europa.eu/rapid/press-release_IP-14-382_en.htm, [accessed Sept. 14, 2014].

European Union (2014), *A Peaceful Europe—The Beginning of Cooperation*, available at: http://europa.eu/about-eu/eu-history/1945-1959/index_en.htm, [accessed May 20, 2014].

European Union (2014), *Thinking about Europe: Jean Monnet Support to European Studies*, Luxembourg: Publications Office of the European Union.

European Union (2014), EU treaties, available at: http://europa.eu/eu-law/decision-making/treaties/index_en.htm, [accessed Mar. 24, 2015].

European Union (2003), *European Security Strategic—A Secure Europe in a Better World*, available at: https://europa.eu/globalstrategy/en/european-security-strategy-secure-europe-better-world, [accessed March 10, 2019].

Fan, M., and Chen, X. (2009), "Zhongguo Daxuesheng Zhuanye Xuanze Diaocha Zhi Jiben Fenxi (A Survey on the Major Choice of Chinese Undergraduates)," *Daxue Jiaoyu Kexue* (*University Education Science*), No.3: 91–96.

Fan, Y. (2006), "Branding the Nation: What is Being Branded?" *Journal of Vocation Marketing*, 12(1): 5–14.

Fan, Y. (2008), "Soft Power: Power of Attraction or Confusion?" *Public Diplomacy and Place Branding*, 4(2): 147–158.

Fan, Y. (2010), "Branding the Nation: Towards A Better Understanding," *Place Branding and Public Diplomacy*, Vol.6: 97–103.

Field, H. (2001), *European Integration Curricula and "Europeanisation": Alternative Approaches and Critical Appreciation*, paper presented to the ECSA Seventh Biennial International Conference, May 31–June 2, 2001, Madison: Wisconsin.

Figel, J. (2011), "Critical Reflection and Reliable Information: The Jean Monnet Community and the Future Course of the European Union," in European Union, (ed.), *20 Years of Support for European Integration Studies*, Luxembourg: Publications Office of the European Union.

Fingleton, W. (2012), *The Influence of Public Diplomacy on EU-China Relations*, speech at conference of the the conference of "the Wisdom of Public Diplomacy: the dialogue among Chinese, American and European scholars" was held on 19th May 2012 in Beijing, by Netherland Institute of International Relation "Clingeneal" and The Charhar Institute, a Chinese non-governmental think-tank for international relations and diplomacy, available at: http://www.charhar.org.cn/newsinfo.aspx?newsid=4629, [accessed Sept. 2, 2015].

Fioramonti, L. and Lucarelli, S, (2010), "Self-representations and External Perceptions—Can the EU Bridge the Gap?" In Lucarelli, S. and Fioramonti, L. (eds.), *External Perceptions of the European Union as a Global Actor*, Hoboken: Taylor and Francis: 218–225.

Fisher, A. (2011), "Looking at the Man in the Mirror: Understanding of Power and Influence in Public Diplomacy," *in Fisher, A. and Lucas, S. (eds.), Trials of Engagement: The Future of US Public Diplomacy*, Leiden: Martinus Nijhoff Publishers: 271–295.

Fisher, A. (2013), *Collaborative Public Diplomacy: How Transnational Networks Influenced American Studies in Europe*, New York: Palgrave Macmillan.

Fisher, A. and Lucas, S. (2011), "Introduction," Fisher, A. and Lucas, S. (eds.), *Trials of Engagement: The Future of US Public Diplomacy*, Leiden: Martinus Nijhoff Publishers: 1–15.

Fitzpatrick K. R. (2007), "Advancing the New Public Diplomacy: A Public Relations Perspective," *The Hague Journal of Diplomacy*, 2(3): 187–211.

Fitzpatrick K. R. (2010), *The Future of U.S. Public Diplomacy: An Uncertain Fate*, Leiden: Koninklijke Brill NV.

Fligstein, N., Polyakova, A., and Sandholtz, W. (2012), "European Identity, Nationalism and European Identity," *JCMS: Journal of Common Market Studies*, 50(1): 106–122.

Forster, C. and Owen, J. (2006), *Understanding Iran: A Solution to the Nuclear Crisis?* London: Foreign Policy Centre, available at: http://fpc.org.uk/fsblob/710.pdf, [accessed May 10, 2016].

Fransen, F. J. (2001), *The Supranational Politics of Jean Monnet: Ideas and Origins of the European Community*, Westport CT: Greenwood Press.

Freedman, L. (2006), "Networks, Culture and Narratives," *The Adelphi Papers*, 45(379): 23

Gao, H. (2012), "After 20 Years of Silence, China Slowly Confronts the 'Great Leap Forward,'" available at: http://www.theatlantic.com/international/archive/2012/05/after-50-years-of-silence-china-slowly-confronts-the-great-leap-forward/257797/, [accessed April 15, 2016].

Gilardi, F. (2012), "Transnational Diffusion: Norms, Ideas, and Polices," in Carlsnaes, W. Risse, T. and Simmons, B. (eds.), *Handbook of International Relations, 2nd edition*, Thousand Oaks: Sage Publication: 453–477.

Gilboa, E. (1998), "Media Diplomacy: Conceptual Divergence and Applications," *The International Journal of Press/Politics*, 3(3): 56–75.

Gilboa, E. (2008), "Searching for a Theory of Public Diplomacy," *Annals of the American Academy of Political and Social Science*, 616(1): 55–77.

Gill, B. & Huang, Y. (2006), "Source and Limits of Chinese Soft Power," *Survival: Global Politics and Strategy*, 48(2): 17–39.

Gillespie, J. (2012), "Developing a Theoretical Framework for Evaluating Rule of Law Promotion in Developing Countries," in Zurn, M., Nollkaemper, A. and Peerenboom, R. (eds.), *Rule of Law Dynamics: In an Era of International and Transitional Governance*, New York: Cambridge University Press: 233–251.

Godement, F. (2013), "Law and Power in Xi's China," *China Analysis*, European Council of Foreign Relations, available at: http://www.ecfr.eu/page/-/China_Analy sis_Law_and_Power_in_Xis_China_December2013.pdf, [accessed May 25, 2016].

Golan, G. J. (2013), "An Integration Approach to Public Diplomacy," *American Behavioural Scientist*, 57(9): 1251–1255.

Goldsmith, B., and Horiuchi, Y. (2009), "Spinning the Globe? U.S. Public Diplomacy and Foreign Public Opinion," *The Journal of Politics*, 71(3): 863–875.

Gregory, B. (2008), "Public Diplomacy: Sunrise of an Academic Field," *The Annals of the American Academy of Political and Social Science*, 616(1): 274–290.

Gregory, B. (2011), "American Public Diplomacy: Enduring Characteristics, Elusive Transformation," *The Hague Journal of Diplomacy*, 6(3-4): 351–372.

Griese, O. (2006), "EU-China Relations—An Assessment by the Communications of the European Union," *Asia Europe Journal*, 4(4): 545–553.

Grunig J. E. (1997), "A Situational Theory of Publics: Conceptual History, Recent Challenges, and New Research," In Moss, D., Macmanus, T. and Vercic, D. (eds.), *Public Relations Research: An International Perspective*, London: International Thomson Business: 3–38

Ham, P. V. (2001), "The Rise of the Brand State: The Postmodern Politics of Image and Reputation," *Foreign Affairs*, 80(5): 2–6.

Ham, P. V. (2008), "Place Branding: The State of the Art," *Annals of the American Academy of Political and Social Science*, 616(1): 126–148.

Han, F. (2011), *Gonggong Waijiao Gailun* (*Introduction to Public Diplomacy*), Beijing: Peking University Press.

Han, Z. (2011), "China's Public Diplomacy in a New Era," in Zhu, Z. (ed.), *The People's Republic of China Today: Internal and External Challenges*, Singapore: World Scientific Publishing: 291–310.

Hannabuss, S. (1996), "Research Interviews," *New Library World*, 97(5): 22–30.

Hartmann, B. (2015), Speech delivered at the routable discussion on China and the Rule of Law, Madariaga Foundation, Brussels, Belgium, 4th Feb 2015.

Hassid, J. and Sun, W., (2015), "Stability Maintenance and Chinese Media: Beyond Political Communication?" *Journal of Current Chinese Affairs*, 44(2): 3–15.

Hayden, C. (2011), *The Rhetoric of Soft Power: Public Diplomacy in Global Context*, Plymouth: Lexington Books.

Headrick, D. R. (1994), "Shortwave Radio and its Impact on International Telecommunication between the Wars," *History and Technology: An International Journal*, 11(1): 21–32.

Heath, R. L., Liao, S. and Douglas, W. (1995), "Effects of Perceived Economic Harms and Benefits on Issues Involvement, Use of Information Source, and Actions: A Study in Risk Communication," *Journal of Public Relations Research*, 7(2): 89–109.

Herlin-Karnell, E. (2012), "The EU as a Promoter of Values and the European Global Project," *German Law Journal*, 13(11): 1225–1246.

Heron, L. (2013a), "Nine Chinese Universities Sign Academic Freedom Pact," *The South China Moring Post*, available at: http://www.scmp.com/news/china/ar ticle/1331803/nine-chinese-universities-sign-academic-freedom-pact, [accessed May 26, 2016].

Hill, C. (2010), "Cheque and Balances: The European Union's Soft Power Strategy," in I. Parmar and M. Cox, (eds.), *Soft Power and US Foreign Policy: Theoretical, Historical and Contemporary Perspectives*, London: Routledge: 182–198.

Hill, C. and Smith, M. (2011), "International Relations and the European Union: Themes and Issues," in Hill, C. and Smith, M. (eds.), *International Relations and European Union (2nd edition)*, the New York: Oxford University press: 3–20.

Hogg, M. A. and Abrams, D. (1988), *Social Identification: A Social Psychology of Intergroup Relations and Group Process*, New York: Routledge.

Holslag, J. (2010), "The Strategic Dissonance between Europe and China," *The Chinese Journal of International Politics*, 3(2): 325–345.

Holslag, J. (2011), "The Elusive Axis: Assessing the EU-China Strategic Partnership," *JCMS: Journal of Common Market Studies*, 49(2): 293–313.

Hong, N.Y. (2014), "EU-China Education Diplomacy: An effective Soft Power Strategy?" *European Foreign Affairs Review*, 19 (3/1), Special Issue: 155–171.

Hopf, T. (1998), "The Promise of Constructivism in International Relations Theory," *International Security*, 23(1): 171–200.

Hovland, C. and Weiss, W. (1951), "The Influence of Source Credibility on Communication Effectiveness," *Public Opinion Quarterly*, 15(4): 635–650

Humanrights.cn, (2014), "Sichuan Daxue Renquan Falv Yanjiu Zhongxin (Research Centre of Human Rights Law at Sichuan University)," available at: http://www.humanrights.cn/html/2014/5_0703/1218_3.html, [accessed May 14, 2016].

Huo, Z. (2005), "Lun Zhongou Zhanlue Guanxi (On China-EU Strategic Relationship)," *Guoji Wenti Yanjiu* [*International Studies*].

Ikenberry, G. J. (2011), "The Future of the Liberal World Order: Internationalism after America," *Foreign Affairs*, 90(3): 56–68.

Jackson, R. and Sørensen, G. (2016), *Introduction to International Relations: Theories and Approaches (6th edition),* Oxford: Oxford University Press.

Jia, Q. (2010), *Continuity and Change: China's Attitude Toward Hard Power and Soft Power*, Brookings East Asia Comment, No. 44.

Joffe, J. (2006), "The Peril of Soft Power," *The New York Times*, http://www.nytimes. com/2006/05/14/magazine/14wwln_lede.html?_r=1&pagewanted=print&oref=slo gin, [accessed Dec. 10, 2013].

Jones, W. J. (2009-2010), "European Union Soft Power: Cultural Diplomacy & Higher Education in Southeast Asia," *Silpakorn University International Journal*, Vol.9-10: 41–70.

Jowett, G. S. and O'Donnell, V. J. (2011), *Propaganda and Persuasion, (fifth edition)*, CA: Sage Publication.

Jungermann, H., Pfister, H. R., and Fischer, K. (1996), "Credibility, Information Preference, and Information Interests," *Risk Analysis*, 16(2): 251–261.

Katz, E. (1957), "The Two-Step Flow of Communication: An Up-To-Date Report on a Hypothesis," *Public Opinion Quarterly*, 21(1): 61–78

Kavanaugh, A. L., Fox, E. A, Sheetz, S. D. (2012), "Social Media Use by Government: From the Routine to the Critical," *Government Information Quarterly*, 29(4): 480–491.

Keck, Z. (2014), "The 4th Plenum: Rule of Law with Chinese Characteristics," *The Diplomat*, available at: http://thediplomat.com/2014/10/4th-plenum-rule-of-law -with-chinese-characteristics/, [accessed Feb. 27, 2016].

Keohane, R. and Nye, J. (2011), *Power and Interdependence, 4th edition*, New York: Longman.

Keohane, Robert, O. and Nye, J. (1987), "Review: Power and Interdependence Revisited," *International Organisations*, 41(4): 725–753.

Keukeleire, S. and Delreux, T. (2014), *The Foreign Policy of the European Union, 2nd Edition*, Hampshire: Palgrave Macmillan.

Keukeleire, S. and MacNaughtan, J. (2008), *The Foreign Policy of the European Union*, Hampshire: Palgrave Macmillan.

King, G., Pan, J. and Roberts, M. E. (2013), "How Censorship in China Allows Government Criticism but Silences Collective Expression," *American Political Science Review*, 107(2): 326–343.

Kirkland, J. (2014), *Soft Power in Higher Education: Friend or Foe?* The Association of Commonwealth Universities, available at: https://www.acu.ac.uk/news -events/blog/soft-power-higher-education, [accessed May 31, 2014].

Knight, J. (2014), *The Limits of Soft Power in Higher Education*, University World News, 31st Jan., available at: http://www.universityworldnews.com/article. php?story=20140129134636725, [accessed May 31, 2014].

Krebs, R. R. and Jackson, P. T. (2007), "Twisting Tongues and Twisting Arms: The Power of Political Rhetoric," *European Journal of International Relations*, 13(1): 35–66.

Kugiel, P. (2017), "End of European Soft Power? Implications for EU Foreign Policy," *The Polish Quarterly of International Affairs*, 26 (1): 59–72.

Kuhn, T. (2012), "Why Educational Programmes Miss Their Mark: Cross-Border Mobility, Education and European Identity," *Journal of Common Market Studies*, 50(6): 994–1010.

La Porte, T. (2011), *The Power of the European Union in Global Governance: A Proposal for a New Public Diplomacy*, Los Angeles: Figueroa Press.

Larsen, H. (2014), "The EU as a Normative Power and the Research on External Perceptions: The Missing Links," *Journal of Common Market Studies*, 52(4): 896–910.

Lasswell, H. (1948), "The Structure and Function of Communication in Society," in Bryson, L. (ed.), *The Communication of Ideas*, New York: Harper & Bros: 37–51.

Lasswell, H. (1971), *Propaganda Technique in World War, The New Edition*, MA: MIT Press.

Law, W. (2013), "Globalization, National Identity, and Citizenship Education: China's Search for Modernization and a Modern Chinese Citizenry," *Frontiers of Education in China*, 8(4): 596–627.

Lazarsfeld, P. F., Berelson, B. and Gaudet, H. (1948), *The People's Choice*, New York: Columbia University Press.

Lehne, S. (2016), *How the Refugee Crisis will Reshape the EU*, Carnegie Europe, available at: http://carnegieeurope.eu/2016/02/04/how-refugee-crisis-will-reshape -eu/itj7, [accessed 11-04-2016].

Leonard, M., Stead, C. and Smewing, C. (2002), *Public Diplomacy*, London: Foreign Policy Centre.

Li, J. (2014), "Educators Have a Duty to Teach about China's Problems: Chinese Newspapers," *South China Moring Post*, available at: http://www.scmp.com/ news/china/article/1660338/educators-have-duty-teach-about-chinas-problems-chi nese-newspaper, [accessed May 27, 2016].

Li, J. (2015), "China's Education Dilemma: Building Harvard-level Universities within a Firm Ideological Lock," *South China Moring Post*, available at: http:// www.scmp.com/news/china/policies-politics/article/1876856/chinas-education-di lemma-building-harvard-level, [accessed May 27, 2015].

Li, R. (2013), "Seven Subjects Off Limits for Teaching, Chinese Universities Told," *South China Morning Post*, available at: http://www.scmp.com/news/china/ar-ticle/1234453/seven-subjects-limits-teaching-chinese-universities-told, [accessed June 7, 2016].

Li, X. (2007), "Chinese Television Coverage and Chinese Perceptions of Sino-EU Relations," in Kerr D, and Liu, F. (eds.), *The International Politics of EU-China Relations*, Oxford: Oxford University Press: 102–177.

Lijphart, A. (1964), "Tourist Traffic and International Potential," *Journal of Common Market Studies*, 2(3): 251–262.

Lima Jr. A. F. (2007), "The Role of International Educational Exchanges in Public Diplomacy," *Place Branding and Public Diplomacy*, 3(3): 234–251.

Lloveras-Soler, J. M. (2011), *The New EU Diplomacy: Learning to Add Value*, European University Institute working paper, http://cadmus.eui.eu/bitstream/han dle/1814/15639/RSCAS_2011_05.pdf?sequence=1, [accessed April 9, 2014].

Lucarelli, S. and Fioramonti, L. (2010), "The EU in the Eyes of the Others—Why Bother?" In Lucarelli, S. and Fioramonti, L. (eds.), *External Perceptions of the European Union as a Global Actor*, Hoboken: Taylor and Francis: 1–10.

Lynch, D. (2005), *Communicating Europe to the World: What Public Diplomacy for the EU?* EPC Working Paper, No. 21.

Ma, X. (2012), *Beyond the Economic Ties: EU in the Chinese Media*, Centre of Public Diplomacy, University of South California, available at: http://uscpublicdiplo macy.org/sites/uscpublicdiplomacy.org/files/legacy/pdfs/XinruMaBestPaper2012. pdf, [accessed July 9, 2014].

Maher, R. (2016), "The Elusive EU-China Strategic Partnership," *International Affairs*, 92(4): 959–976.

Malone, G. (1985), "Managing Public Diplomacy," *The Washington Quarterly*, 8(3): 199–213.

Manheim, J. B. (1994), *Strategic Public Diplomacy and American Foreign Policy: The Evolution of Influence*, New York: Oxford University Press.

Manners, I. (2002), "Normative Power Europe: A Contradiction in Terms?" *Journal of Common Market Studies*, 40(2): 235–258.

Manners, I. (2008), "The Normative Ethics of the European Union," *International Affairs*, 84(1): 65–80.

Manners, I. and Whitman, R. (2013), "Normative Power and Future of EU Public Diplomacy," in Mai'a K. Davis Cross & Melissen, J. (eds.), *European Public Diplomacy: Soft Power at Work*, Hampshire: Palgrave Macmillan: 183–203.

Maresceau, M. (2011), "Tracing the History of the Jean Monnet Programme," in in European Union, (ed.), *20 Years of Support for European Integration Studies*, Luxembourg: Publications Office of the European Union: 274–284.

Mark, S. L. (2010), "Rethinking Cultural Diplomacy: The Cultural Diplomacy of New Zealand, the Canadian Federation and Quebec," *Political Science*, 61(1): 62–83.

Marshall, T. (1970) "The Strategy of International Exchange," in Eide, I. (ed.), *Students as Links between Cultures*, Universitetsforlaget, Oslo, Norway: 3–31.

Martinelli, A. (2017), "The European Identity," *Glocalism: Journal of Culture, Politics and Innovation*, 23. DOI: 10.12893/gjcpi.2017.2.11.

Mattlin, M. (2012), "Dead on Arrival: Normative EU Policy towards China," *Asia Europe Journal*, 10(2): 181–198.

McCombs, M. and Shaw, D. L. (1972), "The Agenda-Setting Function of Mass Media," *The Public Opinion Quarterly*, 36(2): 176–187.

McPhail, T. L. (2010), *Global communication: Theories, Stakeholders and Trends*, West Sussex: Wiley-Blackwell.

Mearsheimer, J. (2002), "Hearts and Minds," *The National Interest*, No. 69.

Melissen, J. (2005), "The New Public Diplomacy: Between Theory and Practice," in Melissen, J. (ed.), *The New Public Diplomacy: Soft Power in International Relations*, New York: Palgrave Macmillan: 3–27.

Melissen, J. (2005), *Wielding Soft Power: The New Public Diplomacy*, Netherlands Institute of International Relations, "Clingendael."

Melissen, J. (2013), "Conclusion and Recommendations on Public Diplomacy in Europe," in Mai'a K. Davis Cross & Jan Melissen (eds.), *European Public Diplomacy: Soft Power at Work*, Basingstoke: Palgrave Macmillan, 205–212.

Men, J. (2012), "The EU and China: Mismatched Partners?" *Journal of Contemporary China*, 21(74): 333–349.

MFA (2014), *China's Policy Paper on the EU: Deepen the China-EU Comprehensive Strategic Partnership for Mutual Benefit and Win-win Cooperation*, available at: http://www.fmprc.gov.cn/mfa_eng/wjdt_665385/wjzcs/t1143406.shtml, [accessed April 26, 2016].

MFA (2016), Wang Yi Meets with Assistant to the US President for National Security Affairs Susan Rice, available at: http://www.fmprc.gov.cn/mfa_eng/zxxx_662805/t1343846.shtml, [accessed April 26, 2016].

Michalski, A. (2005), "The EU as a Soft Power: The Force of Persuasion," in Melissen, J. (ed.), *The New Public Diplomacy: Soft Power in International Relations*, New York: Palgrave Macmillan: 121–146.

Michalski, A. (2012), "China and the EU: Conceptual Gaps in Soft Power," in Pan, Z. (ed.), *Conceptual Gaps in China-EU Relations*, Hampshire and New York: Palgrave Macmillan: 65–79.

Michalski, A. and Pan, Z. (2017), *Unlikely Partners? China, The European Union and the Forging of a Strategic Partnership*, Singapore: Palgrave Macmillan.

Ministry of Education, China (2015), The Notification of the 2015 Project List of National College Student Innovation Fund, available at: http://www.moe.gov.cn/s78/A08/A08_gggs/A08_sjhj/201510/t20151029_216448.html, [accessed May 12, 2016].

Ministry of Foreign Affairs of P. R. China. (2003), *China's Policy Paper on EU*, available at: www.chinamission.be/eng/zywj/zywd/t1227623.htm, [accessed March 6, 2019].

Ministry of Foreign Affairs of P. R. China. (2014), *China's Policy Paper on the EU: Deepen the Chin-EU Comprehensive Strategic Partnership for Mutual Benefits and Win-win Cooperation*, available at: http://www.chinamission.be/eng/zywj/zywd/t1143406.htm, [accessed March 6, 2019]. Ministry of Foreign Affairs of P. R. China. (2018), *China's Policy Paper on the European Union*, available at: http://www.chinamission.be/eng/zywj/zywd/t1623330.htm, [accessed March 6, 2019].

Miskimmon, A., O'Loughlin, B. and Roselle, L. (2012), *Forging the World: Strategic Narratives and International Relations*, Working Paper, Centre for European Politics/ New Political Communication Unit, available at: http://newpolcom.rhul.ac.uk/storage/Forging%20the%20World%20Working%20Paper%202012.pdf, [accessed Nov. 22, 2015].

Miskimmon, A., O'Loughlin, B. and Roselle, L. (2013), *Strategic Narratives: Communication Power and the New World Order*, New York and London: Routledge.

Mitchell, J. M. (1986), *International Cultural Relations*, London: Allen & Unwin.

Mitchell, K. (2015), "Rethinking the 'Erasmus Effect' of European Identity," *Journal of Common Market Studies*, 53(2): 330–348.

Mohrman, K. (2008), "The Emerging Global Model with Chinese Characteristics," *Higher Education Policy*, Vol.21: 29–48.

Monthy, J. T. (1998), "Internal Perspective on Chinese Human Rights Reform: The Death Penalty in the PRC," *Texas International Law Journal*, 33(1): 189–226.

Moran J. and Ponz Canto, F. (2004), *Taking Europe to the World—50 Years of the European Commission's External Service*, EEAS, http://www.eeas.europa.eu/delegations/docs/50_years_brochure_en.pdf , [accessed Jan. 12, 2014].

Moravcsik, A. (2009), "Europe: The Quiet Superpower," *French Politics*, Vol.7: 403–422.

Morini, M. Peruzzi, R. and Poletti, A. (2010), "Eastern Giants: The EU in the Eyes of Russia and China," in Lucarelli, S. and Fioramonti, L. (eds.), *External Perceptions of the European Union as a Global Actor*, Hoboken: Taylor and Francis: 32–51.

Mulcahy, K. V. (1999), "Cultural Diplomacy and the Exchange Programme: 1938–1978," *The Journal of Arts, Management, Law, and Society*, 29(1): 7–28.

Mull, C. and Wallin, M. (2013), Propaganda: A Tool of Strategic Influence, *Fact sheet of American Security Project*, available at: http://www.scribd.com/doc/165110783/FACT-SHEET-Propaganda-A-Tool-of-Strategic-Influence, [accessed Nov. 4, 2014].

Murch, A. W. (1971), "Public Concern for Environmental Pollution," *The Public Opinion Quarterly*, 35(1): 100–106.

Murray, P. (2009), "Model Europe? Reflections on the EU as a Model of Regional Integration," in Pompeo Della Posta, Milica Uvalic and Amy Verdun (eds.), *Globalization, Development and Integration*. Hampshire: Palgrave: 273–289.

NAFSA: Association of International Educators (2003), *In America's Interest: Welcoming International Students*, available at: http://www.nafsa.org/Resource_Library_Assets/Public_Policy/In_America_s_Interest__Welcoming_International_Students/, [accessed May 27, 2014].

Neumann, R. Parry, S. and Becher, T. (2002), "Teaching and Learning in their Disciplinary Contexts: A Conceptual Analysis," *Studies in Higher Education*, 27(4): 405–417.

Niblett, R. (2013), *Strategic Europe: Still a Civilian Power*, Carnegie Europe, available at: http://carnegieeurope.eu/publications/?fa=45665&reloadFlag=1, [accessed June 10, 2014]

Nielsen, K. L. (2013), "EU Soft Power and the Capability-expectations Gap," *Journal of Contemporary European Research*, 9(5): 723–739.

Nisbet, E. C. (2005), "The Engagement Model of Opinion Leadership: Testing Validity within a European Context," *International Public Opinion Research*, 18(1): 3–30.

Nossel, S. (2004), "Smart Power: Reclaiming Liberal Internationalism," *Foreign Affairs*, 81(2): 131–142.

Noya, J. (2005), "The Symbolic Power of Nations," *Place Branding*, 2(1): 53–67.

Nunes, I. F. (2011), "Civilian, Normative, and Ethical Power Europe: Role Claims and EU Discourses," *European Foreign Affairs Review* 16(1): 1–20.

Nye, J. (1990), "Soft Power," *Foreign Policy*, No. 80: 153–171.

Nye, J. (2004), *Soft Power: The Means to Success in World Politics*, New York: Public Affairs.

Nye, J. (2008), "Public Diplomacy and Soft Power," *Annals of the American Academy of Political and Social Science*, 616(1): 94–109.

Nye, J. (2009), "Get Smart: Combining Hard and Soft Power," *Foreign Affairs*, July/August Issue, available at: http://www.foreignaffairs.com/articles/65163/joseph-s-nye-jr/get-smart?page=1, [accessed Aug. 18, 2014].

Nye, J. (2010), *The Future of Power*, New York: Public Affairs.

Nye, J. (2011), *Why Europe Is and Will Remain, Powerful? Utopian.org.* available at: http://www.the-utopian.org/post/2424081389/why-europe-is-and-will-remain-powerful, [accessed May 11, 2015].

Nye. J. (2005), "Soft Power and Higher Education," in *The Internet and the University: Forum 2004*, online publication, available at: http://net.educause.edu/forum/iuf04.asp?bhcp=1, [accessed 27-05-2014].

Oberthür, S. (2009), "The Role of the EU in Global Environmental and Climate Governance," in Telò, M. (ed.), *The European Union and Global Governance*, London: Routledge: 192–209.

Orbie, J. (2006), "Civilian Power Europe: Review of the Original and Current Debates," *Cooperation and Conflict*, 41(1): 123–128.

Orbie, J. (2009), "A Civilian Power in the World? Instruments and Objectives in European Union External Policies," in Orbie, J. (ed.), *Europe's Global Role*, Surrey: Ashgate Publishing Limited: 1–34.

Osler, A., and Starkey, H. (1999), "Rights, Identities and Inclusion: European Action Programmes as Political Education," *Oxford Review of Education*, 25(1–2): 199–215.

Özoğuz-Bolgi, S. (2013), "Is the EU Becoming a Global Power after the Treaty of Lisbon," in Boening, A. Kremer, J-F, and Van Loon, A. (eds.), *Global Power Europe*, Vol. 1, Springer-Verlag Berlin Heidelberg: 3–18.

Pace, M. (2007), "The Construction of EU Normative Power," *Journal of Common Market Studies*, 45(5): 1041–1064.

Pacheco Pardo, R, (2009), "The Political Weakness of the EU in East Asia: A Constructivist Approach," *Asia Europe Journal*, 7(2): 265–280.

Pamment, J. (2012), *New Public Diplomacy in the 21st Century: A Comparative Study of Policy and Practice*, New York and Abingdon: Routledge

Pamment, J. (2014), "Strategic Narratives in US Public Diplomacy: A Critical Geopolitics," *Popular Communication*, 12(1): 48–64.

Pan, Z. (2010), "Managing the Conceptual Gap on Sovereignty in China-EU Relations," *Asia Europe Journal*, 8(2): 227–243.

Pan, Z. (ed.), (2012), *Conceptual Gaps in China-EU Relations*, London: Palgrave Macmillan.

Pech, L. (2009), "The Rule of Law as a Constitutional Principle of the European Union," *Jean Monnet Working Paper 04/09*, NYU School of law.

Peerenboom, R. (2002*), China's Long March toward Rule of Law*, Cambridge: Cambridge University Press.

Peisert, H. (1978). *Die Auswärtige Kulturpolitik Der Bundesrepublik Deutschland. Sozialwissenschaftliche Analysen und Planungsmodelle.* Stuttgart: Klett-Cotta.

People.com.cn, (2014), "Laoshi, Qing Buyao Zheyang Jiang Zhongguo (Teacher, Please Do Not Teach China in This Way)," available at: http://edu.people.com.cn/n/2014/1114/c1006-26025286.html, [accessed May 13, 2016].

Persson, A. (2017), "Shaping Discourse and Setting Examples: Normative Power Europe can Work in the Israeli-Palestinian Conflict," *JCMS: Journal of Common Market Studies*, 55(6): 1415–1431.

Peruzzi, R. P., A. and Zhang, S. (2007), "China's View of Europe: A Maturing Partnership," *European Foreign Affairs Review*, 12(3): 311–330.

Peters, M. A. (2007), "Europa, Europeanisation, and Europe: Constituting New Europeans," in Kuhn, M. (ed.), *Who is the European?—A New Global Player*, New York: Peter Lang Publishing: 71–86.

Peterson, P. M. (2013), *Global Higher Education as a Reflection of International Relations*, European Association for International Education Conference, 12th Sept., Istanbul.

Philippou, S., Keating, A., and Ortloff, D. H. (2009), "Citizenship Education Curricula: Comparing the Multiple Meanings of Supra-national Citizenship in Europe and Beyond," *Journal of Curriculum Studies*, 41(2): 291–299.

Piao, V. (2014), "3 Universities Pledge to Uphold Party Ideals on Campus," *The New York Times*, available at: http://cn.nytimes.com/china/20140904/c04campus/dual/, [accessed May 25, 2016].

Pisani-Ferry, J., Röttgen, N., Sapir, A., Tucker, P. and Wolff, G. B. (2016), *Europe after Brexit: A Proposal for a Continental Partnership*. Available at: https://ces.fas.harvard.edu/uploads/files/Reports-Articles/Europe-after-Brexit.pdf, [accessed July 11, 2018].

Pithers, R. T. and Soden, R. (2000), "Critical Thinking in Education: A Review," *Educational Research*, 42(3): 237–249.

Poletti, A., and Sicurelli, D. (2012), "The EU as Promoter of Environmental Norms in the Doha Round," *West Europe Politics*, 35(4): 911–932.

Polglase, G. (2013), "Higher Education as Soft Power in the Eastern Partnership: The Case of Belarus," *Eastern Journal of European Studies*, 4(2): 111–121.

Porter, W. and Mykleby, M. (2011), *A National Strategic Narrative*, Woodrow Wilson Centre, available at: https://www.wilsoncenter.org/sites/default/files/A%20National%20Strategic%20Narrative.pdf, [accessed April 19, 2016].

Pu, X. (2012), "Socialisation as a Two-way Process: Emerging Powers and the Diffusion of International Norms," *The Chinese Journal of International Politics*, 5(4): 341–367.

Qu, Q. S. and Dumay, J. (2011), "The Qualitative Research Interview," *Qualitative Research in Accounting & Management*, 8(3): 238–264.

Quintin, O. (2009), *20 Years of Support for European Integration Studies*, Jean Monnet Conference (Closing Session), http://ec.europa.eu/education/jean-monnet/doc1567_en.htm, [accessed 10-02-2013].

Rasmussen, S. B. (2010), "The Messages and Practices of the European Union's Public Diplomacy," *The Hague Journal of Diplomacy*, 5(3): 263–287.

Rasmussen, S. B. (2012), "Current Challenge to European Union Public Diplomacy," *Public Diplomacy Magazine*, University of Southern California, available at: http://publicdiplomacymagazine.com/current-challenges-to-european-union-public-diplomacy/, [accessed Nov. 22, 2014].

Rawnsley, G. (1995), "Media Diplomacy: Monitored Broadcasting and Foreign Policy," *Discussion Papers in Diplomacy*. Leicester, UK: Centre for the Study of Diplomacy, University of Leicester.

Rawnsley, G. (2012), "Approaches to Soft Power and Public Diplomacy in China and Taiwan," *The Journal of International Communication*, 18(2): 121–135.

Reinfeldt, A. (2014), "Communicating European Integration: Information vs. Integration," *Journal of Contemporary European Research*, 10(1): 45–56.

Reiterer, M. (2012), *2012: The EU in Asia Year—Facts and Figures Concerning the EU's Engagement in the Asia Pacific*, available at: http://eeas.europa.eu/deleg ations/australia/documents/press_corner/20121025_eu-in-asia-facts-and-figures. pdf, [accessed 09-09-2014].

Reiterer, M. (2014), "The Role of Culture in EU-China Relations," *European Foreign Affairs Review*, 19(3/1), Special Issue: 135–154.

Rettman, A. (2010), "Ashton Designates Six New 'Strategic Partner,'" *EU Observer*, available at: https://euobserver.com/institutional/30828, [accessed March 10, 2019].

Robberecht, J. (2013), *The European Union External Action in Times of Crisis and Change: Public Diplomacy and Discourse*, European Policy Brief, available at: http://www2.warwick.ac.uk/fac/soc/csgr/green/papers/policybriefs/eu20agora20po licy20brief20-20eu20external20action20-public20diplomacy20and20discourse. pdf, [accessed June 24, 2015].

Robles, A. C. Jr. (2003), "The ASEAN Regional Forum and the European Union as a Security System and a Security Actor," *Dialogue and Cooperation*, Singapore: Friedrich-Ebert Stiftung Singapore: 19–34.

Ronfeldt, D. and Arquila, J. (2009), "Noopolitik: A New Paradigm for Public Diplomacy," in Snow, N. and Taylor, P. M., (eds.), *Routledge Handbook of Public Diplomacy*, New York: Routledge: 352–362.

Roselle, L., Miskimmon A., O'Loughlin, B. (2014), "Strategic Narrative: A New Means to Understand Soft Power," *Media, War & Conflict*, 7(1): 70–84.

Rugh, W.A. (2014), *Front Line Public Diplomacy: How US Embassies Communicate with Foreign Publics*, Hampshire and New York: Palgrave Macmillan.

Sabin, G. H. (1912), "Descriptive and Normative Sciences," *The Philosophical Review*, 21(4): 433–450.

Samei, M. F. A. (2015), "The European Union's Public Diplomacy towards the Arab Spring: The Case of Egypt," *The Hague Journal of Diplomacy*, 10(2): 111–138.

Sandrin, P. O. and Hoffmann, A. R. (2018), "Silences and Hierarchies in European Union Public Diplomacy," *Revista Brasileira de Política Internacional*, 61(1): 1–18.

Scheipers, S. and Sicurelli, D. (2007), "Normative Power Europe: A Credible Utopia?" *Journal of Common Market Studies*, 45(2): 435–457.

Schilling, E. (2012), *When the Rising Dragon Sees Fading Stars: China's View of the European Union*, CEPS Special Report, No. 73, Centre for European Policy Studies.

Schmitter, P. C. (2001), *What Is There to Legitimize in the European Union . . . And How Might This be Accomplished*, Institute for Advanced Studies working paper, No.75.

Schneider C. P. (2005), "Culture Communicates: US Diplomacy That Works," In Melissen Jan, (ed.), *The New Public Diplomacy: Soft Power in International Relations*, New York: Palgrave Macmillan: 147–168.

Schneider, C. P. (2006), "Cultural Diplomacy: Hard to Define, but You'd Know it if You Saw It," *The Brown Journal of World Affairs*, 13(1): 191–203.

Scott, D. (2007), "China and the EU: A Strategic Axis for the Twenty-first Century," *International Relations*, 21(1): 23–45.

Scott, D. (2014), "Trust, Structure and Track-2 Dialogue in the EU-China Relationship: Resetting and Resettling a 'Strategic Partnership,'" *Asia Europe Journal*, 12(1–2): 21–34.

Seib, P. (2012), *Real-time Diplomacy: Politics and Power in the Social Media Era*, New York: Palgrave Macmillan

Seib, P. (2013), *Public Diplomacy and the Media in the Middle East*, CPD perspectives on public diplomacy, Centre on Public Diplomacy, University of Southern California.

Seo, Hyunjin (2009), *How the Internet Changes Public Diplomacy: A Case Study of Online Community Run by U.S. Embassy in South Korean*, Conference paper, International Communication Association.

Sevin, E. (2011) "Thinking about Place Branding: Ethics of Concept," *Place Branding and Public Diplomacy*, Vol. 7: 155–164.

Shore, C. (2000), *Building Europe: The Cultural Politics of European Integration*, London and New York: Routledge.

Sicurelli, D. (2015), "The EU as a Norm Promoter Through Trade: The Perceptions of Vietnamese Elites," *Asia Europe Journal*, 13(1): 23–39.

Sigalas, E. (2009), *Does ERASMUS Student Mobility Promote a European Identity?* Webpapers on Constitutionalism and Governance beyond the State, Institute for European Integration Research, Vienna, No. 2.

Signitzer, B. H. and Coombs, T. (1992), "Public Relations and Public Diplomacy: Conceptual Convergences," *Public Relations Review*, 18(2): 137–147.

Simonin, B. L. (2008), "Nation Branding and Public Diplomacy: Challenges and Opportunities," *World Affairs*, 32(3): 19–34.

Skuse, A., Gillespie, M., and Power, G. (eds.), (2011), *Drama for Development: Cultural Translation and Social Change*, New Delhi: Sage India.

Small, A. (2011), "Cooperation between China and the EU in the UN Security Council (1)," in *EU-China: Close Cooperation on the Multilateral Agenda*, EU-China Policy Dialogues Support Facility, July: 44–48

Small, M. L. (2009), "How Many Cases Do I Need? On Science and the Logic of Case Selection in Field-Based Research," *Ethnology*, 10(1): 5–38.

Smith, K. E. (2005), *Beyond the Civilian Power Debate*, London: LSE Research online, available at: http://eprints.lse.ac.uk/812/1/BeyondPDF.pdf, [accessed June 7, 2014].

Smith, K. E. (2014), "Is the European Union's Soft Power in Decline?" *Current History*, March: 104–109.

Smith, M. (2007), "The European Union and International Order: European and Global Dimensions," *European Foreign Affairs Review*, 12(4): 437–456.

Smith, M. (2016), "EU Diplomacy and the EU-China Strategic Relationship: Framing, Negotiation and Management," *Cambridge Review of International Affairs*, 29(1): 78–98.

Smith, M. and Xie, H. (2010), "The European Union and China: The Logics of 'Strategic Partnership,'" *Journal of Contemporary European Research*, 6(4): 432–448.

Snyder, F. (2009), *The European Union and China, 1949-2008: Basic Documents and Commentary*, Oxford and Portland: Hart Publishing.

Snyder, J. T. (2013), *The United States and the Challenge of Public Diplomacy*, New York: Palgrave Macmillan.

Solana, J. (2005), *Speech by Javier Solana, EU Higher Representative for the Common Foreign and Security Policy: Driving forwards the China-EU Strategic Partnership*, Sept. 6, available at: http://www.omct.org/files/2005/09/3088/omct_euro_week_newsletter_30_05.pdf. [accessed March 6, 2019].

Sommerfeldt, N. and Zschapitz, H. (2016), "The End of European 'Soft Power,'" available at: https://gulfnews.com/opinion/op-eds/the-end-of-european-soft-power-1.1850842, [accessed Mar. 24, 2019].

Song, X. (2008), "China's View of European Integration and Enlargement," in Shambaugh, D., Sandschneider E. and Zhou H. (eds.), *China-Europe Relations*, London and New York: Routledge: 144–186.

Song, X. (2010), "European 'Models' and Their Implications to China: Internal and External Perspectives," *Review of International Studies*, 36(03): 755–775.

Song, X. (2012), "Challenges and Opportunities in EU-China Relations," in Vogt, R. (ed.), *Europe and China: Strategic Partners or Rivals?* Hong Kong: Hong Kong University Press: 19–36.

Sowa, P. A. (2002) "How Valuable Are Student Exchange Programmes?" *New Directions for Higher Education*, No.117: 63–70.

Stevenson, C. (2007), "Breaching the Great Firewall: China's Internet Censorship and the Quest for Freedom of Expression in a Connected World," *Boston College International and Comparative Law Review*, 30(1): 531–558.

Stumbaum, M. U. (2012), How *Does Asia View the EU? Security in an Interpolar World*. NFG Working Paper, Series, No. 01, March 2012, NFG Research Group "Asian Perceptions of the EU," Free University of Berlin.

Stumbaum, M. U. and Xiong, W. (2012), "Conceptual Differences of Strategic Partnership in EU-China Relations," in Pan, Z. (ed.), *Conceptual Gaps in China-EU Relations: Global Governance, Human Rights and Strategic Partnership*, Basingstoke: Palgrave Macmillan: 156–170.

Szondi, G. (2008), *Public Diplomacy and Nation Branding: Conceptual Similarity and Difference*, Netherlands Institute of International Relations, "Clingendael."

Taneja, P. (2010), "China-Europe Relations: The Limits of Strategic Partnership," *International Politics*, 47(3/4): 371–387.

Tang, S., Zhang, J. and Cao, X. (2005), "Zhongguo De Diqu Yanjiu: Chengjiu, Chaju He Qidai (Area Studies in China: Achievements, Deficiencies, and Prospects)," *Shijie Jingji Yu Zhengzhi (World Economics and Politics)*, No. 11: 7–16.

Tocci, N. (2008), "The European Union as a Normative Foreign Policy Actor," in Tocci, N. (ed.), *Who Is a Normative Foreign Policy Actor? The European Union and its Global Partners*, Brussels: Centre for European Policy Studies: 24–75.

Toje, A, (2010), *The European Union as a Small Power*, London: Palgrave Macmillan.

Tomusk, V. (2007), "Pizza Bolognese a la Russe: The Promise and Peril of the Bologna Process in Russia," in Tomusk, V. (ed.), *Creating the European Area of Higher Education: Voices from the Periphery*, Dordrecht: Springer: 227–250.

Tsatsou, P. (2014), *Internet Studies: Past, Present and Future Directions*, Burlington, VT and Surrey: Ashgate.

Tuch, H. (1990), *Communicating with the World, U.S. Public Diplomacy Overseas*, New York, ST. Martin's press.

Tulmets, E. (2007), "Can the Discourse on 'Soft Power' Help the EU to Bridge its Capability-Expectation Gap?" *European Political Economy Review*, No.7: 195–226.

Twigg, S. (2005), "Preface," in De Gouveia, P. F. and Plumridge, H., (eds.), *European Infopolitik: Developing EU Public Diplomacy Strategy*, London: Foreign Policy Center.

Uddin, Z. (2011), "Soft and Normative Power: The Power of Attraction in International Politics," *E-International Relations*, 1st Oct., available at: http://www.e-ir.info/2011/10/01/soft-and-normative-power-the-power-of-attraction-in-international-politics/, [accessed May 20, 2014].

United States Advisory Commission on Information, (1952), *Sixth Semi-annual Report of United States Advisory Commission on Information*, available at: http://www.state.gov/documents/organization/175481.pdf, [accessed July 6, 2015].

United States National Intelligence Council, (2008), *Global Trend 2025: A Transformed World*, available at: http://fas.org/irp/nic/2025.pdf, [accessed April 18, 2015].

Urwin, D. W. (2009), "The European Community: From 1945 to 1985," in Cini M. and Borragán N., (eds.), *European Union Politics (3rd edition)*, New York: Oxford University Press: 16–31.

Van Der Mensbrugghe, F. (2015), Speech delivered at the roundtable discussion on China and the Rule of Law, Madariaga Foundation, Brussels, Belgium, 4th Feb 2015.

Van Ham, P. (2005), "Power, Public Diplomacy, and the Pax Americana," in Melissen (ed.), *The New Public Diplomacy: Soft Power in International Relations*, New York: Palgrave Macmillan: 47–66.

Vanhoonacker, S. and Reslow, H. (2010), "The European External Action Service: Living Forwards by Understanding Backwards," *European Foreign Affairs Review*, 15(1): 1–18.

Veg, S. (2014), "China's Political Spectrum under Xi Jinping," *The Diplomat*, available at: http://thediplomat.com/2014/08/chinas-political-spectrum-under-xi-jinping/, [accessed May 25, 2016].

Verhaegen, S., and Hooghe, M. (2015), "Does More Knowledge about the European Union Lead to a Stronger European Identity? A Comparative Analysis among Adolescents in 21 European Member States," *Innovation: The European Journal of Social Science Research*, 28(2): 127–146.

Versluys, H. (2009), "European Union Humanitarian Aid: Lifesaver or Political Tool?" In Jan Orbie, (ed.) *Europe's Global Role: External Policies of the European Union*, Hampshire: Ashgate Publishing Limited: 91–116.

Vickers, R. (2004), "The New Public Diplomacy: Britain and Canada Compared," *The British Journal of Politics and International Relations*, 6(2): 182–194.

Vlasenko, A. (2013), *EU Public Diplomacy Effects on Ukrainian Attitudes towards the EU*, Department of Political Science, Lund University, available at: http://lup.lub.lu.se/luur/download?func=downloadFile&recordOId=3798270&file OId=3798564, [accessed April 6, 2013].

Von Hofmann, N. (2007), "How do Asians Evaluate Europe's Strategic Involvement in East Asia," *Asia Europe Journal*, 5(2): 187–192.

Vončina, T. (2011), "Speaking with One Voice: Statement and Declarations as an Instrument of the EU's Common Foreign and Security Policy," *European Foreign Affairs Review*, 16(2): 169–186.

Vuving, A. L. (2009), *How Soft Power Works* Paper presented at the panel "Soft Power and Smart Power," American Political Science Associate Annual Meeting, 3rd Sept., Toronto.

Wagner, J. (2014), "The Effectiveness of Hard & Soft Power in Contemporary International Relations," *E-International Relations*, 14th May, available at: http://www.e-ir.info/2014/05/14/the-effectiveness-of-soft-hard-power-in-contemporary-international-relations/, [accessed May 21, 2014].

Wallström, M. (2008), *Public Diplomacy and its Role in the EU's External Relations*, Mortara Center for International Studies, Georgetown University, available at: http://europa.eu/rapid/press-release_SPEECH-08-494_en.pdf, [accessed April 3, 2015].

Wang, D. and Mark, G. (2015), "Internet Censorship in China: Examining User Awareness and Attitudes," *ACM Transaction on Computer-Human Interaction (TOCHI)*, 22(6), Article no. 31.

Wang, J. (2005), "Localizing Public Diplomacy: The Role of Sub-national Actors in Nation Branding," *Place Branding*, 2(1): 32–42.

Wang, J. (2006), "Managing National Reputation and International Relations in the Global Era: Public Diplomacy Revisited," *Public Relations Review*, 32(2): 91–96.

Wang, J. and Chang, TK. (2004), "Strategic Public Diplomacy and Local Press: How a High-Profile 'Head-of-State' Visit was Covered in America's Heartland," *Public Relations Review*, 30(1): 11–24

Wang, Y. (2008), "Public Diplomacy and the Rise of Chinese Soft Power," *The Annals of the American Academy of Political and Social Science*, Vol.616: 257–273.

Wang, Y. (2012a), "China and the EU in Global Governance: Seeking Harmony in Identities," in Wouters, J. de Wilder, T. and Defraigne P. (eds.), *China, the European Union and Global Governance*, Cheltenham: Edward Elgar: 50–61.

Wang, Y. (2012b), "The Identity Dilemmas of EU Normative Power: Observations from Chinese Traditional Culture," paper presented at the seminar "International Society and the Rising Power," 2nd, Nov. King's College London, the UK.

Wang, Z. and Popescu, B.G. (201), *Understanding EU's Internal Complexities help increase Chinese Perception of The EU and Europe*, China Policy Center in University of Nottingham, http://www.nottingham.ac.uk/cpi/research/funded-projects/chinese-eu/consortium.aspx, [accessed Oct. 10, 2014].

Weiss, R. (1994), *Learning from Strangers*, New York: Free Press.

Weissmann, M. (2013), *A European Strategy towards East Asia: Moving from Good Institutions to Action*, the Swedish Institute of International Affairs, UI Occasional Paper, No. 19.

Welch, D. (1999), "Power of Persuasion," *History Today*, 49(8): 24–26.

Wen, J. (2004), *Vigorously Promoting Comprehensive Strategic Partnership between China and the European Union*, at the China-EU Investment and Trade Forum in Brussels, May 6, available at: https://www.fmprc.gov.cn/ce/cebe/eng/zt/Topics/t101949.htm, [accessed March 6, 2019].

Wendt, A. (1992), "Anarchy Is What States Make of It: The Social Construction of Power Politics," *International Organisations*, 46(2): 391–425.

Westerman, D., Spence, P.R. and Der Heide, B. V. (2014), "Social Media as Information Source: Recency of Updates and Credibility of Information," *Journal of Computer-Mediated Communication*, 19(2): 171–183.

Whitman, R. G. (2011), "Norms, Power and Europe: A New Agenda for Study of the EU and International Relations," in Whitman, R.G. (ed.), *Normative Power Europe: Empirical and Theoretical Perspectives*, Basingstoke: Palgrave Macmillan: 1–22.

Wiessala, G. (2013), "Social-Cultural and Educational Cooperation between the EU and Asia," in Christiansen, T. Kirchner, E. and Murray, P. B. (eds.), *The Palgrave Handbook of EU-Asia Relations*, Hampshire: Palgrave Macmillan: 221–225.

Wilding, C. M. (2007), *Measuring the Effectiveness of Public Diplomacy: the UK Approach*, available at: http://www.global.asc.upenn.edu/fileLibrary/PDFs/wilding.pdf, [accessed April 3, 2015].

Wilson III E. (2008), "Hard Power, Soft Power, Smart Power," *Annals of the American Academy of Political and Social Science*, 616(1): 110–124.

Wilson, I. (2010), *Are International Exchange and Mobility Programmes Effective Tools of Symmetric Public Diplomacy?* Aberystwyth University, available at: http://cadair.aber.ac.uk/dspace/handle/2160/7177, [accessed Sept. 18, 2014].

Wolfram Cox, J. & Hassard, J. (2005). "Triangulation in Organizational Research: A Re-presentation," *Organization*, *12*(1): 109–133.

Wouters, J. and Duquet, S. (2011), *The EU, EEAS and Union Delegations and International Diplomatic Law: New Horizons*, Katholieke University Leuven working paper 62.

Wu, X., Zhao, C., Zhang, L. (2011), *Ouzhou Zhengzhi Yanjiu Shinian Pingshu (2001–2010) (The Review of European Politics Research [2001–2010])*; Institute of European Studies of Chinese Academy of Social Science, available at: http://ies.cass.cn/Article/cbw/ozzz/201108/4128.asp, [accessed July 29, 2014].

Xing, G. (2009), "'Peaceful Rise': China's Public Diplomacy and International Image Cultivation," in Guo, S. and Hua, S. (eds.), *New Dimensions of Chinese Foreign Policy*, Lanham and Plymouth: Lexington Books: 133–148.

Yang, X. (2014), "Xueke Zhuanye Shezhi Zhengzhi Xuxiang Gaoxiao Rangdu Quanli (The Government Needs to Give Higher Education Institutions Autonomy in Setting Degree Programmes)," *people.com.cn*, available at: http://edu.people.com.cn/n/2014/0225/c1006-24453298.html, [accessed May 13, 2016].

Yepsen, E. A. (2012), *Practicing Successful Twitter Public Diplomacy: A Model and Case Study of U.S. Efforts in Venezuela*, CPD Perspectives on Public Diplomacy, University of Southern California

Yi, D. Shi, J. and Li, Z. (2013), "Oumeng Fazhan De Buqueding Yu Zhongou Guanxi De Weilai (The Uncertain Trend of the EU and Future of Sino-EU Relations)," in *Ouzhou Yanjiu Luncong (European Studies Forum)*, Vol. 15: 21–29.

Youngs, R. (2004), "Normative Dynamics and Strategic Interests in the EU's External Identity," *Journal of Common Market Studies*, 42(2): 415–435.

Yun, S. H. (2006), "Toward Public Relations Theory-Based Study of Public Diplomacy: Testing the Applicability of the Excellent Study," *Journal of Public Relations Research*, 18(4): 287–312.

Zhang, C. (2008), "Renquanguan Chayi Ji Zhongou Guanxi (*Different Concepts of Human Rights and China-EU Relations*)," Doctoral Thesis, Beijing: Peking University.

Zhang, J. (2012), *Ouzhou Guoji Guanxi Yanjiu Shinian Pingshu (2001–2010) (The Review of European International Relations Research [2001–2010])*, Institute of European Studies of Chinese Academy of Social Science, available at: http://ies.cass.cn/Article/cbw/ouwj/201108/4122.asp, [accessed July 29, 2014].

Zhang, Q. (2012), "Jiangou Zhuyi Shijiaoxia Gonggong Waijiao De Xingainian (The New Concept of Public Fiplomacy from the Perspective of Constructivism)," *Journal of University of International Relations*, No.1: 27–33.

Zhong, X. and He, J. (2010), "Yingguo: Cong Wenhua Waijiao Dao Gonggong Waijiao De Yanjin (The UK: An evolution from Cultural Diplomacy to Public Diplomacy)," Guoji Xinwenjie (*Chinse Journal of Journalism & Communication*), No. 7: 19–26.

Zhou, H. (2011), "Zhongou Guanxi Zhong De Renzhi Cuowei (Congitive Dissonance in China-EU Relations)," *Guoji Eenti Yanjiu (International Studies)*, No. 5.

Zhou, H. (2011), *The Past, Present and Future: The Institute of European Studies of Chinese Academy of Social Science*, available at: http://ies.cass.cn/Article/gybs/sq30/201104/3816.asp, [accessed June 12, 2015].

Zhou, H. (2017), "An Overview of the China-EU Strategic Partnership (2003–2013)," in Hong Zhou, (ed.), *China-EU Relations: Reassessing the China-EU Comprehensive Strategic Partnership*, Singapore: Springer: 3–34.

Zwingel, S. (2012), "How Do Norms Travel? Theorising International Women's Rights in Transnational Perspective," *International Studies Quarterly*, 56(1): 115–129.

Index

About the Author

Yifan Yang currently works as a Research Associate in International Politics at East China Normal University. He holds a PhD degree in International Political Economy from King's College London, and his research lies in the field of EU-China relations, public diplomacy, norm diffusion, and the impact of ICTs on Chinese politics/society. His academic papers have appeared in *Journal of European Integration, Journal of Contemporary China, Pacific Focus, European Foreign Affairs Review*, among others.

Lightning Source UK Ltd.
Milton Keynes UK
UKHW012238081019
351248UK00001B/16/P